TERM PAPER
RESOURCE GUIDE TO
NINETEENTH-CENTURY
WORLD HISTORY

TERM PAPER RESOURCE GUIDE TO NINETEENTH-CENTURY WORLD HISTORY

William T. Walker

GREENWOOD PRESS

An Imprint of ABC-CLIO, LLC

A B C ⬥ C L I O

Santa Barbara, California • Denver, Colorado • Oxford, England

Library of Congress Cataloging-in-Publication Data

Walker, William T. (William Thomas), 1942–
    Term paper resource guide to nineteenth-century world history / by William T. Walker.
       p. cm.
    Includes bibliographical references and index.
    ISBN 978–0–313–35404–5 (hard copy : alk. paper) — ISBN 978–0–313–35405–2
    (ebook : alk. paper)
1. History, Modern—19th century—Study and teaching. 2. History, Modern—19th century—
Chronology. 3. History, Modern—19th century—Bibliography. 4. Report writing—Handbooks,
manuals, etc. I. Title.
D359.2.W35   2009
909.81—dc22   2009010169

13 12 11 10 9   1 2 3 4 5

This book is also available on the World Wide Web as an eBook.
Visit www.abc-clio.com for details.

ABC-CLIO, LLC
130 Cremona Drive, P.O. Box 1911
Santa Barbara, California 93116-1911

This book is printed on acid-free paper ∞

Manufactured in the United States of America

To my dear wife

Mildred Pacek Walker

Contents

Acknowledgments   xi

Introduction   xiii

1. Haitian Revolt (1791–1804)   1

2. White Lotus Rebellion (1796–1804)   4

3. Exploration of Australia (1804–1897)   7

4. The Eastern Question (1800–1899)   12

5. Industrial Revolution (1800–1900)   16

6. Establishment of Modern Egypt (1805)   22

7. Venezuelan Independence (1810–1830)   27

8. Massacre of the Mamluks (1811)   30

9. The Cape-Xhosa Wars (1811–1879)   33

10. Eight Trigrams Rebellion (1813)   37

11. Congress of Vienna (1814–1815)   40

12. Straits Question (1815–1878)   44

13. Chilean War of Independence from Spain (1810–1826)   48

14. Founding of Singapore (1819)   52

15. Revolts in Spain, Portugal, and Italy (1820)   56

16. Brazilian Independence (1820–1822)   61

17. Independence of Peru (1821)   63

18. Mexican Independence (1821)   67

19. Greek War for Independence (1821–1832)   71

20. First Ashanti War (1823–1826)   76

21. First Burmese War (1824–1826)   79

22. Decembrist Revolt in Russia (1825)   83

23. Independence of Bolivia (1825)   87

24. Argentinean War of Independence (1810–1818)   91

25. Liberal Revolt in Mexico (1828)   94

26. July Revolution (1830)   97

27. Establishment of the Republic of Ecuador (1830)   101

28. Colombia Gains Independence (1830)   105

29. Algerian Revolt Against France (1832–1840)   109

30. British Abolish Slavery (1833–1834)   112

31. Treaty of Unkiar-Skelessi (1833)   117

32. Carlist Wars (1833–1876)   121

33. The Great Trek (1835–1840)   124

34. Rebellions in Upper and Lower Canada (1837–1838)   128

35. First Opium War (1839–1842)   132

36. First Afghan War (1839–1842)   137

37. Maori Revolts, New Zealand (1844–1865)   140

38. Sayyid Ali Mohammad and the Founding of Babism (1844)   143

39. First Sikh War (1845–1846)   146

40. Establishment of an Independent Liberia (1847)   150

41. War of the Castes (1847–1901)   153

42. Marxism Is Promulgated (1847–1881)   157

43. Revolutions of 1848   163

44. Second Sikh War (1848–1849)   168

45. Schleswig-Holstein Question (1848–1865)   171

46. T'ai Ping Rebellion (1850–1864)   175

47. Second Burmese War (1852–1853)   179

48. Crimean War (1853–1856)   183

49. Nien Rebellion (1851–1868)   189

50. Eureka Stockade (1854)   192

51. Second Opium War (1856–1860)   196

52. Sepoy Mutiny (1857–1858) 199

53. Irish Republican Brotherhood Is Established (1858) 205

54. Discovery of the Source of the Nile (1858–1871) 209

55. Charles Darwin's *The Origin of Species* Is Published (1859) 213

56. Self-Strengthening Movement, Manchu, China 217
(1860–1890)

57. Social Democratic Party Is Founded in Germany 221
(1863–1890)

58. *Syllabus of Errors* Is Issued (1864) 225

59. Paraguayan War (1864–1870) 229

60. Passage of the British North America Act (Constitution Act), 234
Canada (1867)

61. Red River Rebellion in Canada (1869–1870) 237

62. Opening of the Suez Canal (1869) 242

63. Ultramontanism in Quebec (1869–1877) 246

64. Ten Years' War (1868–1878) 249

65. Meiji Restoration (1868–1912) 253

66. Unification of Italy (1870) 257

67. Tientsin Massacre (1870) 260

68. Unification of Germany (1871) 263

69. Second Ashanti War (1873–1874) 269

70. Three Emperors' League and Alliance (1873–1881) 273

71. Founding of Arya Samaj Movement (1875) 278

72. Congress of Berlin (1878) 281

73. Second Afghan War (1878–1880) 285

74. Anglo-Zulu War (1878–1879) 290

75. Panama Canal and the French (1878–1899) 294

76. War of the Pacific (1879–1884) 298

77. Scramble for Africa (1880s–1890s) 301

78. First Boer War (1880–1881) 305

79. Sino-French War (1883–1885) 310

80. Berlin Conference (1884–1885) 313

81. Pandjeh Incident (1884) 317

82. Gaelic Revival in Ireland (1884) 320

83. Third Burmese War (1885) 323

84. North-West Rebellion (1885) 326

85. Indian National Congress Is Established (1885) 333

86. Irish Home Rule Established (1886) 337

87. Discovery of Gold in South Africa (1886) 341

88. Treaty of Uccialli and the Italians in Ethiopia (1889) 344

89. Barings Crisis (1890) 347

90. *Rerum Novarum (On Capital and Labor)* Is Published (1891) 351

91. Siamese Crisis (1893) 354

92. Sino-Japanese War (1894–1895) 357

93. Armenian Massacres (1894–1896) 360

94. Jameson Raid (1895–1896) 364

95. Publication of *The Jewish State* by Theodor Herzl (1896) 367

96. Battle of Adowa (1896) 370

97. Fashoda Crisis (1898) 374

98. Hundred Days of 1898 377

99. Boxer Rebellion (1899–1900) 381

100. Boer War (1899–1902) 385

Index 395

Acknowledgments

A book project is a major undertaking and the finished product is the work of many people. I want to thank my dear wife, Mildred Pacek Walker, for her encouragement and enduring patience as I worked on this book. For more than four decades she has assisted me in so many ways; I have been most fortunate to have her love and support.

I also want to extend my thanks to Sister Mary Josephine Larkin, SSJ, Head Librarian, and Carol Consorto, Interlibrary Loan Coordinator, at the Logue Library at Chestnut Hill College in Philadelphia. Through their kind and exhaustive services, I consulted countless sources both at the Library and its databases, and from numerous other universities and depositories. I also want to thank my editor, Wendi Schnaufer, for her expertise, support, kindness, and patience while working on this volume. Finally, I thank Kathy Breit of BeaconPMG who has done a marvelous job in preparing the manuscript for publication.

WTW
Warminster, Pennsylvania

Introduction

The rationale for this book is to assist students in the selection and development of term papers related to nineteenth-century world history. Unlike previous periods in world history where many cultures had limited or no contact, the nineteenth century witnessed revolutionary changes worldwide in culture, economics, transportation, and politics that deeply affected our sense of historical consciousness. It was the age of the Industrial Revolution and unbridled capitalism; the countercultural ideologies of Marxism and anarchism; mainstream nationalism and conservatism and the new forces of liberalism and social justice; imperialism, racism, and the beginnings of globalization; materialism and secularism; unparalleled growth in population and urbanization; the collapse of the last vestiges of the feudal order and the emergence of democratic institutions; and significant improvements in literacy and communications. It was a century of imperial violence that was paradoxically viewed by perpetrators as progressive and peaceful. Also, it was an era during which interest in history and in maintaining records, documents, and personal and public manuscripts expanded and became part of the culture of many societies. With all of this, my challenge to select 100 from the thousands of major events during the nineteenth century was formidable. The criteria for selecting the events were historical significance, availability of source materials, and my understanding of the interests of high school and undergraduate students. The first two components were based on my knowledge and understanding of world history during the nineteenth century. The elusive third piece in the puzzle—student interest—was based on my in-class work with undergraduates at Chestnut Hill College. I trust that all readers will find topics that interest them.

The primary purposes of a term paper assignment in history are to develop the student's knowledge of the subject, to strengthen the student's understanding of the historical method and the use of primary and secondary materials, to enhance the student's critical thinking skills, and to improve the student's writing skills. This guide is designed to contribute to all of those objectives by presenting students with proposed ideas for term papers that will spark their imaginations—and motivate their skill sets—and provide them with a clear direction on where they may find useful sources for the development of their papers.

USING THIS GUIDE

This guide consists of 100 historically significant events that span the nineteenth century. The events are listed chronologically and each entry consists of the following components:

- An overview in which basic information on the event is provided.
- Term Paper Suggestions: Traditional term paper assignments are listed in this section. Frequently, students have been provided with analytical challenges in which they may elect to compare and contrast historical situations or roles. Keep in mind that students can modify the suggested assignment so that it fits their needs and that of the instructor.
- Alternate Term Paper Suggestions: Alternate formats include the development of podcasts, iMovies, computer-generated historical maps, journal and diary entries, blogs, and news articles and dispatches. In all of these alternate approaches, it is critical to recognize that the finished product must be historically accurate and that there are no contradictions with the historical record. Podcasts and iMovies could consist of interviews of historical participants in an event—either in the time frame of the event or as a reflection after the event. The development of computer-generated maps with narratives may be a useful alternative when researching a topic such as the discovery of the source of the Nile River or a significant shift in geopolitical boundaries. An example, of a critical writing project would be for the student to take on the role of a participant or observer and, through diaries entries, a journal, reports, or dispatches, provide an account and analysis of the event.
- Primary Sources: Several primary sources are provided for each event. They include printed documents, online records, memoirs, and other

personal recollections. Many primary sources have been reprinted or are available as e-books—that information has been included.

- Secondary Sources: The major secondary sources on each of the events have been listed, including histories, biographies, monographs, and collections of historical essays. Most of the sources are very recent but some are classics and others—according to a review of WORLDCAT—are available in many public, college, and university libraries.

- World Wide Web: Web sites have been listed for each event; the number of sites listed varies depending upon the general and scholarly interest in the topic. All sites listed have been based on reliable information and frequently list additional sites as well as bibliographical information.

- Multimedia Sources: This category provides information on videos, audios, illustrations, and interactive maps that relate to the topic. These can be very useful if students are developing their assignments in an alternate format. For example, some voice and video clips have been listed; they can be incorporated into podcasts and/or iMovies.

1. Haitian Revolt (1791–1804)

The Haitian revolt against France began in 1791 when Vincent Ogé, a free black, demanded the right to vote. When he was refused, Ogé and a small group of supporters revolted; Ogé was captured and executed. In a larger context Ogé and other free blacks had been influenced by the ideas of the French Enlightenment and, in particular, by the discussions on the "Declaration of the Rights of Man and the Citizen." African Haitians realized that the French did not intend to extend their concepts of equality and social justice to all; this recognition transformed the Haitian revolt into a revolution against slavery as well as a revolution for independence from France. This brutal rebellion continued through the decade and involved not only French but British and Spanish military intervention. It was not until Toussaint Louverture (1743–1803) emerged as the leader of the rebel forces that progress was made in suppressing the Europeans and gaining some concessions. An authoritarian constitution was imposed in 1801 and the final major conflict of the revolution occurred at the Battle of Vertières on November 18, 1803. In January 1804, Louverture's successor, Jean-Jacques Dessalines (1758–1806), proclaimed Haiti a republic and himself as Emperor Jacques I.

TERM PAPER SUGGESTIONS

1. Write a paper on the impact of the French Enlightenment on the Haitian revolt.
2. Develop a paper on the role of Toussaint Louverture during the Haitian revolt.
3. Write a paper in which you compare French, British, and Spanish involvement in the revolution.
4. Develop a paper on the military developments during the revolt.
5. Write a paper in response to the following question: was the Haitian revolt based on ideology? race? or both?

ALTERNATIVE TERM PAPER SUGGESTIONS

1. Develop a podcast in which Toussaint Louverture is interviewed on the rationale for the revolution and his vision for an independent Haiti.

2. Develop an iMovie in which Vincent Ogé and his colleagues discuss the differences between French ideas and French actions.

3. The revolution is over and independence won. As a soldier in the Haitian revolutionary army, you return home to resume a civilian life. Create a blog on your experiences and your hopes for a free Haiti.

SUGGESTED SOURCES

Primary Sources

Arthur, Charles, and Michael Dash, eds. *A Haiti Anthology: Libète.* Princeton: Marcus Wiener, 1999. Includes some primary materials in the chapter on "Colonialism and Revolution."

"Declaration of the Rights of Man." http://www.pbs.org/wgbh/aia/part3/3h1577t.html. Provides the text of the French document that motivated the Haitian rebels.

Dubois, Laurent, and John D. Garrigus. *Slave Revolution in the Caribbean, 1789–1804: A Brief History with Documents.* New York: Palgrave Macmillan, 2006. Includes valuable primary materials on Haiti.

Howard, Thomas Phipps. *The Haitian Journal of Lieutenant Howard, York Hussars, 1796–1798.* Ed. Roger Norman Buckley. Knoxville: University of Tennessee Press, 1985. A useful memoir by a member of the British force that was involved in the Haitian revolt.

"Letter of Tobias Lear to Secretary of State James Madison." http://www.pbs.org/wgbh/aia/part3/3h491t.html. Dated July 17, 1801, this letter describes conditions in revolutionary Haiti and Lear's meeting with the rebel leader General Toussaint Louverture.

Monti, Laura Virginia. *A Calendar of Rochambeau Papers at the University of Florida Libraries.* Gainesville: University of Florida Libraries, 1972. An excellent work on the French general's correspondence on the Haitian revolt.

Popkin, Jeremy D. *Facing Racial Revolution: Eyewitness Accounts of the Haitian Insurrection.* Chicago: University of Chicago Press, 2007. Includes several personal narratives by participants and eyewitnesses to the Haitian revolt.

Rainsford, Marcus. *An Historical Account of the Black Empire of Hayti* [sic] : *Comprehending a View of the Principal Transactions in the Revolution of Saint Domingo: with its antient and modern state.* London: J. Cundee, 1805. An important contemporary account that includes extensive primary materials.

Secondary Sources

Chin, Pat, ed. *Haiti, A Slave Revolution: 200 Years after 1804.* New York: International Action Center, 2004. A collection of sympathetic essays on the Haitian revolt that focus on the slavery issue.

Coupeau, Steeve. *The History of Haiti.* Westport, CT: Greenwood Press, 2008. Includes very useful chapters on "Early Haiti" and "Independence and Empire."

Davis, Harold P. *Black Democracy, the Story of Haiti.* New York: Dial, 1928. An old but still intriguing account of the revolt that may be useful to some students.

Dubois, Laurent. *Avengers of the New World: The Story of the Haitian Revolution.* Cambridge, MA: Harvard University Press, 2004. One of the best books available on the Haitian revolt—scholarly and very readable.

Fischer, Sibylle. *Modernity Disavowed: Haiti and the Cultures of Slavery in the Age of Revolution.* Durham: Duke University Press, 2004. A seminal study on Haiti's leadership on abolishing slavery and its influence elsewhere.

Garraway, Doris L., ed. *Tree of Liberty: Cultural Legacies of the Haitian Revolution in the Atlantic World.* Charlottesville: University of Virginia Press, 2008. A collection of scholarly essays on the impact of the Haitian revolution.

Geggus, David P., ed. *The Impact of the Haitian Revolution in the Atlantic World.* Columbia: University of South Carolina Press, 2001. Provides nine essays on the impact of the revolt on Haiti and elsewhere—see the essay on slavery.

———. *Haitian Revolutionary Studies.* Bloomington: Indiana University Press, 2002. Includes 13 essays on the revolt. Most students will want to see this book by a prominent authority on Haiti's history.

Heinl, Robert D., and Nancy G. Heinl. *Written in Blood: The Story of the Haitian People, 1492–1995.* 3rd ed. Lanham, MD: University Press of America, 2005. A very good study that includes extensive information on the revolution as well as a very good bibliography.

Munro, Martin, and Elizabeth Walcott-Hackshaw, eds. *Reinterpreting the Haitian Revolution and Its Cultural Aftershocks.* Kingston, Jamaica: University of the West Indies Press, 2006. An excellent analysis of the immediate and far-reaching consequences of the Haitian revolt.

Ott, Thomas O. *The Haitian Revolution, 1789–1804.* Knoxville: University of Tennessee Press, 1973. A dated but useful and reliable study of the revolt.

World Wide Web

"Douglas Egerton, on the Haitian Revolution, Toussaint L'Ouverture, and Jefferson." http://www.pbs.org/wgbh/aia/part3/3i3130.html. Egerton (LeMoyne College) advances his thoughts on the Haitian revolt.

"Haitian Independence and the Limits of the Enlightenment." http://encarta
.msn.com/sidebar_1741573154/haitian_independence_and_the_limits
_of_the_enlightenment.html. An important article by Allan Karras
(University of California, Berkeley) on the influence of the French
Enlightenment in the Haitian revolution.

"Haitian Revolution." http://www.nationmaster.com/encyclopedia/Haitian
-Revolution. A very good history of the revolt and its consequences.

"Revenge Taken by the Black Army." http://www.pbs.org/wgbh/aia/part3/3h90.
html. Describes the treatment of both French and Haitian prisoners and
has an illustration of the hanging of a French soldier.

"The Haitian Revolution." http://www.albany.edu/~js3980/haitian-revolution.
html#Biblio. A comprehensive Web site dedicated to the Haitian
revolution.

"The Haitian Revolution, 1794–1804." http://www.pbs.org/wgbh/aia/part3/
3p2990.html. A good introduction to the revolt with several important
links to related materials.

"The Haitian Revolution, 1794–1804." http://www.haitiposter.com/haitian
-revolution.html. An introduction to the revolt.

"The History of the Haitian Revolution, 1794–1804." http://www.hartford
-hwp.com/archives/43a/index-ag.html. Provides links to many other
relevant sources on this topic.

"The History of the Haitian Revolution and the Economic Adjustment to Emancipation: 1791–1804." http://www.columbia.edu/~ad245/Mehta.pdf.
A seminar paper by Sapna Mehta (Columbia University) that is well documented and addresses an aspect of the revolt that needs to be considered.

"The Revolution on Ste. Dominigue." http://www.zum.de/whkmla/region/
caribbean/haitirev.html. Provides a substantial introduction to the
Haitian revolt.

"Toussaint L'Ouverture." http://www.pbs.org/wgbh/aia/part3/3h326.html. Statement on the leader of the revolt, with a copy of a portrait produced in 1832.

Multimedia Source

"Haiti." http://encarta.msn.com/encyclopedia_761576153_7/haiti.html. Includes
four illustrations on the Haitian revolt and a useful interactive map.

2. White Lotus Rebellion (1796–1804)

The White Lotus movement, which had a Buddhist base, emerged in
the area where the borders of Hubei, Shaanxi, and Sichuan provinces meet,

as a political force during the late eighteenth century in China. It was focused on the overthrow of the Ch'ing Dynasty. The White Lotus movement was a religious-political force supported by the rural poor who were attracted by its anti-tax and anti-corruption agenda and their belief that their involvement in the rebellion would lead to life after death. One of the major factors that gained support for the rebellion was the entrenched corruption at the local level; local officials demanded bribes for all services and actions. In 1796 Emperor Qianlong, who ruled from 1711 to 1799, sent a military force under General Ho-shen to suppress the rebels. White Lotus rebels defeated the government's army. Ho-shen stole much of the funds that the government provided for the army, and this corruption contributed significantly to the defeat. In 1799, Emperor Jiaqing inherited the throne from Qianlong, and he ruled from 1799 to 1820. He removed Ho-shen and reformed the Chinese army. By 1804 the White Lotus Rebellion had been defeated. The most significant legacy of the rebellion was that it had achieved temporary success and, in so doing, demonstrated the vulnerability of the government. A variant of the White Lotus movement appeared during the 1890s and contributed to the xenophobia that led to the Boxer Rebellion.

TERM PAPER SUGGESTIONS

1. Develop a term paper on the White Lotus religious movement and consider its impact on the rebellion that broke out in 1794.

2. Write a paper on the factors that contributed to the rebellion and the early success of the White Lotus rebels.

3. Jiaqing's reforms of the army and local governments were essential components in the defeat of the rebellion. Establish a blog in which you discuss these reforms and their application and significance.

ALTERNATIVE TERM PAPER SUGGESTIONS

1. As an aide to General Ho-shen, you are aware of his corruption. Develop a podcast in which you testify before a government panel investigating Ho-shen, the defeat of the army, and his alleged thefts.

2. Develop a 4–5 minute iMovie on the collapse of the White Lotus Rebellion. Be sure to consider the issues and concerns that affected both sides during the last years of the struggle.

3. As a follower of the White Lotus movement, you are committed to improving the society in which you live. Write a journal of your thoughts from the early 1790s to 1804 when the rebellion was defeated.

SUGGESTED SOURCES

Primary Sources

Cheng, Pei-kai, and Michael Lestz, eds. *The Search for Modern China: A Documentary Collection.* New York: W. W. Norton & Company, 1999. A valuable collection of primary documents that will benefit many students working on the rebellion.

De Bary, William Theodore, and Wing-Tsit Chan, eds. *Sources of Chinese Tradition.* 2 vols. New York: Columbia University Press, 1964. The second volume in this set provides primary materials that should be of use to many students.

Sommer, Deborah, ed. *Chinese Religion: An Anthology of Sources.* New York: Oxford University Press, 1995. Includes a section on the White Lotus movement that is useful in understanding the rise of this movement.

Secondary Sources

Art, Suzanne Strauss. *China's Later Dynasties.* Lincoln, MA: Pemblewick Press, 2002. Provides a useful and accurate introduction to the rebellion.

Borthwick, Mark. *Pacific Century: The Emergence of Modern Pacific Asia.* Boulder, CO: Westview Press, 2007. Includes some retrospective notes on the rebellion and its role in Chinese history.

Eastman, Lloyd E. *Family, Fields, and Ancestors: Constancy and Change in China's Social and Economic History, 1550–1949.* New York: Oxford University Press, 1988. Considers the White Lotus movement and rebellion in the context of Chinese social and economic development.

Ebrey, Patricia Buckley. *The Cambridge Illustrated History of China.* Cambridge: Cambridge University Press, 1996. A very good resource for introductory material.

Esherick, Joseph W. *The Origins of the Boxer Uprising.* Berkeley: University of California Press, 1988. Considers the earlier White Lotus rebellion as a significant predecessor to the xenophobic uprising a century later.

Fairbank, John K. *The Great Chinese Revolution 1800–1985.* New York: Harper Perennial, 1987. An outstanding resource on all aspects of the Chinese revolutionary experience by the foremost American scholar.

Gernet, Jacques. *A History of Chinese Civilization.* Trans. J. R. Foster and Charles Hartman. 2nd ed. New York: Cambridge University Press, 1996. Provides a very good introduction to the White Lotus movement and rebellion.

Goldstone, Jack A. *Revolution and Rebellion in the Early Modern World.* Berkeley: University of California Press, 1993. Examines the rebellion in the context of a global revolutionary tradition.

Gray, Jack. *Rebellions and Revolutions: China from the 1800s to 2000.* 2nd ed. New York: Oxford University Press, 2002. Very good resource on the rebellion with strong bibliography.

Perdue, Peter C. *China Marches West: The Qing Conquest of Central Eurasia.* Cambridge, MA: Harvard University Press, 2005. An important study that includes extensive information on the White Lotus Rebellion.

Ter Haar, B. J. *The White Lotus Teachings in Chinese Religious History.* Leiden: E. J. Brill, 1992. Quite significant in understanding the Buddhist roots of the movement and rebellion.

World Wide Web

"The White Lotus Rebellion." http://www.ibiblio.org/chinesehistory/contents/03pol/c03s03.html. Excellent resource on the rebellion.

"The White Lotus Religion in China." http://www.sjsu.edu/faculty/watkins/whitelotus.htm. Very good and useful site on the religious movement and its connection to the rebellion.

"White Lotus Rebellion." http://www.encyclopedia.com/doc/1E1-WhiteLot.html. Provides a useful introduction to the rebellion.

"White Lotus Rebellion." http://www.infoplease.com/ce6/history/A0852123.html. Adequate introduction to the rebellion.

"White Lotus Rebellion." http://www.britannica.com/EBchecked/topic/642358/White-Lotus-Rebellion#tab=active~checked%2Citems~checked&title=White%20Lotus%20Rebellion%20–%20Britannica%20Online%20Encyclopedia. General introduction to the rebellion.

Multimedia Source

The Conquerors. Directed by Wenji Teng. University of Chicago, 1995. DVD. This dramatic film presents a sympathetic account of the White Lotus rebellions.

3. Exploration of Australia (1804–1897)

While claimed and coastal areas were occupied by the English during the late eighteenth century, very little was known of the extent and the contents of the interior of Australia until well into the nineteenth century.

Myths abounded about a huge interior sea, the extraordinarily primitive native peoples, and the vastness of the continent. Responding to the challenges to acquire information and the potential for fame and fortune, 22 major expeditions of Australia's interior by English and Australian explorers occurred between 1804 and 1897. While significant positive and negative experiences were recorded, these explorers opened up the continent. Among the areas explored were Tasmania, New South Wales, and Western Australia; they discovered the Murray, Blackwood, Avon/Swan, Capel, Moore, Condamine, Finke, and Darling rivers. They also learned that there was no inland sea and the native peoples were primitive but not as barbaric as some of those who were involved with the expeditions. By the end of the century most of Australia was charted and known. Vast lands were opened to cattle and sheep production and wheat farming.

TERM PAPER SUGGESTIONS

1. Write a term paper on the factors that motivated the exploration of central Australia during the nineteenth century.
2. Develop a term paper on the transformation of the Australian interior that resulted from the discoveries of the explorers.
3. Between 1825 and 1840 twelve major expeditions were conducted in Australia. Write a paper on these expeditions and how our view of Australia changed as a result of their discoveries.
4. Write a term paper on the Burke-Wills expedition of 1860. What was discovered?

ALTERNATIVE TERM PAPER SUGGESTIONS

1. As a journalist accompanying the Burke-Wills expedition into the Australian heartland, host a blog for your newspaper in Melbourne in which you describe the progress and problems that the expedition experienced.
2. Develop an iMovie in which you interview Robert O'Hara Burke and William John Wills prior to their expedition. What did they hope to achieve? What was the relationship between them before the expedition?
3. Develop a hyperlink map of the Burke-Wills expedition with accompanying narrative.
4. Develop a podcast in which you interview Charles Sturt ([1795–1869], an Englishman born in India) on his achievements as an explorer of Australia.

SUGGESTED SOURCES

Primary Sources

Eyre, Edward John. *Journals of Expeditions of Discovery into Central Australia and overland from Adelaide to King George's Sound, in the years 1840–1 sent by the colonists of South Australia. . . .* 2 vols. London: T. and W. Boone, 1845. A valuable journal that details Eyre's experiences on this expedition and presents a clear description of the difficulties in organizing and leading such an effort.

Flannery, Tim, ed. *The Explorer: Stories of Discovery and Adventure from the Australian Frontier.* New York: Grove Press, 2000. Includes excerpts from primary materials that may be useful.

Giles, Ernest. *Australia Twice Traversed: The Romance of Exploration Being a Narrative compiled from the Journals of Five Exploring Expeditions into and through Central South Australia and Western Australia from 1872 to 1876.* Victoria Park, Australia: Hesperian Press, 1995; originally published in 1889. Includes extensive primary materials from the journals and six folded maps.

Grey, George. *Journals of Two Expeditions of Discovery in North-west and Western Australia, during the years 1837, 38, and 39, under the authority of Her Majesty's government. . . .* 2 vols. London: T. and W. Boone, 1841. Provides a valuable early description of the regions and the difficulties associated with the expeditions.

McKinley, John. *McKinley's Journal of Exploration in the Interior of Australia.* Melbourne: F. F. Bailliere, 1862. Available as an e-book through Project Gutenberg at http://www.archive.org/details/mckinlaysjournal 13248gut. An absorbing account of the successes and failures of McKinley's effort to develop a map and an understanding of central Australia.

Mitchell, Thomas Livingstone. *Journal of an Expedition into the Interior of tropical Australia, in search of a Route from Sydney to the Gulf of Carpentaria.* London: Longman, Brown, Green, 1848. This journal constitutes a careful and comprehensive list of plants that were discovered during the expedition. Comments on natives, weather, etc., are also included.

———. *Three Expeditions into the Interior of Eastern Australia, with descriptions of the recently explored region of Australia Felix, and of the present colony of New South Wales.* 2nd ed. London: T. and W. Boone, 1839. Mitchell's account is reliable and should be consulted by those working on this period or region.

Sturt, Charles. *The Central Australian Expedition, 1844–1846: The Journals of Charles Sturt.* Ed. Richard C. Davis. London: Hakluyt Society, 2002.

Charles Sturt was one of the most significant explorers of Australia, and this work is the best and most current edition of his journals.

———. *Journal of the Central Australian Expedition, 1844–1845.* Ed. Jill Waterhouse. London: Caliban Books, 1984. A reliable edition that has a good introduction.

Secondary Sources

Beale, Edgar. *Sturt, the Chipped Idol: A Study of Charles Sturt, Explorer.* With a medical commentary by Kenneth Noad. Sydney: Sydney University Press, 1979. An intriguing and scholarly biography of Sturt in which many students find new research topics.

Calvert, Albert F. *The Exploration of Australia.* 2 vols. London: G. Philip, 1895–1896. Available as an e-book at http://books.google.com/books ?id=yRkXAAAAYAAJ. While dated, this is an excellent resource with detailed information on most of the expeditions and some excerpts of primary materials.

Crotty, Martin, and David A. Roberts, eds. *The Great Mistakes of Australian History.* Sydney: University of New South Wales Press, 2006. Includes a very useful chapter on the Burke and Wills expedition of 1860–1861.

Day, Alan. *Historical Dictionary of the Discovery and Exploration of Australia.* Lanham, MD: Scarecrow Press, 2003. An outstanding reference work that should be useful to all working on any aspect of this topic.

Estensen, Miriam. *The Life of Matthew Flinders.* Crows Nest, Australia: Allen and Unwin, 2002. A biography of an explorer of central Australia that is available and reliable. Flinders is credited with naming Australia.

Favenc, Ernest. *The Explorers of Australia and their Life-Work.* London: Whitcombe and Tombs, 1908. An old but worthwhile secondary study that is reliable and that provides details not found in other works.

Feeken, Erwin H., Gerda E. E. Feeken, and O. H. K. Spate. *The Discovery and Exploration of Australia.* Melbourne: Nelson, 1970. A standard history of the exploration of Australia, with extensive information on the nineteenth century.

Henry, William. *The Shimmering Waste: The Life and Times of Robert O'Hara Burke.* Galway, IR: W. Henry, 1997. A fascinating and reliable biography of one of the most celebrated martyrs of Australian exploration in the nineteenth century.

Jack, Robert Logan. *Northmost Australia: Three Centuries of Exploration, Discovery, and Adventure in and around the Cape York Peninsula, Queensland.* London: Simpkin, Marshall, Hamilton, and Kent, 1921. Jack's study is valuable to those researching the particular regions indicated in the title of his book.

Moorehead, Alan. *Cooper's Creek.* London: H. Hamilton, 1963. Still the most thorough and readable account of the Burke and Wills expedition.

Murgatroyd, Sarah. *The Dig Tree: The Extraordinary Story of the Burke and Wills Expedition.* London: Bloomsbury, 2002. A readable and reliable study that students will find fascinating and troublesome.

Perry, Thomas Melville. *The Discovery of Australia: The Charts and Maps of the Navigators and Explorers.* London: H. Hamilton, 1982. A very good reference work that includes nineteenth-century maps and charts.

Williams, Gwenneth. *South Australian Exploration to 1856.* Adelaide: Board of Directors of the Public Library, Museum and Art Gallery of South Australia, 1919. An officially sponsored history that includes maps and illustrations, many relating to the period from the 1820s to 1856.

World Wide Web

"Australian Explorers, Discoverers, and Pioneers." http://gutenberg.net.au/explorers.html. A very worthwhile site that provides information and many valuable links to other sites.

"European Discovery and the Colonisation of Australia." http://www.cultureandrecreation.gov.au/articles/australianhistory/. Provides students with a very good introduction and some information on the nineteenth-century explorers and their achievements.

"Exploration of Australia." http://www.knowledgerush.com/kr/encyclopedia/Exploration_of_Australia/. An extensive site with links to dozens of related Web pages.

"Exploration of Australia between 1770–1876." http://www.planetware.com/map/australia-exploration-of-australia-between-1770-1876-map-aus-aus12.htm. Provides an excellent map that indicates the primary areas of exploration. Students should refer to this Web site.

"Nineteenth Century Exploration of Australia." http://www.wku.edu/~smithch/australia/. A megasite that includes a reproduction of an 1893 map of Australia and links to biographical information on most of the explorers of this period. This is a very helpful site that should be visited by students working on this topic.

Multimedia Source

"Australia." http://uk.encarta.msn.com/medias_761568792/Australia.html.
Includes maps and photographs, many of which relate to the exploration
of Australia during the nineteenth century.

4. The Eastern Question (1800–1899)

Throughout the nineteenth century the European powers were monitoring carefully the disintegration of the Ottoman Empire—both in southeastern Europe and in the Middle East. The century opened with a non-Ottoman restoration of Egyptian power under Mohammad Ali and increasingly strained relations between the Russians and the Turks. Great Britain was focused on the eastern Mediterranean and was intent upon sustaining Russia's lack of access to the Mediterranean. Thus, Britain found itself defending Ottoman interests at the Congress of Berlin in 1878 and with mixed feelings during the Greek war for independence. The Austro-Hungarian Empire was interested in expanding into the Balkans and taking advantage of the weakening Ottoman Empire; however, Austro-Hungarian interests collided with Russian interests in the region and would eventually result in a series of crises during the early twentieth century. The most visible manifestation of the Eastern Question during the nineteenth century occurred during the Russo-Turkish War of 1877–1878 and the subsequent Congress of Berlin in 1878. Russia defeated the Turks and entered into a peace that provided for a large Bulgarian state and Russian access to the Dardanelles Straits. British Prime Minister Benjamin Disraeli refused to recognize these terms, and a crisis emerged during the spring of 1878 that resulted in the Congress of Berlin in which Britain was able to limit the Russian advance into the region. The Eastern Question caused friction among the European powers as well as a realignment of diplomatic strategies.

TERM PAPER SUGGESTIONS

1. Write a paper on the origins of the Eastern Question and its development during the first three decades of the nineteenth century.
2. Develop a paper on the emergence of the Russian-Austrian rivalry in the Balkans that resulted from the Eastern Question.

3. Write a paper on Great Britain's foreign policy *vis à vis* the Eastern Question during the nineteenth century. Compare the policies of Lord Palmerston (Henry John Temple), Disraeli, and William E. Gladstone.

4. Write a paper in which you evaluate the impact of the Eastern Question.

ALTERNATIVE TERM PAPER SUGGESTIONS

1. Develop a podcast in which the Turkish leaders meet to discuss the formation of a long-term policy directed at restoring stability and minimizing European involvement in their affairs.

2. Develop an iMovie in which Disraeli and his Cabinet consider British policy on the Eastern Question.

3. As a contemporary Italian scholar, you witness the polarization of Russia and Austria during the late-nineteenth century. Create a blog that consists of your impressions of the Question and your concerns and recommendations for maintaining the peace.

SUGGESTED SOURCES

Primary Sources

Dilke, Charles Wentworth. *The Eastern Question.* London: Robert Bush, 1878. Available as an e-book at http://books.google.com/books?hl=en&id=tJ8BAAAAQAAJ&dq=The+Eastern+Question&printsec=frontcover&source=web&ots=HH5J5QVWf1&sig=p9qCvU45ZSVSft0FVCOux2r6HQ8&sa=X&oi=book_result&resnum=6&ct=result#PPP7, M1. A copy of Dilke's (Member of Parliament) speech delivered on January 15, 1878.

Johnstone, Henry Alexander Munro Butler. *The Eastern Question.* [n.p.]: [n.p.], 1881. Also available as an e-book at http://books.google.com/books?hl=en&id=gTTJAG86JD0C&dq=The+Eastern+Question&printsec=frontcover&source=web&ots=bxX13mJM14&sig=LmeC3DCW5tXAaFRU2YJ8NMdELAg&sa=X&oi=book_result&resnum=3&ct=result#PPP5,M1. A privately published work by a British official who was involved in many aspects of the Eastern Question.

Marvin, Charles Thomas. *The Russian Advance Towards India: Conversations with Skobeleff, Ignatieff, and other distinguished Russian generals and statesmen, on the Central Asian Question.* Peshawar: Saeed Book Bank, 1984. A valuable resource that provides firsthand Russian comments on the Eastern Question.

Marx, Karl. *The Eastern Question: A Reprint of Letters Written 1853–1856 Dealing with the Events of the Crimean War.* Manchester, NH: Ayer

Publishing, 1968. Also available as an e-book at http://books.google
.com/books?id=Aqva7niucY8C. Marx's critical impressions on the
Question constitute an important contemporary image of the Eastern
Question.

Secondary Sources

Anderson, M. S. *The Eastern Question, 1774–1923: A Study in International
Relations.* New York: St. Martin's, 1966. A classic study that should be
consulted by all students working on this topic.

Argyll, George Douglas. *The Eastern Question from the Treaty of Paris 1856 to the
Treaty of Berlin 1878 and the Second Afghan War.* 2 vols. Chestnut Hill,
MA: Adamant Media/Elibron, 2001. A contemporary account of the
evolution of the Eastern Question that may be helpful to students
working on this period.

Bitts, Alexander. *Russia and the Eastern Question: Army, Government, and Society,
1815–1833.* Oxford: Oxford University Press, 2006. A recent, scholarly study that considers the impact of the Eastern Question on all
aspects of Russian life during the two decades after the Congress of
Vienna.

Canning, Stratford. *The Eastern Question.* London: John Murray, 1881. Available as an e-book at http://books.google.com/books?hl=en&id=Vz0p
AAAAYAAJ&dq=The+Eastern+Question&printsec=frontcover&source
=web&ots=mzKZuz_Tht&sig=wI3gvUWHt6xaxPoZQxugKAs3MzU&sa
=X&oi=book_result&resnum=10&ct=result. Still a very good resource that
includes some excerpts of primary materials.

Drage, Geoffrey. *Russian Affairs.* London: John Murray, 1904. A dated
work focused on Russian interest in the Balkans and the Ottoman
world.

Duggan, Stephen P. *The Eastern Question: A Study in Diplomacy.* London:
P. S. King and Son, 1902. An old classic that dominated European thinking on the Eastern Question during the early twentieth century.

Hozier, Henry M. *The Russo-Turkish War: Including an Account of the Rise and
Decline of the Ottoman Power, and the History of the Eastern Question.
Part 3.* Chestnut Hill, MA: Adamant Media/Elibron, 2001; originally
published in 1878. A contemporary history of the war of 1877–1877
with additional information on the Eastern Question.

MacFie, A. L. *The Eastern Question 1774–1923.* Boston: Addison-Wesley, 1996.
A reliable and comprehensive history of the Eastern Question and its
role in European diplomacy and politics.

Marriott, J. A. R. *The Eastern Question: A Study in European Diplomacy.* Oxford: Oxford University Press, 1940. A very worthwhile study by a prominent British historian of the early twentieth century.

Millman, Richard. *Britain and the Eastern Question 1875–1878.* Oxford: Oxford University Press, 1979. A scholarly examination of the impact of the Question on British politics and Prime Minister Benjamin Disraeli's policies during the Russo-Turkish War and the Congress of Berlin.

Montagu, Robert. *England and the Eastern Question.* London: Chapman, 1877. Also available as an e-book at http://www.archive.org/details/Foreign Policy. An important primary account that had impact on the formulation of British policy.

Seton-Watson, R. W. *Disraeli, Gladstone, and the Eastern Question: A Study in Diplomacy and Party Politics.* New York: W. W. Norton, 1971. One of the best books published on this aspect of the Question. If students are studying the Russo-Turkish War as the focus for their papers, they need to read this book.

Taylor, A. J. P. *Struggle for Mastery in Europe, 1848–1918.* Oxford: Oxford University Press, 1980. A very good and readable study that includes extensive information on the Eastern Question.

World Wide Web

"Eastern Question." http://www.encyclopedia.com/doc/1E1-EasternQ.html. A good introduction to the Eastern Question that includes a map and four illustrations.

"Eastern Question." http://www.infoplease.com/ce6/history/A0816586.html. A good introduction to the history of the Eastern Question.

"The Eastern Question." http://www.saburchill.com/history/chapters/empires/0057.html. Includes links to several useful sites including three maps of the Balkans.

"The Eastern Question." http://countrystudies.us/austria/28.htm. Emphasizes Austria's role in the Eastern Question.

"The Great Powers and the Eastern Question." http://staff.lib.msu.edu/sowards/balkan/lect10.htm. A lecture by Steven Sowards that provides insights into the connections between the major European powers and the Ottoman Empire.

"The Origin of the Eastern Question." http://www.thecorner.org/hist/europe/east-qtn.htm. A very useful outline on the Eastern Question.

Multimedia Source

"Ottoman Empire." http://encarta.msn.com/media_461555303_761575380
_-1_1/Ottoman_Empire.html. Includes maps and illustrations that
relate to the Eastern Question.

5. Industrial Revolution (1800–1900)

While some advancements toward industrialism were evident in the Low
Countries and Switzerland in the eighteenth century, its initial manifestation occurred in Britain in the 1750s and 1760s. The momentum of this
extremely important process was accelerated in Britain during the early decades of the nineteenth century because of market needs, the availability of
investment capital, unencumbered entrepreneurial opportunities, advances
in applied sciences, and improved transportation systems. Many of these
factors were interdependent (for example, transportation supported the
necessary supplies of raw materials and the marketing of finished products);
however, fundamental to industrial expansion was a banking system that
facilitated investment. Technology improved through the application of
steam power, the development of new metals that enabled product development, as well as a revolution in engineering and architecture. The building
of factories, canals, and railroads stimulated new industries throughout
Britain. At the same time, the new industrial order brought new problems
in the abuse of labor, poor sanitation in cities, and inadequate housing.
The population of cities expanded beyond all expectations and, in some
areas, agriculture lacked sufficient labor resources. With the resulting
urbanization of industrial societies, political change accompanied the economic revolution and, in many societies, members of the industrial working class were active in demanding political actions to improve their
conditions. The resulting Industrial Revolution transformed Western and
then global societies during the nineteenth and twentieth centuries. In the
Americas, the United States, Canada, Mexico, Chile, Argentina, and Brazil
became increasingly active in industrial expansion during the second half of
the nineteenth century. In 1868, Japan launched a Westernization program
that was industrially based; other societies followed. Two other factors that
had global ramifications were the need for raw materials to fuel the industrial system and the search for new markets for finished goods.

TERM PAPER SUGGESTIONS

1. Develop a paper on the development of industrialism in Europe during the first half of the nineteenth century. What were the factors that stimulated this development?

2. Write a paper on emerging industrial economies in Latin America during the nineteenth century.

3. Write a paper that addresses the following question: why did the Industrial Revolution first develop fully in Britain?

4. The emergence of an industrial economy involves substantive changes in the life of a nation—demographics, working conditions, dependency on trade, food supplies, banking, transportation, shifts in political power, technology, and the general quality of life. Develop a paper in which you select three of these factors and consider the changes in each in Britain during the nineteenth century.

5. Write a paper of the progress of industrialism in Central and Eastern Europe during the second half of the nineteenth century.

ALTERNATIVE TERM PAPER SUGGESTIONS

1. During the years after the defeat of Napoleon in 1815, the conditions of the English industrial working class were dismal and demands for reform mounted. Develop an iMovie in which workers and reformers meet to develop a petition of grievances that address these conditions.

2. Develop a podcast on the conditions of child labor that resulted in the Factory Act of 1833. Be sure to include the terms and significance of the Act.

3. The use of children in the new industrial order resulted in the abuse and deaths of many minors. You are a journalist for a reform newspaper. You have infiltrated the coal mining business in the Midlands and have firsthand information on the abuses. Develop a blog that is a series of articles that are factual and discuss the need for government intervention.

SUGGESTED SOURCES

Primary Sources

Frader, Laura L. *The Industrial Revolution: A History in Documents*. New York: Oxford University Press, 2006. Includes a wide range of public and private primary sources, and is a valuable resource for most term papers.

"Industrial Revolution." http://www.historyteacher.net/APEuroCourse/ WebLinks/WebLinks-IndustrialRevolution.htm. Provides more than 50 primary sources on the Industrial Revolution.

Lewald, Fanny. *A Year of Revolutions: Fanny Lewald's Recollections of 1848.* Ed. and trans. Hanna Ballin Lewis. Providence, RI: Berghahn, 1997. An account of several continental revolutions by an eyewitness.

Outman, James L. *Industrial Revolution: Primary Sources.* New York: UXL Publishing, 2003. A good selection of useful primary materials.

Pike, Edgar Royston. *Human Documents of the Industrial Revolution in Britain.* New York: HarperCollins, 1967. Excellent source for contemporary sources on social and economic history.

Porter, Roy, and Edward Royle, eds. *Documents of the Early Industrial Revolution.* Cambridge, U.K.: Local Examinations Syndicate, 1983. Porter and Royle have assembled a valuable collection of primary materials that should be of interest to most students working on the Industrial Revolution.

Secondary Sources

Ashton, T. S., and Pat Hudson. *The Industrial Revolution, 1760–1830.* New York: Oxford University Press, 1998. A classic study of the Industrial Revolution that is still useful, arguing that it resulted in significant progress.

Barnett, David. *London, Hub of Industrial Revolution: A Revisionary History, 1775–1825.* London: Tauris, 1998. Barnett advances a London-centric interpretation on the Industrial Revolution that is provocative and worthwhile.

Breunig, Charles, and Matthew Levinger. *The Revolutionary Era, 1789–1850.* 3rd ed. New York: W. W. Norton, 2002. Includes informed perceptions and commentary on the Industrial Revolution during the first half of the nineteenth century.

Church, R. A., and E. A. Wrigley, eds. *The Industrial Revolutions.* 11 vols. Oxford: Blackwell, 1994. A marvelous resource with volumes on the Industrial Revolution in Britain, Europe, North America, and Japan, as well as additional volumes focused on specific industries, textiles, metals, coal and iron, and finances.

Crump, Thomas. *A Brief History of the Age of Steam: The Power that Drove the Industrial Revolution.* New York: Carroll and Graf, 2007. A useful study on the applications of steam during the Industrial Revolution.

Deane, P. M. *The First Industrial Revolution.* Cambridge, U.K.: Cambridge University Press, 1980. Deane focuses on the Industrial Revolution up to 1850 and considers the macrochanges in society that resulted from the revolution.

Dupree, Marguerite. *Family Structure in the Staffordshire Potteries, 1840–1860.* Oxford: Clarendon Press, 1995. A seminal study on the transformation of the family resulting from the new industrial economy.

Engerman, Stanley L. *Trade and the Industrial Revolution, 1700–1850.* Cheltenham, U.K.: E. Elgar, 1996. Engerman argues that a new world economy emerged from the Industrial Revolution—very good source.

Evans, Chris, and Gōran Rydén, eds. *The Industrial Revolution in Iron: The Impact of British Coal Technology in Nineteenth Century Europe.* Aldershot, U.K.: Ashgate, 2005. An intriguing collection of scholarly essays on the transformation of industry resulting from British technological innovations.

Evans, Eric J. *The Forging of the Modern State: Early Industrial Britain, 1783–1870.* 3rd ed. Harlow, U.K.: Longman, 2001. A scholarly argument that connects the Industrial Revolution with the emergence of the structures that supported the new nation-states.

Hobsbawn, Eric J. *Industry and Empire: From 1750 to the Present Day.* Rev. ed. New York: New Press, 1999; originally published in 1968. A very important work by a noted British historian, it includes several chapters on the nineteenth century.

Horn, Jeff. *The Industrial Revolution: Milestones in Business History.* Westport, CT: Greenwood Press, 2007. A very good resource on the development of the industrially based economy in the nineteenth century. A chapter on the changing standard of living is included.

Inikori, J. E. *Africans and the Industrial Revolution in England: A Study in International Trade and Development.* Cambridge, U.K.: Cambridge University Press, 2002. A seminal study in which Inikori examines the impact of slavery on the Industrial Revolution and the economy of Britain.

King, Steven. *Making Sense of the Industrial Revolution.* Manchester, U.K.: Manchester University Press, 2001. An excellent introduction to the history of the Industrial Revolution and its impact on the expansion of the British economy between 1760 and 1880.

Kömer, Axel. *1848—A European Revolution?: International Ideas and National Memories of 1848.* New York: St. Martin's Press, 2000. A scholarly study that approaches the revolutions as a cohesive movement.

Kristofferson, Robert. *Craft Capitalism: Craftworkers and Early Industrialization in Hamilton, Ohio, 1840–1872.* Toronto: University of Toronto Press, 2007. A very solid scholarly study focused on the impact of industrialism on a developing Canadian town.

Marks, Robert. *The Origins of the Modern World: A Global and Ecological Narrative from the Fifteenth to the Twenty-first Century.* 2nd ed. Lanham, MD: Rowman and Littlefield, 2007. Includes an important chapter on the Industrial Revolution that may be useful to students researching a related topic.

Mason, David S. *Revolutionary Europe, 1789–1989: Liberty, Equality, Solidarity.* Lanham, MD: Rowman and Littlefield, 2005. Includes a valuable chapter on the "Industrial Revolution and the Birth of Capitalism."

Mokyr, Joel, ed. *The British Industrial Revolution: An Economic Perspective.* 2nd ed. Boulder, CO: Westview Press, 1999. Includes four useful essays on the Industrial Revolution from 1760 to 1860.

Morgan, Kenneth. *The Birth of Industrial Britain: Social Change, 1750–1850.* New York: Pearson Longman, 2004. Emphasizes the social transformation in Britain that resulted from the industrial economy, and provides excellent documentation.

Morrison-Low, A. D. *Making Scientific Instruments in the Industrial Revolution.* Burlington, VT: Ashgate, 2007. Focuses on the British centers for fine craftsmanship—York, Sheffield, Bristol, Liverpool, Manchester, Birmingham, and London—and considers the marketing of these devices.

O'Brien, P. K. *The Industrial Revolution in Europe.* 2 vols. Oxford: Blackwell, 1994. An excellent comprehensive of industrialism and its consequences.

——— and Roland Quinault, eds.. *The Industrial Revolutions and British Society.* Cambridge, U.K.: Cambridge University Press, 1993. A series of essays on the emergence and impact of industrialism in Britain.

Pollard, Sidney. *Essays on the Industrial Revolution in Britain.* Ed. Colin Holmes. Aldershot, U.K.: Ashgate, 2000. A useful collection of Pollard's essays on a variety of topics related to the Industrial Revolution in Britain.

Rider, Christine, and Micheál Thompson, eds. *The Industrial Revolution in Comparative Perspective.* Malabar, FL: Krieger Publishing, 2000. Provides alternative interpretations on the Industrial Revolution and its impact.

Rodner, William S. *J. M. W. Turner: Romantic Painter of the Industrial Revolution.* Berkeley: University of California Press, 1997. An excellent study of Turner's portrayal and interpretation of the Industrial Revolution in art.

Sale, Kirkpatrick. *Rebels against the Future: The Luddites and their War on the Industrial Revolution: Lessons for the Computer Age.* Reading, MA: Addison-Wesley, 1995. A very good account of the enemies of industrialism that may provide several ideas for term papers.

Sperber, Jonathan. *The European Revolutions, 1848–1851.* New York: Cambridge University Press, 1994. An excellent scholarly study of all of the major revolutions at mid-century. A very good introduction to each of the revolutions is included.

Stearns, Peter N. *The Industrial Revolution in World History*. Boulder, CO: Westview Press, 2007. A penetrating and seminal study on the transformation of the world that resulted from the Industrial Revolution.

——— and John H. Hinshaw. *The ABC-CLIO World History Companion to the Industrial Revolution*. Santa Barbara, CA: ABC-CLIO, 1998. An excellent resource that should be useful in the development of many term papers.

Sunderland, David. *Social Capital, Trust, and the Industrial Revolution, 1780–1880*. London: Routledge, 2007. An important study that considers the Industrial Revolution's impact on class structure, trust in business, and philanthropy.

Thomas, Brinley. *The Industrial Revolution and the Atlantic Economy: Selected Essays*. London: Routledge, 1993. Includes essays on utopian socialist Robert Owen, food supplies in Britain, and energy in Britain that should be very useful to many students.

Tuttle, Carolyn. *Hard at Work in Factories and Mines: The Economics of Child Labor during the British Industrial Revolution*. Boulder, CO: Westview Press, 1999. An excellent study of the crisis in child labor that dominated British society in the early decades of the nineteenth century.

de Vries, Jan. *The Industrial Revolution, Consumer Behavior and the Household Economy, 1650 to the Present*. Cambridge, U.K.: Cambridge University Press, 2008. A seminal study of the emerging industrial economy in which consumerism was a primary characteristic.

Wrigley, E. A. *Continuity, Chance and Change: The Character of the Industrial Revolution*. Cambridge, U.K.: Cambridge University Press, 1990. A stimulating and worthwhile scholarly study of the Industrial Revolution that stresses its revolutionary impact on all aspects of life.

Zlotnick, Susan. *Women, Writing, and the Industrial Revolution*. Baltimore, MD: Johns Hopkins University Press, 1998. A seminal study that may provide several interesting topics for term papers.

World Wide Web

"Industrial Revolution." http://www.fordham.edu/halsall/mod/modsbook14.html. An excellent resource developed by Paul Halsall and maintained by Fordham University that includes primary and secondary sources and links on the agricultural revolution of the seventeenth and eighteenth centuries, the revolution in the manufacture of textiles, the revolution in power, the great engineers, the process of industrialization, social and political effects of industrialism, and the literary response to it.

"Revolution, Liberalism and Nationalism in Europe, 1789–1914." http://www.uncp.edu/home/rwb/hst329_p3.html. Links to primary sources and other sources of information on the Industrial Revolution, maintained by Robert Brown, University of North Carolina, Pembroke.

Multimedia Sources

European History and European Lives, 1715–1914. Teaching Company, 2003. Audio CD. In 36 lectures Jonathan Steinberg examines a wide range of development focused on the impact of the Industrial Revolution.

The Europeans: An Age of Revolutions. Films for the Humanities & Sciences, 2003. DVD. Includes data on the Industrial Revolution and its consequences.

Industrial Revolution. Educational Video Network, 2004. DVD. Provides a general introduction to the Industrial Revolution.

Industrial Revolution. Educational Filmstrip and Video, 2006. DVD. An introduction to the Industrial Revolution.

Just the Facts: The Industrial Revolution. Goldhill Home Media, 2007. DVD. A very good introduction to the Industrial Revolution. Originally produced in 2001.

Middlemarch. BBC/Warner Home Video, 2005. DVD. A video adaptation of George Eliot's novel in which the impact of the Industrial Revolution is portrayed. Originally broadcast in 1994.

Mill Times. PBS, 2006. DVD. A documentary developed and narrated by David Macaulay that utilized old photographs, film of restored mills and homes, and animation to discuss his interest in the interrelationship of people, their workplaces, and environs. Originally produced in 2001.

The Story of the Industrial Revolution. DD Home Entertainment, 2002. VHS. An introduction to the Industrial Revolution presented by Tony Robinson.

6. Establishment of Modern Egypt (1805)

In 1798 Napoleon Bonaparte led a French army to Egypt and scored a major victory over the Mamluk forces in the Battle of the Pyramids. In the fall of 1799 Napoleon abandoned his army after the destruction of the French fleet by the British. Egypt was in a state of disorder, and the Mamluk leadership had not only been defeated but also discredited and demoralized by the Europeans. Into this void stepped Mohammad (Muhammad) Ali (1769–1849; ruler of Egypt, 1805–1848). Ali, an Albanian by birth, immediately began a process to modernize Egyptian government, military, and society. He oriented Egyptian agriculture toward the production of cotton to supply the textile industries in Europe, initiated reforms and expansion of the Egyptian military, and launched policies to improve education and society along European standards. Ali expanded his control south to the Sudan where his army prevailed. He was also interested in expanding Egyptian authority into Palestine, Syria, and parts of present-day Turkey. Twice during his long reign Ali's forces defeated the Ottoman Turks and appeared to be on the verge of replacing them as leaders of the Near East, but Russian and British intervention on behalf of the Turks stifled these plans. Ali established a dynasty that ruled Egypt until 1952.

TERM PAPER SUGGESTIONS

1. Write a paper on the collapse of the Mamluks and the ascendancy of Mohammad Ali.
2. Develop a paper on the domestic achievements that Ali attained in his modernization of Egypt.
3. Ali posed a serious threat for Ottoman leadership during the 1820s and 1830s. Write a paper on Ali's ambitions and his two wars against the Ottoman Turks.
4. Write a paper in which you assess the domestic and foreign policies of Mohammad Ali.

ALTERNATIVE TERM PAPER SUGGESTIONS

1. Develop an iMovie in which the British and French leaders discuss the strategic ascendancy of Egypt under Mohammad Ali.
2. As an aide to Ali during most of the reign, you witness the transformation of the Egyptian state. Develop a blog that consists of excerpts from your memoir of your work with Ali.
3. Develop a podcast in which the Ottoman leadership in Constantinople consider their plans to contain the expansionist Ali.

SUGGESTED SOURCES

Primary Sources

"Firman of Appointment of Muhammad 'Ali as Pasha of Egypt Issued by Ottoman Sultan, 1840." http://historicaltextarchive.com/sections.php ?op=viewarticle&artid=15. Copy of the document that appointed Ali as Pasha of Egypt.

Hassan, Hassan. *In the House of Muhammad Ali: A Family Album, 1805–1952.* New York: American University in Cairo, 2000. Available as an e-book at http://books.google.com/books?id=00tKmHNrKLQC&dq=Hassan +Hassan,+In+the+House+of+Muhammad+Ali&source=gbs_summary_s &cad=0. A rich source of printed primary materials including more than 70 photographs, several relating to Mohammad Ali's role in the establishment of modern Egypt.

Hourani, Albert, ed. *The Modern Middle East: A Reader.* Berkeley: University of California Press, 2004. Includes some primary materials that may be useful.

Secondary Sources

Bayly, C. A. *The Birth of the Modern World: 1780–1914.* New York: Wiley-Blackwell, 2003. Includes information on Mohammad Ali and the establishment of the post-Napoleonic Egyptian state.

Cleveland, William L. *A History of the Modern Middle East.* Boulder, CO: Westview Press, 2004. Provides data on the emergence of Egypt during the nineteenth century.

Daly, M. W. *The Cambridge History of Egypt, Volume 2: Modern Egypt from 1517 to the End of the Twentieth Century.* Cambridge, U.K.: Cambridge University Press, 2008. An excellent resource with considerable information and useful citations; see the article by Khaled Fahmy on Ali.

Falola, Toyin. *Key Events in Africa History: A Reference Guide.* Westport, CT: Greenwood Press, 2002. Includes a very good introduction on the rise of Mohammad Ali of Egypt.

Flower, Raymond. *Napoleon to Nasser: The Story of Modern Egypt.* Washington, DC: First Books Library, 2002. Provides an elementary introduction to the establishment of modern Egypt.

Goldschmidt, Arthur, and Arthur Goldschmidt, Jr. *Modern Egypt: The Formation of a Nation-State.* Boulder, CO: Westview Press, 2004. Also available as an e-book at http://books.google.com/books?id=ZvujoSCdtdgC &pg=PA2&lpg=PA2&dq=Birth+of+Modern+Egypt&source=bl&ots =y5ZLtnIvMF&sig=ydgMTNF7yFqfofDzbs5ZYYyJwaM&hl=en&sa =X&oi=book_result&resnum=7&ct=result. An excellent and useful study with extensive information on the establishment of modern Egypt.

Hunter, F. Robert. *Egypt under the Khedives, 1805–1879: From Household Government to Modern Bureaucracy.* Pittsburgh: University of Pittsburgh Press, 1984. A scholarly study of the structure and administration of the reemergent Egyptian state.

Kedourie, Elie, and Sylvia G. Haim, eds. *Modern Egypt: Studies in Politics and Society.* London: Cass, 1980. A collection of articles on modern Egypt, including some that may be of interest to students working on this topic.

Landau, Jacob M. *Middle Eastern Themes: Papers in History and Politics.* London: Cass, 1973. Includes some useful information that may be of interest to students working on this topic.

McGregor, Andrew. *A Military History of Modern Egypt: From the Ottoman Conquest to the Ramadan War.* Westport, CT: Praeger, 2006. The best study available on the Egyptian military including data on the early nineteenth century.

Manley, Deborah, and Peta Rée. *Henry Salt: Artist, Traveller, Diplomat, Egyptologist.* London: Libri, 2001. A biography of a Western observer who witnessed the establishment of modern Egypt under Mohammad Ali.

Marlowe, John. *Anglo-Egyptian Relations, 1800–1953.* London: Cresset Press, 1954. Includes data on the relationship during the reign of Mohammad Ali and its impact on the formation of the new Egyptian state.

Marsot, Afaf Lutfi Al-Sayyid. *A History of Egypt: From the Arab Conquest to the Present.* 2nd ed. Cambridge, U.K.: Cambridge University Press, 2007. A reliable general history that includes considerable information on the emergence of the new Egyptian state during the early nineteenth century.

———. *Egypt in the Reign of Muhammad Ali.* Cambridge, U.K.: Cambridge University Press, 1984. Also available as an e-book at http://books. google.com/books?id=KCz7N-GYKRcC&dq=Primary+source +mohammad+ali++egypt&pg=PP1&ots=9Bzjr4CHM8&source=in&sig =yN2ZqNFrkV2kjujk5mSN9__7FQw&hl=en&sa=X&oi=book_result &resnum=11&ct=result. A very good study that includes information on Ali's European orientation and preferences.

Perry, Glenn E. *The History of Egypt.* Westport, CT: Greenwood Press, 2004. A very good general history that provides a solid introduction to the founding of the new Egyptian state under Mohammad Ali.

Pollard, Lisa. *Nurturing the Nation: The Family Politics of Modernizing, Colonizing, and Liberating Egypt, 1805–1923.* Berkeley: University of California Press, 2005. An excellent and sophisticated scholarly study that examines the establishment of modern Egypt and its transformation during the nineteenth century.

Rifaat, Mohammed. *The Awakening of Modern Egypt.* London: Longmans, Green, 1947. A dated but useful study on the modern reemergence of Egypt.

Stewart, Desmond. *Young Egypt.* London: Wingate, 1958. The early chapters of this book may be useful to some students.

Sonbol, Amira el-Azhary. *The New Mamluks, Egyptian Society and Modern Feudalism.* Syracuse, NY: Syracuse University Press, 2000. Argues that the earlier Mamluk systems contributed significantly to the emergence of modern Egypt and that Ali built upon them.

Thompson, Jason. *History of Egypt: From Earliest Times to Present.* Cairo and New York: American University in Cairo Press, 2008. The chapter on "The Birth of Modern Egypt" should be useful to all students working on this topic—based on the most current scholarship.

Toledano, Ehud R. *State and Society in Mid-Nineteenth-Century Egypt.* Cambridge, U.K.: Cambridge University Press, 1990. An important scholarly study that provides information on the progress in building modern Egypt during the nineteenth century.

Vatikiotis, P. J. *The History of Modern Egypt: From Mohammad Ali to Mubarak.* 4th ed. Baltimore, MD: Johns Hopkins University Press, 1991. A very good and useful general history of modern Egypt—see the initial chapters and the bibliography.

Weigall, Arthur. *A History of Events in Egypt from 1798 to 1914.* Edinburgh: W. Blackwood and Sons, 1915. An old but reliable history that includes extensive information on early nineteenth-century Egypt.

Young, George. *Egypt.* London: E. Benn, 1927. The early chapters should be useful to many students.

World Wide Web

"History of Egypt under the Mohammad Ali Dynasty." http://www.nation master.com/encyclopedia/History-of-Egypt-under-the-Muhammad-Ali -dynasty. A useful Web site with reliable information on Ali and Egypt.

"Mohammad Ali." http://www.sis.gov.eg/En/History/Modern/08070000 0000000001.htm. Provides biographical data on Ali and links to other sources.

"Muhammad Ali of Egypt, 1805–48: The Father of Modern Egypt." http:// www.travel-to-egypt.net/muhammad-ali.html. Biographical information that introduces students to the life and accomplishments of Ali.

Multimedia Source

"Mohammad Ali (1805–2005)." http://weekly.ahram.org.eg/2005/ mhmdali.htm. A series of 18 articles from *Al-Ahram* (2005) on Ali and his impact on establishing modern Egypt. Each article provides illustrations, cartoons, maps, etc., that should be quite useful to students.

7. Venezuelan Independence (1810–1830)

Venezuelan nationalists seized upon the crisis that confronted Spain when it was invaded by Napoleonic France in 1808 in the Peninsular War. In April 1810 the Spanish governor in Caracas was removed and Francisco de Miranda (1750–1816), a leader of the revolt, declared the independence of the Venezuelan republic on July 5, 1811. However, the Spanish launched a counteroffensive that was aided by an earthquake that decimated the areas that supported independence. Miranda was captured and died in captivity, while his second in command, Simon Bolivar (1783–1830), fled. By the summer of 1812, Bolivar had defeated the Spanish and declared himself "Liberator of Venezuela." This victory was short-lived when Bolivar's forces were again defeated and Bolivar fled to Jamaica. Bolivar organized a new army and returned victorious in 1816. By 1818 the Congress of Angostura met in Caracas and, in the next year, designated Bolivar as the president of the Venezuelan Republic. Bolivar became involved in other successful regional rebellions and formed "Gran Colombia" that included Colombia, Ecuador, and Venezuela— Bolivar was its president. This artificial political creation collapsed during the 1820s. In 1830 Venezuela broke away and established itself as an independent country.

TERM PAPER SUGGESTIONS

1. Write a paper on the role of Francisco de Miranda in initiating the Venezuelan War of Independence.

2. Develop a paper on Bolivar's vision for the new "Gran Colombia."

3. Write a paper on the tenacious royalist support that attempted to suppress the revolutionary forces. What was the composition of the royalist forces?

4. Write a paper on Bolivar's eventual military success over the royalists. Who served in his army? Was Bolivar a gifted military strategist and tactician?

ALTERNATIVE TERM PAPER SUGGESTIONS

1. Develop a podcast in which Miranda and Bolivar are interviewed during the early years of the war on their aspirations for Venezuela and its people.

2. As an aide to Bolivar, you have access to extensive information and all of the personalities associated with the war—you maintain a journal on the struggle.

Create a blog of your journal entries about Bolivar's assumption of leadership to his victory at Carabobo in 1821.

3. Develop an iMovie in which Bolivar explains his plans for "Gran Colombia."

SUGGESTED SOURCES

Primary Sources

Bolivar, Simon. *Selected Writings.* 2 vols. Compil. Vicente Lecuna; ed. Harold Bierck; trans. Lewis Bertrand. New York: Colonial Press, 1951. A very good collection of Bolivar's writings, including many related to Venezuela's independence.

Hanke, Lewis, and Jane M. Rausch, eds. *People and Issues in Latin American History: From Independence to the Present: Sources and Interpretations.* 3rd ed. Princeton, NJ: Markus Weiner, 2008. Includes useful primary sources as well as excerpts from scholarly works.

Hippisley, Gustavus. *A Narrative of the Expedition to the Rivers Orinoco and Apuré in South America; which sailed from England in November 1817, and joined the patriotic forces in Venezuela and Caráccas.* London: John Murray, 1819. Personal recollections of an adventurer who had contact with the Venezuelan rebels.

O'Leary, Daniel Florencio. *The "Detached" Recollections of General D. F. O'Leary.* Ed. R. A. Humphreys. London: Athone Press, 1969. An important memoir by a major participant.

————. *Bolivar and the War of Independence.* Trans. and ed. Robert F. McNerney, Jr. Austin: University of Texas Press, 1970. Provides firsthand insights on Bolivar's leadership and accomplishments.

Vila, Manuel Pérez. *Simon Bolivar: His Basic Thoughts; Biographical Sketch and Selection of Documents.* Caracas: Presidency of the Republic of Venezuela, 1981. An excellent collection of documents on Bolivar that should be very useful to students writing on his role in the war for independence.

Secondary Sources

Bethell, Leslie, ed. *The Independence of Latin America.* New York: Cambridge University Press, 1987. A collection of worthwhile essays on the independence movements (including Venezuela) in Latin America.

Blanchard, Peter. *Under the Flags of Freedom: Slave Soldiers and the Wars of Independence in Spanish South America.* Pittsburgh: University of Pittsburgh Press, 2008. Includes a useful chapter on conditions in Venezuela.

Brading, D. A. *Classical Republicanism and Creole Patriotism: Simon Bolivar (1783–1830) and the Spanish American Revolution.* Cambridge, U.K.:

Cambridge University Press, 1983. A seminal study of Bolivar's ideological and social values and how they shaped the Latin American wars of independence.

Brown, Matthew. *Adventuring through Spanish Colonies: Simón Bolivar, Foreign Mercenaries and the Birth of New Nations.* Liverpool: Liverpool University Press, 2008. An excellent—scholarly yet readable—study that includes extensive information on Venezuela.

Burkholder, Mark A., and Lyman L. Johnson. *Colonial Latin America.* 6th ed. New York: Oxford University Press, 2008. Provides a good background on the origins of the Venezuelan revolt.

Bushnell, David. *Simón Bolivar: Liberation and Disillusion.* New York: Pearson Longman, 2004. Includes information on Bolivar's aspirations for the new Latin American republics.

Chasteen, John. *Americanos: Latin America's Struggle for Independence.* New York: Oxford University Press, 2008. Provides good introductions to the many Latin American revolutions.

Harvey, Robert. *Liberators: Latin America's Struggle for Independence.* New York: Overlook, 2000. A reliable and useful study on the leaders of the conflicts.

Lynch, John. *Simón Bolivar: A Life.* New Haven, CT: Yale University Press, 2006. Perhaps the best biography of Bolivar that includes extensive information on his activities in Venezuela.

———. *The Spanish American Revolution, 1808–1826.* New York: Longman, 2003. A very reliable and comprehensive study of all of the Latin American revolutions.

Nicholson, Irene. *The Liberators, A Study of Independence Movements in Spanish America.* New York: Praeger, 1969. A very good account of the various national movements, including the Venezuelan revolt.

Robertson, William Spence. *Rise of the Spanish-American Republics, as Told in the Lives of Their Liberators.* New York: Free Press, 1948. A classic study by a renowned historian, this volume should be useful to many students.

Scheina, Robert L. *Latin America's Wars.* 2 vols. Dulles, VA: Brassey's, 2003. Excellent scholarship on all of the wars of independence, including Venezuela's.

Tarver, H. Michael, and Julia C. Frederick. *The History of Venezuela.* Westport, CT: Greenwood Press, 2005. A very good general history that includes extensive information on Venezuela's war for independence.

Trend, John B. *Bolivar and the Independence of Spanish America.* Washington: Bolivarian Society of Venezuela, 1951. A very good study on Bolivar's transformational role in Latin American politics.

World Wide Web

"Bolívar's War—Venezuela's War of Independence, 1811–1812." http://www
.experiencefestival.com/bolvars_war_-_venezuelan_war_of_independence
_1811-1812. Provides multiple links to articles on Bolivar and his leader-
ship in the war.

"Timeline—Venezuela." http://timelinesdb.com/listevents.php?subjid=58
&title=Venezuela. A good timeline that includes a section on the war
for Venezuelan independence.

"Venezuelan War of Independence." http://www.economicexpert.com/a/
Venezuelan:War:of:Independence.html. Provides an introduction to the
war with helpful links on Bolivar.

"Venezuelan War of Independence." http://www.bookrags.com/wiki/Venezuelan
_War_of_Independence. A reliable statement on the war with multiple
links to related subjects.

"Venezuelan War of Independence." http://www.mapsofworld.com/venezuela/
history/war-of-independence.html. Provides a good introduction to
the war.

Multimedia Source

Simón Bolívar. Unicorn Video, 1985. VHS. A dramatic film directed by Alessandro
Blasetti.

8. Massacre of the Mamluks (1811)

After a chaotic period of the collapse of the Mamluk leadership and the disruptive invasion of a French army under Napoleon Bonaparte, Mohammad
Ali (1769–1849; ruler of Egypt, 1805–1848) established a new regime
from which the modern Egyptian state would develop. Ali was determined
to eliminate all threats to his position, and his deteriorating relationship
with the Mamluk chieftains led to the infamous massacre of the Mamluks
in 1811. Ali invited the Mamluks to a celebration in Cairo. During a parade
through the citadel area, Ali's forces fired on the unsuspecting Mamluks and
murdered them. Some accounts indicate that as many as 600 tribal leaders
were slain. The massacre continued for several weeks during which approx-
imately 3,000 Mamluks were killed. Some escaped to the Sudan where Ali's
forces pursued them and, at the same time, claimed authority over the
Sudan. Ali's ruthless reputation and his devious methods won him the fear,
distrust, and yet respect of the Arab world.

TERM PAPER SUGGESTIONS

1. Write a paper on the role of the Mamluks during the decades immediate prior to Ali's coming to power in 1805.

2. Develop a term paper on Ali's conclusion that the Mamluks had to be eliminated.

3. Write a paper on the massacre in the citadel and the subsequent actions against the Mamluks.

ALTERNATIVE TERM PAPER SUGGESTIONS

1. Develop a podcast in which Ali is interviewed and provides an explanation for his brutal treatment of the Mamluks.

2. As the son or daughter of a Mamluk who was slaughtered in Cairo, write a blog based on the Mamluk interpretation of the massacre.

3. Develop an iMovie in which the Mamluks discuss whether they would attend the celebration in Cairo.

SUGGESTED SOURCES

Primary Sources

Hassan, Hassan. *In the House of Muhammad Ali: A Family Album, 1805–1952.* New York: American University in Cairo, 2000. Available as an e-book at http://books.google.com/books?id=00tKmHNrKLQC&dq=Hassan +Hassan,+In+the+House+of+Muhammad+Ali&source=gbs_summary_s &cad=0. A rich source of printed primary materials including more than 70 photographs, several relating to Mohammad Ali's role in the establishment of modern Egypt.

Hourani, Albert, ed. *The Modern Middle East: A Reader.* Berkeley: University of California Press, 2004. Includes some primary materials that may be useful.

Secondary Sources

Daly, M. W. *The Cambridge History of Egypt, Volume 2: Modern Egypt from 1517 to the End of the Twentieth Century.* Cambridge, U.K.: Cambridge University Press, 2008. An excellent resource with considerable information and useful citations; see the article by Khaled Fahmy on Ali.

Fage, J. D., John E. Flint, Roland Anthony Oliver, and Roland Oliver. *The Cambridge History of Africa: From C. 1790 to C. 1870,* Cambridge, U.K.: Cambridge University Press, 1977. Includes a description of the massacre and its long-term impact.

Goldschmidt, Arthur, and Arthur Goldschmidt, Jr. *Modern Egypt: The Formation of a Nation-State.* Boulder, CO: Westview Press, 2004. Also available as an e-book at http://books.google.com/books?id=ZvujoSCdtdgC&pg=PA2&lpg=PA2&dq=Birth+of+Modern+Egypt&source=bl&ots=y5ZLtnIvMF&sig=ydgMTNF7yFqfofDzbs5ZYYyJwaM&hl=en&sa=X&oi=book_result&resnum=7&ct=result. An excellent and useful study with extensive information on the establishment of modern Egypt.

Little, D. P. *An Introduction to Mamluk Historiography.* Wiesbaden: Verlag, 1970. This is an excellent study on the wide range of historical approaches and interpretations that have emerged on the Mamluks.

McGregor, Andrew. *A Military History of Modern Egypt: From the Ottoman Conquest to the Ramadan War.* Westport, CT: Praeger, 2006. Also available as an e-book at http://books.google.com/books?id=QZpWx-dgbYcC&dq=Massacre+of+the+Mamluks+1811&source=gbs_summary_s&cad=0. Includes a section on the massacre.

Marsot, Afaf Lutfi Al-Sayyid. *A History of Egypt: From the Arab Conquest to the Present.* 2nd ed. Cambridge, U.K.: Cambridge University Press, 2007. A reliable general history that includes considerable information on the emergence of the new Egyptian state during the early nineteenth century.

———. *Egypt in the Reign of Muhammad Ali.* Cambridge, U.K.: Cambridge University Press, 1984. Also available as an e-book at http://books.google.com/books?id=KCz7N-GYKRcC&dq=Primary+source+mohammad+ali++egypt&pg=PP1&ots=9Bzjr4CHM8&source=in&sig=yN2ZqNFrkV2kjujk5mSN9__7FQw&hl=en&sa=X&oi=book_result&resnum=11&ct=result. A very good study that includes information on Ali's European orientation and preferences.

Shaw, Stanford Jay Shaw, and Ezel Kural Shaw. *History of the Ottoman Empire and Modern Turkey: Reform, Revolution, and Republic: The Rise of Modern Turkey 1808–1975.* Cambridge, U.K.: Cambridge University Press, 1977. Includes information on the massacre and the ascendancy of Ali.

Thompson, Jason. *History of Egypt: From Earliest Times to Present.* Cairo and New York: American University in Cairo Press, 2008. The chapter on "The Birth of Modern Egypt" should be useful to all students working on this topic—based on the most current scholarship.

Ulford, Letitia W. *The Pasha: How Mehemet Ali Defied the West, 1839–1841.* Jefferson, NC: McFarland, 2007. While this work addresses a later topic, the initial chapter should be worthwhile to gain an understanding of Ali's leadership and focus on power.

World Wide Web

"Mamluks." http://encarta.msn.com/encyclopedia_761551963/mamluks.html. A description of the Mamluks and a photograph of a Mamluk vase.

"Mohammed Ali Dynasty." http://www.youregypt.com/ehistory/history/ mohamedali/mali/. Includes a statement on the massacre and a reproduction of a painting of the massacre in the citadel.

"The Mamluks in History." http://www.muslimheritage.com/uploads/ mamluk.pdf. An article by Salah Ziemech that reviews Mamluk history and includes a brief statement on the massacre. It is helpful in understanding the Mamluk tradition and position in Egypt prior to Ali.

"Timeline, 1800–99." http://toolbar.google.com/archivesearch?q=ali+mamluk +mamluks+cairo+muhammad&scoring=t&hl=en&ned=us&sa=N&sugg =d&as_ldate=1800&as_hdate=1899&lnav=hist7. Provides information on the massacre and links to other relevant sites.

Multimedia Sources

"Mamluk Pictures." http://www.lexic.us/definition-of/mamluks. Includes many relevant illustrations of the Mamluks.

"Slide Tour of the Citadel." http://www.nmhschool.org/tthornton/images/ Muhammad_Ali__mosque.jpg and http://www.nmhschool.org/tthornton/ mehistorydatabase/fatimid_mamluk_architecture_cairo.php#citadel. Provides a series of images on the location of the massacre.

9. The Cape-Xhosa Wars (1811–1879)

The Cape-Xhosa Wars (*Cape Frontier Wars or the Kaffir Wars*) consisted of nine conflicts between the European colonists and the Xhosa people in the eastern part of South Africa. As the Europeans were arriving and expanding to the north and west, the Xhosa were migrating with their herds to the south and east. During the nineteenth century there were six Xhosa wars: 1811–1812, 1818–1819, 1834–1836, 1846–1847, 1851–1853, and 1877–1879. In addition, the Xhosa mounted opposition through the "Cattle Killings" of 1856–1858. Under the influence of a young woman prophet, they sacrificed their animals in the belief that their ancestors would save them from the Europeans. The Europeans and the Xhosa were competing for land—for farming and grazing for their animals. The impact of the wars was to drive the Xhosa from the useful land. The British contained the Xhosa and transformed them into laborers who would work the diamond and gold mines.

TERM PAPER SUGGESTIONS

1. Write a paper on the causes, outbreak, and consequences of the four Cape-Xhosa wars during the first half of the nineteenth century.
2. Develop a paper on the "Cattle Killings" of 1856–1858. How did this start? What did the Xhosas think would follow?
3. Write a paper on the ninth Cape-Xhosa war (1877–1879). How did this connect with the Zulu wars and Anglo-Boer relations?

ALTERNATIVE TERM PAPER SUGGESTIONS

1. The Xhosa were a peaceful people who were focused on tending to their animals and the land that was necessary to support them. Develop a podcast in which Xhosa leaders discuss the encroachment of the Boers and British into their homeland and their concerns and plans on how they were going to handle this aggression.
2. The British colonists were very aggressive in seizing the best land for farming and grazing. As a member of a British colonist family, you witness the impact of these seizures on the native Xhosa people. Create a blog of your diary entries on events during the early nineteenth century and consider the moral dilemma that you have—could the land support the needs of both peoples if it was held in common?
3. Develop an iMovie in which the Xhosa prophet Nongquawuse urges the Xhosa to destroy their crops and cattle to gain the support of their ancestors in the struggle with the Europeans.

SUGGESTED SOURCES

Primary Sources

Prichard, Helen M. *Friends and Foes in the Transkei: An Englishwoman's Experiences During the Cape Frontier War of 1877–78.* Whitefish, MT: Kessinger, 2008. A first-rate primary source that all students working on this subject should consult. It includes information on the war and its impact on the peoples of both sides.

Throup, David, ed. *British Documents on Foreign Affairs: Reports and Papers from the Foreign Office Confidential Print. Part I, From the mid-nineteenth century to the First World War, Series G, Africa, 1848–1914.* 25 vols.

Bethesda, MD: University Publications of America, 1995. See volumes 4 through 6 in this work for relevant documents and information on the Cape-Xhosa War.

Secondary Sources

Beckett, Ian F. W. *The Victorians at War*. London: Continuum, 2006. Also available as an e-book at http://books.google.com/books?id=LjBE4Xp LxSwC&dq=Cape+Frontier+Wars&source=gbs_summary_s&cad=0. Includes extensive information on several of the Xhosa wars.

Bundy, Colin. *The Rise and Fall of the South African Peasantry*. 2nd ed. New York: ACLS Humanities, 2008. An important study that examines the impact of the displacement caused by the advance of the Boers and the British in South Africa.

Castle, Ian, and Christa Hook. *British Infantryman in South Africa, 1877–81*. Botley, U.K.: Osprey, 2003. Available as an e-book at http://books.google .com/books?id=CFog2V7uykAC&pg=PA6&lpg=PA6&dq=Cape+Xhosa +War+1878+1879&source=web&ots=mqsWfkylMG&sig=tFSOCbfC qcyJOhXPqQgSwAwymeI&hl=en&sa=X&oi=book_result&resnum =9&ct=result. Includes useful information on the ninth Xhosa war.

Davenport, Rodney. *South Africa: A Modern History*. 5th ed. London: Palgrave Macmillan, 2000. A general history of South Africa that includes information on the wars and their impact on the native population.

Gilionmee, Hermann Buhr. *The Afrikaners: Biography of a People*. Charlottesville: University of Virginia Press, 2003. Provides some information and insights into the Xhosa wars and their impact on both sides.

Meredith, Martin. *Diamonds, Gold, and War: The British, the Boers, and the Making of South Africa*. New York: Public Affairs, 2007. Useful in examining the motives for the later Xhosa wars and the consequences on South African history.

Oliver, Roland, and G. N. Sanderson, eds. *The Cambridge History of Africa, Volume 6, c. 1870–c.1905*. Cambridge, U.K.: Cambridge University Press, 1985. Very reliable and useful resource that includes essays on the European expansion and the impact on the natives—the ninth Xhosa war is discussed.

Olson, James S. *The Peoples of Africa: An Ethnohistorical Dictionary*. Westport, CT: Greenwood Press, 1996. A very useful resource that most students working on this topic will want to see.

Raugh, Harold E. *The Victorians at War, 1815–1914: An Encyclopedia of British Military History*. Santa Barbara, CA: ABC-CLIO, 2004. Available as an e-book at http://books.google.com/books?id=HvE_Pa_ZlfsC&dq =Cape+Frontier+Wars&source=gbs_summary_s&cad=0. This reliable reference work includes information on the fifth through ninth Xhosa wars.

Vandervort, Bruce. *Wars of Imperial Conquest in Africa, 1830–1914.* Bloomington: Indiana University Press, 1998. A scholarly study of the European expansion in Africa that includes data on the Xhosa wars.

Worden, Nigel. *The Making of Modern South Africa: Conquest, Apartheid, Democracy.* New York: Longitude, 2007. A very good and provocative study that examines the consequences on the natives of the imperial wars in South Africa and the historical development of the country to the present. Data on the Xhosa wars are included.

World Wide Web

"Cape Frontier War." http://www.britannica.com/EBchecked/topic/93594/Cape-Frontier-Wars. Provides a brief statement on the war.

"Cape Frontier Wars." http://www.nationmaster.com/encyclopedia/Cape-Frontier-Wars. Includes information on the wars and a timeline.

"Cape Frontier Wars in South Africa." http://www.speirstours.co.za/cape-frontier-wars.htm. A good and accurate introduction to the wars.

"Frontier Wars." http://www.frontierwars.co.za/index.htm. Provides information on the wars along with a good map, illustrations, and photographs.

"Frontier Wars." http://africanhistory.about.com/od/glossaryf/g/def_FrontierWar.htm. Provides introductory level information on the wars between the Boers and the Xhosas.

"South African Oriented Timeline, 1843–1881." http://whitlock.castlewebs.net/whitsend/tl3.htm. A useful timeline on the numerous conflicts in South Africa, including the Xhosa wars.

"South African History Time Line 1488–2000." http://griquatownandersons.com/SouthAfricanHistory.html. A very useful timeline accompanied by a marvelous regional map.

"Xhosa Wars." http://books.google.com/books?id=SARuV5ubf-YC&pg=PA6&lpg=PA6&dq=Cape+Xhosa+War+1878+1879&source=web&ots=6gb0pGNl9H&sig=-_Qn8wubNNSLZ0LGvZGcNv1hajQ&hl=en&sa=X&oi=book_result&resnum=1&ct=result#PPA6,M1. Provides a statement on the wars from *Queen Victoria's Enemies* by Ian Knight and Richard Scollins.

Multimedia Sources

"Decline of the African States." http://www.britannica.com/EBchecked/topic/555568/South-Africa/44071/The-decline-of-the-African-states.

Includes information on the war and 25multimedia components including some maps that are useful on this topic.

"Wargaming the Cape Frontier Wars." http://www.geocities.com/cdferree/xhosa/xhosa.html. Includes a lengthy and accurate statement on the wars and then establishes criteria for a war game based on the historical situations.

10. Eight Trigrams Rebellion (1813)

During the early nineteenth century, northern China was ripe for violent action against the corrupt and dismal Ch'ing Dynasty. At the same time, millenarian sects flourished and served as mediums for criticism of the regime. The most significant of these sects was a variant of the White Lotus ideology known as the Eight Trigrams Movement. It was based on a sixteenth-century religion that worshipped as its principal god the "Eternal and Venerable Mother." The rebels anticipated that their overthrow of the government would usher in a new age of "endless blessings" for all and that Chinese society would be greatly improved. The rebellion lasted for several months and, after the defeat of the rebels in the Forbidden City (Beijing), the government forces prevailed. While some rebels persisted in fighting in the northern province of Honan, most of its leaders were executed and its peasant supporters effectively intimidated. The rebellion was the most violent challenge to Ch'ing power during the early decades of the nineteenth century; the next threat would be the First Opium War in 1840.

TERM PAPER SUGGESTIONS

1. Write a paper on the origins of the Eight Trigrams movement in China. What were its basic tenets? Was it primarily a religious or a peasant resistance movement?

2. Develop a paper on the outbreak and suppression of the Eight Trigrams Rebellion.

3. Write a paper on the place of the Eight Trigrams Rebellion in the context of nineteenth-century Chinese revolutionary history.

ALTERNATIVE TERM PAPER SUGGESTIONS

1. Develop an iMovie in which the leaders of the Eight Trigrams Rebellion discuss their grievances against the Chinese government. Did they think

that they had a reasonable chance of prevailing in the struggle? Why or why not?

2. As an elder in North China who has witnessed the poor performance of the Ch'ing Dynasty in addressing the needs of the people, you support the rebellion. Develop a blog in support of the Eight Trigrams movement. Be sure to provide specific information based on the values of the movement in justifying your complaints against the government.

3. Develop a podcast in which the surviving defeated leaders of the rebellion reflect upon the reasons for their failure and their plans for the future.

SUGGESTED SOURCES

Primary Sources

Ebrey, Patricia B., ed. *Chinese Civilization: A Sourcebook.* 2nd ed. New York: Free Press, 1993. Includes some related sources that may be useful to students working on this topic.

Mair, Victor H., ed. *The Columbia History of Chinese Literature.* New York: Columbia University Press, 2001. Includes early nineteenth century writings related to the Eight Trigrams movement.

Secondary Sources

Allen, Frank, and Tina Chunna Zhang. *The Whirling Circles of Ba Gua Zhang: The Art and Legends of the Eight Trigram Palm.* Berkeley, CA: Blue Snake Books, 2007. Provides information on the legacy of the movement and its values through methods and songs. It is useful for gaining an understanding of the cultural basis of the movement.

Eastman, Lloyd E. *Family, Field and Ancestors: Constancy and Change in China's Social and Economic History, 1550–1949.* New ed. New York: Oxford University Press, 1989. Provides information on early nineteenth century Chinese social history that may be useful to students working on this topic.

Elleman, Bruce A. *Modern Chinese Warfare, 1795–1989.* London: Routledge, 2001. The notions of rebellion and revolution warfare that are considered in the initial chapter may be useful.

Fairbank, John King. *The Great Chinese Revolution, 1800–1985.* New York: Harper Perennial, 1987. Provides information on the rebellion within the context of organized resistance in modern Chinese history.

Haar, Barend J. ter. *Messianism and the Heaven and Earth Society: Approaches to Heaven and Earth Society Texts.* New Haven, CT: Yale University Press, 1985. Provides useful data on the movement and society.

Little, Daniel. *Understanding Peasant China: Case Studies in the Philosophy of Social Science.* New Haven, CT: Yale University Press, 1989. Available as an e-book at http://books.google.com/books?id=u53C6RpEf QYC&dq=Eight+Trigrams+Rebellion&source=gbs_summary_s&cad =0. An analysis of scholarship on Chinese peasant mentality that includes data on the Eight Trigrams movement.

Naquin, Susan. *Millenarian Rebellion in China: Eight Trigrams Uprising of 1813.* New Haven, CT: Yale University Press, 1976. Available as an e-book at https://kb.osu.edu/dspace/bitstream/1811/5983/12/TOCIntroEtc.pdf. The most comprehensive history of the rebellion in English. It is critical for all students working on this topic.

Rinehart, James F. *Revolution and the Millennium: China, Mexico, and Iran.* Westport, CT: Greenwood Press, 1997. A useful comparative study of millenarian movements—including the Eight Trigrams movement—in three very different societies.

Roberts, J. A. G. *The Complete Illustrated History of China.* New ed. London: History Press, 2003. Provides introductory information that should be useful.

Spence, Jonathan D. *The Search for Modern China.* New ed. New York: W. W. Norton, 1991. A general introduction to modern Chinese history by a prominent historian; students should have ready access to this popular work.

World Wide Web

"Eight Trigrams Society." http://www.britannica.com/EBchecked/topic/ 181049/Eight-Trigrams-Society. A good introduction to the ideology and values of the society. It includes comments on the rebellion.

"Links for Chinese Religion and Philosophy." http://www2.kenyon.edu/Depts/ Religion/Fac/Adler/Reln270/links270.htm#POPULAR. A useful site developed by Joseph Adler of Kenyon College, it includes hundreds of links to sites, including some related to the Eight Trigrams movement and rebellion.

Multimedia Sources

Masa, Ron. "An Introduction to the I Ching." Audio-book available at http:// www.learnoutloud.com/Sale-Section/Self-Development/Spirituality/ An-Introduction-to-the-I-Ching/24133. Chapter six includes information on the origins and history of the Eight Trigrams movement.

"Eight Trigrams Society." http://www.britannica.com/EBchecked/topic/ 181049/Eight-Trigrams-Society. Useful introductory site with some multimedia features.

11. Congress of Vienna (1814–1815)

By the spring of 1814 the generation-long upheaval of the wars of the French Revolution and Napoleonic era was drawing to a close. The major powers (Great Britain, Austria, Prussia, and Russia) in the coalition against France were determined to establish a postwar political system that reflected the pre–French Revolutionary conditions in Europe. Thus, the dominant theme that dominated their conversations and communications was the restoration of the "old order" in Europe. Napoleon's initial abdication and exile to Elba occurred in April 1814; the Congress convened in September 1814. By that time the "four" great powers had become "five" with the admission of the new French leadership—the restored Bourbon Louis XVIII. While numerous states sent representatives to Vienna, the five major powers directed the agenda and controlled the outcomes. The dominant personality of the Congress was the Austrian Prime Minister Prince Metternich; Britain was represented by its Foreign Minister Lord Castlereagh and, later, the Duke of Wellington, and France benefited significantly from the talents of Talleyrand. Much of the Congress was spent arguing over exchanges of territory or agreements on territorial boundaries among the victors. Some general international agreements on diplomacy, the protection of diplomats, and the open navigation of international rivers were concluded, but Britain's effort to include an international agreement on abolishing the slave trade failed to gain support. Napoleon's escape from Elba and his infamous "Hundred Days," which resulted in a French defeat at Waterloo in June 1815, did not disrupt the progress of the Congress of Vienna. Its concluding documents were signed on June 9, 1815, during the days immediately prior to Napoleon's defeat. The Congress of Vienna had short-term success, but the forces of liberalism and nationalism posed serious and consistent challenges during the decades ahead and manifested themselves in the revolutions of 1820, 1830, and 1848.

TERM PAPER SUGGESTIONS

1. Develop a paper on the varying approaches to the postwar settlement expressed by the authoritarian regimes of central and eastern Europe (Austria, Prussia, and Russia) with the more liberal western European countries led by Great Britain.
2. Did the Congress of Vienna succeed in restoring the *ancient regime?*

3. Write a paper focused on Metternich's role at the Congress of Vienna. To what degree did he shape its outcomes?

4. How successful were Castlereagh and the British delegation in thwarting any colonial ambitions held by their traditional enemy, France?

5. Was the peace established by the Congress of Vienna bound to collapse because it ran counter to new prevailing historical forces?

6. Did ethics play a role in the development of the final treaty in Vienna?

ALTERNATIVE TERM PAPER SUGGESTIONS

1. Develop a hyperlink online map of the results of the Congress of Vienna and provide commentary on how the Congress shaped nineteenth-century history.

2. Imagine that you were a representative of the United States at the Congress of Vienna. Develop a blog on your experiences at the Congress. How would your values and perspective differ from those of Metternich and the other leading participants?

3. Develop a podcast on the negotiation between Metternich and Castlereagh on their approach to France at the Congress of Berlin.

4. Much of the "business" of the Congress was transacted at social events, such as dances or balls. Develop a 2–3 minute iMovie in which one of Metternich's spies is gathering information from the Russian representatives who are attending such an event.

SUGGESTED SOURCES

Primary Sources

Castlereagh, Robert Stewart Viscount. *Memoirs and Correspondence of Viscount Castlereagh, second Marquess of Londonderry.* Ed. his brother, Charles Vane, Marquess of Londonderry. 12 vols. London: H. Colburn, 1848–1853. The best printed source of primary material by Castlereagh, available in most university libraries.

Metternich, Clemens Wenzel Lothar, First von. *Memoirs of Prince Metternich, 1773–1815.* Ed. Prince Richard Metternich; trans. Mrs. Alexander Napier. 5 vols. New York: H. Fertig, 1970; reprint of 1880 ed. This is the standard source in English for Metternich's personal recollections and reflections.

———. *Metternich, The Autobiography.* Welwyn Garden City, U.K.: Ravenhall Books, 2004. A useful volume of primary material based on the *Memoirs.*

Spiel, Hilde, ed. *The Congress of Vienna: An Eyewitness Account.* Trans. Richard H. Weber. Philadelphia: Chilton Book, 1968. A collection of primary materials on the Congress by those in attendance.

Talleyrand, Prince. *The Correspondence of Prince Talleyrand and King Louis XVIII During the Congress of Vienna.* Whitefish, MT: Kessinger Publishing, 2005. An important primary source to understand the French positions at the Congress.

Wellington, Gerald Wellesley, Seventh Duke of, ed. *Wellington and His Friends: Letters of the First Duke of Wellington to the Rt. Hon. Charles and Mrs. Arbuthnot, the Earl and Countess of Wilton, Princess Lieven, and Miss Burdett-Coutts.* London: Macmillan, 1965. Provides insights and recollections on the Congress and its participants.

Secondary Sources

Chapman, Tim. *The Congress of Vienna: Origins, Processes, and Results.* London: Routledge, 1998. A reliable study that provides a comprehensive introduction to the history of the Congress.

Dallas, Gregor. *The Final Act: The Roads to Waterloo.* New York: Henry Holt, 1996. Includes some valuable commentary on the early months of the Congress and the impact of Napoleon's "Hundred Days" on the proceedings.

Derry, John Wesley. *Castlereagh.* London: A. Lane, 1976. A reliable biography that introduces Castlereagh as a major power at the Congress.

Gash, Norman. *Lord Liverpool: The Life and Political Career of Robert Banks Jenkinson, Second Earl of Liverpool, 1770–1828.* Cambridge, MA: Harvard University Press, 1984. A solid study of the British Prime Minister by a respected scholar.

Harris, Robin. *Talleyrand: Betrayer and Savior of France.* London: John Murray, 2007. A readable and reliable introduction to the complex life of the French foreign minister who survived the turbulence of French politics and won favorable terms for defeated France at the Congress of Vienna.

Haythornthwaite, Philip. *Wellington: The Iron Duke.* Washington, DC: Potomac Books, 2007. An introduction to the soldier-statesman-politician who defeated Napoleon at Waterloo, represented Britain at the Congress, and later served as Prime Minister.

Kissinger, Henry. *A World Restored: Metternich, Castlereagh, and the Problems of Peace, 1812–22.* Boston: Houghton Mifflin, 1973. A useful consideration of the impact of the Congress on the post-Napoleonic era.

King, David. *Vienna 1814: How the Conquerors of Napoleon Made Love, War, and Peace at the Congress of Vienna.* New York: Random House/

Harmony, 2008. This critically acclaimed study provides a new analysis of primary documents and provides vivid portraits of the personalities that gathered in Vienna; for readability, it stands next to Harold Nicolson's classic study.

May, Arthur James. *The Age of Metternich, 1814–1848.* Hinsdale, IL: Dryden Press, 1963. Still a standard and readily available study of Metternich and his impact at the Congress and during the first half of the nineteenth century.

Nicolson, Harold. *The Congress of Vienna: A Study in Allied Unity, 1812–1822.* New York: Grove Press, 2001. This is a new edition of a classic history of the Congress of Vienna. Nicolson was a solid historian and diplomat who was also a stylist.

Sked, Alan. *Metternich and Austria: An Evaluation.* New York: Palgrave Macmillan, 2008. While considering the impact of Metternich's entire career on Austria, this book provides some provocative and challenging notions of Metternich at the Congress.

Straus, Hannah Alice. *The Attitude of the Congress of Vienna toward Nationalism in Germany, Italy, and Poland.* New York: AMS Press, 1968. Considers the opposition to "nationalist" groups from the advocates of "restoration."

Webster, Charles K. *The Congress of Vienna, 1814–1815.* London: Thames and Hudson, 1969. A dependable history of the Congress.

Zamoyski, Adam. *Rites of Peace: The Fall of Napoleon and the Congress of Vienna.* New York: HarperCollins, 2007. Largely based on primary sources, Zamoyski concludes that greed and geopolitical ambitions motivated the victors at the Congress of Vienna.

World Wide Web

"An Austrian View of Alexander I and the Russians at the Congress of Vienna, 1815." http://www.shsu.edu/~his_ncp/Vienna01.html. This is a valuable excerpt describing the Russian position at the Congress from *Readings in Modern European History.* Ed. James Harvey Robinson and Charles Beard. Boston: Ginn and Company, 1908.

Bloy, Marje. "The Congress of Vienna, 1 November 1814–8 June 1815." Available on *The Victorian Web* at http://www.victorianweb.org/history/forpol/vienna.html. An outstanding source on the terms of the Congress of Vienna that is data-rich for new students.

"The Council of Vienna System and Challenges." http://www.fordham.edu/halsall/mod/modsbook16.html. Includes four primary sources by Metternich as well as a copy of the Carlsbad Decrees (1819). This is from the *Internet Modern History Sourcebook,* Conservative Order, Fordham University. Ed. Paul Halsall.

"Europe After the Congress of Vienna, 1815." http://www.rootsweb.ancestry
.com/~wggerman/map/vienna1815.htm. Provides a reliable map
that indicates the major territorial changes that resulted from the
Congress.

Multimedia Sources

Congress Dances. 1931. VHS. Operetta starring Lillian Harvey, directed by Erik
Charell. German with English subtitles. Set in the context of the
Congress of Vienna, this is a fictional tale of an ambitious business
woman. The film was banned by the Nazis because of the number of
Jews who were associated with its production.

"The Age of Metternich: 1814–1848." 2007. Podcast by Margaret Anderson,
University of California, Berkeley. http:www.learnoutloud.com/
Podcast-Directory/History/European-History/The-Age-of-Metternich-
1814-1815-Podcast/. A university lecture on the influence of the
Austrian Foreign Minister from the Congress of Vienna to the outbreak
of the Revolutions of 1848.

"The Hundred Days." 2007. Podcast. http://www.searchpodcast.com/feeds/
56651?page=1&query=Congress+of+Vienna. Based on Napoleon's letters, this podcast provides insights into his thinking during the early
months of the Congress of Vienna in the fall and winter of 1814–
1815.

The Iron Duke. Video Classics, 1935. DVD. Drama starring George Arliss,
Ellaline Terriss, Gladys Cooper, A. E. Matthews, and Allan Aynesworth.
The film opens at the Congress of Vienna and then follows with the
Hundred Days. This obviously dated but worthwhile film glorifies
Wellington as the hero of Waterloo and, later, British politics.

12. Straits Question (1815–1878)

The Straits Question that dominated much of nineteenth- and twentieth-
century European diplomacy was closely related to the Eastern Question.
The focal points were the Bosporus and Dardanelles straits that separated
the Black and Mediterranean seas. During the nineteenth century these
straits were controlled by the decadent Ottoman Empire, which was
vulnerable to extraordinary pressures brought by the great powers. After
the Congress of Vienna (1815) the British came to consider the Mediterranean Sea as a British sphere of influence. At the same time, the

Russia Empire was seeking to gain access to the straits and the Mediterranean Sea so that it could expand its political and economic influence in the region and beyond into the Atlantic Ocean. The Straits Question resulted in a series of crises. A dispute in the 1830s was resolved by the London Straits Convention in 1841 when the European powers agreed that no warships could traverse the Straits. This maintained the Russian isolation from access to the Mediterranean. Between 1854 and 1856 the Crimean War was fought on the Crimea Peninsula (Russia) between Russia and the allies, Great Britain, France, and Sardinia. The Russians continued to be restricted from the Straits. After the Russo-Turkish War of 1877–1878, the Congress of Berlin thwarted Russian plans for the straits and the Balkans when Great Britain pulled off a diplomatic coup with the assistance of Germany, the Ottoman Empire, and Austria-Hungary. As the nineteenth century closed, Britain had prevailed on the Straits Question at the continuing expense of Russia.

TERM PAPER SUGGESTIONS

1. Write a paper in which you compare/contrast the Russian and British policies on the Straits Question during the nineteenth century.

2. Develop a paper on the role and impact of the Straits Question within the larger context of the Eastern Question during the nineteenth century.

3. Write a paper on how the Austrians came to support the British position on the Straits during the 1870s and 1880s.

4. Write a paper on the impact of the Straits Question on the Ottoman Empire during the nineteenth century.

ALTERNATIVE TERM PAPER SUGGESTIONS

1. Develop a podcast in which you interview British Prime Minister Benjamin Disraeli and his Foreign Secretary Robert Salisbury on their rationale for restricting Russia from gaining access to the straits.

2. Develop an iMovie in which Russian diplomats argue their case for gaining access to the straits during the deliberations at the Congress of Berlin.

3. Develop a hyperlink map of the straits with a narrative of all of the conflicts that developed on them during the nineteenth century.

4. As a Russian diplomat you have argued for Russian access to the straits for decades. Develop a blog in which you record your experiences serving the tsar from the 1840s through the early 1880s.

SUGGESTED SOURCES

Primary Sources

Campbell, George Douglas, Duke of Argyll. *The Eastern Question from the Treaty of Paris 1856 to the Treaty of Berlin 1878, and to the Second Afghan War.* London: Strahan, 1879. Also available as an e-book at http://www.archive.org/details/afghanquestionfr00argy. Includes firsthand information by Argyll, a British statesman, on the complex issues associated with the straits within the context of Anglo-Russian and Anglo-Turkish relations.

Holland, Thomas Erskine. *The European Concert in the Eastern Question: A Collection of Treaties and Other Public Acts.* Aalen: Scientia Vertag, 1979; originally published in 1885. Includes texts and announcements related to the Straits Question.

Temperley, Harold, and Lillian M. Pearson, eds. *Foundations of British Foreign Policy from Pitt (1782) to Salisbury (1902): or, Documents, old and new.* Cambridge, U.K.: Cambridge University Press, 1938. An excellent resource that includes several documents connected to the straits issue.

Secondary Sources

Anderson, Matthew S. *The Eastern Question, 1774–1923: A Study in International Relations.* New York: St. Martin's, 1966. Includes information on the Russian ambitions to gain access to the Mediterranean Sea through the straits and the British opposition to such actions.

Bartlett, Christopher John. *Peace, War, and the European Powers, 1814–1914.* London: Macmillan, 1996. Also available as an e-book at http://books.google.com/books?id=eVPQWWqHbi8C. An important and significant work that includes several references to the Straits Question as a source of diplomatic difficulty during the nineteenth century.

Bitis, Alexander. *Russia and the Eastern Question: Army, Government, and Society: 1815–1833.* New York: Oxford University Press for the British Academy, 2006. Includes information on the Russian policies on the straits during the 1820s and 1830s within the context of their national plans.

Bobroff, Ronald. *Roads to Glory: Late Imperial Russia and the Turkish Straits.* London and New York: I. B. Tauris, 2006. The introductory chapter refers to the historic background to the Russo-Turkish conflict on the straits and may be useful to students.

Duggan, Stephen. *The Eastern Question: A Study in Diplomacy.* New York: AMS Press, 1970. A standard source in which Russian access to the straits is raised as a continuing problem for European diplomats during the nineteenth century.

Graves, Philip P. *The Question of the Straits.* London: E. Benn, 1931. A classic study that examines the many manifestations of the straits issue during the nineteenth and twentieth centuries.

Ingram, Edward. *Eastern Question in the Nineteenth Century: The Collected Essays of Allan Cunningham.* London: Routledge, 1993. Some essays are focused on the straits as the key factor in understanding the larger Eastern Question.

Jelavich, Barbara. *Russia's Balkan Entanglements, 1806–1914.* Cambridge: Cambridge University Press, 1991. Also available as an e-book at http://books.google.com/books?id=K9kmX-OBDOEC. While Russia was interested in expanding its influence in the Balkans, the straits issue was never far from being a central issue. This is an outstanding book.

———. *The Ottoman Empire, the Great Powers, and the Straits Question, 1870–1887.* Bloomington: Indiana University Press, 1973. While focused on only 17 years, Jelavich's study is the best work on the Straits Question and its impact on diplomacy and the relationships among the great powers.

Marriott, J. A. R. *The Eastern Question: An Historical Study in European Diplomacy.* 2nd ed. Oxford: Clarendon Press, 1918. Available as an e-book at http://www.archive.org/stream/easternquestiona009777mbp/easternquestiona009777mbp_djvu.txt This old, classic study established the standard interpretation on the Eastern Question and the place of the straits debate in it and is still noteworthy and usable.

Medlicott, William Norton. *The Congress of Berlin and After: A Diplomatic History of the Near Eastern Settlement, 1878–1880.* London: Methuen, 1938. The best diplomatic history of the Congress of Berlin of 1878 in which the straits were among the core issues that had to be resolved.

Millman, Richard. *Britain and the Eastern Question, 1875–1878.* New York: Oxford University Press, 1979. Very good on Prime Minister Benjamin Disraeli's policy to block Russia's access to the straits. It covers the period of the Russo-Turkish War and the Congress of Berlin.

Philipson, Coleman, and Noel Buxton. *The Question of the Bosphorus and Dardanelles.* London: Stevens and Haynes, 1917. Still an important and useful study that includes extensive information of the Straits Question during the nineteenth century.

Puryear, Vernon John. *England, Russia, and the Straits Question.* Hamden, CT: Archon, 1965; originally published in 1931. An outstanding study on the Straits Question as a major obstacle in Anglo-Russian relations during the nineteenth century.

Rozakis, Christos L., and Petros N. Stagos. *The Turkish Straits.* Dordrecht: Martinus Nijhoff Publishers, 1987. Also available as an e-book at

http://books.google.com/books?id=yJc7HWhF-K8C. Includes valuable
information and maps that should be helpful to most students.

World Wide Web

"The Great Powers and the Eastern Question." http://staff.lib.msu.edu/sowards/
balkan/lect10.htm. A lecture by Steven Sowards that provides insights
into the connections between the major European powers and the
Ottoman Empire.
"The Origin of the Eastern Question." http://www.thecorner.org/hist/europe/
east-qtn.htm. A very useful outline on the Eastern Question.
"The Straits Question." http://www.britannica.com/EBchecked/topic/567974/
Straits-Question. A reliable and comprehensive statement on the question as a source of continuing diplomatic difficulty among the great
powers.

Multimedia Sources

"Bosphorus Cruise." http://www.youtube.com/watch?v=zm3SA2M67Cw.
Includes maps and video on the straits.
"Traffic in the Dardanelles." http://uk.encarta.msn.com/encyclopedia
_761552237/Dardanelles.html. Provides a photograph of a ship going
through the Dardanelles Straits.

13. Chilean War of Independence from Spain (1810–1826)

The Chilean War of Independence from Spain was divided into two periods: 1810–1821 and 1821–1826. During the first 11 years of the struggle, most of the actual fighting occurred between the Chileans and the
Spaniards, and Chile's forces prevailed when the Spanish were driven
from the mainland. This phase also included the issuance of the Chilean
Declaration of Independence on February 12, 1818. During the second
period (1821–1826), the war continued on a reduced level until the
Spanish troops on Chiloé (a very large island in southern Chile) surrendered and Chiloé was incorporated into the independent Chilean state.
During the late eighteenth century, the Spanish-appointed *captaincy-gen-
eral* acted with considerable autonomy. In 1808 the beloved Captain-
General Luis Muñoz de Guzmán died, and during the next two years the

difficulties that confronted Chile were aggravated by the political unrest and lack of direction. On September 10, 1816, the war for independence began when the Chilean political leaders could no longer abide by their Spanish overlords. A Chilean *junta* took charge to run the war against Spain; the *junta* was followed by a dictatorship. The war with Spain turned in favor of Chile when the Army of the Andes under the Argentinean José de San Martin (1778–1850) and the Chilean Bernardo O'Higgins (1776–1842) defeated the Spaniards in 1817. O'Higgins declared Chile's independence and San Martin's strategy and tactics defeated the remnants of the Spanish army on Chiloé. Spain recognized Chile's independence in 1840.

TERM PAPER SUGGESTIONS

1. Write a paper on the causes and outbreak of the Chilean War of Independence.
2. Develop a paper on the Spanish defense of their position in Chile.
3. The Chilean *junta* appeared to be unable to win the war. Write a paper in which you analyze the performance of the *junta* and its leadership of the war.
4. Write a paper on the Chiloé campaign and its significance in the independence of Chile.

ALTERNATIVE TERM PAPER SUGGESTIONS

1. Develop a podcast in which San Martin and O'Higgins assess Chile's rebel leaders and their plans for the Army of the Andes.
2. As an influential citizen in Santiago, Chile, during the years of turbulence (1808–1810), you are very concerned about your family's future. Create a blog that consists of a series of letters in which you describe the uncertainty of the period and its principal developments.
3. Develop an iMovie on the development of the Chilean Declaration of Independence and its contents.

SUGGESTED SOURCES

Primary Sources

Callcott, Maria. *Journal of a Residence in Chile during the year 1822; and, A Voyage from Chile to Brazil in 1823.* Ed. Jennifer Hayward. Charlottesville: University of Virginia Press, 2003. Personal recollections of a contemporary traveler in the region who acquired extensive information and met some of those involved in the war.

Cochrane, Thomas. *Narrative of Services in the Liberation of Chile, Peru, and Brazil from Spanish and Portuguese Domination.* Ann Arbor: University Microfilms, 1973; originally published in 1858. A memoir by a major military participant who provided leadership in the defeat of the Spaniards.

Johnston, Samuel B. *Letters Written during a Residence of Three Years in Chile. . . .* Microopaque, NY: Readex Microprint, 1982; originally published in 1816. Johnson's correspondence provides a firsthand account of some of the conditions and events associated with the rebellion.

O'Leary, Daniel Florencio. *The "Detached"' Recollections of General D. F. O'Leary.* Ed. R. A. Humphreys. London: Athone Press, 1969. A memoir by an Irish-born military leader who supported Chilean independence.

Pérez Rosales, Vicente. *Times Gone By: Memoirs of a Man of Action.* Trans. John H. R. Polt. Oxford: Oxford University Press, 2003. The very useful reminiscences of Pérez Rosales (1807–1886), a participant in Chile's war of independence.

Secondary Sources

Bethell, Leslie, ed. *The Independence of Latin America.* New York: Cambridge University Press, 1987. Includes useful data on Chile's independence from Spain.

——— ed. *Chile Since Independence.* Cambridge, U.K.: Cambridge University Press, 1993. Available as an e-book at http://books.google.com/ books?id=86kSD98NY2AC&dq=independence+of+chile&source=gbs _summary_s&cad=0. An excellent collection of essays on the history of Chile, some relate to the independence era.

Burkholder, Mark A., and Lyman L. Johnson. *Colonial Latin America.* 6th ed. New York: Oxford University Press, 2008. Good survey of the conditions in Chile prior to independence.

Chasteen, John. *Americanos: Latin America's Struggle for Independence.* New York: Oxford University Press, 2008. Excellent, well-written study that includes reliable information on Chile.

Chisholm, Adam Stuart. *The Independence of Chile.* Boston: Sherman, French, 1911. Available as an e-book at http://books.google.com/books?id =PuYoAAAAYAAJ&dq=independence+of+chile&source=gbs_summary_s &cad=0. An old but still useful study that is very sympathetic to the Chilean rebels.

Clissold, Stephen. *Bernardo O'Higgins and the Independence of Chile.* New York: Praeger, 1969. Readable study of O'Higgins's military contributions in defeating the Spanish and others.

Collier, Simon. *Ideas and Politics of Chilean Independence 1808–1833.* London: Cambridge University Press, 1967. A scholarly study that is very well documented and is centered in the impact of ideological issues on the outbreak and development of the Chilean war for independence.

———— and William F. Sater. *A History of Chile, 1808–2002.* 2nd ed. New York: Cambridge University Press, 2004. A very useful and reliable history of Chile. The earlier chapters should be useful to most students.

Cordingly, David. *Cochrane: The Real Master and Commander.* New York: Bloomsbury, 2007. An excellent and exciting study of Thomas Cochrane's naval victories in support of Chile's independence.

Haigh, Roger M. *The Formation of the Chilean Oligarchy 1810–1821.* Salt Lake City: Historical S. & D. Research Foundation, 1972. An interesting study of the rise of Chile's new government that emerged during the war for independence.

Harvey, Robert. *Liberators: Latin America's Struggle for Independence.* New York: Overlook, 2000. A very good series of biographical studies on those who led Chile and other Latin American revolutions.

————. *Cochrane: The Life and Exploits of a Fighting Captain.* New York: Carroll and Graf, 2000. A very good biography of Cochrane. The information on his work on behalf of Chile should be helpful to those students working on the naval aspects of the conflict.

Metford, J. C. J. *San Martin, the Liberator.* New York: Philosophical Library, 1950. A dated but solid biography of San Martin that should be useful to many students.

Nicholson, Irene. *The Liberators, A Study of Independence Movements in Spanish America.* New York: Praeger, 1969. Another good study that examines the roles of prominent revolutionaries in the many national movements in which they were involved.

O'Leary, Daniel Florencio. *Bolivar and the War of Independence.* Trans. and ed. Robert F. McNerney, Jr. Austin: University of Texas Press, 1970. Includes information on Bolivar's influence on the Chilean war for independence.

Rector, John L. *The History of Chile.* London: Palgrave Macmillan, 2005. A very good general history that provides extensive information on the independence movement.

Robertson, William Spence. *Rise of the Spanish-American Republics, as Told in the Lives of Their Liberators.* New York: Free Press, 1948. A classic and important work that includes extensive information on Chile.

Tepaske, John H., ed. *Research Guide to Andean History: Bolivia, Chile, Ecuador, and Peru.* Durham, NC: Duke University Press, 1981. Provides bibliographies and other information on the Andean state, and may provide students with term paper topics.

Thomas, Donald. *Cochrane*. New York: Viking, 1976. A reliable biography of Thomas Cochrane (1775–1860) who was involved in the independence movements in Chile and Peru.

Vale, Brian. *Cochrane in the Pacific: Fortune and Freedom in Spanish America*. London: I. B. Tauris, 2008. Another important study on Cochrane as an agent of change in Chile and elsewhere.

World Wide Web

"Chile Wars of Independence, 1810–18." http://www.workmall.com/wfb2001/chile/chile_history_wars_of_independence_1810_18.html. Provides a good introduction to Chile's struggle for independence.

"Chilean War of Independence, 1817–1818." http://www.onwar.com/aced/chrono/c1800s/yr15/fchile1817.htm. Focused on 1817–1818, this site provides information on the last year of the war for independence.

"Struggle for Independence." http://www.britannica.com/EBchecked/topic/111326/Chile/25249/Struggle-for-independence. Reliable introductory information.

"The Wars of San Martin, 1814–1824." http://www.onwar.com/aced/data/sierra/sanmartin1814.htm. Includes information on the contributions of José San Martin in acquiring Chile's independence.

"Timeline on Chile War of Independence." http://www.timelines.info/history/conflict_and_war/18th_&_19th_century_conflicts/chile_war_of_independence/. A detailed timeline that should be very useful to all students writing on this topic.

"War of Independence." http://countrystudies.us/chile/8.htm. A good introduction to Chile's war for independence.

Multimedia Source

"Chile." http://encarta.msn.com/encyclopedia_761572974_8/chile.html. Includes 55 multimedia items, some on independence, and an excellent interactive map.

14. Founding of Singapore (1819)

As early as the sixteenth century, European explorers and their governments recognized the value of trading in Southeast Asia. The Dutch steadily extended their economic interests and connections in the region and by the end of the eighteenth century had established a predominant position. During the Wars of the French Revolution and the Napoleonic era (1792–1815), the Dutch were allied with France against Britain and her allies. During the wars the British invaded Java and successfully challenged the Dutch for its control. After the defeat of France and Napoleon in 1815, the British government was determined to expand its interests in the region. The Congress of Vienna resulted in the acquisition of additional overseas holdings for Britain. Combined with the continuing growth of the new industrial economy and its constant needs for access to raw materials and markets, Britain's sense of "global empire" grew among its colonial leaders. In 1818 Sir Thomas Stamford Raffles (1781–1826), who was involved in the Java and Malay actions earlier against the Dutch, was named as a lieutenant governor of Bencoolen, a small British colony of relatively little importance. Within a few months, he had been granted permission to establish a new British base in the region. On January 29, 1819, Raffles arrived on the island of Singapore (near the southern end of the Malay Peninsula) and determined that it was ideal to expand British economic and political interests. Within a few weeks Raffles overthrew the native government and installed a government that supported Britain. During the six remaining years of Raffles's life, Singapore grew rapidly as a free port where no duties were enacted. Singapore continued to expand during the nineteenth century and was transformed into a major British colony that had political, economic, and military significance for more than a century.

TERM PAPER SUGGESTIONS

1. Write a paper on Britain's rationale for the establishment of Singapore.
2. Develop a paper on Raffles's impact on the founding and early growth of Singapore.
3. Write a paper on the geopolitical impact of the British establishment of Singapore on European influence in the region.
4. The founding of Singapore had an impact on the people of the region. Write a paper on the growth of Singapore during the nineteenth century—be sure to include its influence on the native population.

ALTERNATIVE TERM PAPER SUGGESTIONS

1. Develop a 4–5 minute podcast in which Raffles convinces his reluctant superiors to allow him to establish a new base for British interests in Malay—that

eventually became Singapore. Be sure to include details on his rationale, why his superiors were not initially supportive, and why they changed their minds.

2. Develop an iMovie/documentary on Raffles's founding of Singapore in January 1819. Points to be considered include the geographic benefits, the native population, and the actual seizure of the territory.

3. Raffles's principal aide in Singapore was Major William Farquhar. As Farquhar, develop a blog on Singapore's founding and early development during 1819 and 1820.

SUGGESTED SOURCES

Primary Sources

Buckley, Charles B. *An Anecdotal History of Old Times in Singapore.* 2 vols. Whitefish, MT: Kessinger, 2007. Volume One includes some primary materials that should be of use.

Raffles, Sophia. *Memoir of the Life and Public Services of Sir Thomas Stamford Raffles.* New ed. London: J. Duncan, 1835. A valuable resource by Raffles's second wife, who had access to much of his correspondence.

Raffles, Thomas Stamford. *Letters of Sir Stamford Raffles to Nathaniel Wallich, 1819–1824.* Kuala Lumpur: Malaysian Branch of the Royal Asiatic Society, 1981. Very good on a wide range of Raffles's interests.

Secondary Sources

Alatas, Syed Hussein. *Thomas Stamford Raffles, 1781–1826: Schemer or Reformer? An Account of His Political Philosophy, etc.* Sydney: Angus and Robertson, 1971. An analytical study of Raffles and his achievements.

Bastin, John. *Sir Thomas Stamford Raffles.* Liverpool: Ocean Steam Ship Co., 1969. A solid introduction to the study of Raffles and his adventures.

Boulger, Demtrius Charles. *The Life of Sir Thomas Stamford Raffles.* New ed. Amsterdam: Pepin Press, 1999. A useful and reliable biography that includes a section on the founding of Singapore.

Chandler, David P., and David J. Steinberg. *In Search of Southeast Asia.* Honolulu: University of Hawaii Press, 1988. A regional study that includes data on the establishment of Singapore.

Chew, Ernest, and Edwin Lee, eds. *A History of Singapore.* Melbourne: Oxford University Press, 1991. Excellent scholarly work that is accurate and relevant.

Clair, Colin. *Sir Stamford Raffles, Founder of Singapore.* Leavesden, England: Bruce & Gawthorn, 1963. A reliable and useful biography of Raffles that includes considerable information on the founding of Singapore.

Collis, Maurice. *Raffles.* New York: John Day, 1968. Perhaps the most readable, exciting, and reliable biography of Raffles that is still readily available.

Cook, John Angus. *Sir Thomas Stamford Raffles, Founder of Singapore, 1819, and Some of his Friends and Contemporaries.* London: Arthur H. Stockwell, 1918. An old but still useful biography that includes valuable information on Raffles's colleagues and others.

Corfield, Justin J., and Robin S. Corfield. *Encyclopedia of Singapore.* Lanham, MD: Scarecrow Press, 2006. Indispensable resource for the history of Singapore.

Coupland, Reginald. *Raffles, 1781–1826.* 2nd ed. Oxford: Oxford University Press, 1934. A standard but old biography that some students may find useful.

Hahn, Emily. *Raffles of Singapore, A Biography.* Garden City: Doubleday, 1946. A good introduction to Raffles and the establishment of Singapore.

Hong, Lysa, and Huang Jianli. *The Scripting of a National History: Singapore and its Pasts.* Hong Kong: Hong Kong University Press, 2008. A seminal scholarly study that examines the evolution of the idea and identity of Singapore since its founding.

Liu, Gretchen. *Singapore: A Pictorial History, 1819–2000.* Singapore: Archipelago Press, 1999. Very useful and informative introduction to Singapore history. Also included are numerous illustrations, maps, and, for the later periods, photographs.

Mulliner, K., and Lian The-Mulliner. *Historical Dictionary of Singapore.* Metuchen, NJ: Scarecrow Press, 1991. Very useful resource for all papers on the founding of Singapore.

Pringle, R. D. *A Brief Life of Sir Stamford Raffles, the Founder of Singapore.* Singapore: Methodist House, 1918. A reliable but dated introduction to Raffles's life and his role in the establishment of modern Singapore.

Pearson, Henry Frank. *Singapore: A Popular History, 1819–1960.* Singapore: Eastern Universities Press, 1961. A good introduction to the establishment of Singapore.

Porter, Andrew, and Alaine Low, eds. *The Oxford History of the British Empire: Volume III, The Nineteenth Century.* New York: Oxford University Press, 1999. Provides excellent data on the establishment of Singapore within the context of the greater Empire.

Ryan, Neil. J. *Making of Modern Malaysia and Singapore: A History from Earliest Times to 1966.* New York: Oxford University Press, 1970. A useful introduction to the founding of Singapore.

Turnbull, C. Mary. *A History of Singapore, 1819–1988.* 2nd ed. New York: Oxford University Press, 1989. Considered by many to be the classic standard on Singapore history, Turnbull's examination of its founding is thorough and scholarly.

Wurtzburg, Charles Edward. *Raffles of the Eastern Isles.* New York: Oxford University Press, 1984. An outstanding biography of Raffles with much useful information on the founding of Singapore.

World Wide Web

"Founding of Modern Singapore, 1819–1826." http://libpweb1.nus.edu.sg/bib/sh/ sing1819.html. Provides a very good bibliography on Singapore that was developed by the National University of Singapore Library.
"National Archives of Singapore." http://www.nhb.gov.sg/. A massive archive that has extensive resources on the founding of Singapore.
"Sir Stamford Raffles." http://www.britannica.com/EBchecked/topic/489451/ Sir-Stamford Raffles#tab=active~checked%2Citems~checked&title=Sir %20Stamford%20Raffles%20~%20Britannica%20Online%20Encyclo pedia. A thorough reference entry on Raffles and Singapore.
"Sir Thomas Stamford Raffles." http://www.britishempire.co.uk/biography/ raffles.htm. An introduction to Raffles's life and work.
"Sir Thomas Stamford Raffles." http://www.answers.com/topic/sir-thomas -stamford-raffles. A very good sketch of Raffles's life and the founding of Singapore.

Multimedia Sources

"Raffles Landing Site: Where Heritage Whispers." http://www.youtube.com/ watch?v=6k6vZimbbCo. A brief video on the founding of Singapore by Raffles.
"Singapore Story." Singapore National Archives and Records Administration, 2008. DVD. Provides some information on the founding of Singapore.

15. Revolts in Spain, Portugal, and Italy (1820)

During the years after the defeat of Napoleon and the Congress of Vienna, supporters of liberalism and nationalism continued to advance many of the values associated with the French Revolution. In 1820, liberal revolts broke out in Spain, Portugal, and Italy (the Kingdom of the Two Sicilies). In Spain, the liberals wanted King Ferdinand VII (1784–1833) to rule under the Constitution of 1812. He refused and, during the years after 1815, critics of the regime became increasingly critical of the monarch's arbitrary rule. In 1820 a military mutiny broke out and a rather meager force marched on Madrid. Ferdinand VII, fearing for his life, immediately agreed to abide by the constitution. However, by 1822, he requested the intervention of the European powers in order to restore his absolute power. They responded at the Congress of Verona (January 22, 1823) in which they approved French intervention in Spain. French forces invaded Spain in the spring and succeeded in suppressing the liberals by November. The political situation in Portugal had been altered significantly by the Napoleonic Wars. Between 1808 and 1821, Rio de Janeiro served as the capital of Portugal and Brazil—with the monarch in exiled residence. In 1820 liberal advocates of a Portuguese constitution succeeded in transferring the capital back to Lisbon, but their aspirations for a genuinely liberal regime would have to await the stabilization of the monarchy in the 1830s. In Italy (which was not yet a unified state), a revolution led by the *Carbonari* ("coal burners," a secret society) broke out during 1820 in the Kingdom of the Two Sicilies, and they succeeded in forcing the government into promising that a constitution would be developed. In 1821, the *Carbonari* gained the same concession from the Kingdom of Sardinia. However, these gains were eliminated by the direct military intervention of France and Austria.

TERM PAPER SUGGESTIONS

1. Write a paper in which you compare and contrast the origins of the revolutions of 1820 in Spain, Portugal, and the Italian states.
2. Develop a paper in which you compare and contrast the impact of the Holy Alliance on the revolutions in Spain and Italy.
3. Write a paper on the level of domestic support for a liberal constitution in Spain. What groups in society supported a constitution? What groups were opposed?
4. Write a paper on the legacy of the revolts of 1820.
5. Write a paper on the origins and impact of the *Carbonari* in supporting liberal and nationalist ideals.

ALTERNATIVE TERM PAPER SUGGESTIONS

1. Develop a podcast in which you interview Ferdinand VII of Spain on his opposition to constitutional government and his request for the Great Powers to assist him in eliminating the liberals.

2. As a member of the *Carbonari* in the Kingdom of the Two Sicilies, you are involved in the liberal revolt of 1820. Create a blog in which you record your activities from the revolt's beginning through its failed conclusion.

3. Develop an iMovie on the Congress of Verona among the Great Powers. Why did they agree to support French intervention in Spain?

SUGGESTED SOURCES

Primary Sources

Cowans, Jon, ed. *Modern Spain: A Documentary History.* Philadelphia: University of Pennsylvania Press, 2003. Includes some useful primary materials on this topic.

Smith, John A., and Conde da Carnota. *Memoirs of Field-Marshall the Duke de Saldanha, with Selections from His Correspondence.* Chestnut Hill, MA: Elibron/Adamant Media, 2002; reprint of 1880 edition. This memoir by the leading Portuguese military leader of the 1820s should be a useful resource for those working on that topic.

Volgin, Andrei. *A Journey into Various Parts of Europe; and a Residence in Them, during the Years 1818, 1819, 1820, and 1821: with notes Historical and Classical. . . .* Chestnut Hill, MA: Elibron/Adamant Media, 2001; originally published in 1825. Recollections by an eyewitness to many developments associated with the revolutions of 1820.

Secondary Sources

Brady, Joseph. *Rome and the Neapolitan Revolution of 1820–1821: A Study in Papal Neutrality.* Whitefish, MT: Kessinger, 2006; originally published in 1937. A dated but still useful study on Papal policy and strategy during the revolution in the Kingdom of the Two Sicilies in 1820–1821.

Carr, Raymond. *Spain, 1808–1975.* 2nd ed. Oxford: Clarendon Press, 1982. Provides reliable information on the Spanish revolt and a good bibliography.

Clarke, Henry Butler. *Modern Spain, 1815–1898.* New York: AMS Press, 1969. An older work that students should still find accessible and useful—extensive information on the Spanish revolution.

Di Scala, Spencer M. *Italy: From Revolution to Republic, 1700 to the Present.* 3rd ed. Boulder: Westview, 2004. Provides introductory-level information on the Italian revolutions of the early 1820s and a good bibliography.

Esdaile, Charles J. *Spain in the Liberal Age: From Constitution to Civil War, 1808–1939.* Oxford: Blackwell, 2000. An excellent secondary resource with detailed information on the Spanish Revolution of 1820.

Fehrenbach, Charles W. "Moderados and Exaltados: The Liberal Opposition to Ferdinand VII, 1814–1823." *Hispanic American Historical Review,* L (1970): 52–69. A scholarly article on the crisis in Spain between the conflicting political cultures that resulted in the Revolution of 1820.

Goldsto, Jack A. *The Encyclopedia of Political Revolutions.* New York: Vintage, 1996. A valuable reference book that includes information on all of the revolutions of 1820—Spain, Portugal, and Italy.

Hobsbawn, Eric. *The Age of Revolution: 1789–1848.* New York: Vintage, 1996. A seminal study by one of the foremost historians of the second half of the twentieth century that places the revolutions of 1820 in the context of the revolutionary tradition and culture of the period.

Junco, José Alvarez, and Adrian Shubert, eds. *Spanish History Since 1808.* London: Arnold, 2000. Includes several scholarly essays that relate to the 1820 Revolution in Spain, especially Isabel Brudiel's "Liberal Revolution, 1808–1843."

McCabe, Joseph. *Spain in Revolt, 1814–1931.* New York: D. Appleton, 1932. A dated but still useful study that provides detailed information on the Spanish Revolution of 1820.

Macaulay, Neill. *Dom Pedro: The Struggle for Liberty in Brazil and Portugal, 1798–1834.* Durham, NC: Duke University Press, 1988. A bio-historical study that focuses on the Portuguese leader who had an alternative vision for the political future of his country and its citizens.

Ramos Oliviera, Antonio. *Politics, Economics, and Men of Modern Spain, 1808–1946.* Trans. Teener Hall. London: V. Gollancz, 1946. Spanish economic development was the central theme of this study, which includes information on the Revolution of 1820.

Ringrose, David R. *Spain, Europe and the "Spanish Miracle," 1700–1900.* Cambridge, U.K.: Cambridge University Press, 1996. Ringrose argued that Spain developed economically during the period in spite of entrenched problems and attitudes. Ringrose is supportive of the liberal Revolution of 1820.

Sencourt, Robert. *Spain's Uncertain Crown: The Story of the Spanish Sovereigns, 1808–1931.* London: E. Benn, 1932. Includes considerable information on the Revolution of 1820, foreign intervention, and the impact on the monarchy.

Wrightson, Richard H. *A History of Modern Italy, from the First French Revolution to the Year 1850.* Chestnut Hill, MA: Elibron/Adamant Media, 2005; originally published in 1855. Very old but very good on the liberal revolutions of 1820 in Italy.

World Wide Web

"A New Conservative Order, to 1820." http://www.fsmitha.com/h3/h36
-pol.html. Provides an extensive summary of the developments associated with the revolutions of 1820.

"*Carbonari.*" http://encyclopedia.jrank.org/CAL_CAR/CARBONARI_an
_Italian_word_meani.html. Very good on the role of the *Carbonari* in the Italian revolutions of 1820 and beyond.

"Liberal Revolution of 1820." http://www.nationmaster.com/encyclopedia/
Liberal-Revolution-of-1820. A brief but useful summary of the principal developments associated with the revolutions of 1820.

"Portugal under the Nineteenth Century Constitutional Monarchy." http://
libro.uca.edu/payne2/payne22.htm. An article by Stanley Payne that includes significant information on the political conditions in Portugal during the 1820s; a very useful map has also been provided.

"Results of the Congress of Vienna." http://killeenroos.com/4/RESULTCV.htm.
A worthwhile statement on the immediate consequences of the Congress of Vienna, including the involvement of the great powers in the suppression of the revolutions of 1820.

"Revolt in the Two Sicilies, 1820–1821." http://www.onwar.com/aced/data/
tango/twosicilies1820.htm. A brief but accurate statement on the revolution in the Kingdom of the Two Sicilies (Naples) in 1820.

"Spain, Portugal, and Italy." http://www.saburchill.com/history/chapters/
empires/0037.html. Provides information on the revolutions of 1820 in these three nations.

"The Iberian Peninsula." http://www.bartleby.com/67/1062.html. Includes an extensive paragraph on the revolutions of 1820 in Spain and Portugal.

"The Porto Junta Revolt in Portugal, 1820." http://www.onwar.com/aced/
chrono/c1800s/yr20/fportugal1820.htm. Provides reliable information on the revolt within the context of the civil war that continued until 1834.

Multimedia Sources

"*Carbonari.*" http://www.encyclopedia.com/doc/1O48-Carbonari.html.
Includes copies of four illustrations of the *Carbonari* (charcoal burners) who were involved with the revolutions in 1820.

"Spain." http://encarta.msn.com/encyclopedia_761575057_17/spain.html.
Includes a map of Spain and Portugal and other related multimedia illustrations and photographs.

16. Brazilian Independence (1820–1822)

Unlike other independence movements in Latin America, Brazil's independence from Portugal did not result from a violent overthrow of the colonial government. Rather, it emerged from a complex web of factors that involved European and Portuguese politics as well as the internal forces in Brazil. During the tumultuous era of the Napoleonic Wars, Portuguese King João VI (1767–1826) and his court fled Lisbon in 1808 and were transported to Brazil on British naval ships. Even though Napoleon was defeated in 1815, the Portuguese government continued its sojourn in Brazil until the Portuguese revolution in 1820 forced its return in 1821. The status of Brazil became the central issue between the monarchy and the liberal revolutionaries who seized the government. That situation was complicated further when violence broke out in 1821 in Pernambuco between the departing Portuguese troops and the Luso-Brazilians (Brazilians with Portuguese citizenship). The Brazilians supported the acceptance of João VI's son, Dom Pedro (1798–1834), to remain in Brazil as its protector, but the violence spread in the cities and the countryside. In 1822, Dom Pedro announced the independence of Brazil and the establishment of a Brazilian Empire with himself (Pedro I) as its leader. His reign was troublesome and he was forced to abdicate in 1831, but Brazil's independence had been secured.

TERM PAPER SUGGESTIONS

1. Write a paper on the background and causes for the Brazilian War of Independence (1821–1822) against Portugal.

2. Develop a paper in which you assess the significance of the 1820 Portuguese Revolution on the development of Brazilian independence.

3. Write a paper focused on Dom Pedro's role as a catalyst for Brazilian independence.

4. Develop a term paper on Great Britain's influence on the development of Brazil's independence.

ALTERNATIVE TERM PAPER SUGGESTIONS

1. Develop a podcast in which the Luso-Brazilians petition Dom Pedro to remain in Brazil and serve as its protector.

2. Develop an iMovie in which Pedro I announces the independence of Brazil and shares his vision for its future.

3. You are a journalist for a liberal newspaper in Lisbon reporting from Brazil during 1821 and 1822. Develop a blog for the newspaper on the turbulence in Brazil.

SUGGESTED SOURCES

Primary Sources

Callcott, Maria Graham. *Journal of a Residence in Chile during the year 1822; and, A Voyage from Chile to Brazil in 1823.* Ed. Jennifer Hayward. Charlottesville: University of Virginia Press, 2003. A very useful source by a contemporary who was impacted by the Brazilian War for Independence.

Cochrane, Thomas. *Narrative of Services in the Liberation of Chile, Peru, and Brazil from Spanish and Portuguese Domination.* Ann Arbor: University Microfilms, 1973; originally published in 1858. An important work by a significant participant in the war.

O'Leary, Daniel Florencio. *The "Detached" Recollections of General D. F. O'Leary.* Ed. R. A. Humphreys. London: Athone Press, 1969. A very useful primary source by a prominent revolutionary general.

———. *Bolivar and the War of Independence.* Trans. and ed. Robert F. McNerney, Jr. Austin: University of Texas Press, 1970. Includes firsthand information on Simon Bolivar by a revolutionary colleague.

Secondary Sources

Bethell, Leslie, ed. *The Independence of Latin America.* New York: Cambridge University Press, 1987. A collection of worthwhile essays on the independence movements (including Brazil) in Latin America.

Burkholder, Mark A., and Lyman L. Johnson. *Colonial Latin America.* 6th ed. New York: Oxford University Press, 2008. Provides a good background on the origins of the Brazilian revolt.

Cavaliero, Roderick. *The Independence of Brazil.* London: I. B. Tauris, 1993. A good resource (especially the early chapters) on the outbreak and progress of the Brazilian War for Independence.

Chasteen, John. *Americanos: Latin America's Struggle for Independence.* New York: Oxford University Press, 2008. Provides good introductions to the many Latin American revolutions.

Harvey, Robert. *Liberators: Latin America's Struggle for Independence.* New York: Overlook, 2000. A reliable and useful study.

Kraay, Henrik. *Race, State, and Armed Forces in Independence-Era Brazil: Bahia, 1790s–1840s.* Stanford: Stanford University Press, 2001. A scholarly work on the complex forces in pre- and post-independent Brazil.

Macaulay, Neill. *Dom Pedro: The Struggle for Liberty in Brazil and Portugal, 1798–1834.* Durham, NC: Duke University Press, 1986. An excellent biography of Pedro I.

Mosher, Jeffrey C. *Political Struggle, Ideology, and State Building: Pernambuco and the Construction of Brazil, 1817–1850.* Lincoln: University of Nebraska Press, 2008. A very good study—particularly strong on the early years of the struggle.

Nicholson, Irene. *The Liberators, A Study of Independence Movements in Spanish America.* New York: Praeger, 1969. A very good account of the various national movements, including the Brazilian revolt.

Robertson, William Spence. *Rise of the Spanish-American Republics, as Told in the Lives of Their Liberators.* New York: Free Press, 1948. A classic study by a renowned historian, this volume should be useful to many students.

World Wide Web

"Brazil—Independence." http://historicaltextarchive.com/sections.php?op=viewarticle&artid=352. A good introduction to the development of the Brazilian war against Portugal from the History Text Archive.

"Brazil, The Economy at Independence, 1822." http://www.photius.com/countries/brazil/economy/brazil_economy_the_economy_at_indep-214.html. Provides information on Brazilian trade with regional and international partners during the 1820s and gives insights on the condition of the economy at the time of liberation.

"Brazilian War of Independence, 1821–1825." http://www.onwar.com/aced/nation/bat/brazil/fbrazil1821b.htm. A very good introduction to the Brazilian struggle for independence from Portugal.

"Pedro I." http://www.answers.com/topic/pedro-i. A biography of the Emperor of Brazil.

"The Empire, 1822–89." http://countrystudies.us/brazil/11.htm. Includes a very good description of the Brazilian War for Independence.

Multimedia Source

"Latin American Independence." http://encarta.msn.com/medias_761588450/Latin_American_Independence.html. Includes illustrations and maps of several leading revolutionaries in Latin America including Brazilians.

17. Independence of Peru (1821)

The war for Peru's independence was initiated as a class conflict in 1812 and eventually expanded into a national movement during the next two years. To a large extent, Peru achieved its independence through the work of three powerful pan-Latin revolutionary leaders: Simon Bolivar (1783–1830), José de San Martin (1778–1850), and Thomas Cochrane (1775–1860). Bolivar and San Martin organized the Army of the Andes and defeated the Spanish in several battles. Bolivar became the sixth president of Peru, and San Martin declared Peru's independence on July 28, 1821. A former British naval officer, Cochrane, under San Martin's command, led the rebel navy to victories over the Spanish. On December 9, 1824, the Spanish were defeated in the last major battle of the war at Ayacucho. Peruvian military officers dominated the presidency during the nineteenth century; only three civilians served as president prior to the twentieth century.

TERM PAPER SUGGESTIONS

1. Write a paper on the causes and outbreak of the war for Peruvian independence.
2. Develop a term paper on the development of the war for independence. Include the problems associated with the Creole-*Caudillos* conflict.
3. Write a paper on the Peruvian Declaration of Independence and its contents.
4. Write a paper on the roles of José de San Martin and Simon Bolivar in attaining Peru's independence.

ALTERNATIVE TERM PAPER SUGGESTIONS

1. Develop an iMovie in which Lima's principal business leaders consider their interests when the war for independence began.
2. As a Peruvian dissident, you are involved in the Creole rebellion of Huánuco in 1812 that preceded the main war. Develop a blog about the struggle, and reflect upon the reasons for the rebellion and its progress.
3. Develop a podcast in which San Martin and Bolivar discuss their strategies to gain Peru's independence.

SUGGESTED SOURCES

Primary Sources

Bolivar, Simon. *El Libertador: Writings of Simon Bolivar.* New York: Oxford University Press, 2003. A significant primary source that most students will want to examine, which contains considerable material on Peru.

Cochrane, Thomas, Earl of Dundold. *Narrative of Services in the Liberation of Chile, Peru, and Brazil, from Spanish and Portuguese Domination.* London: J. Ridgway, 1859; also available in microforms, Ann Arbor: University Microfilms, 1973. The memoir of the great naval leader who made significant contributions to Peruvian independence.

Miller, John. *Memoirs of General Miller, in the Service of the Republic of Peru.* 2nd ed. London: Longman, Rees, Orme, Brown, and Green, 1829. Miller's memoir provides information on the military actions against the Spanish as well as evaluative comments on the quality of the combatants.

Secondary Sources

Anna, Timothy. *The Fall of the Royal Government in Peru.* Lincoln: University of Nebraska Press, 1979. A useful history of the collapse of the regime in Peru.

Bethell, Leslie, ed. *The Independence of Latin America.* New York: Cambridge University Press, 1987. A collection of scholarly essays including information on Peru's independence movement.

Blanchard, Peter. *Under the Flags of Freedom: Slave Soldiers and the Wars of Independence in Spanish South America.* Pittsburgh: University of Pittsburgh Press, 2008. This seminal study addresses the usually omitted issue of the "slave soldiers"—the contradictory issues of "freedom" and "slavery" did not appear to concern many of the revolutionaries.

Bushnell, David. *Simon Bolivar: Liberation and Disappointment.* New York: Longman, 2004. Includes information on Bolivar's aspirations for an independent Peru.

Cahill, David. *From Rebellion to Independence in the Andes: Soundings from Southern Peru, 1750–1830.* Amsterdam: Aksant, 2002. A scholarly study for advanced students on the indicators for rebellion that were evident in southern Peru prior to the outbreak of war.

——— and Blanca Tovias, eds. *New World, First Nations: Native Peoples of Mesoamerica and the Andes under Colonial Rule.* Brighton: Sussex Academic Press, 2006. A study of the condition of the native populations in Latin America prior to the overthrow of the European imperial regimes.

Fisher, John R., Allen J. Kuethe, and Anthony McFarlane, eds. *Reform and Insurrection in Bourbon, New Granada, and Peru.* Baton Rouge: Louisiana State University, 1991. A comparative study in a collection of essays on the Peruvian independence movement.

———. *Bourbon Peru, 1750–1824.* Liverpool: Liverpool University Press, 2003. A very good history of Peru prior to the break for independence.

Harrison, Margaret. *Captain of the Andes—The Life of José de San Martin, Liberator of Argentina, Chile, and Peru*. Whitefish, MT: Kessinger, 2008; originally published in 1943. A dated but excellent biography of San Martin with significant information on the independence of Peru.

Hunefeldt, Christine. *A Brief History of Peru*. New York: Facts on File, 2004. Provides adequate introductory material on the independence movement.

Jacobsen, Nils, and Cristóbal Aljvin de Losada. *Political Cultures in the Andes, 1750–1950*. Durham, NC: Duke University Press, 2005. Includes several essays related to Peru's war for independence.

Lynch, John. *The Spanish American Revolution, 1808–1826*. New York: Longman, 2003. A very reliable and comprehensive study of all of the Latin American revolutions, including Peru.

———. *Simon Bolivar: A Life*. New Haven, CT: Yale University Press, 2007. Perhaps the best biography of Bolivar that includes extensive information on his activities in Peru.

Marks, Patricia H. *Deconstructing Legitimacy: Viceroys, Merchants, and the Military in Late Colonial Peru*. University Park: Pennsylvania State University Press, 2007. A significant, recent study of the pre-independence political, economic, and military conditions in Peru that should be considered by students who are working on the causes for the war.

Méndez, G. Cecelia. *The Plebeian Republic: The Huanta Rebellion and the Making of the Peruvian State, 1820–1850*. Durham, NC: Duke University Press, 2005. A seminal study that centers on the sociopolitical factors that contributed to the transformation of Peru.

Petre, F. Loraine. *Simon Bolivar "El libertador": A Life of the Chief Leader in the Revolt against Spain in Venezuela, New Granada, and Peru*. London: J. Lane, 1910. An old but still useful study of Bolivar.

Rink, Paul. *Soldier of the Andes: José de San Martin*. New York: Julian Messner, 1971. A reliable biography of San Martin that includes information on Peru.

Rodriquez, Jaime E. *The Independence of Spanish America*. New York: Cambridge University Press, 1998. Includes useful information on Peru's independence movement.

Scheina, Robert L. *Latin America's Wars*. 2 vols. Dulles, VA: Brassey's, 2003. Excellent scholarship on all of the wars of independence, including Peru's.

Sherwell, Guillermo A. *Simon Bolivar, the Liberator: Patriot Warrior Statesman, Father of Five Nations*. Charleston, SC: BiblioBazaar, 2007. A very sympathetic biography of Bolivar as the founding liberator in Latin America.

Walker, Charles. *Smouldering Ashes: Curco and the Creation of Republican Peru, 1780–1840*. Durham, NC: Duke University Press, 1999. Very good on the long-term development of republican values in late colonial Peru.

Wilgus, A. Curtis, ed. *South American Dictators During the First Century of Independence.* Washington, DC: George Washington University Press, 1937. Includes an essay on Peru by N. A. N. Cleven.

World Wide Web

"Independence." http://www.hammond.swayne.com/independ.htm. A valuable site with information on the British officers who assisted in Peru's war of independence,

"Independence: Politics and Economics in the 19th Century." http://www.casahistoria.net/Peru.htm#4._Independence:_Politics_&_Economics_in_the_19th_century. Useful site with multiple links to related sites.

"Peru, Independence Imposed from Without, 1808–1824." http://www.workmall.com/wfb2001/peru/peru_history_independence_imposed_from_without_1808_24.html. A good article that stresses the importance of San Martin's intervention in realizing independence for Peru.

"Peruvian War of Independence." http://www.mundoandino.com/Peru/Peruvian-War-of-Independence. Provides introductory information on the struggle and links to many other relevant sites.

"Wars of Independence, 1810–1824." http://www.nationmaster.com/encyclopedia/History-of-Peru#Wars_of_independence_.281810.E2.80.931824.29. A brief introduction to the study with valuable links. Also includes emphasis on the roles of San Martin and Bolivar.

Multimedia Sources

"*Bolivar Soy Yo* (Bolivar I am)." Directed by Jorge Ali Triana. Venevision, 2003. DVD. English subtitles. A dramatic film that provides a unique interpretation of Bolivar and his ideas.

"Independence of Peru." Video. Spanish with English subtitles. http://www.youtube.com/watch?v=KM4h-j331Kc. Provides a general introduction to the war for independence.

"Peru." http://encarta.msn.com/media_461533950_761570790_-1_1/Peru_Flag_and_Anthem.html. Includes 50 multimedia sources, many of which relate to the war for independence.

18. Mexican Independence (1821)

The war for Mexican independence went through several phases and enjoyed varying levels of support from the Mexican people. Some revolutionaries were interested in social and economic improvements and others in the political advancement of their ideology or class, but all came to agree that Spanish authority had to be eliminated. The war for independence started on September 15, 1810, when Father Miguel Hidalgo y Costilla issued a declaration of war against the Spanish colonial government and initiated military actions that at first were successful. The Spanish army gained the advantage by 1811, and Hidalgo was captured and executed. Rebel leader Agustin de Iturbide unified the rebel armies and defeated the Spanish. The Spanish, exhausted by war at home and multiple insurrections throughout Latin America and outnumbered militarily by a ratio of 5:1, recognized the futility of their position in Mexico and signed the Treaty of Córdoba on August 21, 1821, which recognized the independence of Mexico.

TERM PAPER SUGGESTIONS

1. Develop a term paper on the background and causes for the outbreak of the Mexican war for independence.
2. Write a paper on the coalition of revolutionary leaders that contributed to Mexican independence. Address the following questions: What were their differences? What held them in common? How were rivalries resolved?
3. Develop a paper on Spanish policy and resistance during the Mexican war for independence.
4. Write a paper on the Hidalgo Revolt and consider its impact on the independence movement.

ALTERNATIVE TERM PAPER SUGGESTIONS

1. Develop a 5 minute podcast in which Hidalgo and José María Morelos discuss their views on the role the Mexican Catholic hierarchy should have played versus what they actually played during the Mexican war for independence.
2. As an educated Mexican youth in 1820, develop a blog on the independence movement and what your aspirations are for a new independent Mexico.
3. Develop an iMovie in which a group of Criollos, Mestizos, Zambos, and Amerindians meet to discuss their peoples' roles in achieving Mexican independence.

SUGGESTED SOURCES

Primary Sources

Leiby, John S. *Report to the King: Colonel Juan Camargo y Cavallero's Historical Account of New Spain, 1815.* New York: Peter Lang, 1984. Very useful resource that includes a translation of Camargo y Cavallero's memoir of New Spain, including California.

O'Leary, Daniel Florencio. *The "Detached" Recollections of General D. F. O'Leary.* Ed. R. A. Humphreys. London: Athone Press, 1969. An absorbing and reliable personal account of a major military leader in the Mexican war for independence.

———. *Bolivar and the War of Independence.* Trans. and ed. Robert F. McNerney, Jr. Austin: University of Texas Press, 1970. Includes information on Bolivar's influence on the Mexican War of Independence.

Secondary Sources

Anna, Timothy E. *The Mexican Empire of Iturbide.* Lincoln: University of Nebraska Press, 1990. A scholarly work on the life and influence of Agustin de Iturbide.

Archer, Christon I., ed. *The Birth of Modern Mexico, 1780–1824.* Wilmington, DE: Scholarly Resources, 2003. Includes nine useful essays on varying topics related to Mexican independence.

Bethell, Leslie, ed. *The Independence of Latin America.* New York: Cambridge University Press, 1987. A collection of essays on the Latin American revolutions, including an essay on Mexico.

——— ed. *Mexico Since Independence.* New York: Cambridge University Press, 1998. The early essays in this volume may be of use to students working on the immediate impact of Mexican independence.

Brading, D. A. *Classical Republicanism and Creole Patriotism: Simon Bolivar (1783–1830) and the Spanish American Revolution.* Cambridge, U.K.: Cambridge University Press, 1983. Includes information on Bolivar's influence on the Mexican war for independence.

Burkholder, Mark A., and Lyman L. Johnson. *Colonial Latin America.* 6th ed. New York: Oxford University Press, 2008. A very useful volume in which the later chapters provide insights into the Mexican revolution.

Caruso, John Anthony. *The Liberators of Mexico.* New York: Pageant, 1954. Includes useful information on Miguel Hidalgo y Costilla, Agustin de Iturbide, and José Maria Morelos.

Chasteen, John. *Americanos: Latin America's Struggle for Independence.* New York: Oxford University Press, 2008. An excellent scholarly study that includes information on the Mexican revolution.

Fisher, Lillian Estella. *The Background of the Revolution for Mexican Independence.* Boston: Christopher Publishing House, 1934. A dated but still useful study on the causes and background of the Mexican war for independence.

Florescano, Enrique. *Memory, Myth, and Time in Mexico: From the Aztecs to Independence.* Trans. Albert G. Bork and Kathryn R. Bork. Austin: University of Texas Press, 1994. An intriguing and seminal study that provides reliable information on the Mexican revolt.

Hamil, Hugh M. *The Hidalgo Revolt, Prelude to Mexican Independence.* Gainesville: University of Florida Press, 1966. This important work on Father Miguel Hidalgo places this revolt in its proper context and credits it as being critical to the movement.

Hamnett, Brian R. *Roots of Insurgency: Mexican Regions, 1750–1824.* Cambridge, U.K.: Cambridge University Press, 1986. Very good on the eighteenth-century insurgencies that precipitated the Mexican revolution.

Harvey, Robert. *Liberators: Latin America's Struggle for Independence.* New York: Overlook, 2000. Provides valuable information on the generation of revolutionary leaders who contributed to Mexican and other Latin American revolutions.

Joseph, Gilbert M. *The Mexico Reader: History, Culture, Politics.* Durham, NC: Duke University Press, 2002. A very good resource that should be useful to students.

Ladd, Doris M. *The Mexican Nobility at Independence, 1780–1828.* Institute of Latin American Studies, Latin American monographs, no. 40. Austin: University of Texas Press, 1976. An important study that focuses on the Mexican nobility's varying responses to the revolutionary movements of the late eighteenth and early nineteenth centuries.

Leone, Bruno. *The Mexican War of Independence.* San Diego: Lucent, 1996. A good history of the revolution against Spain.

Nicholson, Irene. *The Liberators, A Study of Independence Movements in Spanish America.* New York: Praeger, 1969. A very good account of the various national movements, including the Mexican revolt.

Rink, Paul. *Warrior Priests and Tyrant Kings: The Beginnings of Mexican Independence.* Garden City, NY: Doubleday, 1976. A very readable and reliable introduction to the Mexican war for independence.

Robertson, William Spence. *Rise of the Spanish-American Republics, as Told in the Lives of Their Liberators.* New York: Free Press, 1948. A classic and important study that includes significant information on the Mexican war for independence.

Rodriquez, Jaime E. *The Independence of Mexico and the Creation of the New Nation.* Berkeley: University of California Press, 1989. A scholarly assessment of the Mexican revolt that should be very useful to many students.

Timmons, Wilbert H. *Morelos: Priest, Soldier, Statesman of Mexico.* El Paso: Texas Western College Press, 1963. A reliable biography of the revolutionary leader José María Morelos.

Trend, John B. *Bolivar and the Independence of Spanish America.* New York: Bolivarian Society of Venezuela, 1951. A very good account of Bolivar's influence throughout Latin America.

Van Young, Eric. *The Other Rebellion: Popular Violence, Ideology, and the Mexican Struggle for Independence, 1810–1821.* Stanford, CA: Stanford University Press, 2001. An excellent comprehensive study of the Mexican revolution.

Varona, Frank De. *Miguel Hidalgo y Costilla: Father of Mexican Independence.* Minneapolis, MN: Millbrook Press, 1995. A reliable biography of Hidalgo.

World Wide Web

"Blogs About: The Mexican War of Independence." http://wordpress.com/tag/mexican-war-of-independence/. A very useful online discussion tool on the Mexican revolution.

"Mexican War of Independence, 1810–1821." http://www.onwar.com/aced/nation/may/mexico/fmexico1810b.htm. A very good introduction to the Mexican war against Spain that includes statistical information on the armed forces.

"Mexican War of Independence, 1810–1821." http://www.bookrags.com/wiki/Mexican_War_of_Independence. A good introduction to the revolution.

"Mexican War of Independence, Father Miguel Hidalgo's Revolt." http://www.historynet.com/mexican-war-of-independence-father-miguel-hidalgos-revolt.htm. A good account of the Hidalgo phase of the Mexican revolution.

"The History of Mexican Independence." http://www.mexonline.com/mexican-independence.htm. Provides information on the background and causes for the revolution; includes three illustrations.

Multimedia Source

"Pictures of Guanajuato and the Mexican War of Independence: Photo Images History." http://www.downtheroad.org/Photo/4CenMex/WarofInd2PHOTO.htm. Interesting photographs of sites and monuments related to the Mexican war for independence.

19. Greek War for Independence (1821–1832)

Throughout the early modern era, the Greeks had attempted several times to overthrow the rule of the Ottoman Turks but were unsuccessful. In the late eighteenth and early nineteenth centuries the rise of nationalism and the historic antipathy against the Turks—who proved unable to safeguard the people from outlaws—once again resulted in a Greek revolution for independence. During the 1790s Rigas Feraios (1757–1798) emerged as the leader of the nationalist cause. He advocated the establishment of a Balkan republic and achieved widespread support. Feraios was declared an outlaw, arrested by Austrian officials in Trieste in 1797, and turned over to the Turks. On June 13, 1798, he was murdered by Turkish troops in Belgrade. His execution reinforced the cause of Greek nationalism, and a new wave of leaders emerged and in 1814 organized the *Filiki Eteria*, a secret society to bring about Greek independence. In 1820 Alexander Ypsilantis (1792–1828) became the leader of *Filiki Eteria* and developed a plan to launch a war of independence. He hoped that there would be a general uprising of all Christians against the Islamic Turks, and in March 1821 he initiated actions against the Ottoman Turks. A series of regional declarations of war followed and the war for independence began. The Turks were supported by the Egyptians immediately, and, in the fall of 1821, it appeared that the Greek cause was doomed. However, the Greek rebels survived and were later supported financially by western Europeans. European support for the Greeks centered on the actions of the British Foreign Secretary George Canning (1770–1827), who organized an alliance of Great Britain, France, and Russia against the Turks. They provided significant support in naval battles. The war continued throughout the decade and tens of thousands died. In 1832, after the Turks were weakened, the European powers convened at the London Conference and recognized the independence of Greece.

TERM PAPER SUGGESTIONS

1. Write a paper on the background and outbreak of the Greek War for Independence in 1821.

2. The British poet Lord Byron supported the Greek War for Independence. Write a paper on Byron's rationale and his involvement in the struggle.

3. Write a paper on the progress of the rebellion and the impact of foreign intervention in the war. Would the Greek revolt have succeeded without the assistance of the European powers?

4. Develop a paper on this question: How did the Turks lose this war?

5. Write a paper on the rationale of the European powers' support for the Greeks.

ALTERNATIVE TERM PAPER SUGGESTIONS

1. Develop a podcast in which you interview Alexander Ypsilantis on his decision to launch the war. What is his strategy?

2. As a companion to Byron in Greece, develop a blog on your experiences and impressions of the Greek War for Independence up to Byron's death.

3. Develop an iMovie in which you interview George Canning on Britain's support for Greek independence.

SUGGESTED SOURCES

Primary Sources

Dwight, Sereno Edwards. *The Greek Revolution: An Address, delivered in Park Street Church, Boston, on Thursday, April 1st: and repeated at the request of the Greek Committee, in the Old South Church on the evening of April 14, 1824.* 2nd ed. Boston: Crocker and Brewster, 1824. Includes a three-page address from the Greek rebels to the American people in which political and financial support for the war are requested.

Hughes, Thomas Smart. *Considerations upon the Greek Revolution: With a Vindication of the Author's "Address to the People of England" from the Attack of Mr. C. B. Sheridan.* Athens: Historike kai Ethnologikē Hertairia tēs Hellados, 1974; originally published in 1823. A valuable resource for those studying the debate within England on the Greek revolt. Support from British citizens played an important part in supporting the revolt.

Humphreys, W. H. *W. H. Humphreys' First "Journal of the Greek War of Independence" (July 1821–February 1822).* Stockholm: Almquist and Wiksell, 1967. For the first year of the war, Humphreys's *Journal* is one of the best primary sources in English.

Jarvis, George. *George Jarvis: His Journal and Related Documents.* Ed. George G. Ammakis. Thessaloniki: Institute for Balkan Studies, 1965. Provides an American participant's perspective on the Greek revolt. The document section should be checked by all students working on this topic for specific primary materials that may relate to their papers.

Kolokotrōnēs, Theodōros. *Memoirs from the Greek War of Independence, 1821–1833.* Trans. E. M. Edmonds. Chicago: Argonaut, 1969; originally published in 1892. This is an important memoir by a participant in the war for independence; Kolokotrōnēs was involved in combat as a general in the Greek army and has been considered the most significant individual in the revolution.

Russia, Foreign Ministry. *Russia and Greece during the Regency of King Othon, 1832–1835: Russian Documents on the First Years of Greek Independence.*

Thessaloniki: Institute of Balkan Studies, 1962. Includes correspondence between the Russian Foreign Ministry and the Russian officials in Bavaria about the Greek War and the establishment of the new government.

Swan, Charles. *Journal of a Voyage up the Mediterranean: Principally among the Islands of the Archipelago, and in Asia Minor, including many interesting particulars relative to the Greek Revolution.* . . . 2 vols. London: C. and J. Rivington, 1826. This is an eyewitness account to many incidents in the war during its early phases.

Secondary Sources

Athanassoglou-Kallmy, Nina M. *French Images from the Greek War of Independence, 1821–1830: Art and Politics under the Restoration.* New Haven, CT: Yale University Press, 1989. Includes scores of copies (with narrative) of French paintings, prints, and sculpture influenced by the Greek War of Independence.

Brewer, David. *The Greek War of Independence: The Struggle for Freedom from Ottoman Oppression and the Birth of the Modern Greek Nation.* Woodstock, NY: Overlook Press, 2001. An obviously sympathetic history of the revolt that includes an extensive bibliography.

Clogg, Richard, ed. *The Struggle for Greek Independence: Essays to Mark the 150th Anniversary of the Greek War of Independence.* Hamden, CT: Archon, 1973. Most of these essays will be of interest to students working on this topic. Generally the essays are sympathetic to the Greek cause, but they are not uncritical.

———. *A Concise History of Greece.* 2nd ed. Cambridge, U.K.: Cambridge University Press, 2002. Clogg's *History* is a good starting point to gain a reliable base of introductory knowledge on the Greek War for Independence.

Dakin, Douglas. *British and American Philhellenes, During the War of Greek Independence, 1821–1833.* Thessaloniki: Institute for Balkan Studies, 1955. An absorbing account of British and American support for the Greeks in their war with the Ottoman Turks.

———. *The Greek Struggle for Independence, 1821–1823.* Berkeley: University of California Press, 1973. A reliable and readable scholarly account that focuses on the critical early years of the rebellion; an extensive bibliography is appended to the text.

Diamandouros, Nikiforos, ed. *Hellenism and the First Greek War of Liberation, 1821–1830: Continuity and Change.* Thessaloniki: Institute for Balkan Studies, 1976. A series of related scholarly papers that were presented at a conference at Harvard University in 1971.

Howe, Samuel G. *An Historical Sketch of the Greek Revolution.* Rev. ed. Austin: Center for Neo-Hellenic Studies, 1966. An accurate and detailed introduction to the war that may be useful to students.

Jelavich, Barbara. *History of the Balkans, 18th and 19th Centuries.* New York: Cambridge University Press, 1983. The chapter on the Greek revolt by this outstanding scholar provides valuable insights into the scope and significance of the establishment of modern Greece.

Koumoulides, John T. *Cyprus and the War of Greek Independence, 1821–1829.* San Francisco: Zeno, 1974. Provides a basis point on the origins of the Cyprus problem between the Greeks and the Turks.

Pappas, Paul Constantine. *The United States and the Greek War for Independence, 1821–1828.* East European Monographs, no. 173. New York: Columbia University Press, 1985. A scholarly analysis of the generally positive support that Americans provided to the Greek rebels during the 1820s and 1830s.

Paroulakis, Peter H. *The Greek War of Independence.* Athens: Hellenic International Press, 1984. A reliable and useful history of the war that is sympathetic to the Greeks, as well as a good bibliography and documentation.

Phillips, W. Allison. *The War of Greek Independence, 1821 to 1833.* Whitefish, MT: Kessinger, 2007; originally published in 1897. Also available as an e-book at http://www.archive.org/stream/warofgreekindepe00philiala/ warofgreekindepe00philiala_djvu.txt. Phillips was on the faculty at Oxford University. This book was not based on primary research but was written for the general public and supports the Greek interpretation of the war.

Stavrianos, L. S. *The Balkans Since 1453.* London: C. Hurst, 2000. A general history by a prominent scholar that includes information on the Greek revolt of the 1820s.

World Wide Web

"Greek Revolution, 1821–1829." http://www.nostos.com/greekrev/. Provides nine biographies (with illustrations) of the Greek heroes of the revolution.

"Greek War of Independence." http://members.fortunecity.com/fstav1/1821/ fort1821/struggle.html. A major site that provides information and links to other sites; illustrations, music, and maps are also included.

"Greek War of Independence, 1821–1832." http://www.onwar.com/aced/ chrono/c1800s/yr20/fgreece1821.htm. In addition to the summary history of the war, this site provides statistics on the number of casualties from all of the nations that were involved.

"The Greek War of Independence." http://www.fsmitha.com/h3/h36-2gr.html. Includes a detailed summary of the war, three illustrations, and a very useful map.

"Greek War of Independence: Timeline." http://www.timelines.info/ history/conflict_and_war/18th_&_19th_century_conflicts/greek_war _of_independence/. A valuable timeline of the war that details the chronology of events.

Multimedia Sources

"Greek War of Independence, 1821." http://www.youtube.com/watch?v =r0E1J1O2Ny4. A video with period music that provides numerous images of the war from the art of the era.

"The Greek Adventure: The War of Independence, 1821–27." Recorded Books, 1982. Audiobook Cassette. 6 audio cassettes. Written by David Howarth. Narrated by Tom West. Presents a reliable history of the Greek war for independence,

20. First Ashanti War (1823–1826)

By the beginning of the nineteenth century the balance of power among the African tribes in West Africa (Ghana/Gold Coast) was shifting. The Ashanti tribe expanded and threatened the Fanti who dominated the coastal areas and had experience with British and other European traders. British efforts to use diplomacy to placate the Ashanti failed and hostilities commenced in 1823. In 1824 a British force (1,000 British and mostly natives) under Sir Charles MacCarthy (1764–1824) met the Ashantis (10,000) in the Battle of Nsamankow (January 22, 1824). The British were defeated and MacCarthy was killed. In 1826, the Ashantis launched another invasion. The British and their African allies responded in the following year by organizing a force of 400 well-equipped British troops and 4,600 natives to go against the Ashanti army of 15,000. At the Battle of Dodowa the British won a decisive victory and the Ashantis withdrew to the interior. The Ashantis also suffered from diseases that decimated their numbers. By 1831, the British and the Ashanti accepted the Pra River as the boundary between the Ashanti sphere of influence and the British protectorate over the coastal areas. However, the conflict between the British and Ashantis would erupt on several additional occasions during the nineteenth century.

TERM PAPER SUGGESTIONS

1. Write a paper in which you analyze the growth of the Ashanti empire in West Africa prior to the outbreak of the war. How did Ashanti ambitions conflict with British imperialism in West Africa?

2. Develop a paper on the outbreak and development of the First Ashanti War.

3. Write a paper on the consequences of the First Ashanti War.

ALTERNATIVE TERM PAPER SUGGESTIONS

1. Develop a podcast in which you interview Sir Charles MacCarthy before he launches his action against the Ashanti. What does he expect from the Ashanti warriors? Is he confident of victory?

2. As an aide to MacCarthy, you have maintained a diary of your experiences during the early years of the First Ashanti War. Because of illness, you miss the battle in which MacCarthy and the remainder of his force are slaughtered. After that tragedy, you develop a blog for the British government based on your diary entries and other experiences.

3. Develop an iMovie in which the leaders of the British Foreign and Colonial Offices meet to discuss their strategy after the defeat at Nsamankow.

SUGGESTED SOURCES

Primary Sources

West-African Sketches: Compiled from the Reports of Sir G. R. Collier, Sir Charles MacCarthy and Other Official Sources. Whitefish, MT: Kessinger, 2007; originally published in 1824. These firsthand reports provide valuable information on British perceptions of West Africa and their role in the region immediately prior to the outbreak of the First Ashanti War.

Metcalfe, George Edgar. *Great Britain and Ghana, Documents of Ghana History, 1807–1957.* London: T. Nelson, 1964. This extensive collection of documents includes several on the Ashanti wars of the nineteenth century.

Secondary Sources

Callwell, C. E. *Small Wars: Their Principles and Practices.* 3rd ed. Lincoln: University of Nebraska Press, 1996. A classic study on military history that provides information on the Ashanti wars.

Claridge, William W. *A History of the Gold Coast and Ashanti, from the Earliest Times to the Commencement of the Twentieth Century.* 2 vols. 2nd ed. New York: Barnes and Noble, 1964. An exhaustive secondary study on the Ashanti that includes information on all of the Ashanti conflicts of the nineteenth century.

Edgerton, Robert B. *The Fall of the Asante Empire: The Hundred-Year War for Africa's Gold Coast*. New York: The Free Press, 1995. A highly readable and reliable study of the collapse of the Ashanti hegemony in West Africa. Among the many factors that explain their fall were British weapons and tactics, disease, and a lack of depth in their organization.

Farwell, Byron. *The Encyclopedia of Nineteenth-century Land Warfare: An Illustrated World View*. New York: W. W. Norton & Company, 2001. A very useful reference book that provides information on the military aspects of the Ashanti wars.

Goldstein, Erik. *Wars and Peace Treaties, 1816–1991*. London: Routledge, 1992. A useful text that provides information on general and colonial wars (including Ashanti wars) during the nineteenth and twentieth centuries.

Lloyd, Adam. *The Drums of Kumasi: The Story of the Ashanti Wars*. London: Longmans, 1964. A readable and reliable narrative history of the Ashanti wars of the nineteenth century.

McCarthy, Mary. *Social Change and the Growth of British Power in the Gold Coast: The Fante States, 1807–1874*. Lanham, MD: University Press of America, 1983. A scholarly study of the impact of British expansion in the Gold Coast and other areas in West Africa. Although the focus is on the coastal areas, the continuing concern with the Ashantis is addressed.

Raugh, Harold E. *The Victorians at War, 1815–1914: An Encyclopedia of British Military History*. Santa Barbara, CA: ABC-CLIO, 2004. Also available as an e-book at http://books.google.com/books?id=HvE_Pa_ZlfsC. An excellent reference tool that includes information on the Ashanti wars of the nineteenth century.

Shillington, Kevin. *History of Africa*. New York: St. Martin's, 1996. A general text that is reliable and well organized. It provides introductory information on the Anglo-Ashanti conflicts in West Africa during the nineteenth century.

Ward, William E. *A History of Ghana*. Rev. 3rd ed. London: Allen and Unwin, 1968. A standard text that provides information on the Ashanti wars throughout the century and their impact on British interests and the other regional tribes.

Wilks, Ivor. *Asante in the Nineteenth Century: The Structure and Evolution of a Political Order*. Cambridge, U.K.: Cambridge University Press, 1975. An interesting study of the transformation of the Ashanti political system during the nineteenth century.

World Wide Web

"Anglo-Ashante Wars." http://www.newworldencyclopedia.org/entry/Anglo -Asante_Wars. Provides comprehensive statements on the Ashanti wars of the nineteenth and twentieth centuries.

"First Ashanti War, 1823–1826." http://www.heritage-history.com/www/ heritage.php?R_menu=OFF&Dir=wars&FileName=wars_ashanti.php. A well-written description of the First Ashanti War with a brief bibliography.

"First Ashanti War, 1824–1831." http://www.onwar.com/aced/data/alpha/ asante1824.htm. Provides a detailed and accurate description of the war and its consequences; some statistical information on casualties is included.

"Sir Charles MacCarthy." http://www.nationmaster.com/encyclopedia/Sir -Charles-MacCarthy. A biography of MacCarthy that provides information on his African experiences, including his part in the First Ashanti War.

Multimedia Sources

Asanti. Tango Entertainment, 2005. DVD. A dramatic film (filmed in 1979) on the Anglo-Ashanti wars that reflects the imbalance and the cultural significance of the conflicts.

"Ashanti Kingdom." http://encarta.msn.com/medias_761580620/ashanti _kingdom.html. Provides a very good map, four illustrations, and a sample of traditional Ashanti music.

21. First Burmese War (1824–1826)

While the British were gaining a stronghold in India by defeating the French during the 1780s and 1790s, they found themselves confronted with an expansionist Burma Kingdom. After 1817 Burma invaded a frontier state in Northwest India and, in 1819, the state of Manipur was attacked and plundered. The British, whose aid was sought by the leaders of other frontier states, were more concerned about the possibility of the French obtaining ports in the region than they were about an attack on British India. The British position changed on September 23, 1823, when Burmese forces attacked a border area in India and killed six members of the British Army in India. In January 1824, they attacked Cachar, which was under British protection. In response to these provocations and not being responsive to negotiations, the British declared war on Burma on

March 5, 1824. During the next two years, most of the conflict was fought on Burmese territory. Both sides made errors in judgment. The British did not appreciate the Burmese pattern of withdrawal and the impact of long lines of supply and disease on its troops, while the Burmese did not value British firepower and the resolve that they brought to the war. In the end the Burmese were defeated and signed the Treaty of Yandabo on February 24, 1826. The treaty restored the areas militarily occupied by Burma, gained new concessions for trade and access to Burmese markets, and compensated the British East India Company for its costs of the war.

TERM PAPER SUGGESTIONS

1. Write a paper on the Burmese vision of its role in South Asia during the early nineteenth century.

2. Develop a paper on the Burmese offensive operations in the region from 1817 to the British declaration of war in 1824.

3. Compare and contrast the errors made by both sides during the war.

4. Write a paper in which you analyze the Treaty of Yandabo. What impact did it have on future Anglo-Burmese relations?

5. Develop a paper on the human (combatant and noncombatant) cost of this war.

ALTERNATIVE TERM PAPER SUGGESTIONS

1. Develop an iMovie in which you interview the negotiators at Yandabo. Why did they agree to sign the peace treaty? Did they intend to abide by it?

2. As an aide to Burmese King Bagyidaw, you have access to the inner circle of Burmese leadership. Develop a blog of your diary entries for between 1819 and 1826 that are focused on Burmese policy and aspirations.

3. Develop a podcast on conversations between representatives of the British Foreign and Colonial Offices during the winter of 1824 on the developing crisis in Burma.

SUGGESTED SOURCES

Primary Sources

Allcott, Anna. *The End of the First Anglo-Burmese War: The Burmese Chronicle Account of How the 1826 Treaty of Yandabo Was Negotiated.* Bangkok: Chulalongkorn University Book Center, 1994. An important primary source that provides insights into the opposing views on the Treaty of Yandabo.

Butler, John. *With the Madras European Regiment in Burma—The Experience of an Officer of the Honorable East India Company's Army during the First Anglo-Burmese War, 1824–1826*. London: Leonaur, 2007. Includes Officer Butler's personal recollections of the war and a history of the Indian army.

Doveton, Frederick Brickdale. *Reminiscences of the Burmese War, in 1824-5-6*. Chestnut Hill, MA: Adamant/Elibron, 2005; originally published in 1852. An important and credible memoir by a participant in the war.

Gillian, Thomas. *Journal of Thomas Gillian . . . During the First Burmese War*. London: Hiscoke and Son, 1900. A useful source by a contemporary and eyewitness to many events.

Marks, John Ebenezer. *Forty Years in Burma*. Ed. W. C. B. Purser. London: Hutchinson, 1917. The personal recollections of a missionary who served many years in Burma.

Rhé-Philipe, George William de. *A Narrative of the First Burmese War, 1824–26: With the Various Official Reports and Despatches Describing the Operations of Naval and Military Forces . . . Progress, and Conclusion of the Contest*. Calcutta: Office of the Superintendent of Government Printing, India, 1905. A reliable mix of personal recollections, printed official documents, and historical analysis.

Snodgrass, J. J. *War Beyond the Dragon Pagoda: A Personal Narrative of the First Anglo-Burmese War, 1824–1826*. London: Leonaur, 2007. An eyewitness account of many of the events in the First Burmese War.

Wilson, Horace Hayman. *Narrative of the Burmese War, in 1824–25*. Ithaca, NY: Cornell University Library, 1852. Personal recollections of a contemporary.

Secondary Sources

Blackburn, Terence R. *The British Humiliation of Burma*. Bangkok: Orchid Press, 2000. A critical assessment of the British domination of Burma during the nineteenth and twentieth centuries—includes information on the First Burmese War.

Cooler, Richard M. *British Romantic Views of the First Anglo-Burmese War, 1824–1826*. DeKalb: Northern Illinois University Press, 1977. A critical analysis of the positions of the British government and public on the prosecution of the First Burmese War.

Ghosh, Parimal. *Brave Men of the Hills: Resistance and Rebellion in Burma, 1825–1932*. Honolulu: University of Hawaii Press, 2000. A scholarly study of the Burmese resistance movement against foreign intervention.

Hack, Karl, and Tobias Rettig, eds. *Colonial Armies in Southeast Asia*. Routledge Studies in the Modern History of Asia, no. 33. London: Routledge, 2006. Includes an essay on the British in Burma by Robert Taylor that may be useful, as well as maps that are quite good.

Hall, Daniel G. *Europe and Burma: A Study of European Relations with Burma to the Annexation of Thibaw's Kingdom, 1886.* New York: Oxford University Press, 1945. A scholarly account of Burma's unfortunate relationships with the European states prior to its collapse.

Harvey, Godfrey E. *British Rule in Burma, 1824–1942.* London: Faber and Faber, 1946. A useful study of the British governance in Burma—includes information on all of the Anglo-Burmese wars.

Henty, G. A. *On the Irrawaddy: A Story of the First Burmese War.* Whitefish, MT: Kessinger, 2008; originally published in 1897. Includes illustrations by W. H. Overend and a dated but useful account of the war.

Htin Aung, U. *The Stricken Peacock: Anglo-Burmese Relations, 1752–1948.* The Hague: M. Nijhoff, 1965. A critical analysis of Britain's role in Burma that includes information on the Anglo-Burmese wars.

Koenig, William J. *The Burmese Polity, 1752–1819: Politics, Administration, and Social Organization in the Early Kon-baung Period.* Ann Arbor: Center for South and Southeast Asian Studies, University of Michigan, 1990. An interesting study of Burmese leadership and policy prior to the British incursions of the nineteenth century.

Pollak, Oliver B. *Empires in Collison: Anglo-Burmese Relations in the Mid-Nineteenth Century.* Westport, CT: Greenwood Press, 1979. Excellent seminal study that all students working on this topic should consult.

Robertson, Thomas Campbell. *Political Incidents of the First Burmese War.* London: Richard Bentley, 1853. Available as an e-book at http://www.archive.org/details/politicalinciden00robeuoft. A very old classic study of the war that may still be useful to students who are focusing on the political aspects of the struggle.

Seekins, Donald M. *Historical Dictionary of Burma.* Lanham: Scarecrow, 2006. Most students will want to refer to this reference book that includes extensive information on the Anglo-Burmese wars.

Trager, Helen Gibson. *Burma Through Alien Eyes: Missionary Views of the Burmese in the Nineteenth Century.* New York: Praeger, 1966. Using the accounts of missionaries, Trager presents a vivid and distinctive interpretation of Burmese attitudes during the nineteenth century.

Wheeler, James T. *A Short History of India and the Frontier States of Afghanistan, Nipal, and Burma.* London: Macmillan, 1894. An old but still useful study that includes information on the Anglo-Burmese wars.

World Wide Web

"First Anglo-Burmese War, 1823–1826." http://www.historyofwar.org/articles/wars_angloburma1.html. An introduction to the war by J. Rickard.

"First Anglo-Burmese War, 1823–1826." http://www.onwar.com/aced/nation/ bat/burma/fburma1823.htm. Provides reliable introductory information on the war.

"First Burmese War, Autumn 1825–Spring 1826." http://www.experience festival.com/first_burmese_war_-_autumn_1825__spring_1826. Provides a list of links to articles on the war.

"The First Burmese War." http://www.rakhapura.com/scholars-column/ the-first-burmese-war.asp. The account of the war by Maung Boon, a tutor to a prominent British representative and an eyewitness, as translated by San Shwe Bu.

Multimedia Sources

"Multimedia: British Empire." http://encarta.msn.com/media_70176 6307_761566125_-1_1/British_Empire.html. Includes ten maps and photographs, two of which relate to Burma.

"The First Burmese War, 1824–1826." http://www.somerset.gov.uk/archives/sli/1 burmese.htm. Includes a photograph of a watercolor print of an incident in the conflict and a statement on the causes of the war.

22. Decembrist Revolt in Russia (1825)

The Decembrist Revolt occurred on December 26, 1825 in St. Petersburg when a group of Russian officers rallied about 3,000 men in opposition to Nicholas I's ascending the tsarist throne after his older brother Constantine declared that he was not interested in serving as the Russian leader. The origins of the dissident conspiracy that manifested itself in the Decembrist Revolt can be traced to the Union of Salvation that was established by several officers in 1816. It was radicalized by Pavel Pestel and split into two groups—the moderate Northern Society and the radical Southern Society that Pestel dominated. These dissidents were interested in reforming Russian law, improving the condition of the working class, and incorporating a wide sweeping liberal political agenda. When the rebels refused to recognize Nicholas I as tsar, a revolt was led by the Northern Society. Violence broke out and Nicholas used artillery to brutally suppress the insurrection. The Southern Society was devastated when Pestel was arrested. Many Decembrists were tried and convicted. Pestel and four others were hung and many were sent into exile in Siberia. The Decembrist Revolt quickly was transformed into a legend and its importance was sustained by other nineteenth- and twentieth-century Russian reformers.

TERM PAPER SUGGESTIONS

1. Develop a term paper on the background and causes of the Decembrist Revolt.
2. Write a paper on the outbreak of the Revolt—why did it occur in December 1825?
3. Develop a paper on the reasons for the failure of the Revolt—were any of its objectives realized?
4. What is the "place/image" of the Decembrist Revolt in the Russian revolutionary tradition in the nineteenth century?
5. The Decembrist Revolt occurred a decade after the defeat of Napoleon and the "French Revolutionary ideas." Write a paper on the question of whether the Decembrists were "romantics" or "rationalists."

ALTERNATIVE TERM PAPER SUGGESTIONS

1. Imagine that you are a *confidente* of the Decembrist leader Pavel Pestel. Develop a podcast of a private conversation in which Pestel shares with you the reasons for the Revolt and his plans for it.
2. As a correspondent for a Paris newspaper, you have infiltrated the Decembrist conspiracy with which you have great sympathy. Develop a blog of your dispatches to your paper that will be published immediately upon the outbreak of the Revolt. The dispatches must be fact-filled and reflect a criticism of the Russian tsarist system.
3. Develop an iMovie of the trial of the Decembrist conspirators. Was this a fair trial?
4. Develop a blog that includes entries by the Decembrist rebels in which they justify their revolt and call for others to join them. What was their vision for the future of Russia?

SUGGESTED SOURCES

Primary Sources

Dmytryshyn, Basil, ed. *Imperial Russia: A Source Book, 1700–1917.* Gulf Breeze, FL: Academic International Press, 1999. A very good source of primary materials including some on the Decembrist Revolt.

Giblan, George, ed. *The Portable Nineteenth-Century Russian Reader.* New York: Penguin, 1993. A compendium of contemporary literary, political, and philosophical sources, includes resources on the Decembrists.

Jackman, Sydney W., ed. *Romanov Relations, The Private Correspondence of Tsars Alexander I, Nicholas I and the Grand Dukes Constantine and Michael with Their Sister, Queen Anna Pavlovna, 1817–1855.* London: Macmillan, 1969. A valuable resource in which the tsars confided in Pavlovna who was the queen of the Netherlands.

Offord, D. C., ed. *A Documentary History of Russian Thought: From the Enlightenment to Marxism.* Trans. William J. Leatherbarrow. New York: Ardis, 1987. A very good collection of documents on Russian intellectual and cultural developments in the nineteenth century, including the Decembrists.

Pope-Hennessey, Una. *A Czarina's Story, Being an Account of the Early Married Life of the Emperor Nicholas I of Russia Written by His Wife.* London: Nicholson and Watson, 1948. Includes some useful commentary on the Decembrists and the post-Decembrist era.

Secondary Sources

Crankshaw, Edward. *The Shadow of the Winter Palace: Russia's Drift to Revolution, 1825–1917.* Cambridge, MA: DeCapo Press, 2000. An excellent study by a recognized scholar, this volume places the Decembrist Revolt in the context of the Russian revolutionary tradition.

Cross, Anthony. *St. Petersburg, 1703–1825.* New York: Palgrave-Macmillan, 2003. A scholarly work that consists of nine essays and concludes with the ascendancy of Nicholas I and the Decembrist Revolt.

Figes, Orlando. *Natasha's Dance: A Cultural History of Russia.* London: Picador, 2003. This outstanding study of Russian thought provides insights and anecdotes that are not found elsewhere and that should be very useful.

Grunwald, Constantin de. *Tsar Nicholas I.* Trans. Brigit Patmore. London: L. D. Saunders, 1954. A standard but dated biography of Nicholas I that includes information on the Decembrist Revolt.

Leighton, Lauren G. *The Esoteric Tradition in Russian Romantic Literature: Decembrism and Freemasonry.* University Park: The Pennsylvania State University Press, 1994. An important work by a reputable scholar that connects the revolt to Russian literary development.

Lincoln, W. Bruce. *Nicholas I, Emperor and Autocrat of All the Russians.* Bloomington: Indiana University Press, 1980. A solid and reliable biography that includes data on the Decembrist movement.

Mayne, F. *The Life of Nicholas I, Emperor of Russia; With a Short Account of Russia and the Russians.* Whitefish, MT: Kessinger Publishing, 2007. A dated but still useful biography of Nicholas I that includes data on the Decembrist Revolt and the treatment of the conspirators.

Mazour, Anatole Gregory. *The First Russian Revolution, 1825: The Decembrist Movement, its Origins, Development, and Significance.* Stanford, CA: Stanford University Press, 1961. A very good and reliable scholarly study of the Revolt that should be consulted.

Michelsen, Edward H. *The Life of Nicholas I: Emperor of All the Russians.* Whitefish, MT: Kessinger Publishing, 2007. A classic and traditional study of Nicholas I and his reaction to the Decembrists.

Miller, Alexei, and Alfred J. Rieber, eds. *Imperial Rule.* Budapest and New York: Central European University Press, 2004. Includes an outstanding essay by Miller on the "imagination" of Russian nationalism.

O'Meara, Patrick. *The Decembrist Pavel Pestel: Russia's First Republican.* New York: Palgrave-Macmillan, 2004. Based on archival work, O'Meara's book is the best and most thorough study of Pestel with emphasis on the period from 1816 to 1825.

Presniakov, A. E. *Emperor Nicholas I of Russia: The Apogee of Autocracy, 1825–1855.* Ed. and trans. Judith C. Zacek. Gulf Breeze, FL: Academic International Press, 1974. A dated but still useful work that is critical of Nicholas I on his treatment of the Decembrists.

Rabow-Edling, Susanna. "The Decembrists and the Concept of Civic Nation." *Nationalities Papers* 35, no. 2 (May 2007): 369–391. A seminal study on the impact of the Decembrist ideology on nineteenth-century Russian political thought.

Raeff, Marc. *The Decembrist Movement.* Englewood Cliffs, NJ: Prentice-Hall, 1966. A good introduction to the movement and its place in Russian history.

Riasanovsky, Nicholas V. *Nicholas I and Official Nationality in Russia, 1825–1855.* Berkeley: University of California Press, 1959. A meaningful study of the idea of nation, nationality, and nationalism in nineteenth-century Russia.

Saunders, David. *Russia in the Age of Reaction and Reform, 1801–1881.* London and New York: Longman, 1992. This is a worthwhile study that interprets the Decembrist movement as a reform movement in the larger context of European political history in the nineteenth century.

Seton-Watson, Hugh. *The Russian Empire, 1801–1917.* Oxford: Clarendon Press, 1988. Includes a good introduction to the background, outbreak, and consequences of the Revolt.

World Wide Web

Cunynghame, Daisy. "Position Paper on the Decembrists." http://www.st -andrews.ac.uk/~pvteach/imprus/papers/02b.html. An excellent resource on the Decembrist Revolt from Paul Vyšný's Seminar on Russian Society and Outlook in the Early Nineteenth Century, University of St. Andrews.

"The Decembrist Disaster." http://www.bl.uk/onlinegallery/features/bkackeuro/pushkindisaster.html. This British Library site connects the Decembrist rebels with Alexander Pushkin and his *Ode to Freedom.* It includes three related images.

"Decembrist Revolt, 1825." http://www.thenagain.info/WebChron/East Europe/DecRevolt.html. Provides an introduction to the Revolt and a brief bibliography.

Hamilton, Dominic. " 'Love Tyrannises All The Ages': The Decembrists of Siberia." http://www.nomadom.net/russia/decembrists.htm. An intriguing site that focuses on the lives of the Decembrists in Siberia.

Multimedia Sources

Captivating Star of Happiness. Russian Cinema Council, 1975. DVD released 2003. Produced by Ruscico. In Russian with English subtitles. A dramatic film on the Decembrist Revolt and the subsequent exile to Siberia of many of its supporters and their families. This is a sympathetic account of the revolt and its victims.

Russia—Land of the Tsars. A&E Home Video, 2003. DVD. A docudrama that includes a section on the Decembrist Revolt.

Stoppard, Tom. *The Coast of Utopia;* published as *The Coast of Utopia, Voyage, Shipwreck, Salvage.* New York: Grove, 2007. The Decembrist Revolt serves as the starting point of this nearly eight-hour play, which proceeds to follow the lives of Russian revolutionary thinkers for several decades.

23. Independence of Bolivia (1825)

Political change in Upper Peru (Bolivia) was affected by shifts of power in Spain and the dominance of the Bonaparte family. During 1807–1808 French forces invaded Spain, forced the abdication of Ferdinand VII (1784–1833), and named Joseph Bonaparte (1768–1844) as king of Spain. In the Latin American colonies, allegiance was divided between the old order and the Bonapartes. In Bolivia most members of the ruling classes supported the new government, anticipating a wave of liberal reforms. Some others supported the family of the old king, and others (*criollos,* people born in Latin America with no native blood) wanted complete and immediate independence. In 1809 a *criollos* revolt proclaimed an independent state in Upper Peru in the name of

Ferdinand VII, but it was suppressed by forces of the Viceroyalty of Peru in Lima. However, Upper Peru—difficult to invade—found itself enjoying a limited degree of freedom during the years that the other Latin American states were fighting for their independence. It was not until the defeat of the royalist army in the Battle of Ayacucho (December 9, 1824) that Upper Peru moved to full independence as Bolivia. Simon Bolivar (1783–1830) wrote Bolivia's first constitution.

TERM PAPER SUGGESTIONS

1. Write a paper in which you compare and contrast the roles of Pedro Domingo Murillo, Pedro Antonio de Olanneta, and Antonio José de Sucre on the Bolivian independence movement.

2. Develop a paper on the Battle of Ayacucho and its significance in Bolivian history.

3. Write a paper in which you analyze Bolivia's first constitution (1825).

4. Write a paper in which you respond to this question: why did it take 16 years for Bolivia to achieve its independence?

ALTERNATIVE TERM PAPER SUGGESTIONS

1. Develop a podcast in which you interview General Antonio José de Sucre after the Battle of Ayacucho. What was his analysis of the battle and the independence of Bolivia?

2. Develop an iMovie in which Pedro Domingo Murillo discusses his 1809 revolt against the Viceroyalty of Peru.

3. As a radical *criollos* in Upper Peru, you are focused on the need for independence. Develop a blog in which you recorded your impressions of the phases and events from 1809 to 1825 that ultimately led to Bolivian independence.

SUGGESTED SOURCES

Primary Sources

Bolivar, Simon. *Selected Writings*. 2 vols. Compil. Vicente Lecuna; ed. Harold Bierck; trans. Lewis Bertrand. New York: Colonial Press, 1951. A very good collection of Bolivar's writings, including some related to Bolivia's independence. Bolivar wrote the first constitution of Bolivia.

Hanke, Lewis, and Jane M. Rausch, eds. *People and Issues in Latin American History: From Independence to the Present: Sources and Interpretations*. 3rd ed. Princeton, NJ: Markus Weiner, 2008. Includes useful primary sources as well as excerpts from scholarly works on the Latin American (including Bolivia's) independence movements.

Pazos, Vicente. *Letters on the United Provinces of South America, addressed to the Hon. Henry Clay, Speaker of the House of Representatives of the United States.* Trans. Platt H. Crosby. New York: J. Seymour, 1819. Also available as a microform book from Chester, VT: Readex, 2007. These letters from a participant of the Argentine and Bolivian wars for independence provide an important commentary of the era.

Vila, Manuel Pérez. *Simon Bolivar: His Basic Thoughts; Biographical Sketch and Selection of Documents.* Caracas: Presidency of the Republic of Venezuela, 1981. An excellent collection of documents on Bolivar that should be very useful to students writing on his role in the wars for independence, including Bolivia.

Secondary Sources

Alexander, Robert J. *Bolivia: Past, Present, and Future of Its Politics.* New York: Praeger, 1982. The introductory chapters provide information on the independence movement in Bolivia.

Amande, Charles W. *The Emergence of the Republic of Bolivia.* New York: Russell and Russell, 1970. An intriguing study of Bolivia's long path to the establishment of a republic in the nineteenth century.

Barton, Robert. *A Short History of the Republic of Bolivia, Being an Account of all that has taken place in Upper Peru from Earliest Times to the Present.* 2nd ed. La Paz: Editorial Los Amigos del Libro, 1968. The early sections of this study provide data on the independence movement—a good introduction.

Bethell, Leslie, ed. *The Independence of Latin America.* New York: Cambridge University Press, 1987. A collection of worthwhile essays on the independence movements (including Bolivia) in Latin America.

Brown, Matthew. *Adventuring through Spanish Colonies: Simón Bolivar, Foreign Mercenaries and the Birth of New Nations.* Liverpool: Liverpool University Press, 2008. An excellent—scholarly yet readable—study that includes some information on Bolivar's support and involvement with the Bolivian independence movement.

Burkholder, Mark A., and Lyman L. Johnson. *Colonial Latin America.* 6th ed. New York: Oxford University Press, 2008. Provides a good background on the conditions in pre-independent Bolivia.

Bushnell, David. *Simón Bolivar: Liberation and Disillusion.* New York: Pearson Longman, 2004. Includes information on Bolivar's aspirations for the new Latin American republics.

Chasteen, John. *Americanos: Latin America's Struggle for Independence.* New York: Oxford University Press, 2008. Provides good introductions to the many Latin American revolutions including Bolivia.

Fifer, J. Valerie. *Bolivia: Land, Location, and Politics since 1825.* Cambridge Latin American Studies, no. 13. Cambridge, U.K.: Cambridge University Press, 1972. This study may be useful to students researching the years immediately following independence.

Harvey, Robert. *Liberators: Latin America's Struggle for Independence.* New York: Overlook, 2000. A reliable and useful study on the leaders of the conflicts including Bolivar, San Martin, and Sucre.

Jacobsen, Nils, and Cristobal Aljovin de Losada, eds. *Political Cultures in the Andes, 1750–1950.* Durham, NC: Duke University Press, 2005. A collection of essays on Andean history, some related to Bolivia.

Klein, Herbert S. *A Concise History of Bolivia.* Cambridge, U.K.: Cambridge University Press, 2003. A reliable and useful text that includes information on Bolivia's war for independence.

Lynch, John. *Simón Bolivar: A Life.* New Haven, CT: Yale University Press, 2006. Perhaps the best biography of Bolivar that includes extensive information on his contributions to the independence of Bolivia.

———. *The Spanish American Revolution, 1808–1826.* New York: Longman, 2003. A very reliable and comprehensive study of all of the Latin American revolutions.

Morales, Waltraud Q. *A Brief History of Bolivia.* New York: Facts on File, 2003. A reference work that should be useful in researching Bolivia's war of independence.

Nicholson, Irene. *The Liberators, A Study of Independence Movements in Spanish America.* New York: Praeger, 1969. A very good account of the various national movements, including that of Bolivia.

Scheina, Robert L. *Latin America's Wars.* 2 vols. Dulles, VA: Brassey's, 2003. Excellent scholarship on all of the wars of independence, including Bolivia's war for independence, especially the Battle of Ayacucho.

Tepaske, John. *Research Guide to Andean History: Bolivia, Chile, Ecuador, and Peru.* Durham, NC: Duke University Press, 1981. An excellent resource in gathering information on all aspects of Andean history.

World Wide Web

"Antonio José de Sucre." http://www.answers.com/topic/antonio-jos-de-sucre. A biographical statement on this important Ecuadorian rebel leader who also served as the first constitutionally elected president of Bolivia.

"Bolivian Independence War." http://www.mundoandino.com/Bolivia/Bolivian-Independence-War. A brief, accurate account of Bolivia's war for independence.

"Bolivia Struggle for Independence." http://www.workmall.com/wfb2001/bolivia/bolivia_history_struggle_for_independence.html. Provides a description and outline of Bolivia's multiphase war for complete independence.

"Independence from Spain." http://countrystudies.us/bolivia/8.htm. A well-written and accurate statement on Bolivia's independence movement from Spain/Peru.

Multimedia Source

Simón Bolivar. Unicorn Video, 1985. VHS. A dramatic film directed by Alessandro Blasetti.

24. Argentinean War of Independence (1810–1818)

Spanish control over the Viceroyalty of the Rio de la Plata, which included parts of Argentina, Bolivia, Paraguay, and Uruguay, was focused in an appointed Viceroy and Spanish troops. Spain used its Latin American colonies to enhance its own economic interests; the colonies' trade with other states was prohibited. This restriction created resentment and led many Buenos Aires businessmen to violate it—especially with English traders. Spanish influence was weakened further by the Napoleonic Wars. Napoleon's offensive against Spain (the Peninsular War) resulted in the Argentineans being attracted to the ideas of the republicanism and, at the same time, their recognition of Spain's increased vulnerability. In May 1810 news of Napoleon's advances arrived in Buenos Aires. Within a few days, a revolutionary First Junta was established and seized control of the government, which remained "loyal" to the Spanish monarch. There was fear that the French would seize the Rio de la Plata after the defeat of Spain. A Second or Big Junta was established shortly thereafter to advance Argentinean revolutionary ideas. During 1810–1811 the Second Junta launched two military initiatives—the Alto Peru and the Paraguay campaigns—to consolidate control over the revolutionary movements. These conflicts, as well as the Second Alto Peru campaign of 1812–1813, the Third Alto Peru campaign of 1815, and the Chile campaign of 1817, were among the native revolutionary forces. The Argentinean Declaration of Independence was announced in 1816. By 1818, the Argentineans had achieved their goal of independence and had begun the process of aligning themselves into the new geopolitical reality of the Rio de la Plata.

TERM PAPER SUGGESTIONS

1. Develop a term paper on the causes and early development of the Argentine struggle for independence.
2. Write a term paper on the formulation of the Argentine Declaration of Independence. What values did it espouse? What structure of government did it establish?
3. Develop a paper on the role of Manuel Belgrano in the Argentine independence movement.
4. Write a paper in which you compare and contrast the impact of José de San Martín, Bernardo O'Higgins, and William Brown on Argentinean independence.
5. Develop a paper on the impact of Argentina's successful revolution against Spain on other Latin American revolutions.

ALTERNATIVE TERM PAPER SUGGESTIONS

1. Develop a 5 minute podcast in which Begrano and Martín share their aspirations for a free Argentina and the cause of nationalism throughout Latin America.
2. As a longtime Spanish royalist in Buenos Aires, you resist the wave of revolutions that has gripped Latin America. Develop a blog of your diary entries between 1810 and 1818.
3. Develop an iMovie on the formulation of the Argentine Declaration of Independence—be sure to include the debates on the fundamental issues.

SUGGESTED SOURCES

Primary Sources

"Manuel Belgrano, Archival Collection, University of Notre Dame." http://www.library.nd.edu/rarebooks/collections/manuscripts/latin_american/sc_history/belgrano.shtml#DESCRIPTION. Includes a range of documents on Belgrano up to 1818 that should be very useful to students writing on this topic.

Nouzeilles, Gabriela, and Graciela Montaldo, eds. *The Argentina Reader: History, Culture, Politics.* Durham, NC: Duke University Press, 2002. Provides a wide range of primary sources, including several related to the Argentinean War of Independence.

Secondary Sources

Bethell, Leslie, ed. *The Independence of Latin America.* New York: Cambridge University Press, 1987. A collection of scholarly essays, including one on Argentina.

Chasteen, John. *Americanos: Latin America's Struggle for Independence.* New York: Oxford University Press, 2008. Includes information on Argentina and places that revolution for independence in the context of the region's general revolt against Spain and Portugal.

Harrison, Margaret Hayne. *Captain of the Andes: The Life of Don José de San Martin, Liberator of Argentina, Chile and Peru.* New York: R. R. Smith, 1943. Still a useful and readable account of San Martin's involvement in the Argentine revolt.

Harvey, Robert. *Liberators: Latin America's Struggle for Independence.* New York: Overlook, 2000. A very good series of biographical studies on those who lead the Argentine and other Latin American revolutions.

Metford, J. C. J. *San Martin, the Liberator.* New York: Philosophical Library, 1950. A dated but solid biography of San Martin that should be useful to many students.

Nicholson, Irene. *The Liberators, A Study of Independence Movements in Spanish America.* New York: Praeger, 1969. Another good study that examines the roles of prominent revolutions in the many national movements in which they were involved.

Robertson, William Spence. *Rise of the Spanish-American Republics, as Told in the Lives of Their Liberators.* New York: Free Press, 1948. A classic and important work that includes extensive information on Argentina.

World Wide Web

"Argentine Independence." http://everydaysaholiday.wordpress.com/2008/07/09/argentine-independence/. A useful general introduction to the independence movement in Argentina.

"Argentine Independence—Political Issues." http://historicaltextarchive.com/sections.php?artid=402&op=viewarticle. A worthwhile site that provides reliable information on the myriad political issues that were associated with the Argentine revolt against Spain.

"Argentine War of Independence, 1810–1816." http://www.onwar.com/aced/nation/all/argentina/fargentina1810.htm. An introduction to the chronology and the principal developments of the war for independence.

"Argentine War of Independence." http://www.mundoandino.com/Argentina/Argentine-War-of-Independence. An introduction to the war that includes some useful information not found elsewhere.

"The Economic Consequences of Argentine Independence." http://ideas.repec.org/a/ioe/cuadec/v38y2001i115p275-290.html. A downloadable article by Carlos Newland and Javier Ortiz that examines the extensive economic impact that resulted from Argentina's successful revolt against Spain.

Multimedia Source

"Argentine Independence." http://www.britannica.com/EBchecked/topic/33657/Argentina/33071/Independence#tab=active-checked%2Citems-checked&title=Argentina%20%3A%3A%20Independence%20-%20Britannica%20Online%20Encyclopedia. Includes maps and videos of geographic areas that were involved in the conflict for independence from Spain.

25. Liberal Revolt in Mexico (1828)

During the 1820s the economic condition of the newly independent Mexico declined. The government assumed the debts of the colonial government and spent more than it could afford in developing the new government. As a result, the government was reaching a point where it could not support the debt level. In addition to this economic crisis, conservatives launched an unsuccessful rebellion in 1827 that was quickly suppressed. With a very uncertain economic and political environment, Mexicans voted for a new president in September 1828. The two primary candidates were the conservative Manuel Gómez Pedraza (1789–1851) and the liberal Vicente Guerrero (1782–1831). The election results clearly favored the conservatives, but the liberals refused to recognize their victory; two governments were established with some military units supporting each side. In the end, the liberals prevailed when Pedraza succumbed to the pressures of leading generals—this was the liberal revolution of 1828. Guerrero became the second president of Mexico in 1829.

TERM PAPER SUGGESTIONS

1. Write a paper on the economic and political crises that contributed to the liberal revolution in 1828.

2. Develop a paper in which you compare and contrast the positions of Manuel Gómez Pedraza and Vicente Guerrero.

3. Write a paper on the impact of the Mexican military on the liberal revolution of 1828.

4. General Santa Ana played a key role in settling the crisis of 1828. Write a paper based on his assessment of the situation and his vision for the role of the military in Mexico's political future.

ALTERNATIVE TERM PAPER SUGGESTIONS

1. Develop a podcast in which Pedraza and Guerrero are interviewed on their claims to the presidency.

2. Develop an iMovie in which prominent citizens in Mexico City evaluate the constitutional crisis of 1828.

SUGGESTED SOURCES

Primary Sources

Hardy, Robert William. *Travels in the Interior of Mexico, in 1825, 1826, 1827, and 1828.* London: H. Colburn and R. Bentley, 1829. A memoir by a British traveler in Mexico prior to the revolution of 1828 provides insights into the conditions of the society and the political aspirations of the people.

Penny, Edward B. *A Sketch of the Customs and Society of Mexico: In a series of familiar letters and a Journal of travels in the interior, during the years 1824, 1825, and 1826.* London: Longman, 1828. Also available as an e-book at http://books.google.com/books?hl=en&id=g9uosD3 weW0C&dq=Penny,+Edward+B.+A+Sketch+of+the+Customs+and +Society+of+Mexico&printsec=frontcover&source=web&ots=CwI91H 0j33&sig=uQhLbL6vkM3_2rPQIbevUL7oBT4&sa=X&oi=book_result &resnum=2&ct=result. Personal recollections of an extended visit to Mexico during the period between the achievement of independence and the revolution of 1828.

Tayloe, Edward T. *Mexico, 1825–1828: The Journal and Correspondence of Edward Thornton Tayloe.* Ed. C. Harvey Gardiner. Chapel Hill: University of North Carolina Press, 1959. Tayloe's (private secretary to Joel Poinsett, the first American minister to Mexico) works should be very useful and significant for students working on this topic.

Secondary Sources

Arrom, Silvia M. "Popular Politics in Mexico City: The Parián Riot, 1828." *Hispanic American Historical Review*, LXVIII, no. 2 (May 1988): 245–268. Also available at http://www.jstor.org/pss/2515514. An excellent scholarly study that needs to be read by students working on the 1828 revolt.

Calcott, Wilfrid. *Church and State in Mexico, 1822–1857*. Durham, NC: Duke University Press, 1926. Provides data on the 1828 revolt and its impact on society.

DePalo, William A. *The Mexican National Army, 1822–1852*. College Station: Texas A&M University Press, 1997. Includes an early section on the position and role of the army during the 1828 revolution.

Di Tella, Torcuato S. *National Popular Politics in Early Independent Mexico, 1820–1847*. Albuquerque: University of New Mexico Press, 1996. An important scholarly work that includes data in the liberal revolt. It may provide a range of potential approaches for term papers, and it is well documented.

Fowler, Will. *Mexico in the Age of Proposals, 1821–1853*. Westport, CT: Greenwood Press, 1998. An acclaimed study that includes useful information on the liberal revolt of 1828.

———. "Valentin Gomez Farias: Perceptions of Radicalism in Independent Mexico, 1821–1847." *Bulletin of Latin American Research* XV, no. 1 (1996): 39–62. Includes useful data on the political views of the radical physician and politician Valentin Gomez Farias (1781–1857).

Hale, Charles Adams. *Mexican Liberalism in the Age of Mora, 1821–1853*. New Haven, CT: Yale University Press, 1968. Includes extensive information on the impact of José Maria Luis Mora and his influence on Mexican politics and life.

Stevens, Donald F. *Origins of Instability in Early Republican Mexico*. Durham, NC: Duke University Press, 1991. A scholarly study that considers the impact of tensions emerging from the political, economic, and social conditions and aspirations in Mexico.

World Wide Web

"Mexican History Chronology: Independence through the French Intervention." http://historicaltextarchive.com/sections.php?op=viewarticle &artid=327. A useful timeline on early and mid-nineteenth century Mexican history.

"Mexico: The Federalist Republic, 1824–36." http://www.country-data.com/ cgi-bin/query/r-8697.html. Includes useful information on the liberal revolution and its consequences.

"Vicente Guerrero." http://www.britannica.com/hispanic_heritage/article
-9038379. Useful data on Guerrero who attained the presidency of
Mexico as a result of the liberal revolt.

Multimedia Source

"Pictures of Guanajuato and the Mexican War of Independence: Photo Images
History." http://www.downtheroad.org/Photo/4CenMex/WarofInd2
PHOTO.htm. Interesting photographs of sites and monuments
related to the Mexican war for independence and the liberal revolution
of 1828.

26. July Revolution (1830)

After the defeat of Napoleon in 1815 the victorious powers restored the
Bourbon Dynasty to power in France in the person of King Louis XVIII
(1755–1824), who ruled from 1814 to his death in 1824. He was succeeded by his brother, Charles X (1757–1836), who had little tolerance
for criticism from any and all quarters. These last Bourbon kings were fundamentally conservative, and some would classify Charles X as a reactionary. During the six years of his reign, Charles X became increasingly
intolerant of dissent and surrounded himself with authoritarians who
moved the king closer to the right. Among the measures that Charles X
enacted that alienated him from many were the decrees that mandated
the death penalty for abusing the Roman Catholic communion and
another that provided the victims, usually the rich, with restitution for
losses incurred during the French Revolution of 1789. Opposition in the
press to Charles X reached a high point during the summer of 1830.
In July 1830 Charles X issued the July Ordinances that placed further
restrictions on the press (censorship) and assembly. The July Revolution
occurred during a three-day period—July 27–29, 1830. It was confined
to Paris for the most part and supported by the middle class, reformers
who wanted a liberal constitution, and students. Charles X's government
did not mount any substantive defense of the regime and Charles X abdi-
cated in favor of his cousin Louis Philippe (1773–1850). Charles X fled
the country and first went into exile in England and later in Prague where
he died in 1836. The July Revolution resulted in the disappointing
18-year reign of an increasingly conservative Louis Philippe.

TERM PAPER SUGGESTIONS

1. Write a paper on the background and causes for the July Revolution of 1830.
2. Develop a paper on the leadership of the July Revolution. What did they intend to accomplish by replacing Charles X with his cousin Louis Philippe?
3. How revolutionary was the July Revolution?
4. Develop a paper on Louis Philippe's vision and plans for France in 1830.

ALTERNATIVE TERM PAPER SUGGESTIONS

1. Develop a 5 minute podcast in which the revolutionary conspirators discuss their plans and motives for the overthrow of Charles X.
2. As a young professional in Paris, you support the forced abdication of Charles X and the ascendancy of the new constitutionally appointed Louis Philippe. Develop a blog with your parents in Artois. Be sure to include the rationale for your position and comment on the day-to-day events and the consequences of the revolution.
3. Develop an iMovie in which the old aristocracy assesses the impact of the July Revolution on them and their interests.

SUGGESTED SOURCES

Primary Sources

Belk, Paul H. *Louis Philippe and the July Monarchy.* Princeton, NJ: Anvil, 1965. The second half of this book provides documents and primary materials that should be useful to many students working on aspects of this topic.

Carpenter, William. *Anecdotes of the French Revolution of 1830.* London: W. Strange, 1830. A very good primary source that includes personal recollections and extensive quotations from relevant documents.

Hone, William. *Full Annals of the Revolution in France, 1830: Illegal Ordinances of Charles X, Military Execution to Enforce Them. Battles and Victories of the People ... Bravery; Memoirs of the Duke of Orleans. ...* London: T. Tieg, 1830. Available as an e-book at http://www.archive.org/details/fullannalsofrevo00honeiala. Provides information and documents to justify the overthrow of Charles X.

Turnbull, David. *The French Revolution in 1830: The Events that Produced it, and the Scenes by which It Was Accompanied.* London: H. Colburn and R. Bentley, 1830. Available as an e-book at http://www.archive.org/details/frenchrevolution00turnrich. Includes primary and secondary materials that should be useful to many students.

Secondary Sources

Alexander, R. S. *Re-writing the French Revolutionary Tradition.* Cambridge, U.K.: Cambridge University Press, 2003. A work for advanced students who are investigating varying interpretations and perspective of the July Revolution.

Beach, Vincent W. *The Fall of Charles X of France: A Case Study of Revolution.* University of Colorado Studies. Westport, CT: Greenwood Press, 1961. Available as an e-book at http://books.google.com/books?id =om8TAAAAIAAJ&q=Beach,+Vincent+W.+The+Fall+of+Charles+X +of+France:+A+Case+Study+of+Revolution.+1961.&dq=Beach,+Vincent +W.+The+Fall+of+Charles+X+of+France:+A+Case+Study+of+Revolution. +1961.&pgis=1. A classic study of the July Revolution that should be referred to by most students working on this topic.

———. *Charles X of France: His Life and Times.* Boulder, CO: Pruett, 1971. Available as an e-book at http://books.google.com/books?id=jzte AAAAIAAJ&q=Beach,+Vincent+W.+The+Fall+of+Charles+X+of +France:+A+Case+Study+of+Revolution.+1961.&dq=Beach,+Vincent +W.+The+Fall+of+Charles+X+of+France:+A+Case+Study+of+Revolution .+1961.&pgis=1. Beach's biography still stands as one of the best studies available.

Burton, Richard D. *Blood in the City: Violence and Revelation in Paris, 1789– 1945.* Ithaca, NY: Cornell University Press, 2001. Focused on Paris and its citizens, the sociopolitical scholarly study is quite excellent and should attract student interest.

Collingham, H. A. C. *The July Monarchy.* New York: Longman, 1988. See the early chapters in this book for useful and reliable information on the revolution.

Harsin, Jill. *Barricades: The War of the Streets in Revolutionary Paris, 1830–1848.* New York: Palgrave Macmillan, 2002. A well-researched and well-written study that appropriately reinforces the role of Paris and Parisians in the revolution.

Loades, Judith. *Louis Philippe, The July Monarchy.* Burford, U.K.: Davenant Press, 2000. A reliable and useful biography. The chapters on 1830 should be useful to many students.

Lucas-Dubreton, J. *Restoration and the July Monarchy.* Oldwick, NJ: Arms Press, 1967. Covers the period from 1814 through the reign of Louis Philippe.

Merriman, John. *1830 in France.* New York: New Viewpoints, 1975. Available as an e-book at http://books.google.com/books?id=J-BnAAAAMAAJ&q =Beach,+Vincent+W.+The+Fall+of+Charles+X+of+France:+A+Case +Study+of+Revolution.+1961.&dq=Beach,+Vincent+W.+The+Fall+of +Charles+X+of+France:+A+Case+Study+of+Revolution.+1961.

&pgis=1. A useful study of the revolution that includes data not found elsewhere.

Pinkey, David H. *The French Revolution of 1830.* Princeton, NJ: Princeton University Press, 1972. Available as an e-book at http://quod.lib.umich.edu/cgi/t/text/text-idx?c=acls;idno=heb01309.0001.001. Still a very worthwhile history of the July Revolution—very good on the background and causes.

Pilbeam, Pamela. *The 1830 Revolution in France.* London: Palgrave Macmillan, 1991. A very good history of the July Revolution and its impact on France.

Prothero, Iorwerth J. *Religion and Radicalism in July Monarchy France: The French Catholic Church of the Abbe Chatel.* Studies in French Civilization. Lewiston, NY: Edwin Mellon Press, 2005. A seminal study that students need to read if they are pursuing a topic in which the roles of the Church and its priests are the focus.

Rader, Daniel L. *The Journalists and the July Revolution in France: The Role of the Political Press in the Overthrow of the Bourbon Restoration 1827–1830.* The Hague: Nijhoff, 1973. A scholarly and significant account of the impact of the "fourth estate" on the July Revolution.

Sarrans, Bernard. *Lafayette, Louis Philippe and the Revolution of 1830.* 2 vols. Whitefish, MT: Kessinger, 2007; originally published in 1832. A very important contemporary history that connects the leaders of the French revolutionary tradition. Some primary sources have been inserted in this work.

Woodward, Ernest L. *French Revolutions.* Oxford: Clarendon Press, 1934. A dated resource but it provides useful and reliable information on the July Revolution.

World Wide Web

"Étienne Maurice Gérard." http://www.infoplease.com/ce6/people/A0820592.html. Biography of a supporter of the July Revolution against Charles X.

"July Revolution." http://www.encyclopedia.com/doc/1E1-JulyRevo.html. A very good introduction to the revolution with four illustrations and links to other sites.

"July Revolution." http://www.britannica.com/EBchecked/topic/308028/July-Revolution. A reliable and useful introduction to the July Revolution.

"July Revolution." http://www.questia.com/library/encyclopedia/july_revolution.jsp. A brief but fact-filled statement on the July Revolution with some links to other relevant sources.

"The July Revolution in France 1830." http://www.onwar.com/aced/data/
foxtrot/france1830.htm. A very good introduction to the revolution that
is very critical of Charles X.

"The July Revolution and Heinrich Heine." http://www.nthuleen.com/papers/
141papereng.html. An excellent article on the impact of the July Revolution on the German intellectual and reformer Heinrich Heine.

Multimedia Source

"Léon Cogniet, Scenes of July 1830, a painting alluding to the July revolution of
1830." http://www.freebase.com/view/wikipedia/images/commons_id/
260801. An artist's rendering of the significance of the revolution
through images of three flags.

27. Establishment of the Republic of Ecuador (1830)

In 1808 Napoleon's armies invaded Spain and the crisis on the Iberian
peninsula motivated the supporters of both Spain and a free Ecuador to
take action. Those who were loyal to the Spanish king, Ferdinand VII
(1784–1833), rebelled against the French-appointed leadership on
August 10, 1809. Their victory was short-lived, and the supporters of
the French appointees rallied and regained control of the city. Within
two years the Spanish-French struggle was transformed into a war for
independence of Quito. In 1811 a constitution for Quito was formed
and a government established. However, that effort was crushed when
Spanish forces from Peru arrived and restored Spanish authority in
1812. In 1820 Ecuadorians under the leadership of José Joaquin Olmedo
(1780–1847), inspired by the success of Simon Bolivar (1783–1830) and
José de San Martin 1778–1850), rebelled in Guayaquil and requested
support from the two great revolutionary leaders. Bolivar sent an army
under Antonio José de Sucre Alcalá (1795–1830), but that force was
defeated by the Spanish. San Martin sent additional units and the combined forces for independence defeated the Spanish at the Battle of
Pichincha on May 24, 1822. Under Bolivar's plan, Ecuador became a part
of "Gran Colombia," which also included Bolivia and Venezuela. In May
1830 Ecuador withdrew from "Gran Colombia" and became a fully independent state.

TERM PAPER SUGGESTIONS

1. Write a paper on the initial (French-Spanish) phase of Ecuador's long road to independence.

2. Develop a paper in which you evaluate the impact on Ecuador's independence of Bolivar, Martin, and Olmedo.

3. Write a paper on the leadership of Juan José Flores in attaining independence for Ecuador.

4. The Spanish commitment to retaining control of Quito and the rest of Ecuador was high. Write a paper on the level of Spanish support during all phases of this struggle. Did the Spanish make any serious errors in their management of this war?

ALTERNATIVE TERM PAPER SUGGESTIONS

1. Develop a podcast in which Olmedo, Bolivar, and Martin meet to discuss their strategy and tactics in bringing about the defeat of the Spanish.

2. Develop an iMovie in which Bolivar presents his vision for "Gran Colombia" and Ecuador's place in it.

3. As a student in Quito, you support the wars against the supporter of a French regime as well as the Spanish. However, you have mixed feelings about Ecuador's inclusion in "Gran Colombia" and develop a blog of articles on that issue.

SUGGESTED SOURCES

Primary Sources

Bolivar, Simon. *Selected Writings.* 2 vols. Compil. Vicente Lecuna; ed. Harold Bierck; trans. Lewis Bertrand. New York: Colonial Press, 1951. A very good collection of Bolivar's writings, including many related to Ecuador's independence.

Hanke, Lewis, and Jane M. Rausch, eds. *People and Issues in Latin American History: From Independence to the Present: Sources and Interpretations.* 3rd ed. Princeton, NJ: Markus Weiner, 2008. Includes useful primary sources as well as excerpts from scholarly works.

Torre, Carlos de la. *The Ecuador Reader: History, Culture, Politics.* Durham, NC: Duke University Press, 2008. Includes some relevant primary materials.

Vila, Manuel Pérez. *Simon Bolivar: His Basic Thoughts; Biographical Sketch and Selection of Documents.* Caracas: Presidency of the Republic of Venezuela, 1981. An excellent collection of documents on Bolivar that should be very useful to students writing on his role in the war for independence.

Secondary Sources

Benavides, O. Hugo. *Making Ecuadorian Histories: Four Centuries of Defining Power.* Austin: University of Texas Press, 2004. A valuable study on the Ecuadorian historiography that assesses the range and quality of historical sources—both primary and secondary.

Bethell, Leslie, ed. *The Independence of Latin America.* New York: Cambridge University Press, 1987. A collection of worthwhile essays on the independence movements (including Ecuador) in Latin America.

Blanchard, Peter. *Under the Flags of Freedom: Slave Soldiers and the Wars of Independence in Spanish South America.* Pittsburgh: University of Pittsburgh Press, 2008. Includes information on Ecuador and its war for independence.

Blankstein, George I. *Ecuador: Constitutions and Caudillos.* Berkeley: University of California Press, 1951. A very good scholarly study in which the early chapters relate to the independence era.

Brading, D. A. *Classical Republicanism and Creole Patriotism: Simon Bolivar (1783–1830) and the Spanish American Revolution.* Cambridge, U.K.: Cambridge University Press, 1983. A seminal study of Bolivar's ideological and social values and how they shaped the Latin American wars of independence.

Brown, Matthew. *Adventuring through Spanish Colonies: Simón Bolívar, Foreign Mercenaries and the Birth of New Nations.* Liverpool, U.K.: Liverpool University Press, 2008. An excellent—scholarly yet readable—study that includes extensive information on Ecuador.

Burkholder, Mark A., and Lyman L. Johnson. *Colonial Latin America.* 6th ed. New York: Oxford University Press, 2008. Provides a good background on the origins of the Ecuadorian revolt.

Bushnell, David. *Simón Bolívar: Liberation and Disillusion.* New York: Pearson Longman, 2004. Includes information on Bolivar's aspirations for the new Latin American republics.

Chasteen, John. *Americanos: Latin America's Struggle for Independence.* New York: Oxford University Press, 2008. Provides good introductions to the many Latin American revolutions including Ecuador.

Harvey, Robert. *Liberators: Latin America's Struggle for Independence.* New York: Overlook, 2000. A reliable and useful study on the leaders of the conflicts.

Lowry, Walker. *Tumult at Dusk: Being an Account of Ecuador, Its Indians, Its Conquerors, Its Colonists, Its Rebels, Its Dictators, Its Politicians, Its Landowners, and Its Priests.* San Francisco: Grabhorn Press, 1963. A useful resource that is comprehensive in scope.

Lynch, John. *Simón Bolívar: A Life.* New Haven, CT: Yale University Press, 2006. Perhaps the best biography of Bolívar that includes extensive information on his activities in Ecuador.

———. *The Spanish American Revolution, 1808–1826.* New York: Longman, 2003. A very reliable and comprehensive study of all of the Latin American revolutions.

Nicholson, Irene. *The Liberators, A Study of Independence Movements in Spanish America.* New York: Praeger, 1969. A very good account of the various national movements, including the Ecuadorian revolt.

Robertson, William Spence. *Rise of the Spanish-American Republics, as Told in the Lives of Their Liberators.* New York: Free Press, 1948. A classic study by a renowned historian, this volume should be useful to many students.

Rodriguez, Linda Alexander. *The Search for Public Policy: Regional Politics and Government Finances in Ecuador, 1830–1940.* Berkeley: University of California Press, 1985. The early chapters may be useful to students working on this topic.

Scheina, Robert L. *Latin America's Wars.* 2 vols. Dulles, VA: Brassey's, 2003. Excellent scholarship on all of the wars of independence, including Ecuador's.

Spindler, Frank M. *Nineteenth Century Ecuador: A Historical Introduction.* Fairfax, VA: George Mason University Press, 1987. Includes excellent data on the independence movement and the early years of freedom.

Tepaske, John H., ed. *Research Guide to Andean History: Bolivia, Chile, Ecuador, and Peru.* Durham, NC: Duke University Press, 1981. A valuable resource that most students will want to examine.

Trend, John B. *Bolívar and the Independence of Spanish America.* Washington: Bolivarian Society of Venezuela, 1951. A very good study on Bolívar's transformational role in Latin American politics.

Van Aken, Mark. *King of the Night: Juan José Flores and Ecuador, 1824–1864.* Berkeley: University of California Press, 1989. A very good biography of Flores during the war and the early years of an independent Ecuador.

World Wide Web

"Antonio José de Sucre." http://www.answers.com/topic/antonio-jos-de-sucre. A biographical statement on this important Ecuadorian rebel leader who also served as the first constitutionally elected president of Bolivia.

"Ecuador Gains Independence." http://www.timelineindex.com/content/view/1762. A useful timeline on Ecuador's history and the war of independence.

"Ecuador: The Struggle for Independence." http://www.workmall.com/wfb2001/
    ecuador/ecuador_history_the_struggle_for_independence.html. A reli-
    able statement on Ecuador's war for independence.
"Juan José Flores." http://www.encyclopedia.com/doc/1E1-Flores-J.html.
    Biographical data on the rebel general who became the leader of Ecuador
    in 1830.
"The Struggle for Independence." http://www.ecuadorexplorer.com/html/struggle
    _for_independence.html. Provides a very good and well-written history
    of the war for independence, two illustrations, and links to additional sites.

Multimedia Sources

"Colombia and Panama." http://www.learnoutloud.com/Catalog/Politics/
    Global-Politics/Colombia-and-Panama/21381. Audiobook, CD, 2006.
    Written by Joseph Stromberg; narrated by Richard C. Hottelet. This
    is an account of how Spain's "New Granada" and Bolivar's "Gran
    Colombia" evolved into Venezuela, Ecuador, Panama, and modern
    Colombia.
"Images of Juan José Flores." http://images.google.com/images?hl=en&q=Juan
    +Jose+Flores&um=1&ie=UTF-8&sa=X&oi=image_result_group
    &resnum=4&ct=title. Multiple illustrations of images of General Juan
    José Flores of Ecuador.

28. Colombia Gains Independence (1830)

Inspired by the Haitian revolutionaries, the Colombia independence movement emerged in 1810 when the initial attacks on the Spanish began. Under the inspirational leadership of Simón Bolivar (1783–1830), the resistance movement gained momentum and was combined with similar rebellions in Venezuela, Panama, and Ecuador. Bolivar's forces scored a major victory over Spain in the Battle of Boyacá on August 7, 1819. He established the Grand Republic of Colombia shortly thereafter, which included Colombia, Panama, Venezuela, and Ecuador. From the outset, Venezuelan and Ecuadorian nationalists opposed this arrangement and worked to undo it. After a decade of mounting protest, Venezuela and Ecuador separated from Colombia—Panama remained as the northern province of Colombia for the remainder of the nineteenth century. In 1831 the Republic of Colombia adopted a new constitution.

TERM PAPER SUGGESTIONS

1. Develop a term paper on Bolivar's plan for the Grand Republic of Colombia. Why did he include Panama, Venezuela, and Ecuador in it?

2. Spain was confronted by a widespread rebellion in this region. Write a paper on the Spanish strategy to maintain control and comment on the Spanish performance in the Battle of Boyacá.

3. Write a paper on the Venezuelan and Ecuadorian opposition to the Grand Republic of Colombia during the 1820s.

4. Write a paper on why Panama was retained in the new Republic of Colombia in 1830.

ALTERNATIVE TERM PAPER SUGGESTIONS

1. Develop an iMovie in which Bolivar addresses his colleagues on his vision and rationale for establishing the Grand Republic of Colombia in 1819.

2. Develop a podcast in which the Venezuelan and Ecuadorian nationalists discuss their discontent with the Grand Republic and develop their plans to break away from it.

3. As a Panamanian nationalist, you witness the separation of Venezuela and Ecuador from the Grand Republic. Develop a blog in which you argue the case for Panamanian independence and reflect your frustration with the failure of your plans.

SUGGESTED SOURCES

Primary Sources

Bolivar, Simon. *El Libertador: Writings of Simon Bolivar.* New York: Oxford University Press, 2003. A significant primary source that most students will want to examine. It contains considerable material on Colombia.

Cochrane, Charles Stuart. *Journal of a Residence and Travels in Colombia during the Years 1823 and 1824.* 2 vols. London: Henry Colburn, 1825. Personal recollections of a British adventurer during the period of the war for Colombian independence.

O'Leary, Daniel Florencio. *Bolivar and the War of Independence.* Trans. and ed. Robert F. McNerney, Jr. Austin: University of Texas Press, 1970. Includes firsthand information on Bolivar by a revolutionary colleague.

Secondary Sources

Bethell, Leslie, ed. *The Independence of Latin America.* New York: Cambridge University Press, 1987. A collection of worthwhile essays on the independence movements (including Colombia) in Latin America.

Blanchard, Peter. *Under the Flags of Freedom: Slave Soldiers and the Wars of Independence in Spanish South America.* Pittsburgh: University of Pittsburgh Press, 2008. Includes a useful chapter on conditions in Colombia.

Burkholder, Mark A., and Lyman L. Johnson. *Colonial Latin America.* 6th ed. New York: Oxford University Press, 2008. Provides a good background on the origins of the Colombian revolt.

Bushnell, David. *Simon Bolivar: Liberation and Disappointment.* New York: Longman, 2004. Includes information on Bolivar's aspirations for the new Latin American republics.

Chasteen, John. *Americanos: Latin America's Struggle for Independence.* New York: Oxford University Press, 2008. Provides good introductions to the many Latin American revolutions.

Earle, Rebecca. *Spain and the Independence of Colombia, 1810–1825.* Exeter, U.K.: University of Exeter Press, 2000. A scholarly and useful history on Spain management of the Colombian war for independence; very well documented.

Fisher, John R., Allan J. Kuethe, and Anthony McFarlane, eds. *Reform and Insurrection in Bourbon New Granada and Peru.* Baton Rouge: Louisiana State University Press, 1990. A collection of essays that provides insights and information on Colombia's war for independence.

Harvey, Robert. *Liberators: Latin America's Struggle for Independence.* New York: Overlook, 2000. A reliable and useful study.

Henao, Jesus Maria, and Gerardo Arrubia. *History of Columbia.* Trans. and ed. J. Fred Rippy. Chapel Hill: University of North Carolina Press, 1938. A general history that includes relevant material on the Colombian revolt.

Lasso, Marixa. *Myths of Harmony: Race and Republicanism During the Age of Revolution, Colombia, 1795–1831.* Pittsburgh: University of Pittsburgh Press, 2007. Includes information on Colombia's short-lived first republic and life stories of Afro-Colombian patriots.

Lynch, John. *The Spanish American Revolution, 1808–1826.* New York: Longman, 2003. A very reliable and comprehensive study of all of the Latin American revolutions.

———. *Simon Bolivar: A Life.* New Haven, CT: Yale University Press, 2007. Perhaps the best biography of Bolivar that includes extensive information on his activities in Colombia.

McFarlane, Anthony. *Colombia before Independence: Economy, Society, and Politics under Bourbon Rule*. New York: Cambridge University Press, 1993. A first-rate study of Colombian institutions and life before gaining its independence.

Nicholson, Irene. *The Liberators, A Study of Independence Movements in Spanish America*. New York: Praeger, 1969. A very good account of the various national movements, including the Colombian revolt.

Niles, John Milton. *A View of South America and Mexico: Comprising their History, the Political Condition, Geography, Agriculture, Commerce, etc. of the Republics of Mexico, Guatemala, Colombia, Peru, the United Provinces of South America and Chili, with a Complete History of the Revolution in Each of These Independent States*. New York: H. Huntington, 1826. A contemporary account by a noted early nineteenth century historian that provides reliable and useful information.

Robertson, William Spence. *Rise of the Spanish-American Republics, as Told in the Lives of Their Liberators*. New York: Free Press, 1948. A classic study by a renowned historian, this volume should be useful to many students.

Rodriquez, Jaime E. *The Independence of Spanish America*. New York: Cambridge University Press, 1998. Includes useful information on Colombia's independence movement.

Scheina, Robert L. *Latin America's Wars*. 2 vols. Dulles, VA: Brassey's, 2003. Excellent scholarship on all of the wars of independence, including Colombia's.

Sherwell, Guillermo A. *Simon Bolivar, the Liberator: Patriot Warrior Statesman, Father of Five Nations*. Charleston, SC: BiblioBazaar, 2007. A very sympathetic biography of Bolivar as the founding liberator in Latin America.

Thurner, Mark, and Andrés Guerrero, eds. *After Spanish Rule: Postcolonial Predicaments of the Americas*. Durham, NC: Duke University Press, 2003. Includes an essay by Joanne Rappaport that may be of interest.

World Wide Web

"Colombia." http://www.infoplease.com/ipa/A0107419.html. A useful introduction to Colombia's war for independence.

"Colombia, The Independence Movement." http://www.workmall.com/wfb2001/colombia/colombia_history_the_independence_movement.html. Provides an extensive statement on the movement and links to other sites.

"Independence Movement." http://countrystudies.us/colombia/12.htm. A good introduction to Colombia's independence movement.

"Map of Colombia." http://www.worldatlas.com/webimage/countrys/samerica/
co.htm. A very good and useful map that covers the territory involved
in the struggle.

"South America, 1800–1900." http://www.metmuseum.org/toah/ht/10/sa/ht10
sa.htm. A useful timeline on the Latin American revolutions.

"The History of the Republic of Colombia." http://www.hartford-hwp.com/
archives/42/index-d.html. Includes links to several important Web sites.

"The Independence Movement." http://www.country-data.com/cgi-bin/query/
r-2990.html. Good introduction to the war and its consequences.

Multimedia Sources

"Colombia: Revolution and Independence." http://www.britannica.com/
EBchecked/topic/126016/Colombia/25336/Revolution-and-independence.
Multimedia site with 25 illustrations and maps, many related to the inde-
pendence movement.

"Map of Colombia." http://encarta.msn.com/map_701510601/colombia.html.
An excellent interactive map that will assist students working on this topic.

29. Algerian Revolt Against France (1832–1840)

In January 1830, France, under the leadership of King Charles X (1824–
1830), decided to invade Algeria. The invasion began in June 1830 and
France quickly gained a secure position. The motives for the invasion
were complex. While the nation was told that the Algerians had insulted
France when the Dey of Algeria purportedly hit the French Consul with
his fan in 1827, Charles X's government was coming under mounting
criticism for its right-wing domestic policies, and an invasion of Algeria
was thought to be an effective diversion to lessen the criticism of the
government. While the action had the desired effect for a few days,
Charles X's government fell in the July Revolution of 1830 that brought
in King Louis-Philippe. The new government continued the Algerian
invasion and soon found that the war would be more extended than
planned. The Sultan of Morocco, who had sympathy for the Algerians,
condemned the alleged Christian massacres of Moslems. The French
responded with harsh measures—some authorities argued that more than
25 percent of the Algerian population was eliminated by the French during the 1830s. Nonetheless, Algerian patriots and their supporters

continued to resist the French occupation. France annexed Algeria in 1834 and began the process of establishing a French political and economic system that could exploit the resources of the country. Algerian resistance (under leaders such as Abd el-Kader [b. 1807], who was designated as leader of the anti-French *jihad*) continued until 1840 when, exhausted from the effort and outnumbered by better equipped and led French troops, it collapsed as an organized force.

TERM PAPER SUGGESTIONS

1. Write a paper on the background and immediate causes for the French invasion of Algeria in 1830.
2. Develop a paper on French policies and actions in establishing a permanent colony in Algeria during the 1830s.
3. From the perspective of Abd el-Kader and other resistance leaders, write a term paper on the impact of the French invasion on Algeria and its people.

ALTERNATIVE TERM PAPER SUGGESTIONS

1. As leader of the Algerian resistance, Abd el-Kader feared the loss of Algerian independence and the imposition of French culture and institutions. In an iMovie, conduct an interview with Abd el-Kader in which you discuss the conflict with France and its impact on Algeria.
2. The regime of Charles X was overthrown in July 1830 and replaced with the new government of King Louis Philippe. Develop a podcast in which the leaders of the new government discuss whether they should continue the French action in Algeria.
3. You are a French enlisted soldier. Develop a blog with your relatives and friends on your several years of service in Algeria.

SUGGESTED SOURCES

Primary Sources

Gerard, Jules. *The Life and Adventures of Jules Gerard, Containing a History and Description of Algeria*. Whitefish, MT: Kessinger, 2007. A valuable life story of a French explorer and geographer who specialized in North Africa. It provides useful information on the French invasion of Algeria.

Tocqueville, Alexis de. *Writings on Empire and Slavery*. Ed. and trans. Jennifer Pitts. Baltimore, MD: Johns Hopkins University Press, 2001. Includes six important documents on Algeria during the 1830s and 1840s. Most students will need to refer to this volume.

Secondary Sources

Ageron, Charles Robert. *Modern Algeria: A History from 1830 to the Present.* London: C. Hurst, 1991. Provides a very good account of the French invasion and the suppression of the native Algerian forces and their allies.

Bennoune, Mahfoud. *The Making of Contemporary Algeria, 1830–1987: Colonial Upheavals and Post-Independence Development.* New York: Cambridge University Press, 1988. A scholarly study that includes an excellent chapter on the French invasion in 1830.

Clancy-Smith, Julia A. *Rebel and Saint: Muslim Notables, Populist Protest, Colonial Encounters (Algeria and Tunisia 1800–1904).* Berkeley: University of California Press, 1997. A seminal study that provides insights into the personalities and their causes that came into conflict in Algeria during the 1830s.

Heggoy, Alf Andrew. *The French Conquest of Algiers, 1830: An Algerian Oral Tradition.* Athens: Center for International Studies, Ohio University, 1986. An important resource that should be useful to most students working on this topic.

———— and Robert R. Crout, eds. *Historical Dictionary of Algeria.* Metuchen, NJ: Scarecrow, 1981. Indispensable resource that should be referred to by all students working on the French invasion of Algeria.

Lorcin, Patricia M. E., ed. *Algeria and France 1800–2000: Identity, Memory, Nostalgia.* Syracuse, NY: Syracuse University Press, 2006. A scholarly volume of essays on the French in Algeria. Several essays may be useful for a term paper on this topic.

McDougall, James. *History and the Culture of Nationalism in Algeria.* Cambridge Middle East Studies. New York: Cambridge University Press, 2006. An excellent source from the Algerian perspective.

Newman, Edgar Leon, and Robert Lawrence Simpson, eds. *Historical Dictionary of France from the 1815 Restoration to the Second Empire.* Westport, CT: Greenwood Press, 1987. Excellent resource, many relevant entries on the French invasion of Algeria in 1830 and the subsequent developments.

Quandt, William B., and Benjamin Stora. *Algeria, 1830–2000: A Short History.* Trans. Jane Marie Todd. Rev. ed. Ithaca, NY: Cornell University Press, 2001. An adequate introduction to the French in Algeria during the 1830s and after.

Sessions, Jennifer Elson. *Making Colonial France: Culture, National Identity, and Colonization in Algeria, 1830–1851.* Ann Arbor: University Microfilms, 2005. A very good scholarly examination of transforming Algeria into a French colony.

Woolrich, Kathleen. *A Pictorial History of Colonial Algeria.* N.p.: Kathleen Woolrich, 2006. A valuable, self-published study that includes illustrations and early photographs of the French in Algeria.

World Wide Web

"France in Algeria, 1830–1962." http://countrystudies.us/algeria/18.htm. Provides accurate information on the French invasion of 1830.

"French Colonization." http://www.algeria-un.org/default.asp?doc=-history. Includes a useful chronology on the revolution during the 1830s.

"The Land and the Colonizers." http://countrystudies.us/algeria/19.htm. Provides data on the work of Bertrand Clauzel, the first French Governor of Algeria.

Multimedia Source

The War Against Colonialism, 100 Years of Terror. The History Channel, 2000. VHS. Includes the French invasion of Algeria.

30. British Abolish Slavery (1833–1834)

The concepts of humanity and human rights had been discussed throughout the eighteenth century. One of the outcomes of that discussion was the emergence of an alliance between British religious and political reformers who maintained that the slave trade and slavery itself constituted a violation of God's and nature's value of all human life. During the 1790s the London Anti-Slavery Society was joined by a reformer whose views were shaped by both religious and rationalist arguments—William Wilberforce. He became the primary political advocate of abolishing British involvement in the slave trade and slavery. Supported by a complex network of groups and opposed by those whose income came from the trade, Wilberforce prevailed when Parliament ended slave trade in 1807. In the following decades, other groups, such as the new Anti-Slavery Society, surfaced and British party politics changed. Under the leadership of the reform Prime Minister Earl Grey (1764–1845) and his Secretary of State Edward Stanley (1799–1869), Parliament passed the

Slavery Abolition Act of 1833, which specified that slavery would cease in the "plantation colonies" on July 21, 1834. Excepted from the act were the colonies administered by the East India Company, Ceylon, and St. Helena. A system of apprenticeships was instituted to facilitate the change and slave owners were compensated. A fund of £20,000,000 was established to liberate the 776,000 slaves that were involved.

TERM PAPER SUGGESTIONS

1. Some argue that one person cannot make a real difference, that history is driven by impersonal forces and trends that control its direction. Write a paper on this contention in light of Wilberforce's impact on the antislavery movement in Britain.
2. Develop a paper on the coalition that emerged to support the abolition of the slave trade and slavery within the British Empire.
3. Was the abolition of the slave trade and slavery the triumph of religious values?
4. In the United States the issue of slavery was divisive, how did Great Britain manage to eliminate it peacefully? Describe the details of the process.
5. Develop a term paper on the "politics of abolition" and how Grey and Stanley responded to the new political values in Britain during the 1830s.

ALTERNATIVE TERM PAPER SUGGESTIONS

1. Develop a podcast in which Wilberforce is interviewed on his positions on slavery and the slave trade.
2. Develop an iMovie in which Grey and Stanley determine their strategy to abolish slavery in the British Empire.

SUGGESTED SOURCES

Primary Sources

Belmonte, Kevin, ed. *A Practical View of Christianity.* Peabody, MA: Hendrickson Publishing, 2006. This is Wilberforce's classic book in which he argued that the reality of Christianity required all to live the faith—and oppose slavery.

Bunn, Thomas. *An Essay on the Abolition of Slavery Throughout the British Dominions.* Whitefish, MT: Kessinger Publishing, 2007; reprint of 1833. Available in its entirety on Google Book Search. An important contemporary document on the end of slavery in the British colonies.

Cropper, James. *Letters Addressed to William Wilberforce, M.P.: Recommending the Encouragement of the Cultivation of Sugar in our Dominions in the East Indies, as a Natural and Certain Means of Effecting the General and Total Abolition of the Slave-Trade.* London: Longman, Hurst, 1822; available on microfilm, London: World Microfilms, 1978. A key primary source on understanding the argumentation that was used to advance the anti-slavery case.

London Anti-Slavery Society. *Statements and Observations on the Working of the Laws on the Abolition of Slavery throughout the British Colonies: and on the Present State of the Negro Population.* Ithaca, NY: Cornell University Library, 1836. A brief (68 pages) but important statement on the progress that had been achieved regarding the abolition of slavery in the British Empire.

Smith, William. *A Letter to William Wilberforce, Esq. M.P. on the Proposed Abolition of the Slave Trade, at Present under Consideration by Parliament.* London: Longman, Hurst, Rees, and Orme, 1807. An important contemporary's public letter to Wilberforce during the months immediately prior to the vote in the Parliament.

Snyder, James, ed. *William Wilberforce, Greatest Works.* Alachua, FL: Bridge-Logos Publishers, 2007. An excellent, award-winning selection of Wilberforce's writings with many related to the abolition of the slave trade and slavery in the British Empire.

Wilberforce A. M., ed. *Private Papers of William Wilberforce.* New York: B. Franklin, 1968; reprint of 1897 edition. Provides excellent material on the abolition of the slave trade and slavery.

Wilberforce, William. *A Letter on the Abolition of the Slave Trade: Addressed to the Freeholders and Other Inhabitants of Yorkshire.* London: Cadell and Davies, 1807; available on microfilm, London: World Microfilms, 1978. Provides a clear and precise understanding of Wilberforce's arguments against the slave trade.

———. *Wilberforce: Slavery, Religion, and Politics.* Marlborough, U.K.: Adam Matthew, 2004. A guide to the Wilberforce papers in the Bodleian Library, Oxford. It provides a valuable glimpse into the energy and depth of Wilberforce's commitment in opposition to slavery.

———. *An Appeal to the Religion, Justice, and Humanity of the Inhabitants of the British Empire: In Behalf of the Negro Slaves in the West Indies.* London: J. Hatchard and Son, 1823; available in microfilm and microform book, London: World Microfilms, 1978. Wilberforce argues for the emancipation of the slaves using principles of religion and natural law.

———. *The Correspondence of William Wilberforce.* Ed. his sons, Robert Isaac Wilberforce and Samuel Wilberforce. 2 vols. London: J. Murray, 1840.

Still a reliable collection of letters that is usually available in college and university libraries.

————. *Real Christianity.* Ed. Bob Beltz. Rev. ed. Ventura, CA: Regal Books, 2007; originally published in 1797. In this volume Wilberforce asserts his core belief that Christianity had to be practiced to be real—that opposition to injustice and inhumanity was required to be a real Christian.

Secondary Sources

Baehr, Ted, Susan Wales, and Ken Wales. *The Amazing Grace of Freedom: The Inspiring Faith of William Wilberforce.* Green Forest, AZ: New Leaf Publishing Group, 2007. A Christian interpretation of Wilberforce's struggle by three veteran writers and producers who are devoted to his legacy.

Belmonte, Kevin. *William Wilberforce: A Hero for Humanity.* Grand Rapids, MI: Zondervan, 2007. An inspirational biography of an inspirational leader in the cause of freedom and justice in nineteenth-century Britain.

Black, Jeremy. *The Slave Trade.* London: Social Affairs Unit, 2007. A comprehensive study of the slave trade in the Atlantic and beyond. Black places slavery in the context of a source of labor in the tradition of serfs and indentured servants.

Brown, Ford K. *Fathers of the Victorians: The Age of Wilberforce.* Cambridge, U.K.: Cambridge University Press, 1961. The emphasis in this study is on religion as the driving force in Wilberforce's career.

Cormack, Patrick. *Wilberforce: The Nation's Conscience.* Basingstoke, U.K.: Pickering and Inglis, 1983. Emphasis is on Wilberforce's role as a moral leader in the struggle against slavery.

Derry, John W. *Charles, Earl Grey: Aristocratic Reformer.* Oxford: Blackwell, 1992. Very good on Grey's support of the abolition of slavery as part of the reform agenda.

Furneaux, Robin. *William Wilberforce.* Vancouver, BC: Regent College Publishing, 2006; originally published in 1974. A detailed and sympathetic biography of Wilberforce with excellent information on the abolition of the slave trade and slavery.

Hague, William. *William Wilberforce: The Life of the Great Anti-Slave Trade Campaigner.* Orlando: Harcourt, 2008. A sympathetic yet solid life of Wilberforce by a leader of Britain's Conservative Party and current shadow Foreign Secretary.

Hochschild, Adam. *Bury the Chains: The British Struggle to Abolish Slavery.* London: Pan/Macmillan Books, 2006. An important study of the abolitionist movement that minimizes Wilberforce's contribution and impact.

Jordan, Michael. *The Great Abolition Sham: The True Story of the End of the British Slave Trade*. Charleston, SC: The History Press, 2005. A very solid study of the opposing internal forces in British life that were involved in the debate on the slave trade.

Lean, Garth. *God's Politician: William Wilberforce's Struggle*. London: Darton, Longman and Todd, 1980. A very good examination of the religious, economic, and political forces and values in British society during the era of the abolitionist movement.

Morgan, Kenneth. *Slavery and the British Empire: From Africa to America*. New York: Oxford University Press, 2008. A good comprehensive study of slavery and slave trade throughout the British Empire, supplemented with six maps.

———. *Slavery, Atlantic Trade and the British Economy, 1660–1800*. New Studies in Economic and Social History. Cambridge, U.K.: Cambridge University Press, 2001. An excellent resource on the impact of the slave trade and slavery on the developing British Empire to the era of the abolitionist debate.

Piper, John. *The Roots of Endurance: Invincible Perseverance in the Lives of John Newton, Charles Simeon, and William Wilberforce*. Wheaton, IL: Crossway Books, 2006. The focus on Wilberforce and his battle against slavery is on his religious values.

Pollock, John Charles. *Wilberforce*. New York: St. Martin's Press, 1978. A good bibliography with illustrations and worthwhile bibliography.

Reddie, Richard. *Abolition: The Struggle to Abolish Slavery in the British Empire*. Oxford: Lion Hudson, 2007. This is an excellent scholarly treatment of slavery and the slave trade and the transformation of British policy that brought both to an end.

Sherwood, Marika. *After Abolition: Britain and the Slave Trade since 1807*. London: I. B. Tauris, 2007. A worthwhile examination of the evolution of British policy through the abolition of slavery and beyond.

Smith, E. A. *Lord Grey, 1764–1845*. New York: Oxford University Press, 1990. A very good biography of the reformer prime minister who supported the abolition of slavery in 1833.

Tomkins, Stephen. *William Wilberforce: A Biography*. Grand Rapids, MI: Wm. B. Eerdmans, 2007. A well-written and research biography that examines the challenges that Wilberforce confronted—both personally and politically.

Walvin, James. *Atlas of Slavery*. London: Longman, 2005. A dependable reference with maps, tables, and commentary.

Warner, Oliver. *William Wilberforce and His Times.* London: Batsford, 1962. Provides a good introduction to Wilberforce's attacks on all aspects of slavery in the context of his era.

World Wide Web

"Abolition on British Slavery—Interactive Map." http://www.bbc.co.uk/history/british/abolition/launch_anim_slavery.shtml. An excellent resource developed by the BBC to enhance an understanding of the scope and complexity of the issues associated with eliminating slavery in the British Empire.

"British History Online." http://www.british-history.ac.uk/search.aspx?query=Abolition%20of%20Slavery. Provides more than 200 public documents on the abolition of slavery.

"The Victorian Web." http://www.victorianweb.org/misc/htsearchvt2.cgi?words=Abolition+of+Slavery&config=vict&name=search. Provides 28 excellent documents on the abolition of the slave trade and slavery.

Multimedia Sources

Amazing Grace. 20th Century Fox, 2007. DVD. Directed by Michael Apted. A dramatic video account of William Wilberforce's struggle to end the slave trade and then slavery in the British Empire.

Amazing Grace: William Wilberforce and the Heroic Campaign to End Slavery. Tantor Media, 2007. Audiobook (MP3/CD formats). A reading of Eric Metaxas's book by Johnny Hellor.

Snyder, James, ed. CD that accompanies *William Wilberforce, Greatest Works.* Alachua, FL: Bridge-Logos Publishers, 2007. Provides more than 80 minutes of reading select letters and articles by Wilberforce.

The Better Hour: The Legacy of William Wilberforce. PBS Video, 2008. DVD. Directed by Phil Cooke and Brian Head. An excellent one-hour introduction to the issue of slavery in the British political and economic life and Wilberforce's efforts to abolish it.

William Wilberforce. Vision Video, 2006. DVD documentary. A survey of Wilberforce's life.

31. Treaty of Unkiar-Skelessi (1833)

The Treaty of Unkiar-Skelessi was signed between the Ottoman and Russian Empires on July 8, 1833. These two powers had been at war with one another during 1828–1829. In 1831 Mohammad Ali of Egypt attacked the Ottoman Turks and posed a threat to Constantinople, the Turkish capital. The Egyptian forces scored significant victories over the Turks and established Ali's dominance in Syria and Arabia. The Russians, fearing that the Egyptians would gain control of the Dardanelles and thus restrict their access to the Mediterranean Sea, allied themselves with their former enemy in the Treaty of Unkiar-Skelessi. It was a mutual self-defense alliance but Russia assumed the major responsibility. The British concerns over Russian expansion in the eastern Mediterranean were aggravated by the treaty.

TERM PAPER SUGGESTIONS

1. Write a term paper on the ascendancy of Ali's Egypt in the Middle East in 1831. Did it threaten the balance of power?
2. Develop a paper on the transformation of the Russo-Turkish relationship between 1829 and 1833.
3. Write a paper on the terms and significance of the Treaty of Unkiar-Skelessi.

ALTERNATIVE TERM PAPER SUGGESTIONS

1. Develop a podcast in which Turkish and Russian diplomats discuss the Egyptian threat and their plans to confront it.
2. Develop an iMovie in which Mohammad Ali is interviewed about his intentions—what is his vision for Egypt in a new Middle East?
3. As a member of the British Embassy in Constantinople, you have followed Ali's expansion and what appears to be a realignment in the Ottoman-Russian relationship. Develop a blog of your dispatches back to London on the crisis.

SUGGESTED SOURCES

Primary Sources

Albermarle, George Thomas. *Narrative of a Journey across the Balcan.* London: H. Colburn and R. Bentley, 1831. An Englishman's recollections of travels during the war.
Chesney, Francis R. *The Russo Turkish Campaigns of 1828 and 1829: With a View of the Present State of Affairs in the East.* Ann Arbor: Scholarly Publishing Office, University of Michigan, 2005; originally published in 1854. A very good primary resource with extensive descriptions of the battles and excerpts from primary materials.

Dmytryshyn, Basil, ed. *Imperial Russia: A Source Book, 1700–1917.* 3rd ed. New York: Harcourt Brace, 1990. Includes primary sources that should be useful.

Hertslet, Edward. *The Map of Europe by Treaty: Showing the Various Political and Territorial Changes which Have Taken Place Since the General Peace of 1814.* 2 vols. London: Buttersworths, 1875. Also available as an e-book at http://books.google.com/books?id=bNgLAAAAYAAJ&dq=treaty+of +unkiar+skelessi&source=gbs_summary_s&cad=0. Includes the text of the treaty and accompanying maps.

Pushkin, Aleksandr. *A Journey to Arzrum.* Trans. Birgitta Ingemanson. Ann Arbor: Ardis, 1974. Russian poet Pushkin's impressions of the Russo-Turkish-Egyptian conflict.

Secondary Sources

Acton, John Emerich Edward Dalberg, William Ward, George Walter Prothero, Stanley Mordaunt Leathes, and Ernest Alfred Benians. *The Cambridge Modern History.* Cambridge, U.K.: The University Press, 1907. Also available as an e-book at http://books.google.com/books?id=T6 EFAAAAIAAJ&dq=treaty+of+unkiar+skelessi&source=gbs_summary _s&cad=0. Includes a section on the treaty with extensive data.

Baker, R. L. "Palmerston on the Treaty of Unkiar Skelessi." *English Historical Review* 43 (1928): 83–89. Available at http://www.rhs.ac.uk/bibl/ wwwopac.exe?&database=dcatalo&rf=000154856&SUCCESS=false &SRT2=ti&SEQ2=ascending. Emphasis on the British concerns on Russian expansion and potential access to the Mediterranean Sea.

Fuller, William C., Jr. *Strategy and Power in Russia, 1600–1914.* New York: Free Press, 1992. Includes useful information on the origins of the war, its prosecution, and outcome.

Hamburg, Gary, Thomas Sanders, and Ernest Tucker. *Russian-Muslim Confrontation in the Caucasus: Alternative Visions of the Conflict between Iman Shamil and the Russians, 1830–1859.* London: Routledge/Curzon, 2004. The earlier chapters in this book should be very useful to students working on this topic.

Heyman, Neil M. *Russian History.* New York: McGraw Hill, 1992. Provides general information on the conflict and the treaty.

Hobsbawn, Eric. *The Age of Revolution, 1789–1848.* New York: Vintage, 1996. An extremely important seminal study of the period. It places the Russo-Turkish-Egyptian conflict in the context of larger issues.

Ingram, Edward. *Eastern Questions in the Nineteenth Century: The Collected Essays of Allan Cunningham.* London: Routledge, 1993. Scholarly essays that relate to the war and treaty.

Karsh, Effraim. *Empires of the Sand: The Struggle for Mastery in the Middle East.* Cambridge, MA: Harvard University Press, 2001. Reliable study that examines the war within the larger geopolitical situation in the Middle East.

Petrie, Charles. *Diplomatic History 1713–1933.* London: Hollis and Carter, 1946. Provides valuable information and insights on the war and treaty.

Riasanovsky, Nicholas V. *A History of Russia.* Oxford, U.K.: Oxford University Press, 1984. Provides some relevant information.

Woodward, Llewellyn. *The Age of Reform, 1815–1870.* 2nd ed. New York: Oxford University Press, 1962. Also available as an e-book at http:// books.google.com/books?id=VoRImrfk0UQC&dq=treaty+of+unkiar +skelessi&source=gbs_summary_s&cad=0. Includes data on the British concerns with Russian expansion and access to the Straits.

World Wide Web

"Karl Robert Nesselrode." http://www.1911encyclopedia.org/Karl_Robert, _Count_Nesselrode. Provides important information on this leading participant in the war and the resulting treaty.

"London Straits Convention." http://www.nationmaster.com/encyclopedia/ London-Straits-Convention. Emphasis on the British containment of Russian access to the Straits and the Mediterranean Sea.

"The Story of the Life of Lord Palmerston by Karl Marx." http://www .marxists.org/archive/marx/works/1853/palmerston/ch05.htm. Includes extensive information on the treaty and the British reaction to it.

"Treaty of Unkiar-Skelessi." http://www.answers.com/topic/treaty-of-unkiar -skelessi. Provides a good introduction to the treaty, its provisions, and the circumstances that led to it.

"Treaty of Unkiar-Skelessi." http://www.nationmaster.com/encyclopedia/Treaty -of-Unkiar_Skelessi. Introduction to the treaty and its results.

"Treaty of Unkiar-Skelessi." http://www.onpedia.com/encyclopedia/treaty -of-unkiar-skelessi. Provides data on the treaty and the war that it ended.

Multimedia Source

"Regions of the Ottoman Empire." http://encarta.msn.com/media_701766311 _761570351_-1_1/Regions_of_the_Ottoman_Empire.html. A very useful eighteenth-century map that illustrates the geopolitical tensions between the Turks, the Egyptians, and the Russians.

32. Carlist Wars (1833–1876)

During the nineteenth century Carlism (Spanish political movement of the 1820s that supported traditional Royalist values) emerged as a challenge to the Spanish succession as established by Ferdinand VII who arranged for his daughter, Isabella II (1830–1904), to ascend to the throne rather than his reactionary brother, Don Carlos. At issue was the right of a female to succeed to a position of power in Spain. However, the conflict was more than a dynastic squabble. Ferdinand VII recognized that capitalism and modernity were beginning to develop Spanish life. Social and economic transformation was inevitable, and the leadership of the government had to recognize these forces and support the regions of the country that were affected positively and negatively. The Basque region in the north became more turbulent and calls for Basque independence were being heard. The Roman Catholic Church feared the progressive changes that were becoming evident and expressed sympathy with the Carlists. The Carlist Wars were cultural conflicts in which the supporters of the old order, the Church, the peasantry, and many others found themselves at odds with the liberalism that was being espoused by the government. There were three Carlist Wars during the nineteenth century—the First Carlist War (1833–1840), the Second Carlist War (1847–1849), and the Third Carlist War (1872–1876). In all three of these unsuccessful efforts, the Carlists attempted to gain power through military actions; in most instances, guerilla warfare tactics were utilized against the government's forces. The defeat of the ultraconservatives in the Third Carlist War did not eliminate the right as an opposition force in Spanish politics. Carlism gained momentum in the 1930s with many supporting the conservatives during the Spanish Civil War that concluded in 1939.

TERM PAPER SUGGESTIONS

1. Write a paper on the background and outbreak of the First Carlist War. Were the causes that resulted in this conflict sustained and did they contribute to the other Carlist Wars?

2. Develop a paper in which you analyze the progress of the wars and their outcomes.

3. Write a paper on the role of the Roman Catholic Church in the Carlist Wars of the nineteenth century.

4. Regional interests played an important part in determining affiliations during the Carlist wars. Write a term paper on the Basque area and its role during these struggles.

ALTERNATIVE TERM PAPER SUGGESTIONS

1. Develop a podcast in which the anti-Carlist leaders discuss why the Carlist insurrection cannot be allowed to succeed and why their movement was dangerous for Spain.

2. Construct an iMovie in which you, a member of the Roman Catholic hierarchy, analyze the positive and negative values of Carlism from the perspective of the Church in the short and long terms.

3. As a member of a family that had supported the Carlists during the three wars, reflect upon the reasons that you and your relatives have followed such a path in the form of a blog created shortly after the outbreak of the Third Carlist War.

SUGGESTED SOURCES

Primary Sources

Hardman, Frederick. *The Student of Salamanca: A Tale of the Carlist War of Spain.* Whitefish, MT: Kessinger Publishing, 2008; reprint of 1848 edition. A contemporary primary account that should be useful to students working on the early Carlist Wars.

Henty, G. A. *With the British Legion: A Story of the Carlist Wars.* Whitefish, MT: Kessinger, 2007; originally published in 1902. A valuable primary source by a participant in the later Carlist War.

Kennett-Barrington, Vincent. *Letters from the Carlist War: 1874–76.* Ed. Alice L. Lascelles and J. M. Alberich. Exeter, U.K.: University of Exeter Press, 1987. Excellent and perceptive resource by an eyewitness and participant.

Milman, E. A. *The Wayside Cross: Or the Raid of Gomez, a Tale of the Carlist Wars.* London: John Murray, 1861. A contemporary description of an event during the Second Carlist War.

Montagu, Irving. *Wanderings of a War Artist.* London: W. H. Allen, 1889. A unique account by an eyewitness to the Third Carlist War.

Secondary Sources

Barahona, Renato. *Vizcaya on the Eve of Carlism: Politics and Society, 1800–33.* Reno: University of Nevada Press, 1991. A scholarly account on the origins and early development of Carlism in Spain.

Brett, Edward M. *The British Auxiliary Legion in the First Carlist War, 1835–8: A Forgotten Army.* Dublin: Four Courts Press, 2005. A very good and readable history of the legion in the Carlist struggle.

Coverdale, John F. *The Basque Phase of Spain's First Carlist War.* Princeton, NJ: Princeton University Press, 1984. Excellent scholarly work on the evolution of Basque national identity during the Carlist War. The initial chapter may provide several term paper topics.

Conversi, Daniele. *The Basques, the Catalans, and Spain: Alternative Routes to Nationalist Mobilisation.* Reno: University of Nevada Press, 1997. Early chapters will be useful in examining the sectionalism of the Carlist era.

Gallardo, Alexander. *Britain and the First Carlist War.* Norwood, PA: Norwood Editions, 1978. A valuable examination of British interests in Spanish affairs during the early nineteenth century.

Hayens, Herbert. *The British Legion: A Tale of the Carlist War.* London: Thomas Nelson and Sons, 1898. A lengthy account of the legion in Spain by a popular contemporary author.

Holt, Edgar. *The Carlist Wars in Spain.* Chester Springs, PA: Dufour, 1967. The best general history of the Carlist Wars, which will be of value to most students who work on this topic.

Muro, Diego. *Ethnicity and Violence: The Case of Radical Basque Nationalism.* New York: Routledge, 2008. An important and worthwhile study, and the early chapters are relevant.

Nunez, Luis C. *The Basques: Their Struggle for Independence.* Cardiff, Wales: Welsh Academic Press, 1997. A very good history on the Basques that places the wars in the context of the larger movement.

Payne, Stanley G. *Basque Nationalism.* Reno: University of Nevada Press, 1975. A significant study by a prominent historian, which includes the Carlist Wars.

World Wide Web

"Balmero Espartero, duque de la Victoria, conde de Luchana." http://www.encyclopedia.com/doc/1E1-Esparter.html. A brief biography of a leading anti-Carlist general.

"Carlists." http://www.bartleby.com/65/ca/Carlists.html. A fact-based introduction to the Carlists and their movement.

"Carlists." http://www.encyclopedia.com/doc/1O142-Carlists.html. Includes four contemporary illustrations of the Carlists.

"Ramón Cabrera, conde de Morella." http://www.encyclopedia.com/doc/1E1-CabreraR.html. A brief biography of a major Carlist general.

"The Carlist Wars." http://www.everything2.org/e2node/The%2520Carlist %2520wars. A good introduction to the three Carlist wars.

Multimedia Source

"History of Spain (1796–1843) Peninsular war, Ferdinand VII. . . ." http:// www.youtube.com/watch?v=XYYO5Bhftwg. Includes information on Carlism and the First Carlist War.

33. The Great Trek (1835–1840)

The Great Trek was the migration of about 13,000 Boers (also called Voortrekkers) from the Cape Colony in South Africa to areas across the Orange River in search of new land in which they would be free of British rule. The Boers, most of whom traced their roots to the Netherlands, were opposed to racial integration and British economic and political dominance. Some Boers were attracted to Natal (which was soon annexed by Britain in 1843), and others moved on to what came to be called the Transvaal and the Orange Free State. This expansion was opposed by the Zulus under Chief Dingane ka Senzangakhona, who inflicted a serious defeat on the Boers at Ithaleni (1838). The Boers, under Andries Pretorius, responded with a resounding victory over the Zulus at the Battle of Blood River on December 16, 1838—reportedly the Zulus suffered more than 3,000 killed to three for the Boers. The Boers interpreted this victory as direct support from God—rather than recognizing that they held an extremely effective defensive position and a massive edge in technology (firepower). During the 1840s the Boers were able to establish permanent settlements in the Transvaal and the Orange Free State where they developed extensive farms and other businesses. Boer animosity toward the British did not dissipate; rather it continued to develop during the decades ahead and resulted in the two Boer Wars of the late nineteenth century.

TERM PAPER SUGGESTIONS

1. Develop a paper that examines the animosity that the British and Boers had for each other during the early decades of the nineteenth century in South Africa. Why could they not live together? Why could their differences not be resolved?

2. Write a paper on the process of the Great Trek and the difficulties that the Boers encountered with the African natives.

3. Where did the Boers originate? What did they believe and want? Develop a term paper focused on these two questions and connect your responses to the rationale for the Great Trek.

4. Develop a paper on Boer leadership and organization. Was Pretorius considered an agent of God? Was he a new "Moses" leading the people to a "promised land"?

5. Write a paper on the consequences of the Great Trek. Did it shift geopolitics in South Africa among the European settlers or the African native population?

ALTERNATIVE TERM PAPER SUGGESTIONS

1. Develop a Web page that includes a map of the Great Trek and accompanying personal narratives of important events by participants in the Trek.

2. You are the 17-year-old daughter or son of a Boer family that has embarked on the Great Trek. Write diary entries of your experiences during 1837 and 1838.

3. Develop a podcast of a conversation of Boer leaders who are deciding on and planning the Great Trek—they express their rationale and their aspirations for this decision.

4. Develop an iMovie in which you capture the most difficult days of the Great Trek—be sure to introduce each segment with historical information.

5. As a young African, you were threatened by the Boer incursion into your homeland. Now, decades later, you are telling the story to your grandchild. Develop an oral history of the impact of the Trek on your life.

SUGGESTED SOURCES

Primary Sources

Kruger, Paul. *The Memoirs of Paul Kruger: Four Times President of the South African Republic.* Port Washington, NY: Kennikat Press, 1970. Kruger was 12 years old when he participated in the Great Trek—a defining moment in his life.

Robinson, David, ed. *Sources of the African Past.* Bloomington, IN: AuthorHouse, 1999. A useful collection of documents on a wide range of African historical topics.

Secondary Sources

Cana, Frank Richardson. *South Africa from the Great Trek to the Union.* New York: Negro Universities Press, 1969. An interesting survey of South

African history with valuable information on the impact of imperialism on the native population.

Etherington, Norman. *The Great Treks: The Transformation of Southern Africa, 1815–1854*. London: Longman, 2001. A provocative study of the Great Trek of the Boers and the trek of the Africans (the Mfecane) in response to the expansion of the Zulus.

———. "The Great Trek in Relation to the Mfecane: A Reassessment." *South African Historical Journal* 25 (1991): 3–21. A very important article on the impact of the Trek on the African native population by a reputable scholar.

Fisher, William Edward. *The Transvaal and the Boers, A Brief History*. New York: Negro Universities Press, 1969. A short but good introduction to the Trek and the settlement of the Transvaal.

Hattersley, A. F. "Historical Revisions. 57: The Great Trek, 1835–1837." *History*, New Series (1931): 16ff. A seminal, scholarly account of the Trek that is worthwhile.

Holden, William C. *History of the Colony of Natal*. Cape Town: C. Struik, 1963. Includes information on the Trek and the establishment of Natal.

Laband, John, ed. *Daily Lives of Civilians in Wartime Africa: From Slavery Days to Rwandan Genocide*. Westport, CT: Greenwood Press, 2007. Includes a very good chapter by Laband on the impact of war on the Zulu civilians, 1817–1879.

Liebenberg, B. J. *Andries Pretorius in Natal*. Palo Alto, CA: Academica, 1977. A scholarly study of Pretorius's impact on the establishment of Natal.

Meintjes, Johannes. *The Voortrekkers: The Story of the Great Trek and the Making of South Africa*. London: Cassell, 1973. A rather sympathetic account of the Boer Great Trek.

Meredith, Martin. *Diamonds, Gold, and War: The British, the Boers, and the Making of South Africa*. New York: Public Affairs, 2007. Includes a worthwhile treatment of the Trek and its impact on the Boers and their history.

Moodie, T. Dunbar. *The Rise of Afrikanerdom: Power, Apartheid, and the Afrikaner Civil Religion*. Berkeley: University of California Press, 1975. Provides important insights into the Boer mentalité.

Nutting, Anthony. *Scramble for Africa: The Great Trek to the Boer War*. London: Constable, 1970. A standard introduction to nineteenth-century South African history.

Ransford, Oliver. *The Great Trek*. London: J. Murray, 1972. Dated but still a good history of the Great Trek.

Theal, George McCall. *History of the Boers in South Africa, or, The Wanderings and Wars of the Emigrant Farmers from Their Leaving the Cape Colony to the Acknowledgment of Their Independence by Great Britain.* New York: Negro Universities Press, 1969. A very interesting scholarly history of the Anglo-Boer antagonism in South Africa with substantive consideration given to its impact on the native African population.

Venter, C. *The Great Trek.* Cape Town: Don Nelson, 1985. A rather simple but factually accurate introduction to the history of the Great Trek.

Walker, Eric Anderson. *The Frontier Tradition in South Africa: A Lecture delivered before the University of Oxford at Rhodes House on 5th March 1930.* London: Oxford University Press, 1930. A brief but meaningful study that includes the Boers and the Great Trek.

———. *The Great Trek.* London: A. & C. Black, 1934. Emphasis on the Boers as pioneers that is quite sympathetic but still useful.

World Wide Web

"Africa: Imperialism and Colonialism." http://www.emints.org/ethemes/resources/S00001799.shtml. Provides extensive list of links to Web sites on all aspects of European imperialism in Africa.

"African Political Entities Before the Scramble." http://www.artsci.wustl.edu/~anthro/courses/306/polities.htm. Includes a controversial map of Africa prior to most European imperial seizures.

"Great Trek, A Wisdom Archive on Great Trek." http://www.experiencefestival.com/great_trek. An excellent resource that provides links to many Web sites related to the Great Trek.

"Great Trek." http://www.britannica.com/EBchecked/topic/243837/Great-Trek. A reliable introduction to the history of the Great Trek.

"The Kings of the Zulu." http://www.visitzululand.co.za/zulukings.html. Provides information on the Zulu kings and the important events of their times from 1780 through 1968.

Multimedia Sources

"History of Afrikaner in South Africa." http://www.youtube.com/watch?v=nzrZKnO9pXo. A series of video clips from an Africaner documentary on the Great Trek. While not in English, it is readily understood.

A Pictorial History of the Great Trek: Visual Documents Illustrating the Great Trek. Cape Town: Tafelberg, 1978. An outstanding collection of illustrations and maps on the Great Trek.

34. Rebellions in Upper and Lower Canada (1837–1838)

During the 1830s Canada was organized into three major areas: Lower Canada (Quebec and the surrounding areas), Upper Canada (Ontario and the lands that bordered the United States to the south), and Rupert's Land (owned by the Hudson's Bay Company, the land to the north and west of Lower Canada). During the years after the War of 1812, another wave of Americans fled to Canada because they identified with the British and sided with them in the war. In addition, thousands of British migrated to Canada after the Napoleonic Wars, looking for economic opportunities.

The French speaking people of Lower Canada believed that their culture was threatened by the encroachment of the English-speaking immigrants. Opposing parties and lists of demands appeared in the 1830s. The most important was advanced by the Patriote Party, but it was rejected by the British government when it issued the Ten Russell Resolutions. Leaders of the Patriote Party denounced the British action and were arrested. The Patriotes enjoyed one victory (in six battles) over the British before they suppressed this rebellion.

The rebellion in Upper Canada was not as widespread as in the northern Lower Canada. Many recent American immigrants supported the rebellion. Through the Reform Party political unions were organized and an economic boycott was instituted. It also tried to institute a new constitution for Upper Canada. After a few violent actions, the rebellion collapsed when it was evident that it did not have much support.

The most significant consequence of the rebellions was the adoption and imposition of the Act of Union of 1840, which established a united Canada in 1841.

TERM PAPER SUGGESTIONS

1. Write a paper in which you compare the origins and outbreak of the rebellion in Upper and Lower Canada.
2. Develop a paper on the development and suppression of the rebellion in Upper and Lower Canada.
3. Write a paper on the consequences of the rebellion.
4. Compare and contrast the development and consequences of the rebellions in Upper and Lower Canada.

5. Write a paper in which you consider the aspirations of those who supported the rebellion—be sure to include comments on the cultural, economic, and social complexities that contributed to their dissatisfaction.

ALTERNATIVE TERM PAPER SUGGESTIONS

1. Develop a podcast in which you interview the principal participants in the rebellions and discuss the causes for their actions.

2. Develop an iMovie in which you monitor the planning and progress of the suppression of the rebellions.

3. Develop a Web page in which you provide hyperlink maps of Lower and Upper Canada that indicate significant developments in the rebellion. The Web page should also provide a narrative with data on the rebellions and a bibliography of the sources that you used.

4. Develop a blog between you as a teenage son or daughter of a leader of the rebellion in Upper Canada and a young relative who is the child of a leader of the rebellion in Lower Canada. The blog should reflect shared and different experiences, values and positions held in common and those that were different, and the impact of the rebellions on your communities and families.

SUGGESTED SOURCES

Primary Sources

Greenwood, F. Murray, and Barry Wright, eds. *Canadian State Trials. Volume 2: Rebellion and Invasion in the Canadas, 1837–1839*. Toronto: The Osgoode Society and University of Toronto Press, 2002. Provides detailed information on most aspects of the rebellion, as well as accurate transcripts of the trials.

Read, Colin, and Ronald J. Stagg, eds. *The Rebellion of 1837 in Upper Canada: A Collection of Documents*. Toronto: Champlain Society in cooperation with the Ontario Heritage Foundation and Carleton University, 1985. An excellent collection of significant primary sources on the rebellions.

"The Rebellion of 1837 and 1838." *Canada in the Making*. http://www .canadiana.org/citm/specifique/rebellions_e.html. Includes links to 13 primary sources including "The Ninety-Two Resolutions, 1834" and "Lord John Russell's Ten Resolutions, 1837."

"Upper Canada Rebellion, 1837: The End." http://www.sg-chem.net/UC1838/. Includes "Letter from James Buchanan [U.S. Secretary of State] to Sir George Arthur (March 10, 1838)," "Chief Justice's Address to Samuel Lount and Peter Matthews (April 4, 1838)," "Executive Council Minute

(March 31, 1838)," "Letter from John Ryerson to Egerton Ryerson (April 12, 1838)," and several other valuable primary sources.

Secondary Sources

Boyce, Betsy. *The Rebels of Hastings.* Toronto: University of Toronto Press, 1992. A readable and reliable account of the Hastings uprising—this book may provide ideas for term papers on the rebellion that are related to local history.

Buckner, Philip. *Canada and the British Empire.* Oxford History of the British Empire Companion. New York: Oxford University Press, 2008. An outstanding comprehensive history that provides a solid introduction to most aspects of Canadian history and a very good bibliography.

Craig, Gerald. *Upper Canada: The Formative Years, 1784–1841.* Toronto: McClelland and Stewart, 1963. Still a very reliable and useful introduction to the background and development of the rebellions.

Fryer, Mary Beacock. *Volunteers and Redcoats, Rebels and Raiders: A Military History of the Rebellions in Upper Canada.* Toronto: Dundurn Press/National Museums of Canada, 1987. A very useful military description and analysis of the conflict in Upper Canada that includes detailed information on the combatants.

Buckner, Philip, ed. *Canada and the British Empire.* New York: Oxford University Press, 2008. An excellent volume edited and written by an outstanding historian of Canada that includes a very good introduction to the rebellions and their place in nineteenth-century Canadian history.

———. *The Transition to Responsible Government: British Policy in British North America 1815–1850.* Westport, CT: Greenwood Press, 1985. A valuable scholarly study on the British position and policy to Canada during the first half of the century.

Creighton, Donald. *The Empire of the St. Lawrence.* Toronto: Macmillan, 1956. An adequate introduction to the rebellions along the St. Lawrence River.

Francis, Donald, Richard Jones, and Donald B. Smith. *Origins: Canadian History to Confederation.* Toronto: Harcourt Brace, 1992. Excellent essays on the rebellions and the tensions that developed with the expansion of Canada.

Greer, Allan. *The Patriots and the People: The Rebellion of 1837 in Rural Lower Canada.* Toronto: University of Toronto Press, 1993. A well-researched and well-written study of the conflicting forces that dominated the rebellion in Lower Canada.

Martin, Ged. *Britain and the Origins of Canadian Confederation, 1837–1867.* Vancouver: University of British Columbia Press, 1995. A solid and useful history of the constitutional transformation of Canada that emerged after the rebellions in Upper and Lower Canada, the Durham Report, and other contributing developments.

Ouellet, Fernand. *Social and Economic History of Québec.* Toronto: Macmillan, 1980. An important study by a respected authority on the economic and social evolution of Québec and its impact on politics and political identity.

———. *Lower Canada 1791–1840: Social Change and Nationalism.* Trans. Patricia Claxton. Toronto: McClelland and Stewart, 1980. A very useful scholarly study of the conditions and tensions that contributed to the rebellion in Lower Canada.

Read, Colin. *The Rising in Western Upper Canada, 1837–8: The Duncombe Revolt and After.* Toronto: University of Toronto Press, 1980. An important study of aspects of the rebellion in Upper Canada that contributed to the general distress of the period. It includes very good documentation.

Read, David Breakenridge. *The Canadian Rebellion on 1837.* Toronto: C. B. Robinson, 1896. An early but still useful comprehensive study of the rebellion. It is available in libraries and in e-book collections.

Senior, Elinor Kyte. *Redcoats and Patriotes: The Rebellions in Lower Canada, 1837–1838.* Stittsville, Ontario: *Canada's* Wings, 1985. An excellent history of the events in Lower Canada. Well researched and written, Senior's history is useful to general readers and scholars.

Verney, Jack. *O'Callaghan: The Making and Unmaking of a Rebel.* Ottawa: Carleton University Press, 1994. A useful case study of a participant in the rebellion.

World Wide Web

"Province of Canada, 1841–67." http://www.thecanadianencyclopedia.com/index.cfm?PgNm=TCE&Params=A1ARTA0006530. Addresses the post-uprising situations in Lower and Upper Canada.

"Rebellions of 1837." http://www.thecanadianencyclopedia.com/index.cfm?PgNm=TCE&Params=A1SEC827046. This article by Philip Buckner provides an excellent and reliable introduction to the rebellions in Lower and Upper Canada.

"The 1837 Rebellions." http://www.edunetconnect.com/cat/rebellions/index.html. A comprehensive Web site that includes data on most aspects of the rebellions.

"The 1837 Rebellions." http://collections.ic.gc.ca/charlottetown/glossary/rebellion.html. Includes description of the events on the rebellions.

"The 1837 Rebellions." http://www.nlc-bnc.ca/2/18/h18-2001-e.html#b. Description of the 1837 Rebellion in Upper Canada. Includes the Durham Report and the Act of Union.

Multimedia Sources

"Rebellion of 1837." http://www.canadianheritage.ca/galleries/warsbattlesrebel lions0600.htm#Rebellion%20of%201837. Includes six illustrations and paintings on topics related to the rebellion.

"The Lower Canada Rebellion." http://www.vtap.com/topic.html?da=pc &pg=s&W=&no_crawl=1&usrc=YouTube&usrn=jademoore03. A video on the rebellion in Lower Canada.

35. First Opium War (1839–1842)

The origins of the First Opium War were based on the British importation of opium to China during the late eighteenth and early nineteenth centuries. By the 1830s estimates contend that more than two million Chinese were addicted to opium and its variants. In response to that situation and a decline in the trade of gold and silver with Britain, the Qing Emperor Daoguang (1782–1850) initiated a program to eliminate the trade and use of opium in China. In 1839 he appointed Lin Zexu (1785–1850) as governor of Canton where the abuse of the product was most evident. Lin launched a program to eliminate the sale, distribution, and consumption of opium. His actions included restricting British access to Canton and dispatching a petition to Queen Victoria (1819–1901) requesting her personal intervention in stopping the importation of opium into China. Cantonese officials destroyed opium wherever they found it—including that being held by British merchants. In response to these developments, the British government started the war by seizing Hong Kong. They demanded compensation for the seized opium and access to the Chinese market for opium. Several thousand British marines were deployed, and in 1841 they defeated Chinese forces in the battles at Ningbo and Chinghar. The war ended with the Treaty of Nanking. This imposed agreement resulted in the attainment of all of the British objectives and destabilized the Qing Dynasty.

TERM PAPER SUGGESTIONS

1. Write a paper on the background and outbreak of the First Opium War.
2. Develop a paper on the debate in the British government over whether the First Opium War was a "just" war.

3. Write a paper in which you examine and analyze Lin Zexu's actions in stopping the opium trade in Canton. Were his actions provocative?

4. Develop a paper in which you analyze the Treaty of Nanking and its impact on China and Anglo-Chinese relations.

ALTERNATIVE TERM PAPER SUGGESTIONS

1. Develop an iMovie in which Emperor Daoguang and Lin Zexu discuss their plans to end the impact of opium on China. Did they expect that their anti-drug policy would lead to war?

2. As a Christian missionary opposed to the opium trade, you witness the developments of the First Opium War. Develop a blog with your colleagues in England in which you find yourself opposed to the British policy.

3. Develop a podcast in which the British Cabinet considers the issues that are involved in this struggle.

SUGGESTED SOURCES

Primary Sources

Belcher, Edward. *Narrative of a Voyage Round the World: Performed in Her Majesty's Ship "Sulphur," during the Years 1836–1842, including Details of the Naval Operations in China from December 1840 to November 1841.* London: H. Colburn, 1843. Excellent resource with extensive firsthand information from the British perspective.

Forbes, Robert B. *Personal Reminiscences.* 2nd ed. Boston: Little, Brown, 1882. A useful account by an eyewitness and participant.

Loch, Granville G. *The Closing Events of the Campaign in China: The Operations in the Yang-tze-kiang and the Treaty of Nanking.* London: Murray, 1843. Also available as an e-book at http://books.google.com/books?id =F_eyJPTERisC&pg=PR3&lpg=PR3&dq=Loch,+Granville+G.+The +Closing+Events+of+the+Campaign+in+China:+The+Operations+in +the+Yang-tze-kiang+and+the+Treaty+of+Nanking&source=bl&ots =iYmJu0Zll_&sig=6LwhbeVAEEBOQUTX_OzhBnPG8m0&hl=en&sa =X&oi=book_result&resnum=1&ct=result. Very good primary source by a leading British participant.

"Treaty of Nanking, August 29, 1842." http://web.jjay.cuny.edu/~jobrien/refer ence/ob24.html. The text of the treaty that ended the First Opium War.

Waley, Arthur. *The Opium War Through Chinese Eyes.* London: Routledge, 2005; originally published in 1958. Includes excerpts from contemporary Chinese diaries, records, and other documents that relate to the war.

Wei, Yüan. *Chinese Account of the Opium War.* Trans. E. H. Parker. Wilmington, DE: Scholarly Resources, 1972; originally published in 1888. Wei (1794–1857) was a witness and participant in the conflict.

Secondary Sources

Beeching, Jack. *The Chinese Opium Wars.* New York: Harvest Books, 1977. Good introduction to the two wars with Britain.

Collis, Maurice. *Foreign Mud: Being an Account of the Opium Imbroglio at Canton in the 1830s and the Anglo-Chinese War That Followed.* New York: Knopf, 1947. A well-written and researched study on the background and outbreak of the First Opium War.

Coston, W. C. *Great Britain and China, 1833–1860.* London: Oxford University Press, 1968; originally published in 1937. Very worthwhile but dated study that includes extensive information on both of the Opium Wars.

Fay, Peter Ward. *The Opium War 1840–1842: Barbarians in the Celestial Empire in the Early Part of the Nineteenth Century and the War by which They Forced Her Gates Ajar.* Chapel Hill: University of North Carolina Press, 1997. A reliable, balanced, and well-written history of the First Opium War.

Gelber, Harry Gregor. *Opium, Soldiers, and Evangelicals: Britain's 1840–42 War with China and Its Aftermath.* New York: Palgrave Macmillan, 2004. A well-developed study that connects the trade, the military, and the religious factors in establishing a position of power for Britain in China.

Grasso, June M., Jay Corrin, and Michael Kort. *Modernization and Revolution in China: From the Opium Wars to World Power.* 3rd ed. Armonk, NY: M. E. Sharpe, 2004. An excellent and reliable study that includes data on the Opium Wars.

Gray, Jack. *Rebellions and Revolutions: China from the 1800s to 2000.* 2nd ed. New York: Oxford University Press, 2003. A worthwhile study of the forces of change in China—both internal and external—during the nineteenth and twentieth centuries.

Hanes, William Travis, and Frank Sanello. *Opium Wars: The Addiction of One Empire and the Corruption of Another.* Naperville, IL: Sourcebooks, 2002. A very good reference for the Opium Wars that should be consulted by students working on this topic.

Hevia, James L. *English Lessons: The Pedagogy of Imperialism in Nineteenth Century China.* Durham, NC: Duke University Press, 2003. Includes information on the Opium Wars and other British actions in China.

Hoe, Susanna, and Derek Roebuck. *The Taking of Hong Kong: Charles and Clara Elliot in China Waters*. Richmond, UK: Curzon Press, 1999. Focused on the Elliots (Charles Elliot held the title British Plenipotentiary in Chinese Waters), this is a unique study of the Opium War.

Holt, Edgar. *The Opium Wars in China*. New York: Putnam, 1964. Reliable and well-written study of both of the Opium Wars. It considers the impact on both China and Britain and the resulting relationship.

Janin, Hunt. *The India-China Opium Trade in the Nineteenth Century*. Jefferson, NC: McFarland, 1999. Includes information on the two Anglo-Chinese Opium Wars.

McKown, Robin. *Opium War in China, 1840–1842: The British Resort to War in Order to Maintain Their Opium Trade*. London: Franklin Watts, 1974. A good study, especially on the causes and outbreak of the First Opium War.

Melancon, Glenn. *Britain's China Policy and the Opium Crisis: Balancing Drugs, Violence, and National Honour, 1833–1840*. Aldershot, U.K.: Ashgate, 2003. Very good scholarly study on the background to the war with emphasis on Britain's rationale for the conflict.

Napier, Priscilla Hayler. *Barbarian Eye: Lord Napier in China 1834: The Prelude to Hong Kong*. London: Brassey's, 1995. A sympathetic yet not uncritical study of William Napier's (British Chief Superintendent of Trade in Canton) visit to China that provides insights into the background to the conflict and the British interest in Hong Kong.

Olson, James Stuart, and Robert Shadle, eds. *Historical Dictionary of the British Empire*. Westport, CT: Greenwood Press, 1996. Includes information on the Treaty of Nanking that concluded the war.

Rait, Robert S. *The Life and Campaigns of Hugh, First Viscount Gough, Field-Marshal*. Westminster: A. Constable, 1903. Biography of a leading British military leader in the conflict.

Schoppa, R. Keith. *The Columbia Guide to Modern Chinese History*. New York: Columbia University Press, 2000. An indispensable resource for studying any topic in modern Chinese history.

Têng, Ssǔ-yü. *Chang His and the Treaty of Nanking, 1842*. Chicago: University of Chicago Press, 1944. An examination of the treaty that ended the war from the Chinese perspective.

Wakeman, Frederic E. *Strangers at the Gate: Social Disorder in South China, 1839–1862*. Berkeley: University of California Press, 1966. An examination of the internal social, economic, and political conditions in China from the beginning of the First Opium War to the 1860s.

Ya plan zhan zheng. *The Opium War.* Beijing: Foreign Languages Press, 1976. A Chinese interpretation of the war as an imperialist-capitalist assault on China.

World Wide Web

"Anthony Blaxland Stransham." http://www.bambooweb.com/articles/a/n/ Anthony_Blaxland_Stransham.html. Provides biographical information on the leader of the Royal Marines during the First Opium War.

"China: First Opium War." http://web.jjay.cuny.edu/~jobrien/reference/ob36. html. Includes a description, an illustration of a naval battle, and a small excerpt from a primary source.

"England and China: The Opium Wars, 1839–1860." http://www.victorianweb .org/history/empire/opiumwars/opiumwars1.html. Provides extensive information on both of the Anglo-Chinese Opium Wars.

"First Opium War." http://www.mahalo.com/First_Opium_War. Includes a description of the war, a timeline, and links to other sources.

"First Opium War." http://www.koreanhistoryproject.org/Ket/C18/E1802.htm. Considerable detail on the Chinese resistance to the British attack.

"The First Opium War." http://www.suite101.com/article.cfm/oriental_history/ 19388. A narrative on the war by Maria Christensen.

"First Opium War." http://www.bambooweb.com/articles/f/i/First_Opium _War.html. A good introduction to the war and its impact on the region.

"The Opium Wars." http://wsu.edu/~dee/CHING/OPIUM.HTM. A comprehensive description of the wars with commentary on their impact on Chinese political and economic life.

"Timeline: First Opium War." http://www.timelines.info/history/conflict_and _war/18th_&_19th_century_conflicts/opium_wars/first_opium_war/. A valuable and useful timeline that students should find very helpful.

"William Jardine." http://www.bambooweb.com/articles/w/i/William _Jardine.html. Important information on Jardine, the merchant who contributed to the outbreak of the First Opium War.

Multimedia Sources

"The First Opium War." BBC-4 Radio, 2006. http://www.bbc.co.uk/radio4/ history/empire/episodes/episode_47.shtml. Episode 47 in the *This Sceptred Isle: Empire* series.

"The Opium War." Divisa Red, 1997. DVD. Directed by Jin Xie. Chinese/ Spanish with English subtitles. Dramatic film on the First Opium War. The drama is set in the royal court and includes the negotiations between the Chinese and British.

36. First Afghan War (1839–1842)

The First Anglo-Afghan War began a series of conflicts and interventions by Great Britain during the nineteenth and twentieth centuries. Fearing continuing Russian expansion in Central and South Asia that could jeopardize British interests in India and the region, the British government concluded that it needed to establish a presence, or, at the very least, an understanding that Afghanistan was a British sphere of influence. The plan for the First Anglo-Afghan War was developed by Lord Auckland and executed by several incompetent generals—Sir John Keane, Sir Willoughby Cotton, and Sir William Elphinstone. The war was a disaster from the British perspective with more than 5,000 troops and 12,000 British civilians killed compared with 7,000 Afghan casualties. While Britain attained some short-lived successes, it had to withdraw in a humiliating retreat and the Russians continued to slowly develop their influence in the region.

TERM PAPER SUGGESTIONS

1. Develop a term paper on the conditions in Afghanistan during the 1830s and consider their impact on the origins of the First Afghan War.

2. Write a paper on the British rationale for this war. Be sure to address the traditional British fear of Russian expansion in South Asia.

3. Discuss the military operations in this war—were there any surprises?

4. Develop a paper on the consequences of the war—were the goals of either side achieved?

5. Wars require political and economic support. The First Afghan War was the initial struggle during Queen Victoria's reign. Develop a term paper on the British home front during this war, including political, social, and economic factors.

ALTERNATIVE TERM PAPER SUGGESTIONS

1. Develop a podcast in which you play the role of Lord Auckland when he presents his manifesto calling for British action in Afghanistan.

2. Develop a 3–5 minute iMovie in which intermediate-level British military officers consider the wisdom of the British invasion of Afghanistan in 1838.

3. A a journalist for the *Times* (London), develop a blog of dispatches during the horrendous retreat from Kabul.

SUGGESTED SOURCES

Primary Sources

Atkinson, James. *Afghan Expedition—Notes and Sketches from the First British Afghan War of 1839–1840.* Available as an e-book at http://books .google.com/books?id=lcwNAAAAIAAJ&dq=Atkinson+James+Afghan +Expedition&printsec=frontcover&source=bl&ds=k4nDfWPVkW &sig=1YBgOETuB41_LkYKp2Z6hhmiOc&hi=en&ei=UabHSar QKMSJtgfZltXKCg&sa=X&oi=book_result&resnum=2&ct=result. A detailed description of the first year of this war by a scholar and artist who was traveling with the British forces.

Durand, Henry Marion. *The First Afghan War and Its Causes.* New Delhi: Lancer Publishers, 2008; reprint of 1879 edition. A memoir of the war by Major General Sir Henry Marion Durand of the Corps of Bengal Engineers— very useful.

Gupta, Hari Ram. *Panjab, Central Asia, and the First Afghan War: Based on Mohan Lal's Observations.* 2nd ed. Lahore: Publication Bureau/Panjab University, 1987. Largely based on Lal's contemporary account of the crisis. It includes printed primary sources.

Haughton, Colonel C. S. I. *Char-Ee-Kar and Service There with the 4th Goorkha Regiment in 1841: An Episode of the First Afghan War.* Uckfield, U.K.: Naval and Military Press, 2005; reprint of the second edition, 1877. An account by an officer who saw extensive action in the First Afghan War.

Sale, Florentia. *A Journal of the First Afghan War.* Ed. Patrick Macrory. New York: Oxford University Press, 2003. A firsthand account by a survivor of the Kabul massacre of January 1842.

Williams, Charles Reynolds. *The Defence of Kahan: A Forgotten Episode to the First Afghan War: Being a Narrative Compiled from a Journal Kept during the Siege and Original Letters.* London: W. H. Allen, 1886. An exciting and detailed description of the struggle for Kahan.

Secondary Sources

Dockerty, Paddy. *The Khyber Pass: A History of Empire and Invasion.* Somerville, MA: Union Square Press, 2008. A good and reliable survey of the war.

Forbes, Archibald. *Britain in Afghanistan I: The First Afghan War 1839–1842.* London: Lenonaur, 2007. The emphasis in this book is on the causes for the British failures in the war. It provides a good history.

Henty, G. A. *To Herat and Cabul: A Story of the First Afghan War.* Whitefish, MT: Kessinger Publishing, 2007; reprint of the 1902 edition. Still a useful story of the British youth who finds himself in the war and is rescued by an Afghan tribal chieftain.

Iqbal, Afzal. *Circumstances Leading to the First Afghan War*. Lahore: Research Society of Pakistan, 1976. A useful study of the background and origins of the war.

James, Lawrence. *The Rise and Fall of the British Empire*. New York: St. Martin's, 1994. A reliable standard text that places the specific incidents in British imperial history in the context of the sweep of British imperialism as an historical force. It includes a very good bibliography.

Kaye, John William. *History of the War in Afghanistan*. 3 vols. Chestnut Hill, MA: Adamant Media/Elibron, 2001. [Reprint of 1878 edition published by W. H. Allen (London and Calcutta).] One of the most frequently used and cited sources on the war that provides detailed information and extensive documentation.

Moore, Geoffrey. *Vincent and the 41st: A Soldier's Battles in the First Afghan and Crimean Wars*. Huntingdon, U.K.: Self-published, 1979. A study of Thomas Vincent of the 41st and his experiences in the war at Kandahar and Kabul.

Norris, J. A. *The First Afghan War, 1838–1842*. Cambridge, U.K.: Cambridge University Press, 1967. An excellent history of the war by a solid scholar.

Richards, D. S. *The Savage Frontier, A History of the Anglo-Afghan Wars*. London: Macmillan, 1990. A reliable study based on primary and secondary sources with photographs of important locations and of individuals.

Stone, Alex G. *The First Afghan War, 1839–1842, and its Medals*. London: Spink, 1967. A fascinating demonstration of imperial Britain's commemoration to a rather poor colonial war.

Trotter, L. J. *The Earl of Auckland and the First Afghan War*. New Delhi: Cosmo Publications, 2004. A critical study of Auckland's role in Britain's failures during the First Afghan War.

Waller, John H. *Beyond the Khyber Pass: The Road to British Disaster in the First Afghan War*. Austin: University of Texas Press, 1993. A scholarly and well-written account of the British failure in Afghanistan. Waller noted that the Afghan tribal leaders were outraged and further motivated by the sexual activities of some of the British troops with Afghan women.

World Wide Web

"Battle of Ghuznee" (July 23, 1839). http://www.britishbattles.com/first-afghan-war/ghuznee.htm. A reliable account of the battle between the British/Indian armies and the Afghans led by Dost Mohammed. Includes a battlefield map and 11 illustrations.

"Siege of Jellalabad" (November 12, 1841–April, 13, 1842). http://www.britishbattles.com/first-afghan-war/siege-jellalabad.htm. An accurate account of the victory of the British/Indian force under Sir Robert Sale over the Afghan/Ghilzai tribesmen. Includes a siege map and four illustrations.

"Battle of Kabul" (January 13–17, 1842). http://www.britishbattles.com/first -afghan-war/kabul-gandamak. A detailed account of the battle between the British forces under General Elphinstone and the Afghans under the leadership of the Ameers of Kabul and the Ghilzai tribal chiefs. This was a disaster for the British who lost more than 12,000 troops killed; they were forced to retreat to Gandamak. A battlefield map and five illustrations are included.

"Battle of Kabul" (August–October 1842). http://www.britishbattles.com/first -afghan-war/kabul-1842.htm. A solid account of the British/Indian victory in this prolonged and final battle of the First Afghan War in which the British/Indian force prevailed. Includes a battlefield map and 13 illustrations.

Multimedia Source

Henty, G. A. *To Herat and Cabul: A Story of the First Afghan War.* 2003. Audiofly Digital Audiobook on chip. Read by Patrick Cullen. Can be played on PCs and MACs. Still a useful story of the British youth who finds himself in the war and is rescued by an Afghan tribal chieftain.

37. Maori Revolts, New Zealand (1844–1865)

While the Maori tribe of New Zealand had made contact with Europeans as early as the mid-seventeenth century, it was not until the founding of a penal colony in Australia in 1788 that regular contact developed. During the 1830s, trade with the Maoris increased significantly and a colony was developed in Wellington that grew rapidly. Conflict between the British settlers and the Maori was based on two opposing views on land ownership. The British view of land was that it was either an asset or a liability depending upon its use and profitability. The Maori culture held land ownership in an entirely different context. In addition to its economic implications, the Maori viewed land in social terms. Land ownership connected generations with their ancestors and usually was transferred on a family or hereditary basis. The first Maori revolt was known as the First New Zealand War or the Flagstaff War (1844–1846). It began when a Maori chief, Hone Heke, repudiated British claims to land. During 1845, the Maoris won two skirmishes with the British, but in January 1846 the Maori force was defeated at Ruapekapeka when they confronted artillery. The British imposed a harsh peace on the Maori, which resulted in mounting Maori concerns about British intentions and their violations of the Maori cultural view of the land. By the late 1850s the British were determined to prevail, and they provoked a Second New Zealand War (1860–1861), which did not resolve anything but which did lead to the loss of more lives. In 1863, the Third New Zealand War (1863–1864) broke when the British launched an invasion of the Waikato region under General Duncan Cameron. It was intended to suppress the militant Maoris permanently. The British won the war but did not achieve their objective of gaining absolute control. Intermittent Maori violence actions continued through the remainder of the nineteenth century and into the twentieth century.

TERM PAPER SUGGESTIONS

1. Write a paper on the origins of the Maori revolts. Were they provoked? Were these fundamentally cultural conflicts?

2. Develop a paper on the impact of colonialism on the Maoris.

3. Write a paper on the immediate and long-range consequences of the Maori wars.

ALTERNATIVE TERM PAPER SUGGESTIONS

1. Develop a podcast in which Maori leaders discuss how they should approach the influx of settlers.

2. Develop an iMovie in which General Duncan Cameron is interviewed about his strategy for the Third New Zealand War.

3. Develop a hyperlink map of colonial New Zealand in which you indicate all of the significant developments of the three Maori wars.

SUGGESTED SOURCES

Primary Sources

Hadfield, Octavius. *One of England's Little Wars: A Letter to the Right Hon., the Duke of Newcastle, Secretary of State for the Colonies.* London: Williams and Norgate, 1860. Includes information on the Maori resistance and their suppression.

Manning, Frederick Edward. *Old New Zealand: A Tale of the Good Old Times; and a History of the War in the North against the Chief Heke, in the year 1845, told by an old chief of the Ngapuhi Tribe; also Maori Traditions.* Chestnut Hill, MA: Elibrion/Adamant Media, 2001; originally published in 1906. One of the few accessible important primary sources on the revolts in New Zealand. Detailed information on the Maoris and their military methods are included.

Marjouram, William. *Memorials of Sergeant William Marjouram, Royal Artillery; Including Six Years' Service in New Zealand during the Maori War.* Whitefish, MT: Kessinger, 2007. Another important primary source on the Maoris and the war. In addition to the information on the conflict, Marjouram provides descriptions of the land and the seaports.

Secondary Sources

Ballara, Angela. *Taua: Musket Wars, Land Wars, or Tikanga? Warfare in Maori Society in Early Nineteenth Century.* London: Penguin, 2003. Provides information on inter-Maori conflict as well as that between the European settlers and the Maori.

Belich, James. *The Victorian Interpretation of Racial Conflict: The Maori, the British, and the New Zealand Wars.* McGill-Queen's Studies in Ethnic History, no. 7. Kingston, Ontario: McGill-Queen's University Press, 1990. An argument against the application of Social Darwinism in an enlightened manner.

Burnett, Robert I. *Executive Discretion and Criminal Justice: The Prerogative of Mercy: New Zealand 1840–1853.* Wellington, Australia: Institute of Criminology, Victoria University of Wellington, 1977. Includes information on the distinction between the treatment of Maori and European criminals.

Cowen, James. *The New Zealand Wars: A History of the Maori Campaigns and the Pioneering Period.* 2 vols. New York: AMS Press, 1969; originally published in 1955. The most comprehensive study on the Maori wars that has been published.

Gibson, Tom. *The Maori Wars: The British Army in New Zealand, 1840–1872.* London: L. Cooper, 1974. Excellent military history on the British prosecution of the Maori wars.

Graham, Jeanine. *Frederick Weld.* Auckland: Auckland University Press, 1983. A study of the role of British and Australian naval actions in support of the suppression of the revolts.

Miller, John. *Early Victorian New Zealand: A Study of Racial Tension and Social Attitudes, 1839–1852.* New York: Oxford University Press, 1958. Miller's analysis of the crisis between the British settlers and the Maoris is based on cultural distinctions. The greed and barbarity of the settlers was horrendous.

Petrie, Hazel. *Chiefs of Industry: Māori Tribal Enterprise in Early Colonial New Zealand.* Auckland: Auckland University Press, 2006. An interesting study on the adaptation of the Maori to some aspects of British culture and their success.

Sinclair, Keith. *Origins of the Maori Wars.* New ed. Oxford: Oxford University Press, 1975. A scholarly account on the outbreak of the Maori wars. Sinclair argues that the Maori were defending their culture as well as their idea of land rights.

Smith, Neil C. *Mariners and Maoris: British and Australian Sailors in the New Zealand Wars.* Gardenvale, Victoria, AU: Mostly Unsung Military History Research and Publications, 2003. A useful study on the impact and performance of British and Australian naval forces in actions against the Maoris.

World Wide Web

"New Zealand Maori Wars, 1844–6, 1860–1 and 1863–5." http://www .wartimesindex.co.uk/infopage.php?menu=wars&display=NewZealand. An excellent introduction to the causes, development, and consequences of the wars. This is produced by *War Times Index.*

Multimedia Source

"Utu." Kino Studio/Distributors, 2000. DVD. Directed by Geoff Murphy. This acclaimed dramatic film, originally filmed in 1983, focuses on incidents in the Maori revolts and recognizes the cultural conflict that was paramount.

38. Sayyid Ali Mohammad and the Founding of Babism (1844)

Religious identity in Persia (Iran) during the first half of the nineteenth century was not uniform. While the majority of people were Moslems, theological speculation was evident and, on occasion, attracted many followers. Sayyid Ali Mohammad (1819–1850) was raised in an intense religious environment in which he was led by relatives and friends to believe that he was destined to be revealed as a great prophet. By 1840 he came under the influence of the Shaykhi movement—a dissident sect. Within four years, he was identifying himself as the "Bab"—the "Gate" to the "hidden Imam." In 1844 he traveled to Mecca and found that his views were not acceptable. He continued developing his religious tenets and was imprisoned for heresy on several occasions. In 1848 some of his followers announced that they would join a "Babi jihad," and opponents imprisoned many of the Bab's followers. The Bab was tried and sentenced to death; he was executed on July 9, 1850. Orthodox Babism faded away within a few years after his death but it had a significant impact on the development of the Bahá'í religion.

TERM PAPER SUGGESTIONS

1. Write a paper on the origins of Babism. Was it a threat to Islam? Why?
2. Develop a paper on the development of Babism between 1844 and the violent death of the Bab in 1850.
3. Write a paper in which you consider the following questions: Why did Babism collapse after the death of the Bab, but, at the same time, how did it contribute to the establishment of the Bahá'í religion? What is the role of the Bab in Bahá'í?
4. Develop a paper in which you compare and contrast the basic tenets of Babism with those of Shi'ism.

ALTERNATIVE TERM PAPER SUGGESTIONS

1. Develop a podcast in which you interview the Bab on the origins of his theological views.
2. Develop an iMovie in which members of the Bahá'í faith discuss the place of the Bab in their religion.
3. Develop a PowerPoint program on the basic tenets/doctrines of Babism and how these ideas could be considered heretical by orthodox Moslems.

SUGGESTED SOURCES

Primary Sources

Dolgorukov, Dimitri Ivanovich. "Excerpts from Dispatches written during 1848–1852 by Prince Dolgorukov, Russian Minister to Persia." *World Order* I (1966): 17–24. These documents relate the Russian ambassador's concern about Babism as a disruptive force in the region.

The Bab. [Sayyid 'Ali Muhammad Shirazi]. *A Compilation of Passages from the Writings of the Bab.* New Delhi: BPT, 1980. A compendium of primary doctrines and tenets that were advanced by the Bab.

———. *Inspiring the Heart.* London: Bahá'í Publishing Trust, 1981. Considered to be a major work of the Bab in which the fundamental beliefs of the religion are extended.

———. *Selections from the Writings of the Bab.* Haifa: Bahá'í World Center, 1982. Also available at http://www.sacred-texts.com/bhi/bab/swb.txt. A handbook of Bab beliefs and teachings.

————. *Some Prayers of the Bab.* London: Bahá'í Education Committee of the National Spiritual Assembly of the Bahá'ís of the U.K., n.d. A Bab prayer book in which the basic tenets of the faith are advanced.

Secondary Sources

Amanat, Abbas. *Resurrection and Renewal: The Making of the Babi Movement in Iran, 1844–1850.* Ithaca, NY: Cornell University Press, 1989. An excellent scholarly study on the founding of the movement and the life and thoughts of the Bab.

Balyuzi, H. M. *Khadijih Bagum: The Wife of the Bab.* Oxford: George Ronald, 1981. A brief biography of the Bab's first wife, his cousin Khadija Bagum.

————. *The Bab.* Oxford: George Ronald, 1973. A very good biography that provides an accurate account with bibliographic references.

Bayat, Mangol. *Mysticism and Dissent: Socioreligious Thought in Qajar Iran.* Syracuse, NY: Syracuse University Press, 1982. Three chapters in this book relate to Babism.

Elwell-Sutton, L. P. *Bibliographical Guide to Iran.* Brighton/Totowa: Harvester Press, 1983. This reference work may be very helpful for students working on this topic because it is comprehensive in scope.

Keddie, N. R. "Religion and Irreligion in Early Iranian Nationalism." *Comparative Studies in Society and History* IV (1962): 265–95. An article that considers the place of Babism in nineteenth-century Iranian religion and politics.

MacEoin, Denis. *The Sources for Early Babi Doctrine and History: A Survey.* Leiden: E. J. Brill, 1992. A scholarly analysis of the origins of Babism and the emergence of its earliest tenets.

————. "Divisions and Authority Claims in Babism (1850–1866)." *Studia Iranica* (Leiden) XVIII (1989): 93–129. Covers the collapse of Babism during the years after the death of the Bab.

Martyrdom of the Báb: A Compilation. Los Angeles: Kalimát Press, 1992. Includes extensive information on the violent death and burial of the Báb.

Saledi, Nader. *Gate of the Heart: Understanding the Writings of the Báb.* Waterloo, ON: Wilfrid Laurier University Press, 2008. A concordance to accompany the writings of the Bab.

Smith, Peter. *The Babi and Baha'i Religions: From Messianic Shi'ism to a World Religion.* Cambridge, U.K.: Cambridge University Press, 1987. A scholarly history of Babism and its impact on the emergence of the Bahá'í movement.

World Wide Web

"An Introduction to Bab'i Faith." http://www.islamawareness.net/Deviant/ Bahais/babis.html. An edited article from the *Encyclopedia of Religion*, 2nd ed., by Lindsay Jones, that provides a comprehensive introduction to Babism.

"Babism." http://www.nationmaster.com/encyclopedia/Babism. Provides a relatively brief but accurate introduction to Babism.

"Baha'i." http://mb-soft.com/believe/txo/bahai.htm. Provides useful information on the origins of the movement and its fundamental tenets.

"History and Doctrines of the Babi Movement." http://aaiil.org/text/books/ mali/historydoctrinesbabimovement/historydoctrinesbabimovement .shtml. A comprehensive statement on history and doctrine that should serve students as a frequent reference while working on this topic.

"Letters of Sayyid 'Ali Muhammad Shirazi 'the Báb' to Muhammad Shah Qajar (Part II)." http://irfancolloquia.org/60/quinn_shah. Presented in 2005, this paper by Sholeh Quinn examines the later Tablets of the Báb to Muhammad Shah Qajar (r. 1834–1848), whose reign covered the earlier years of Sayyid 'Alí Muhammad the Báb's ministry (1844–1850).

"The Babi and Baha'i Religions: An Annotated Bibliography: History." http:// bahai-library.com/books/biblio/babi.history.html. An excellent bibliographic resource with many sources in English, some polemic and others scholarly.

Multimedia Source

"Shiism." http://www.encarta.co.uk/medias_761570168/Shiism.html. Includes two photographs of mosques in Iran connected to Babism.

39. First Sikh War (1845–1846)

The background and causes of the First Sikh War in India were in many ways emblematic of the origins of the wars of imperialism of the nineteenth century. Since the late eighteenth century the British presence in India was exercised through the British East India Company. This quasi-private organization was supported by the British government and military. After the defeat of Napoleonic France, the British East India Company extended its influence and power in India through increasing its military strength and suppressing the native leadership. At the same time, Maharaj Ranjit, the leader of the Sikh Kingdom in Punjab, strengthened the Sikh position through military and economic improvements. Diplomatically, Ranjit balanced the British threat against the Afghan threat from the ambitious Dost Mohammed Khan. This precarious balance was sustained until Ranjit's death in 1839. Shortly thereafter, Punjab was thrown into domestic disorder that resulted from political assassinations. The British viewed these developments both as a potential danger to British outposts and interests and as an opportunity to further extend their influence. Relations between Sikhs and the British declined and, in 1845, diplomatic relations were broken. A British/Indian army under General Sir Hugh Gough marched toward Sikh territory, and the Sikhs countered by moving their forces to frontier towns near British positions. A series of battles between these forces followed, and the British victories at Aliwal (January 28, 1846) and Sobraon (February 10, 1846) were among the more notable. The fragmented Sikh government was forced to accept the Treaty of Lahore (1846). Britain's position in Lahore was recognized and the Sikhs were forced to withdraw their claim to Kashmir. The peace was short-lived and was followed by the Second Sikh War.

TERM PAPER SUGGESTIONS

1. Write a paper on the leadership and government of Maharaj Ranjit. Why did this government fail to survive Ranjit's death?
2. Between 1839 and 1845 the Sikh Kingdom experienced turbulence in leadership and a disintegration of the effectiveness of its government. Develop a paper that considers the causes of this collapse and details its development.
3. Was the British East India Company responsible for the outbreak of the war in 1845?
4. From the perspective of regional strategic interests and the potential for conflict, was the First Sikh War inevitable?
5. Explain the defeat of the Sikh Kingdom in this war. Did it result from the superiority of the British forces or did it come about as a consequence of internal Sikh political squabbles?

ALTERNATIVE TERM PAPER SUGGESTIONS

1. Develop a hyperlink map of the region during the 1840s and indicate the major military actions that occurred during the war. Provide detailed annotations on the military operations.

2. Imagine that you are the aging and ailing Maharaj Ranjit early in 1839. For more than a decade you have seen your kingdom flourish in part, as a result of the delicate balance of power that you controlled between the British and the Afghans. Knowing that your days are few, develop online guidelines for your successor on how to sustain this peace.

3. Develop a podcast in which the British leaders develop their strategic objectives and operational plans to defeat the Sikh kingdom in 1845–1846.

4. Develop a 3 minute iMovie on the negotiations that lead to the Treaty of Lahore.

5. As an admirer of the late Ranjit and a member of the Sikh aristocracy, you are dismayed by the disintegration of Sikh politics and effective Sikh resistance to the British. As a contemporary, develop a blog on the paralysis that gripped post-Ranjit Punjab.

SUGGESTED SOURCES

Primary Sources

Anglesey, Marquess of. *Sergeant Pearman's Memoirs, Being Chiefly His Account of Service with the Third (King's Own) Light Dragoons in India from 1846 to 1853, Including the First and Second Sikh Wars.* London: Jonathan Cape, 1968. A useful and reliable primary account of the military actions of a British army regular who served in both Sikh wars.

Baldwin, J. A. *A Norfolk Soldier in the First Sikh War—a Private Soldier Tells the Story of His Part in the Battles for the Conquest of India.* London: Leonaur, Ltd., 2006. This is an excellent account of the battles of Moodkee, Ferozeshah, and Sobroan and provides a perspective by an enlisted soldier of the activities of the British army in India.

Guy, Alan J., ed. *Military Miscellany: Manuscripts from the Seven Years War, the First and Second Sikh Wars and the First World War.* Stroud, U.K.: Sutton Publishing for the Army Records Society, 1991. A good collection of primary materials on the two Sikh wars that provide personal insights to the expectations and uncertainties associated with these conflicts.

Humphries, James. *The Hero of Aliwal: The Campaigns of Sir Harry Smith in India, 1843–1846. During the Gwalior War and the First Sikh War.* London: Leonaur, Ltd., 2007. This reprint edition of a contemporary source includes valuable printed primary sources.

Parshad, Dewan Aljudhia. *Waqai-jang-i-Sikhan: Events of the (First) Anglo-Sikh War, 1845–46: Eye-witness account of the Battles of Pheroshahr and Sobraon.* Chandigarh, India: Punjab Itihas Prakashan, 1975. Provides native insight into the war with a focus on the two battles of Pheroshahr and Sobraon.

Secondary Sources

Burton, Reginald George. *The First and Second Sikh Wars.* 2nd ed. Yardley, PA: Westholme Publishing, 2007. A reliable and readable history of the two Anglo-Sikh wars, based on primary and secondary sources.

Farwell, Byron. *Queen Victoria's Little Wars.* New ed. Ware, Hertfordshire, U.K.: Wordsworth Editions, 1999. Highly recommended and readable chapters on the Sikh wars.

Featherstone, Donald F. *All for a Shilling a Day: The Story of H. M. 16th, the Queen's Lancers, during the First Sikh War 1845–1846.* London: Jarrolds, 1968. A history of the war from the perspective of the enlisted British soldier.

Gupta, H. R., ed. *Punjab on the Eve of the First Sikh War.* Chandigarh, India: Panjab University, 1956. A noteworthy collection of essays on the prewar conditions in Punjab that contributed to the outbreak of hostilities.

Hernon, Ian. *Blood in the Sand: More Forgotten Wars of the Nineteenth Century.* Stroud, U.K.: Sutton, 2001. Includes a very good chapter on the First Sikh War, concise but authoritative.

James, Lawrence. *The Rise and Fall of the British Empire.* New York: St. Martin's, 1994. A reliable standard text that places the specific incidents in British imperial history in the context of the sweep of British imperialism as an historical force and includes a very good bibliography.

World Wide Web

"Anglo-Sikh Wars." http://www.kabira.freeservers.com/angloskhwars.html. Solid introduction to the two wars with statistics on military engagements.

"First Anglo-Sikh War." http://www.asht.info/anglosikh/107/first-anglo-sikh-war.html. Emphasizes the military aspects of the war and includes good links. Produced by the Anglo-Sikh Heritage Trail.

"First Anglo-Sikh War (1845–46)." http://sify.com/itihaas/fullstory.php?id=13258253. A good introduction to the First Sikh War that includes a good summary of the terms of the Lahore Treaty.

"Battle of Moodkee." http://www.britishbattles.com/first-sikh-war/moodkee.htm. An excellent source on the opposing forces in the opening battle of the First Sikh War on December 18, 1845. In addition to text and a copy of a painting on the battle and seven illustrations, an accurate battle map of the Sikh and British/Indian forces was provided.

"Battle of Ferozeshah." http://www.britishbattles.com/first-sikh-war/ferozeshah .htm. Provides a detailed account of the second battle of the First Sikh War on December 21, 1845. It includes a battlefield map, one photograph, and 11 illustrations.

"Battle of Aliwal." http://www.britishbattles.com/first-sikh-war/aliwal.htm. A reliable and detailed account of the battle on January 28, 1846. It includes a very good battlefield map and eight illustrations.

Multimedia Sources

"Empire and Faith, Kinship and War: A Century of Sikh Photographs (1849–1948)." http://www.swfftoronto.com/exhibition/exhibition.php. Provides photographs of locations and individuals who were significant in both of the Anglo-Sikh Wars, exhibited at the Fifth Annual Spinning Wheel Film Festival, 2007, at the Isabel Bader Theatre, Toronto, Ontario.

"First Sikh War—Military Art Prints." http://www.war-art.com/new_page_10. htm. Accurate prints of battle scenes produced by Cranston Fine Arts.

"This Sceptred Isle: Empire, The First Sikh War." BBC/Radio 4 (February 22, 2006). Written by Christopher Lee; narrated by Juliet Stevenson, with readings by Christopher Eccleston. http://www.bbc.co.uk/radio4/schedule/ 2006/02/22/day. Also available at http://www.bbc.co.uk/radio4/history/ empire/episodes/episode_48.shtml. In addition to the First Sikh War, this program provides useful information on the Second Sikh War.

40. Establishment of an Independent Liberia (1847)

Since the beginning of the nineteenth century, a growing number of Americans thought that freed slaves should be provided with an opportunity to return to Africa. Through the acquisition of land by military actions and finances, Liberia in West Africa was identified and acquired as a refuge for the freed slaves. The American Colonization Society was established in 1816 and gained the support of prominent abolitionists for the "back to Africa" movement as a safe haven for the freed slaves. They received an enthusiastic response from African Americans, of whom the most prominent was Joseph Jenkins Roberts. During the 1820s the American Colonization Society purchased coastal land near what is today

Monrovia and established a small settlement of fewer than 100. Other settlements were established nearby during the next 20 years. In 1847 Roberts declared the independence of Liberia, then with a population of 3,000 freed slaves. A constitution was adopted the same year that reflected the structure and values of the American constitution. Ironically, the Liberian constitution denied the right of citizenship and the vote to the native population.

TERM PAPER SUGGESTIONS

1. Write a term paper on the emergence of the American Colonization Society. What interests supported its goals and objectives? Why?

2. Develop a paper on an analysis of the Liberian Constitution. Consider the options that the Liberians had. Why did they elect to follow the American model?

3. Write a paper on the reaction of the American government to the establishment of Liberia.

4. Develop a paper on Roberts's leadership and achievements in establishing an independent Liberia.

5. Write a paper that focuses on the rationale to establish the new state in West Africa. Why was the specific location selected?

ALTERNATIVE TERM PAPER SUGGESTIONS

1. Develop a 4–5 minute podcast in which Roberts discusses his aspirations and plans for a new country, Liberia.

2. As one of the earlier settlers to Liberia during the 1830s, develop a blog with letters to relatives in the United States describing what is being done to establish the new state.

3. Develop an iMovie in which prominent political leaders of the slave states consider the potential impact of the establishment of Liberia on them.

SUGGESTED SOURCES

Primary Sources

Crummell, Alexander. *Destiny and Race: Selected Writings, 1840–1898.* Ed. Wilson J. Moses. Amherst: University of Massachusetts, 1992. The letters and presentations of Alexander Crummell, who worked as a missionary in Liberia.

Fairhead, James, ed. *African-American Exploration in West Africa: Four Nineteenth-Century Diaries.* Bloomington: Indiana University Press, 2003. Includes the diaries of James Sims, George Seymour, Benjamin Anderson, and Benjamin J. K. Anderson.

New York State Colonization Society. *Emigration to Liberia: One-Thousand Applicants for a Passage to Liberia in 1848. An Appeal in Behalf of Two Hundred Slaves Liberated by Captain Isaac Ross: A Brief History of the Ross Slaves.* Ithaca, NY: Cornell University Library, 1848. An important primary document related to a specific incident that supported Liberian development.

"The Declaration of Independence." http://onliberia.org/con_declaration.htm. The text of the Liberian Declaration of Independence in 1847.

Secondary Sources

Clegg, Claude A., III. *The Price of Liberty: African Americans and the Making of Liberia.* Chapel Hill: University of North Carolina Press, 2003. A very good history of African American contributions to the establishment of an independent Liberia.

Hyman, Lester S. *United States Policy Towards Liberia, 1822 to 2003.* Cherry Hill, NJ: Africana Homestead Legacy Publishers, 2007. Important work on the critical issue of American support for Liberia.

Johnson, Harry Hamilton. *Liberia.* London: Hutchinson, 1906. An early history of Liberia, its people, and the land by a prominent British scholar.

McPherson, J. H. T. *History of Liberia.* Baltimore, MD: Johns Hopkins University Press, 1891. Provides extensive information on the establishment of Liberia.

Reef, Catherine. *This Our Dark Country: The American Settlers of Liberia.* New York: Clarion, 2002. A study of the American colonists in Liberia.

Somah, S. L. *Historical Settlement of Liberia and its Environmental Impact.* Lanham, MD: University Press of America, 1994. Includes extensive information on the emigration of African Americans to Liberia during the mid-nineteenth century.

West, Richard. *Back to Africa: History of Sierra Leone and Liberia.* London: Jonathan Cape, 1970. Provides information on the American immigration to Liberia.

Tyler-McGraw, Marie. *An African Republic: Black and White Virginians in the Making of Liberia.* Chapel Hill: University of North Carolina Press, 2007. A very important and seminal study of integrated support for the Liberian exodus.

World Wide Web

"Early Independence." http://personal.denison.edu/~waite/liberia/history/ 49-71.htm. A review of the first years of Liberia's independence with emphasis on gaining recognition from the European states.

"History of Liberia." http://www.britannica.com/EBchecked/topic/339290/ history-of-Liberia. Includes reliable information on the origins of Liberia.

"History of Liberia." http://www.globalsecurity.org/military/world/liberia/ history.htm. A comprehensive introduction to the history of Liberia with extensive information on the independence era.

"Independence for Liberia." http://www.americaslibrary.gov/cgi-bin/page.cgi/jb/ reform/liberia_1. Includes information on the origins of Liberia, the roles of Joseph Jenkins Roberts and Daniel Webster, and a copy of an 1830 map of the region.

"Maps of Liberia, 1830–1870." http://memory.loc.gov/ammem/gmdhtml/ libhtml/libhome.html. This Library of Congress Web site includes 20 maps from the pre-independence period and the early decades of the Liberian nation.

"Timeline of Liberian History." http://www.thewomenoffire.org/timeline_of _liberian_history.htm. A very useful timeline on Liberia.

Multimedia Sources

America's Stepchild. PBS, 2002. DVD. Written and directed by Nancee Oku Bright and Zvi Dor-Ner. This documentary includes information on the founding of Liberia.

Tellewoyan, Joseph. *The Years The Locust Eaten: Liberia 1816–1996.* Audiobook, CD. http://pages.prodigy.net/jkess3/Locust.htm. Includes extensive information on Liberian independence.

41. War of the Castes (1847–1901)

During the Mexican war for independence from Spain, the revolutionary leadership spoke of the equality of all. But, as was frequently the case, the success of the revolt did not result in equality for the "lower" members of society. In the Yucatan Peninsula the remnants of the Maya civilization and other native peoples were disappointed with the new Mexican government's position on their rights and place in society. Yucatan was governed by the *Yucatecos,* a minority group of European ancestry.

They controlled the local businesses and government and ruled over the Mayas or *Indios*. In 1847 three Mayans were charged with treason for planning a revolution and were executed. The Mayas rose in a general uprising that was motivated as much by social factors as their call for political liberties. They were interested in maintaining their communal lands rather than dividing the land into private properties. The Mayas were very successful during the initial year of the war. The *Yucatecos* found themselves isolated and under siege in a few outposts. However, by August 1848, the Mexican government had developed an effective strategy and regained some control over the Yucatan. The Mexican success was due in large part to the availability of funds that they had acquired from the United States after the Mexican War. The Americans had provided compensation for the territories (southwestern United States) that they had seized. The Mayas continued to resist, but the Yucatan provincial government declared victory in 1855. Both sides continued to practice genocide tactics for decades. The Mayas established autonomous communities with the largest being Chan Santa Cruz, which existed until 1894 when the Mexican government forced its dissolution. Outbreaks of violence occurred occasionally during the 1860s to the 1890s. In 1893 a treaty between Mexico and the United Kingdom resolved the long-standing boundary dispute between Mexico and British Honduras. The treaty also prohibited all trade with Chan Santa Cruz. With this treaty in hand, the Mexicans were determined to eliminate the Mayan power in Yucatan. In 1901 the Mayas were defeated and the War of the Castes came to an end. However, violence in the region continued for decades.

TERM PAPER SUGGESTIONS

1. Write a term paper on the causes of the Caste War of the Yucatan. Include in your paper responses to these questions: Was the Caste War an ethnic war? Were the primary differences between the Mexicans and the Mayas political or cultural? What economic factors were associated with the origins of the Caste War?

2. Develop a paper on the prosecution of the war between 1847 and 1855.

3. Write a paper on the impact/involvement of the United States and Great Britain on the Mayas and the Mexicans during the War of the Castes.

4. Develop a paper on the development and collapse of Chan Santa Cruz during the war.

ALTERNATIVE TERM PAPER SUGGESTIONS

1. Develop an iMovie in which Maya leaders discuss their disappointment with the new Mexican government and their concerns that their cultural traditions and local freedoms were endangered.

2. As an 18-year-old *Yucatecos* you are a victim of the Maya seige of your town in late 1847. Develop a blog of your diary entries of your experiences and views of the war, the Maya people, and the Mexican government.

3. Develop a 5 minute podcast of a range of Maya voices who evoke personal explanations for the war and their personal experiences during its early years.

SUGGESTED SOURCES

Primary Sources

Reed, Nelson. *The Caste War of Yucatan.* Rev. ed. Stanford, CA: Stanford University Press, 2001. Available as an e-book at http://books.google.com/books?hl=en&id=e2KhyOCebJkC&dq=caste+war+of+yucatan&printsec=frontcover&source=web&ots=zpW2wu-T7p&sig=6csoJNZylZK1CYL8aG8jMyQCsjo&sa=X&oi=book_result&resnum=2&ct=result. Includes primary documents that should be useful to many students.

Stephens, John L. *Incidents of Travel in Central America, Chiapas and Yucatan.* N. Chelmsford, MA: Courier Dover, 1969; originally published in two volumes in 1841. Stephens's firsthand account of the problems in Yucatan provide primary insights into the background and causes of the Caste war.

Womack, John, Jr., ed. *Rebellion in Chiapas: An Historical Reader.* New York: New Press, 1999. Includes some primary materials that may be useful.

Secondary Sources

Alexander, Rani T. *Yaxcabá and the Caste War of Yucatan: An Archaeological Perspective.* Albuquerque: University of New Mexico Press, 2004. An outstanding scholarly study that will be an important resource to students working on this topic.

Cline, Howard Francis. *Related Studies in Early 19th Century Yucatan Social History.* Chicago: University of Chicago Library, 1950. A dated but still useful study of the ethnic conflicts that precipitated the Caste War.

Dumond, Don E. *The Machete and the Cross: Campesino Rebellion in Yucatan.* Lincoln: University of Nebraska Press, 1997. A well-written scholarly account of one of the actions of the Caste War.

Gabbert, Wolfgang. *Becoming Maya: Ethnicity and Social Inequality in Yucatan since 1500.* Tucson: University of Arizona Press, 2004. Places the Caste War in the context of long-term social and political conflict.

Jones, Grant D., ed. *Anthropology and History in Yucatan.* Austin: University of Texas Press, 1977. A collection of essays; some may be of value to students working on the Caste War.

Landa, Diego de. *Yucatan Before and After the Conquest.* Trans. William Gates. New York: Dover, 1978; originally published in 1937. A classic study by a prominent authority. Most students will want to refer to Landa during their research.

Reed, Nelson. *The Caste War of Yucatán.* Rev. ed. Stanford: Stanford University Press, 2001. Available as an e-book at http://books.google.com/books?hl=en&id=e2KhyOCebJkC&dq=caste+war+of+yucatan&printsec=frontcover&source=web&ots=zpW2wu-T7p&sig=6csoJNZylZK1CYL8aG8jMyQCsjo&sa=X&oi=book_result&resnum=2&ct=result. The best book on the Caste War. Nelson's study is well-written, well-documented, and comprehensive.

Robins, Nicolas A. *Native Insurgencies and the Genocidal Impulse in the Americas.* Bloomington: Indiana University Press, 2005. A seminal study that should attract students who are considering the genocide of the Caste War.

Rugeley, Terry, ed. *Maya Wars: Ethnographic Accounts from Nineteenth-Century Yucatan.* Norman: University of Oklahoma Press, 2001. Another important study that should be accessible and of interest to students.

———. *Yucatan Maya Peasantry and the Origins of the Caste War.* Austin: University of Texas Press, 1996. A readable and scholarly study focused on the background and outbreak of the Caste War.

Sullivan, Paul. *Xuxub Must Die: The Lost Histories of a Murder on the Yucatan.* Pittsburgh: University of Pittsburgh Press, 2004. This book may be useful to a student working on this specific topic.

World Wide Web

"Caste War, 1847–1904." http://www.northernbelize.com/hist_caste.html. A good introduction to the Caste War and its excessive violence.

"Caste War of the Yucatan." http://ambergriscaye.com/pages/mayan/castewar.html. A very substantive introduction to the Caste War.

"Tales from the Yucatan." http://www.planeta.com/ecotravel/mexico/yucatan/tales/0303yucatan.html. A very good and well-written analysis of the Caste War by Jeanine Kitchel, which includes copies of illustrations.

Multimedia Sources

"Tales from the Yucatan." http://www.belize.com/tales-from-the-yucatan.html. Includes one of the few remaining photographs of the original Yucatan Caste War Mural at the Corozal Town Hall painted by Manuel Villamor.

"The Caste War of Yucatan, 1847–1849." http://www.genocidetext.net/gaci _yucatan.htm. Includes six important photographs of sites and art works concerning the Caste War.

42. Marxism Is Promulgated (1847–1881)

Marxism was established by the German Karl Marx (1818–1883), with assistance from Friedrich Engels, during the mid-nineteenth century. Marxism was a political, economic, and social philosophy predicated upon a worldview or philosophy of history as a continuum of class struggles. Marx believed that humanity had been corrupted by artificial institutions of its own making—religion, states, economic structures, and an exploitative class system. Only when these institutions were eliminated could humanity regain its inherent natural goodness. Marx and Engels, who were deeply influenced by the French Revolution and the subsequent thoughts of Georg Hegel (dialectic process), produced *The Communist Manifesto* in 1847 in which they clearly outlined this sense of history. Marx's later works, especially *Das Kapital* (Capital), published in 1864, expanded his thoughts and gained many followers. In many ways, Marxism assimilated the earlier ideas of "humanism" and "rationalism" that had characterized modern thought between the Renaissance and the nineteenth century. During the last three decades of the nineteenth century, Marxism was manifested in new political organizations such as the Fabian Society and the Independent Labour Party in Britain, and the Social Democratic Party in Germany. Marxism was not unified and there were many variations and offshoots of it. Nonetheless, by the end of the nineteenth century, Marxist organizations considered themselves the force of the modern world that would eliminate superstitions and exploitative institutions and practices and bring about a new world order.

TERM PAPER SUGGESTIONS

1. Write a paper on the emergence of Marx as a revolutionary philosopher. What motivated him? What was his vision of the future of humanity?

2. Marx advanced a so-called scientific socialism that challenged the existing "utopian socialism." Develop a term paper on how these two approaches differed and the tensions that developed between them.

3. *Das Kapital* is considered Marx's most important and complex work. Develop a term paper in which you analyze the most significant propositions that he advances in this work.

4. Write a paper on Marx's life as a scholar and writer in London. Why did he reside in London? How did he support his family? Was he a responsible husband and father?

5. Marxism as a political force gained support during the second half of the nineteenth century. Write a paper on the influence of Marxism on new political parties and structure in England, France, and Germany.

ALTERNATIVE TERM PAPER SUGGESTIONS

1. Develop a 4–5 minute iMovie in which Marx and Engels organize the main outline and content of *The Communist Manifesto.*

2. Sidney and Beatrice Webb, Keir Hardie, and George Bernard Shaw were among the founders of the Marxist Fabian Society in London. Develop a podcast in which they determine their agenda for improving life in Britain during the 1880s.

3. Imagine that you are a young but nonetheless significant member of the new Social Democratic Party (SPD) in Germany. Create a blog based on the platform of the new party during the 1890s.

SUGGESTED SOURCES

Primary Sources

Marx, Karl. *The Portable Karl Marx.* Ed. and trans. Eugenia Kamenka. New York: Penguin, 1983. An excellent collection of important primary sources by Marx and his colleagues. Be sure to read the introduction and the introductory remarks on most of the entries.

———. *Karl Marx: A Reader.* Ed. Jon Elster. Cambridge, U.K.: Cambridge University Press, 1986. A worthwhile volume of selected primary materials with a good introduction.

———. *Readings from Karl Marx.* Ed. Derek Sayer. London: Routledge, 1989. Very good and readable selections from Marx's most important writings.

———. *Karl Marx: The Essential Writings.* 2nd ed. Ed. Frederic L. Bender. Boulder, CO: Westview Press, 1986. A solid selection of useful primary documents.

———. *Capital: An Abridged Edition.* Ed. David McLellan. Oxford: Oxford University Press, 1999. A well-edited edition of *Das Kapital* that captures the most critical and significant sections of Marx's massive study.

——— and Friedrich Engels. *The Marx-Engels Reader.* 2nd ed. Ed. Robert C. Tucker. New York: W. W. Norton, 1978. Tucker's selection of primary materials is excellent. This volume should be useful to most student's writing papers on Marxism.

———. *The Communist Manifesto.* Ed. Gareth Stedman. New York: Penguin, 2002. The Stedman edition of this classic is one of the best; read the introduction.

———. *The Communist Manifesto.* Ed. and trans. L. M. Findlay. Peterborough, Ontario: Broadview Press, 2004. Another worthwhile edition of Marx and Engels's most frequently cited work.

———. *The Communist Manifesto.* Trans. Samuel Moore and introduced by Vladimir Pozner. New York: Bantam, 1992. A very good introduction by Pozner is poignant and useful.

Secondary Sources

Appelbaum, Richard P. *Karl Marx.* Newbury Park, CA: Sage Publications, 1988. A very good biography of Marx and his philosophy.

Banerjee, Deb Kumar, ed. *Marx and His Legacy: A Centennial Appraisal.* Calcutta: K. P. Bagchi, 1988. A collection of scholarly essays on Marx and communism.

Barzun, Jacques. *Darwin, Marx, Wagner: Critique of a Heritage.* 2nd ed. Garden City, NY: Doubleday, 1958. Perhaps the most seminal study on Marx produced in the twentieth century. Students using this book should possess a fundamental knowledge of Marx's life and thought.

Berlin, Isaiah. *Karl Marx: His Life and Environment.* 4th ed. New York: Oxford University Press, 1996. Berlin's critical biography of Marx is still the best introduction to the philosopher and his life thought.

Blaug, Mark, ed. *Karl Marx (1818–1883).* Brookfield, VT: Edward Elgar, 1991. A collection of articles on Marx, economic history, and communism.

Briggs, Asa, and John Callow. *Marx in London: An Illustrated Guide.* Rev. ed. London: Lawrence and Wishart, 2008. Traces Marx's life and work in London, and includes useful illustrations. This was published with the assistance of the Marx Memorial Library.

Burns, Tony, and Ian Fraser, eds. *The Hegel-Marx Connection.* New York: St. Martin's Press, 2000. A collection of scholarly essays on the influence (including dialectical process) that Hegel had upon Marx.

Carver, Terrell, ed. *The Cambridge Companion to Marx.* Cambridge, U.K.: Cambridge University Press, 1991. A one-volume collection of facts, sources, and interpretations on Marx and Marxism.

Dussel, Enrique D. *Towards an Unknown Marx: A Commentary on the Manuscripts of 1861–63.* Trans. Yolanda Angulo and ed. Fred Moseley. London and New York: Routledge, 2001. A important work by a Spanish scholar. The focus is on documents that were written paralleling Marx's work on *Das Kapital.*

Eagleton, Terry. *Marx.* New York: Routledge, 1999. A well-written and accurate life story of Marx that emphasizes his development as a philosopher.

Elster, Jon. *An Introduction to Karl Marx.* Cambridge, U.K.: Cambridge University Press, 1986. An elementary study of Marx and his thought for first-time, serious students.

Furet, François. *Marx and the French Revolution.* Ed. Lucien Calvié and trans. Deborah Kan Furet. Chicago: University of Chicago Press, 1988. Approaches Marx and his philosophy within the French Revolutionary tradition.

Gottlieb, Roger S. *Marxism, 1844–1990: Origins, Betrayal, Rebirth.* New York: Routledge, 1992. A very good account of the development of Marxism from its birth to the collapse of communist governments in 1990.

Hampster-Monk, Iain. *A History of Modern Political Thought: Major Political Thinkers from Hobbes to Marx.* Oxford: Blackwell, 1992. The chapter on Marx provides an accurate and useful introduction to Marx.

Henderson, William Otto. *Marx and Engels and the English Workers; and Other Essays.* London: Cass, 1989. The essay on the English proletariat is a classic and could be useful to students writing papers on relevant topics.

Kolakowski, Leszek. *Main Current of Marxism: The Founders, The Golden Age, The Breakdown.* New York: W. W. Norton, 2008. A Marxist scholar examines the origins and decline of Marxism. This volume consists of segments of published work from the 1970s.

Leopold, David. *The Young Karl Marx: German Philosophy, Modern Politics, and Human Flourishing.* Cambridge, U.K.: Cambridge University Press, 2007. A fascinating and sympathetic study of the forces that motivated Marx during the 1840s.

Mason, David S. *Revolutionary Europe, 1799–1989: Liberty, Equality, Solidarity.* Lanham, MD: Rowman and Littlefield, 2005. Includes a valuable chapter on "Marx, Marxism, and Socialism" that should be useful to many students.

McLellan, David. *Karl Marx: A Biography.* 4th ed. New York: Palgrave Macmillan, 2006. A very good and reliable biography that should be useful to most students.

Meikle, Scott, ed. *Marx*. Burlington, VT: Ashgate/Dartmouth, 2002. A collection of essays on Marx as political philosopher.

Morrison, Kenneth. *Marx, Durheim, Weber: Formations of Modern Social Thought*. 2nd ed. London: Sage Publications, 2006. An examination of Marxism as it contributed and intersected with the philosophies of other social reformers in the nineteenth and early twentieth centuries.

Nimtz, August H. *Marx and Engels: Their Contribution to the Democratic Breakthrough*. Albany: State University of New York Press, 2000. A sympathetic interpretation of Marx and Marxism as a major force in gaining acceptance of democratic principles.

Schecter, Darrow. *The History of the Left from Marx to the Present: Theoretical Perspectives*. New York: Continuum, 2007. Includes two useful chapters on "Marx" and "Western Marxism" that should be considered by students focusing on philosophical issues.

Schmitt, Richard. *Introduction to Marx and Engels: A Critical Reconstruction*. Boulder, CO: Westview Press, 1987. Worthwhile introduction to Marxism.

Singer, Peter. *Marx: A Very Short Introduction*. Oxford: Oxford University Press, 2000. A very good introduction to Marxist thought by a prominent scholar.

Steenson, Gary P. *After Marx, Before Lenin: Marxism and Socialist Working-Class Parties in Europe, 1884–1914*. Pittsburgh: University of Pittsburgh Press, 1991. An intriguing study of the growth of socialist parties and organizations during the three decades prior to the outbreak of the First World War.

Tucker, Robert C. *Karl Marx*. Utrecht/Antwerp, United Netherlands: Aula-boeken, 1961. A popular and worthwhile life of Marx that is useful for novices.

Wheen, Francis. *Karl Marx*. London: Fourth Estate, 1999. An excellent biography of Marx that has received critical acclaim. It includes materials that should be useful to most students.

————. *Marx's "Das Kapital": A Biography*. New York: Atlantic Monthly Press, 2007. Wheen's scholarly analysis of *Das Kapital* has received a positive reception and is a very good resource for students working on relevant topics.

White, James D. *Karl Marx and the Intellectual Origins of Dialectical Materialism*. New York: St. Martin's Press, 1998. A very good study of the influence of Hegel on Marx and Marx's evolution of dialectical materialism as a core tenet of his philosophy.

Wood, Allen W. *Karl Marx*. 2nd ed. New York: Routledge, 2004. A reliable and useful biography that should be available and useful to most students.

Worsley, Peter. *Marx and Marxism*. Rev. ed. New York: Routledge, 2002. A useful and general book on the man and his philosophy.

World Wide Web

"Biography of Karl Marx." http://www.econlib.org/library/Enc/bios/Marx.html. A useful introduction to Marx's life from the *Concise Encyclopedia of Economics*.

"Marxists Internet Archive." http://www.marxists.org/. A very comprehensive Web site on Marx and Marxism. Students writing papers on Marxism should refer to this site.

"Women and Marxism." http://www.marxists.org/subject/women/index.htm. An excellent resource for papers relating to Marxist-feminist concerns.

Multimedia Sources

Hegel and Marx. BBC/Films for the Humanities and Sciences, 1987. DVD. Peter Singer and Bryan Magee discuss the thinking of Hegel and Marx and its impact.

Karl Marx. Films for the Humanities and Sciences, 2006. DVD. Using primary materials and commentary by Merold Westphal (Fordham University), this short film provides an introduction to the philosophical biography of Marx.

Karl Marx: Das Kapital: *From Capitalist Exploitation to Community Revolution*. Blackstone Audio, 2006. Audio CD. Written by David Ramsay Steele; read by Louis Rukeyser. An explanation of Marx's major work.

Marx in 90 Minutes. Blackstone Audio, 2006. Audio CD. Script by Paul Strathern; narrated by Robert Whitfield. Useful introduction to Marx and his philosophy.

Marxism: The Theory that Split a World. Phoenix Learning Group, 2008. DVD. A part of *The Shaping of the Western World* series. A very good introduction to the ideology and the impact of Marxism.

Marxism: Philosophy and Economics. Blackstone Audio, 1998. Audio Tape. Read by Louis Lotorto. An important and useful eight-hour commentary on Marxism by Thomas Sowell (Stanford University).

Steinberg, Jonathan. *European History and European Lives, 1715–1914*. 2003. The Teaching Company. Audio CD. Includes a lecture on "Marx and Engels: The Perfect Collaboration."

The Europeans: An Age of Revolutions. Films for the Humanities & Sciences, 2003. DVD. Includes data on Marx and his impact on nineteenth-century European revolutions.

43. Revolutions of 1848

The Revolutions of 1848 constituted a European-wide political upheaval that challenged the remnants of the order that emerged from the Congress of Vienna in 1815. Only Britain and Russia among the major states failed to experience the revolutions. The causes of these revolutions were complex and multifaceted. In many states, crop failures were frequent during the 1840s and led to hunger and emigration. Other factors that contributed to the outbreak of revolutions included mounting urban unemployment, a general lack of confidence in the existing regimes, a growing sense of helplessness among the working classes, unrealized national aspirations, increased criticism of the status quo by students, newspapers, and social critics, and finally, but still extremely important, a developing belief that a revolutionary outburst was inevitable. From Sicily in January, France in February, and the other states during the late winter and early spring of 1848, the revolutions broke, the existing regimes collapsed quickly, and then stalemate occurred. By the summer of 1848 the revolutionaries were fighting among themselves, and by 1849 there appeared little to credit to the revolutionaries. However, such was not the case—the Revolutions of 1848 did have an impact on the states and societies in which they occurred. In France the Second French Republic preceded the Second Empire of Napoleon III but, even within the Empire, the requirements of the modern age were addressed through changes in the government. In Central Europe, the advocates for constitutional government found an unlikely supporter in Prussia. Hungarian and Italian revolutionaries moved their agendas forward and soon realized substantive progress within the next two decades.

TERM PAPER SUGGESTIONS

1. Develop a paper on the background and causes for the outbreak of the French revolution in February 1848.

2. Write a paper in which you compare and contrast the outbreak and development of the revolutions in the German states (including Austria and Prussia) in 1848.

3. The revolutions of 1848 in the Italian states varied considerably because of conditions and aspirations. Write a paper in which you compare and contrast the causes, development, and consequences of these revolutions—be sure to include the Papal States.

4. During 1849, it was apparent that most of the revolutions had failed. Write a paper in which you discuss and analyze the collapse of the revolutionary movements.

5. Write a paper on the legacy of the revolutions of 1848—in Europe and throughout the world.

ALTERNATIVE TERM PAPER SUGGESTIONS

1. As a conspirator in Paris during January and February 1848, you are involved in a series of meetings with co-conspirators considering the need to overthrow the regime of King Louis Philippe. Develop a podcast of these meetings—be sure to include a range of individuals who hold critical but diverse views of the government and its policies.

2. The revolutions in the German states reflected liberal and national values. Develop a 4–5 minute iMovie in which you interview dissenters in Frankfurt, Vienna, and Budapest.

3. Develop a Web site in which you provide a map that indicates the scope of the revolutions of 1848, accompanying narrative, and comparative data (level of support, immediate and long-term results, and leadership) on the revolutions.

4. As a Hungarian student in Vienna, you are attracted by the revolutionary developments in the Austrian Empire. Develop a blog of your diary entries during the late winter and spring of 1848 in which you indicate the course of the revolutions and your increasing anxiety with the course of the revolutions.

SUGGESTED SOURCES

Primary Sources

Lamartine, Alphonse de. *History of the French Revolution of 1848*. London: Bohn, 1849. An important "history" of the French Revolution by a leading participant—biased but valuable nonetheless.

Lewald, Fanny. *A Year of Revolutions: Fanny Lewald's Recollections of 1848*. Trans. and ed. Hanna Ballin Lewis. Providence, RI: Berghahn, Books, 1997. A very useful and perceptive memoir by an eyewitness to many significant events in 1848.

MacKenna, Benjamin Vicuna. *The Girondins of Chile: Reminiscences of an Eyewitness*. Trans. and ed. John Polt. New York: Oxford University Press, 2003; originally published in 1876. The European revolutions of 1848 influenced an important segment of Chile's educated youth and led to a failed Chilean revolution in 1850–1851.

Marx, Karl. *The Revolutions of 1848: Political Writings.* 2 vols. New York: Penguin, 1993. While not a significant leader of the revolutions in 1848, Marx was moved by the events and provided a socialist interpretation of these events in volume one of this set.

Phipps, Constantine Henry. *A Year of Revolution: From a Journal Kept in Paris in 1848 by the Marquis of Normandy.* Chestnut Hill, MA: Elibron/Adamant Media, 2000; originally published in 1857. An important and useful memoir by an eyewitness to many events in Paris.

Tocqueville, Alexis de. *Recollections: The French Revolution of 1848.* Ed. J. P. Mayer and A. P. Kerr. Garden City, NY: Doubleday, 1970. Also available as an e-book at http://books.google.com/books?id=6Hhz6q5hsYcC&pg=PT1 &lpg=PT1&dq=Tocqueville,+Alexis+de.+Recollections:+The+French +Revolution+of+1848.+Edited+by+J.+P.+Mayer+and+A.+P.+Kerr. &source=web&ots=WH2cuLvbDZ&sig=LBou3TYr-jO81LeJLsaYWoh mkII&hl=en&sa=X&oi=book_result&resnum=1&ct=result. An important memoir by an astute contemporary.

Secondary Sources

Clark, T. J. *Image of the People: Gustave Courbet and the 1848 Revolution.* 2nd ed. London: Longman, 1995. A useful study on French artist Courbet's role and influence during the 1848 revolution.

Deak, Istvan. *Lawful Revolution: Louis Kossuth and the Hungarians, 1848–1849.* London: Phoenix Press, 2001. A seminal study of Kossuth and the revolution that he led in Hungary.

Duveau, Georges. *1848: The Making of Revolution.* Cambridge, MA: Harvard University Press, 1984. A good introduction to the scope and significance of the revolutions of 1848.

Eastwood, James, and Paul Tabori. *'48. The Year of Revolutions.* London: Meridian, 1948. Still a worthwhile general history of the revolutions.

Elton, Godfrey. *The Revolutionary Idea in France, 1789–1871.* New York: AMS Press, 1971. A very important study on ideology as a fundamental basis for revolutionary action in France.

Evans, R. J. W., and Hartmut Pogge von Strandmann, eds. *The Revolutions in Europe, 1848–1849: From Reform to Reaction.* New York: Oxford University Press, 2002. An important collection of essays on the origins and collapse of the revolutions of 1848–1849.

Eyck, Frank, ed. *The Revolutions of 1848–49.* New York: Barnes and Noble, 1972. A useful collection of essays and documents on the European revolutions.

Fasel, George. *Europe in Upheaval: The Revolutions of 1848.* Chicago: Rand McNally, 1970. An important study of the impact of the revolutions on European institutions and the order established at the Congress of Vienna.

Fortescue, William. *France and 1848: The End of Monarchy.* London: Routledge, 2005. Very good on the aspirations of the revolutionaries and the progress of the revolution in 1848–1849.

Hobsbawn, E. J. *The Age of Revolution: 1789–1848.* Cambridge, U.K.: Cambridge University Press, 1980. An extremely important scholarly study that unifies the initial revolution and the Revolution of 1848, as well as stresses economic, social, and political factors.

Jones, Peter. *The 1848 Revolutions.* 2nd ed. Seminar Studies in History. London: Longman, 1995. An excellent resource on the revolutions, and a possible source of term paper topics.

Kale, Steven. *French Salons: High Society and Political Sociability from the Old Regime to the Revolution of 1848.* Baltimore, MD: The Johns Hopkins University Press, 2005. An excellent scholarly study of the transformation of the life-style of the French aristocracy caused by the many revolutions in France.

Kömer, Axel, ed. *1848—A European Revolution?: International Ideas and National Memories of 1848.* New York: St. Martin's Press, 2000. A collection of important essays on the issues of national identity and historical consciousness that were significant in the mid-nineteenth century.

Moggach, Douglas, and Paul Leduc Browne, eds. *The Social Question and the Democratic Revolution: Marx and Legacy of 1848.* Ottawa: University of Ottawa Press, 2000. Eleven essays by prominent authorities on a range of relevant topics that are useful for most papers on Marx and the revolutions.

Namier, Louis. *1848: The Revolution of the Intellectuals.* 8th ed. New York: W. W. Norton, 1974. A classic study that still stands as an important work on the revolutions of 1848.

Noyes, P. H. *Organization and Revolution: Working-Class Associations in the German Revolutions of 1848–1849.* Princeton, NJ: Princeton University Press, 1966. A scholarly examination of the role of the associations in advancing the revolutionary agenda in the major German states during 1848–1849.

Price, Roger. *The Revolutions of 1848.* Atlantic Heights, NJ: Humanities Press, 1989. A general history of the revolutions that is reliable and useful.

Robertson, Priscilla Smith. *Revolutions of 1848: A Social History.* Princeton, NJ: Princeton University Press, 1967; originally published in 1952. Still an outstanding source on the social aspects of the revolutions in Europe.

Sewell, William H. *Work and Revolution in France: The Language of Labor from the Old Regime to 1848.* Berkeley: University of California Press, 1999.

A valuable and important book by a noted historian of the social and cultural connections with revolution.

Siemann, Wolfram. *The German Revolution of 1848–49.* Trans. Christiane Banerji. New York: St. Martin's, 1988. Still the best history of the revolutions in the German states.

Sperber, Jonathan. *The European Revolutions, 1848–1851.* Cambridge, U.K.: Cambridge University Press, 1994. Very good comprehensive history that should be useful to most students.

Stearns, Peter N. *1848: The Revolutionary Tide in Europe.* New Brunswick, NJ: Transactions Publishers, 1987. An outstanding history by a trusted historian—most students will want to look at Stearns's classic study.

———. *The Revolutions of 1848.* London: Weidenfield and Nicolson, 1974. Excellent in all regards—most public and university libraries should still hold this title.

Thomson, Guy, ed. *The European Revolutions of 1848 and the Americas.* London: Institute of Latin American Studies, 2002. A very useful and reliable collection of essays on the impact of the European revolutions on Latin America societies.

World Wide Web

"1848: The Course of Events and 19th Century Liberalism." http://www.fordham.edu/halsall/mod/lect/mod18.html; and "1848: Europe in Revolt." http://www.fordham.edu/halsall/mod/modsbook19.html. The Internet Modern History Sourcebook, developed by Paul Halsall and maintained by Fordham University, section of the revolutions includes primary and secondary sources on France, Austria, and Prussia/Germany, a timeline, and links to other sources.

"Mass Politics and the Revolutions of 1848." http://web.bham.ac.uk/1848/. A valuable study and tutorial by John Breuilly that includes a chronology on the revolutions.

Multimedia Sources

"Revolutions of 1848." http://uk.encarta.msn.com/encyclopedia_761553485/revolutions_of_1848.html. Includes 11 copies of illustrations and photographs of revolutionary and conservative leaders.

"Street Fighting in Vienna" and "Five Days in Milan." http://encarta.msn.com/media_941547556_761553485_-1_1/Street_Fighting_in_Vienna_1848.html. Includes copies of contemporary illustrations.

The Europeans: An Age of Revolutions. Films for the Humanities & Sciences, 2003. DVD. Includes data on the revolutions of 1848 and their consequences.

44. Second Sikh War (1848–1849)

The Second Sikh War followed the closure of the initial Anglo-Sikh conflict by two years. This war was not simply the continuation of the First Sikh War; it reflected the complexities, the disintegration, and the vulnerability of Sikh independent political institutions and life. Not only was the British and Sikhs conflict evident, it was aggravated by the Sikh separatist culture within the context of the larger Muslim-Hindu among Indian population. These conflicts manifested themselves within an Indian feudal order that confronted a determined Afghan foe on one frontier and the British Empire on another in the form of the British East India Company. Feudal versus national, Islam versus Hindu, and eastern versus western—these were the parameters of the struggle for the Punjab in the middle of the nineteenth century. And yet, these lines were blurred by Muslims who fought with the British along with Hindu troops—it was not a simple era. The Second Sikh broke out in April 1848 when the viceroy of Multan, Dewan Mulraj, plotted rebellion against the Lahore government. British officials were murdered and insurrection gained momentum. By September 1848 the war was underway. While the Sikh rebels enjoyed some limited success in the early encounters during the fall, the British forces under Sir Hugh Gough gained the upper hand by December and, during the spring of 1849, the British won major battles against the Sikhs. By March 1849 the military phase of the war was concluded. The Sikhs lost because of the failure of administration, a shortage of food, some Muslim support for the British, and the British military capabilities in leadership, men, and material.

TERM PAPER SUGGESTIONS

1. Compare and contrast the origins and significance of the First and Second Sikh Wars.

2. Develop a paper that is focused on the internal political and social chaos with the Sikh kingdom during the two years prior to the outbreak of the war.

3. Write a paper on the immediate causes for the outbreak of the Second Sikh War.

4. Develop a paper on the geopolitical transformation of India that resulted from the collapse of the Sikh kingdom. Include a map that reflects the primacy of Britain after its victory.

5. Compare and contrast the performance of the Sikh and British armies during the Second Sikh War.

ALTERNATIVE TERM PAPER SUGGESTIONS

1. As a Sikh teenager who was taught to admire the "Golden" age of Ranjit Singh, write a blog giving your assessment of the collapse of law and government during the decade following his death in 1839.

2. Develop a visual graphic that represents the developing anarchy in Sikh society between 1846 and 1848.

3. Write and develop a 3–5 minute podcast that assesses the progress of the Second Sikh War through 1848.

4. Develop a 3 minute iMovie (with graphics) that reflects the British policies and strategy during the Second Sikh War.

SUGGESTED SOURCES

Primary Sources

Anglesey, Marquess of. *Sergeant Pearman's Memoirs, Being Chiefly His Account of Service with the Third (King's Own) Light Dragoons in India from 1846 to 1853, including the First and Second Sikh Wars.* London: Jonathan Cape, 1968. A worthwhile printed primary source written by a reliable eyewitness and edited by a scholar.

Gough, Sir Charles, and Arthur D. Innes. *The Sikhs and the Sikh Wars.* London: Innes, 1897. This volume provides many printed primary sources.

Guy, Alan J., ed. *Military Miscellany: Manuscripts from the Seven Years War, the First and Second Sikh Wars and the First World War.* Stroud, U.K.: Sutton Publishing for the Army Records Society, 1991. A good collection of primary materials on the two Sikh wars that provide personal insights to the expectations and uncertainties associated with these conflicts. Included are Daniel George Robinson's (1826–1877; British military cartographer) letters from India, 1845–1849.

Sandford, Daniel A. *A Journal of the Second Sikh War: The Experiences of an Ensign of the 2nd Bengal European Regiment during the Campaign in the Punjab, India, 1848–49.* London: Leonaur, Ltd., 2007. Excellent resource by an intelligent and perceptive participant.

Thackwell, Edward J. *Narratives of the Second Sikh War in 1848–49 with a Detailed Account of the Battles of Ramnugger, the Passage of the Chenats, Chillianwallha, Goojorat, etc.* 2nd ed. Uckfield, U.K.: Naval and Military

Press, 2006. Thackwell provides credible and detailed information not found elsewhere.

Secondary Sources

Bruce, George. *Six Battles for India: Anglo-Sikh Wars, 1845–46 and 1848–49.* Worthing, U.K.: Littlehampton Book Services, 1969. Very good on the military aspects of the conflicts.

Burton, Reginald George. *The First and Second Sikh Wars.* 2nd ed. Yardley, PA: Westholme Publishing, 2007; reprint of the 1911 edition. Still a reliable and readable history of the two Anglo-Sikh wars, based on primary and secondary sources.

Cook, H. C. B. *The Sikh Wars 1845–49.* Delhi: Leo Cooper, 1975. A balanced interpretation of the wars and the impact that they had on India and Britain.

Hasrat, Bikrama Jit. *Anglo-Sikh Relations, 1799–1849: A Reappraisal of the Rise and Fall of the Sikhs.* Hoshiarpur: [n.p.], 1968. A Sikh interpretation of the wars and their impact on the Sikhs.

Hernon, Ian. *Blood in the Sand: More Forgotten Wars of the Nineteenth Century.* Stroud, U.K.: Sutton, 2001. Includes a very good chapter on the Second Sikh War, concise but authoritative.

James, Lawrence. *The Rise and Fall of the British Empire.* New York: St. Martin's, 1994. A reliable standard text that places the specific incidents in British imperial history in the context of the sweep of British imperialism as an historical force. It provides a very good bibliography.

World Wide Web

"Anglo-Sikh War II." http://www.sikhiwiki.org/index.php/Anglo_Sikh_War_II. An introduction to the war from the *Sikh Encyclopedia.*

"Anglo-Sikh Wars." http://www.kabira.freeservers.com/anglosikhwars.html. A solid introduction to the two wars with statistics on military engagements.

"Battle of Ramnagar" (November 22, 1848). http://www.britishbattles.com/second-sikh-war/ramnagar.htm. A detailed and accurate account of the battle in which the British leaders, General Charles Cureton and Colonel William Havelock, were killed. Included are one photograph and five illustrations.

"Battle of Chillianwallah" (January 13, 1849). http://www.britishbattles.com/second-sikh-war/chillianwallah.htm. A valuable account of an indecisive but important battle in the Second Sikh War. Included are a battlefield map and eight illustrations.

"Battle of Goojerat" (February 21, 1849). http://www.britishbattles.com/second-sikh-war/goojerat.htm. An excellent account of the battle between the British Major General Sir Hugh Gough and the Sikh leader, Shere Singh. Included are a battlefield map and nine illustrations.

Multimedia Sources

"Empire and Faith, Kinship and War: A Century of Sikh Photographs (1849–1948). http://www.swfftoronto.com/exhibition/exhibition.php. Provides photographs of locations and individuals who were significant in both of the Anglo-Sikh Wars, exhibited at the Fifth Annual Spinning Wheel Film Festival, 2007, at the Isabel Bader Theatre, Toronto, Ontario,

"This Sceptred Isle: Empire, The First Sikh War." BBC/Radio 4 (February 22, 2006). Written by Christopher Lee; narrated by Juliet Stevenson, with readings by Christopher Eccleston. http://www.bbc.co.uk/radio4/schedule/2006/02/22/day. Also available at http://www.bbc.co.uk/radio4/history/empire/episodes/episode_48.shtml. In addition to the First Sikh War, this program provides useful information on the Second Sikh War.

45. Schleswig-Holstein Question (1848–1865)

Schleswig and Holstein were duchies located between Denmark and the German Confederation during the mid-nineteenth century. Both of the duchies had historic links with the Danish throne and German principalities. From 1848 to 1865, a period of increased nationalist identity and agitation, the status of the duchies became a major diplomatic issue when the German majority in Schleswig and Holstein revolted against Denmark when King Frederick VII (1808–1863), while granting them a liberal constitution, announced that they were part of Denmark. When Prussia sent troops to defend the local people from the Danish army in 1848, the First Schleswig-Holstein War commenced. It ended in 1851 when the Danish army was driven from Schleswig. The status of the duchies was not altered by the London Protocol that brought an end to the hostilities, but it remained a major point of contention between the Danes and the German Confederation. In 1864 the Danes again attempted to annex the duchies. Their actions resulted in the disastrous Second Schleswig-Holstein War (1864–1865) that involved a joint

Austrian-Prussian attack against Denmark. The Danes were defeated and the duchies were to be jointly administered by the Austrians and the Prussians. The Prussian Chancellor, Otto von Bismarck (1815–1898), manipulated the Austro-Prussian administration and brought about the German Civil War in 1866, after which Prussia openly assumed leadership of the German nationalist movement.

TERM PAPER SUGGESTIONS

1. Develop a term paper on the outbreak and prosecution of the First Schleswig-Holstein War.
2. Write a paper on the outbreak and prosecution of the Second Schleswig-Holstein War.
3. Write a paper on the role that Bismarck played in seizing the duchies from the Danes. What was his motive?
4. Develop a paper on the consequences of the Second Schleswig-Holstein War and the system that was established for the joint administration of the duchies.

ALTERNATIVE TERM PAPER SUGGESTIONS

1. Develop a podcast in which Bismarck and Moltke consider the opportunities that Prussia may have with the evolving crisis over Schleswig-Holstein.
2. As a young Dane living in Schleswig, you find yourself in a very difficult position in 1864. Create a blog on the crisis, your thoughts on nationalism and nationality, and your decision on whether you will stay and become a Dane living under German control or migrate to Denmark.
3. Develop an iMovie that consists of two parts: Part 1: the Austrian and Prussian representatives establish the terms of their joint administration of the duchies in 1864, and Part 2: the same representatives meet in 1866 to complain about the failure of the process.

SUGGESTED SOURCES

Primary Sources

Bismarck, Otto von. *Reflections and Reminiscences.* Ed. Theodore S. Hamerow. New York: Harper and Row, 1968. An excellent selection of Bismarck's writings, including information on the Schleswig-Holstein Question.
Moltke, Helmuth Graf von. *Strategy: Its Theory and Application: The Wars for German Unification, 1866–1871.* Westport, CT: Greenwood Press,

1971. This is an excellent primary source by the Prussian field commander during the Austro-Prussian and Franco-Prussian wars.

Salisbury, Robert Arthur. *Essays by the Late Marquess of Salisbury.* 2 vols. New York: Dutton, 1905. Available as an e-book at http://www.archive.org/details/essaysbylatemarq00sali. Includes valuable information and insights on Schleswig-Holstein.

Solger, Reinhold. *Memorial on the Schleswig-Holstein Question: Addressed to the Hon. Bradford R. Wood, Minister to the Court of Denmark, Copenhagen.* Chestnut Hill, MA: Elibron/Adamant, 2005; originally published in 1862. Provides primary materials within the text, all relating to the multiple issues associated with the question.

Wurm, Christian Frederick. *A Letter to Viscount Palmerston Concerning the Question of Schleswig-Holstein (1850).* London: Longman, Brown, Green, 1850. Available as an e-book at http://www.archive.org/details/lettertoviscount00wurmrich. An open letter to the British Foreign Secretary on the complexities of the issue, written shortly after the Revolutions of 1848–1849.

Secondary Sources

Bucholz, Arden. *Moltke and the German Wars, 1864–1871.* New York: Palgrave, 2001. This is an outstanding account of Marshal Helmuth Graf von Moltke's leadership of Prussian forces during the Schleswig-Holstein War, the Austro-Prussian War, and the Franco-Prussian War.

Carr, William. *The Origins of the Wars of German Unification.* New York: Longman, 1991. Two chapters of this well-written book address the causes for the Schleswig-Holstein War of 1864 and the Austro-Prussian War of 1866.

———. *Schleswig-Holstein, 1815–48: A Study in National Conflict.* Manchester: Manchester University Press, 1963. An excellent history of the question and its place in Danish and German national histories.

Darmstaedter, Friedrich. *Bismarck and the Creation of the Second Reich.* Piscataway, NJ: Transaction Publishers, 2008. Includes extensive information on Schleswig-Holstein and the German-Danish War.

Farmer, Alan, and Andrina Stiles. *The Unification of Germany 1815–1919.* 3rd ed. London: Hodder Murray, 2007. Includes information on the question and the war between Denmark and the Prussian and Austrian allies.

Hjelholt, Holger. *Great Britain, the Danish-German Conflict and the Danish Succession 1850–1852. From the London Protocol to the Treaty of London (the 2nd of August 1850 and the 8th of May 1852.)* Kobenhavn: Munksgaard, 1971. A very reliable and absorbing account of the Schleswig-Holstein question during the early 1850s.

Jorgensen, Adolf Ditler. *The Dano-German Question.* Copenhagen: H. Hagerup, 1900. A dated but useful study of the question and its impact on Danish-German relations.

Leman, Katherine Anne. *Bismarck.* New York: Pearson Longman, 2004. Very good on Bismarck's manipulation of the Schleswig-Holstein Question.

Müller, Frederick M. *Last Essays: Essays on Language, Folklore, and Other Subjects.* New York: AMS Press, 1978; reprint of the original 1901 edition. Includes an excellent essay on the complexities associated with the Schleswig-Holstein Question.

Pflanze, Otto. *Bismarck and the Development of Germany: The Period of Unification, 1815–1871.* Princeton, NJ: Princeton University Press, 1990. This is volume one of a three volume study on Bismarck and Germany, and it remains as the standard on the subject. Pflanze's scholarship reflects his mastery of the primary sources and his in-depth knowledge of the nineteenth-century German world.

———. *The Unification of Germany, 1848–1871.* Melbourne, FL: Krieger, 1979. In this valuable collection of excerpts from sources, Pflanze compares interpretations on German unification.

Sandiford, Keith A. *Great Britain and the Schleswig-Holstein Question 1848–64: A Study in Diplomacy, Politics, and Public Opinion.* Toronto: University of Toronto Press, 1975. A scholarly account of British involvement with the question and how it adjusted to Prussian dominance on the provinces.

Showalter, Dennis E. *The Wars of German Unification.* London: Arnold, 2004. Excellent on the Schleswig-Holstein Question.

Steefel, Lawrence D. *The Schleswig-Holstein Question.* Cambridge, MA: Harvard University Press, 1932. An old but very reliable and useful history of the Schleswig-Holstein Question with outstanding maps and documentation.

Svendsen, Nick. *The First Schleswig-Holstein War 1848–50.* Tulsa, OK: Helion, 2008. Excellent on all aspects of the struggle—causes, military, and consequences.

Twiss, Travers. *On the Relations of the Duchies of Schleswig and Holstein to the Crown of Denmark and the German Confederation, and on the treaty-engagements of the great European powers in reference thereto.* London: Longman, Brown, Green. 1848. Available as an e-book at http://www.archive.org/details/onrelationsofduc00twisuoft. A contemporary account that includes extensive information that should be useful.

World Wide Web

"Lord Palmerston Quotes." http://thinkexist.com/quotation/the_schleswig-holstein_question_is_so_complicated/340148.html. Includes the famous Palmerston statement on the Schleswig-Holstein Question.

"Schleswig-Holstein Question." http://www.britannica.com/EBchecked/topic/
527640/Schleswig-Holstein-question. Reliable information on the question and the crisis that ensued.

"Schleswig-Holstein Question." http://everything2.com/?node_id=1237519.
Provides introductory information on the question and its significance.

"Schleswig-Holstein Question." http://www.encyclopedia.com/doc/1B1
-377940.html. Provides a general introduction to the issue.

Multimedia Sources

Hedwig, Douglas. "National Song, Schleswig-Holstein," from the album *The Art
of the Posthorn—From Countryside to Concert Hall.* Elmsford, NY: MSR
Classics, 2006. Performed by Jorge Parodi. Available for MP3 download.
Schleswig-Holstein/Hamburg. Kiel: Lamdesvermessungsamt Schleswig-Holstein,
1998. CD. Provides excellent topographic maps of Schleswig-Holstein.

46. T'ai Ping Rebellion (1850–1864)

The T'ai Ping Rebellion was a fierce and bloody civil war in China
between the Imperial Government and its forces and the followers of the
Christian mystic Hong Xiuquan (1814–1864). During the 1840s China
was in a weakened and chaotic state. The Imperial Government was
poorly led and administered and suffered from extensive corruption, and
the European powers were extending their authority in Hong Kong and
other regions that they could exploit economically. Hong Xiuquan organized a sect that was focused on reforms: predominance of the Christian
Bible; communal rather than private property; a classless and egalitarian
society; and prohibitions against slavery, prostitution, polygamy, and the
use of alcohol, opium, and tobacco. Hong attracted millions of
Chinese to his program and, in 1851, he formally established his movement as the Heavenly Kingdom of T'ai Ping. The movement spread rapidly and mounted a serious challenge to the Imperial Government.
Hong's forces repeatedly defeated the Imperial army and inflicted
100,000s of casualties during the early years of the rebellion. The Imperial
government responded to the revolt by expanding its forces. By the late
1850s the Imperial forces had inflicted a series of casualties on the rebel
armies. In 1860 the rebel forces failed to take Shanghai, which was
defended by Chinese troops under the leadership of British officers,
including General Charles G. Gordon (1833–1885). Hong withdrew

from the active leadership of the rebellion, and by 1864 Imperial forces had gained control of the lands that had been under rebel control. Hong committed suicide to avoid capture. Some authorities contend that the T'ai Ping Rebellion resulted in over 15 million Chinese deaths.

TERM PAPER SUGGESTIONS

1. Write a paper on Hong Xiuquan's aspirations for a new reformed China.
2. Develop a paper on the conditions that attracted many Chinese to Hong's ideas and values.
3. Write a paper on the military aspects of the rebellion. What was the turning point in the conflict?
4. Write a paper on the consequences of the T'ai Ping Rebellion.
5. Develop a paper on the role of Charles G. Gordon in suppressing the rebellion.

ALTERNATIVE TERM PAPER SUGGESTIONS

1. Develop a podcast in which you interview Hong Xiuquan on his beliefs and plans for China.
2. Develop an iMovie in which the five "kings" of the Heavenly Kingdom meet to discuss the mounting threat to their positions by the rejuvenated Imperial army.
3. As an American correspondent covering the rebellion, you are appalled by the magnitude of the violence and the loss of life that is occurring during the rebellion. Develop a blog on the rebellion.

SUGGESTED SOURCES

Primary Sources

Cheng, James Chester. *Chinese Sources for the Taiping Rebellion, 1850–1864.* New York: Oxford University Press, 1963. An excellent work that examines the Chinese sources on the Rebellion.

Clarke, Prescott, and J. S. Gregory, eds. *Western Reports on Taiping: A Selection of Documents.* Honolulu: University of Hawaii Press, 1982. A useful collection of documents that may assist in understanding the contemporary Euro-American analysis of the Rebellion.

Giquel, Prosper. *A Journal of the Chinese Civil War, 1864.* Ed. Steven A Leibo. Trans. Steven A. Leibo and Debbie Weston. Honolulu: University of Hawaii Press, 1985. The memoir of a French eyewitness to much that occurred during the last year of the Rebellion.

Gordon, Charles G. *Events in the Taiping Rebellion.* London: W. H. Allen, 1891. Recollection by a prominent British general who was involved in China during the 1850s and 1860s.

Great Britain. *Further Papers Relating to the Rebellion in China: In Continuation of Papers Presented to Parliament, May 2, 1862: Presented to Both Houses of Parliament by Command of Her Majesty.* San Francisco: Chinese Materials Center, 1975; originally published in 1862. Official British documents relating to the Taiping Rebellion.

Michael, Franz H. *The Taiping Rebellion: History and Documents.* 3 vols. Seattle: University of Washington Press, 1966–1971. The best collection of documents on the Rebellion—students will want access to this rich depository.

Morse, Hosea Ballou. *In the Days of the Taipings: Being the Recollections of Ting Kienchang, otherwise Meisun. . . .* San Francisco: Chinese Materials Center, 1974; originally published in 1927. A worthwhile primary source by a prominent Chinese participant.

Scarth, John. *Twelve Years in China: The People, the Rebels, and the Mandarins, by a British Resident.* Wilmington, DE: Scholarly Resources, 1972; originally published in 1860. Scarth's memoir includes extensive information on the movement that should be very useful.

Williams, Frederick Wells. *The Life and Letters of Samuel Wells Williams, LL.D., Missionary, Diplomatist, Sinologue.* New York: G. P. Putnam's Sons, 1889. Includes firsthand information on the Taiping movement.

Secondary Sources

Boardman, Eugene Powers. *Christian Influence Upon the Ideology of the Taiping Rebellion, 1851–1864.* Madison: University of Wisconsin Press, 1952. A dated but still useful study that focuses on the Christian origins of the movement.

Chien, Yu-wen. *The Taiping Revolutionary Movement.* New Haven, CT: Yale University Press, 1973. An excellent history of the movement and its place in the Chinese revolutionary tradition.

Chin, Shunshin. *The Taiping Rebellion.* Trans. Joshua A. Fogel. Armonk, NY: M. E. Sharpe, 2001. A worthwhile and accessible history that should be helpful to most students.

Grasso, June M., Jay Corrin, and Michael Kort. *Modernization and Revolution in China: From the Opium Wars to World Power.* 3rd ed. Armonk, NY: M. E. Sharpe, 2004. An excellent and reliable study that includes data on the rebellion.

Gray, Jack. *Rebellions and Revolutions: China from the 1800s to 2000*. 2nd ed. New York: Oxford University Press, 2003. A worthwhile study of the forces of change in China—both internal and external—during the nineteenth and twentieth centuries.

Hall, William James. *Tsêng Kuo-Fan and the Taiping Rebellion: With a Short Sketch of his Later Career*. New Haven, CT: Yale University Press, 1927. A good biography of a leader of the movement and insurrection.

Heath, Ian. *The Taiping Rebellion 1851–66*. Oxford: Osprey, 1994. Excellent on all aspects of the military conflicts.

Olson, James Stuart, and Robert Shadle, eds. *Historical Dictionary of the British Empire*. Westport, CT: Greenwood Press, 1996. Includes information on the T'ai Ping Rebellion.

Reilly, Thomas H. *The Taiping Heavenly Kingdom: Rebellion and the Blasphemy of Empire*. Seattle: University of Washington Press, 2004. A scholarly study that examines the cultural threat posed by the T'ai Ping Rebellion.

Schoppa, R. Keith. *The Columbia Guide to Modern Chinese History*. New York: Columbia University Press, 2000. An indispensable resource for studying any topic in modern Chinese history.

Smith, Richard J. *Mercenaries and Mandarins: The Ever-Victorious Army in Nineteenth Century*. Millwood, NY: KTO Press, 1978. A very good history of military activities in China during the 1850s and 1860s.

Spence, Jonathan D. *The Taiping Vision of a Christian China 1836–1864*. Waco, TX: Markham, 1996. An intriguing study of this idea by a prominent American scholar of China.

———. *God's Chinese Son: The Taiping Heavenly Kingdom of Hong Xiuquan*. New York: W. W. Norton, 1997. Excellent scholarly work that is well written and argued. Students working on papers related to Hong should refer to this book.

Têng, Ssǔ-yü. *Historiography of the Taiping Rebellion*. Cambridge, MA: Harvard University Press, 1962. While dated, Têng's analysis of the literature on the rebellion is still unsurpassed.

———. *The Taiping Rebellion and the Western Powers: A Comprehensive Survey*. Oxford: Clarendon, 1971. A detailed study of the response of the West to the outbreak of the rebellion and its development.

———. *New Light on the History of the Taiping Rebellion*. Cambridge, MA: Harvard University Press, 1950. A seminal study on the rebellion that impacted later works.

Wagner, Rudolf G. *Reenacting the Heavenly Vision: The Role of Religion in the Taiping Rebellion*. Berkeley: University of California Press, 1982. A very good scholarly study on the spiritual origins of the movement.

Wakeman, Frederic E. *Strangers at the Gate: Social Disorder in South China, 1839–1862.* Berkeley: University of California Press, 1966. An examination of the internal social, economic, and political conditions in China from the beginning of the First Opium War to the T'ai Ping Rebellion and the Second Opium War.

World Wide Web

"Taiping Rebellion." http://www.bambooweb.com/articles/t/a/Taiping _Rebellion.html. A very good introduction to the rebellion and additional links.

"Taiping Rebellion." http://www.history.com/encyclopedia.do?articleId =223600. Provides a good introduction to the rebellion and its place in nineteenth-century Chinese history.

"Taiping Rebellion." http://www.lycos.com/info/taiping-rebellion.html. A compilation of articles on the rebellion; collectively they present an extensive history of the revolt.

"The Taiping Rebellion." http://wsu.edu/~dee/CHING/TAIPING.HTM. An extensive description of the movement and the rebellion that should be useful.

"The Taiping Rebellion." http://gencobb.com/think/history-pages/the-taiping -rebellion/. An excellent introduction to the rebellion and its development.

"The Taiping Rebellion and Second Opium War." http://www.fsmitha.com/h3/ h38china.htm. Provides reliable information on the rebellion and the war.

Multimedia Sources

"Taiping Rebellion Army vs. Government troop 1." http://www.youtube.com/ watch?v=C-k4M9gb5fM. Excellent footage of a dramatic reenactment of a battle, in Chinese with English subtitles.

"Taiping Rebellion Army vs, Government troop 2." http://www.youtube.com/ watch?v=RLTghC8_Qqc&feature=related. A continuation of the previous site.

47. Second Burmese War (1852–1853)

A brief struggle initiated over British accusations that Burma was violating minor terms of the Treaty of Yandabo, which had concluded the First Burmese War in 1826. Lord Dalhousie, Governor General of India, sent a representative to Rangoon to threaten the Burmese with war unless they complied with British demands. The Burmese acquiesced but a British naval force blockaded the port of Rangoon and the war began. British victories at Martaban and Rangoon were taken in April 1852, and other victories ensued in May and June. By the end of the summer most of the hostilities were concluded. The British seized the prominent city of Prome in October. British intentions were quite obvious. Dalhousie, whose long-term goal was the annexation of all of Burma, was satisfied with the annexation of the valuable province of Pegu. Dalhousie announced that annexation on January 20, 1853, and declared that the war was over. There was no negotiated treaty. This announcement resulted in the overthrowing of the Burmese government and continuing civil unrest.

TERM PAPER SUGGESTIONS

1. Develop a paper on the background and causes of the Second Burmese War.
2. Write a paper on the prosecution of the war. Compare and contrast the strengths and weaknesses of both combatants.
3. Write an analysis of British policy in Burma. Was there any hope that an independent Burma could survive?
4. Develop a paper on the impact of the Second Burmese War on Burma and its people.

ALTERNATIVE TERM PAPER SUGGESTIONS

1. Develop a podcast in which the Burmese leaders attempt to resolve the crisis of 1852, which was initiated by the British.
2. As a young member of the British House of Commons in 1852, you are aware of British policies and actions in Burma. Create a blog in which you assess this policy and consider its political, diplomatic, economic, and ethical issues.
3. Develop an iMovie in which Dalhousie and his staff discuss their vision for Britain in Burma—what are the advantages and disadvantages of moving forward with annexation?

SUGGESTED SOURCES

Primary Sources

Dalhousie, James Andrew. *The Dalhousie-Phayre Correspondence, 1852–1856.* Ed. D. G. E. Hall. London: Oxford University Press, 1932. A very useful primary source that is focused on Burma through the correspondence between Dalhousie and Arthur Purves Phayre.

Laurie, William F. B. *Pegu: Being a Narrative of Events during the Second Burmese War, from August 1852 to Its Conclusion in June 1853; with a succinct continuation down to February 1854.* London: Smith, Elder, 1854. A valuable primary source by a leading military figure in the conflict.

———. *The Second Burmese War: A Narrative of the Operations at Rangoon in 1852.* Whitefish, MT: Kessinger, 2007; originally published in 1854. A very good edition of Laurie's work that should be available to students.

———. *The Second Burmese War: A Narrative of the Operations at Rangoon in 1852.* Chestnut Hill, MA: Adamant/Elibron, 2002; originally published in 1853. Another useful edition of the same work.

———. *Our Burmese Wars and Relations with Burma: Being an Abstract of Military and Political Operations, 1824-25-26, and 1852–1853.* 2nd ed. London: W. H. Allen, 1885. Both memoir and history, this volume by Laurie should be helpful to some students.

Marks, John Ebenezer. *Forty Years in Burma.* Ed. W. C. B. Purser. London: Hutchinson, 1917. The personal recollections of a missionary who served many years in Burma.

Secondary Sources

Bečka, Jan. *Historical Dictionary of Myanmar.* Metuchen, NJ: Scarecrow Press, 1995. A very reliable and useful reference work that includes information on the Burmese wars.

Blackburn, Terence R. *The British Humiliation of Burma.* Bangkok: Orchid Press, 2000. A critical assessment of the British domination of Burma during the nineteenth and twentieth centuries—includes information on the First Burmese War.

Ghosh, Parimal. *Brave Men of the Hills: Resistance and Rebellion in Burma, 1825–1932.* Honolulu: University of Hawaii Press, 2000. A scholarly study of the Burmese resistance movement against foreign intervention.

Hack, Karl, and Tobias Rettig, eds. *Colonial Armies in Southeast Asia.* Routledge Studies in the Modern History of Asia, no. 33. London: Routledge, 2006. Includes an essay on the British in Burma by Robert Taylor that may be useful. The maps are quite good.

Hall, Daniel G. *Europe and Burma: A Study of European Relations with Burma to the Annexation of Thibaw's Kingdom, 1886.* New York: Oxford University Press, 1945. A scholarly account of Burma's unfortunate relationships with the European states prior to its collapse.

Harvey, Godfrey E. *British Rule in Burma, 1824–1942.* London: Faber and Faber, 1946. A useful study of the British governance in Burma—includes information on all of the Anglo-Burmese wars.

Htin Aung, U. *The Stricken Peacock: Anglo-Burmese Relations, 1752–1948.* The Hague: M. Nijhoff, 1965. A critical analysis of Britain's role in Burma—includes information on the Anglo-Burmese wars.

James, Lawrence. *The Rise and Fall of the British Empire.* New York: St. Martin's, 1994. Provides reliable information on the Anglo-Burmese wars.

Nisbet, John. *Burma under British Rule—and Before.* Westminster: A. Constable, 1901. A dated but useful work that is sympathetic to the British actions in Burma.

Pollak, Oliver B. *Empires in Collision: Anglo-Burmese Relations in the Mid-Nineteenth Century.* Westport, CT: Greenwood Press, 1979. Excellent seminal study that all students working on this topic should consult.

Seekins, Donald M. *Historical Dictionary of Burma.* Lanham, MD: Scarecrow, 2006. Most students will want to refer to this reference book that includes extensive information on the Anglo-Burmese wars.

Trager, Helen Gibson. *Burma Through Alien Eyes: Missionary Views of the Burmese in the Nineteenth Century.* New York: Praeger, 1966. Using the accounts of missionaries, Trager presents a vivid and distinctive interpretation of Burmese attitudes during the nineteenth century.

Wheeler, James T. *A Short History of India and the Frontier States of Afghanistan, Nipal, and Burma.* London: Macmillan, 1894. An old but still useful study that includes information on the Anglo-Burmese wars.

World Wide Web

"James Andrew Broun Ramsay, marquess and 10th earl of Dalhousie." http://www.britannica.com/EBchecked/topic/150159/James-Andrew-Broun-Ramsay-Marquess-and-10th-Earl-of-Dalhousie/1697/Second-Burmese-War#tab=active~checked%2Citems~checked&title=James%20Andrew%20Broun%20Ramsay%2C%20marquess%20and%2010th%20earl%20of%20Dalhousie%20%3A%3A%20Second%20Burmese%20War.%20–%20Britannica%20Online%20Encyclopedia. Provides information on the Second Burmese War when Dalhousie was Governor General of India.

"Second Burmese War." http://www.experiencefestival.com/second_burmese_war. Provides a list of articles and links on the Second Burmese War.

"The British Conquest of Burma: The Second Anglo-Burmese War." http://www.suite101.com/article.cfm/east_asian_history/112094. Provides a good survey of the war.

Multimedia Source

"Multimedia: British Empire." http://encarta.msn.com/media_701766307
_761566125_-1_1/British_Empire.html. Includes ten maps and photographs, two of which relate to Burma.

48. Crimean War (1853–1856)

The Crimean War was the most significant conflict among the European powers between the fall of Napoleonic France in 1815 and the outbreak of the First World War in 1914. The conflict in Crimea (North Black Sea) was contended by Imperial Russia and, in opposition, Great Britain, France, the Ottoman Empire, and, during the last year of the war, Sardinia. The war lasted from late 1853 until its conclusion with the Treaty of Paris in 1856. Initially, Russia had expressed interest in serving as the protector of Christians, especially Orthodox Christians, in the Holy Lands. Until this time the Ottoman Turks had provided this protection with cooperation from France. In fact, Russia was interested in expanding its influence in the eastern Mediterranean and in the Balkans —at the expense of the Turks. The Ottoman Empire was in a weakened condition and needed support to contain the Russians, because they feared Russian access to the Straits of Dardanelles and to the Mediterranean Sea. Britain and France responded to this Russian challenge and the war was expanded. In 1855, the Kingdom of Sardinia (Piedmont) joined the anti-Russian alliance hoping to gain great power recognition and some spoils of being affiliated with the victors.

The war itself was a military disaster on all sides. The Charge of the Light Brigade was an infamous military blunder that was representative of the general performance of units in the war. Disease also inflicted extensive casualties on the warring armies. The war concluded with the Treaty of Paris with little change. Russia did not gain its major objectives.

TERM PAPER SUGGESTIONS

1. Write a paper on Russian interests and ambitions in the "Holy Lands" and the Near East.

2. Develop a term paper on the establishment of the anti-Russian alliance that fought in the Crimean War? Why did England, France, and Sardinia go to war with Russia?

3. How did the Crimean War reflect larger issues that caused tensions among European states during the nineteenth century?

4. Write a paper on the "state and condition" of the Ottoman Empire on the eve of the Crimean War.

5. Construct a term paper on the consequences of the Crimean War.

6. Write a paper on the military operations of the Crimean War.

ALTERNATIVE TERM PAPER SUGGESTIONS

1. Develop an iMovie on the decision-making process that led to the Charge of the Light Brigade.

2. You are the spouse of a British participant in the war. Develop a blog on the public impression on the progress of the war with frontline combat soldiers.

3. Develop a podcast on the negotiations between the Russian and coalition diplomats that resulted in the peace settlement.

4. You are a Russian journalist covering the war, and you are embedded in the Russia army in the Crimea. Write a series of dispatches from the front and private diary entries that record your honest thoughts and impressions.

SUGGESTED SOURCES

Primary Sources

Admiralty, Great Britain. *Russian War, 1854: Baltic and Black Sea; Official Correspondence.* Ed. D. Bonner-Smith and A. C. Dewar. London: Navy Records Society, 1943. Includes correspondence between the Admiralty and Vice-Admiral Sir C. Napier (Baltic Sea Commander) and Vice-Admiral Sir James Deans Dundas (Black Sea Commander.)

Douglas, George Brisbane, ed. *The Panmure Papers: Being a selection from the Correspondence of Fox Maule, second Baron Panmure, afterwards eleventh Earl of Dalhousie, K. T.* London: Hodder and Stoughton, 1908. A valuable collection of papers of a participant in the Crimean War.

Duberly, Frances Isabella. *Mrs. Duberly's War: Journal and Letters from the Crimea, 1854–6.* Ed. Christine Kelly. Oxford: Oxford University Press, 2007. Includes the diaries, correspondence, and other personal reflections on the war by Frances Duberly (1829–1902), who was married to Captain Henry Duberly and traveled with the army during the war.

Evelyn, George Palmer. *A Diary of the Crimea.* London: Duckworth, 1954. A personal narrative by a participant that provides valued information and insights.

Gowing, Timothy. *A Soldier's Experience, or, A Voice from the Ranks, . . .* Nottingham, U.K.: T. Forman, 1903. A worthwhile memoir of an enlisted soldier in the British army.

Henderson, Gavin Burns. *Crimean War Diplomacy and Other Historical Essays.* Glasgow, U.K.: Jackson, 1947. Henderson's study is dated but includes perceptions of the diplomatic aspects of the war that are still valuable.

Hudson, Roger, ed. *William Russell, Special Correspondent of the Times.* London: The Folio Society, 1995. Includes primary source materials related to Russell's coverage of the Crimean War.

Lawson, George. *Surgeon in the Crimea, The Experiences of George Lawson Recorded in Letters to His Family 1854–1855.* Ed. Victor Bonham-Carter. London: Constable, 1968. Lawson's letters are focused on hospitals and medical care and give insight into the devastation of the war.

Luddy, Maria, ed. *The Crimean Journals of the Sisters of Mercy, 1854–56.* Portland, OR: Four Courts Press, 2004. Provides the diaries of Sister M. Francis Bridgeman, Sister M. Doyle, and Sister M. Croke, all of whom worked in hospitals in the Crimea.

Marx, Karl. *The Eastern Question: A Reprint of Letters Written 1853–1856 Dealing with the Events of the Crimean War.* Ed. Eleanor Marx Aveling and Edward Aveling. New York: B. Franklin, 1968; reprint of 1897 edition. Karl Marx was a contemporary who was critical of the war as another manifestation of capitalism.

Mawson, Michael H., ed. *Eyewitness in the Crimea: The Crimean Letters (1854–1856) of Lt. Col. George Frederick Dallas, sometime Captain, 46th Foot, and ADC to Sir Robert Garrett.* Mechanicsburg, PA: Stackpole Books, 2001. A collection from the correspondence of a British field officer during the Crimean War.

Nightingale, Florence. *Florence Nightingale: Letters from the Crimea, 1854–56.* Ed. Sue M. Goldie. New York: St. Martin's Press, 1997. A very important collection of letters by the famous frontline nurse who led medical support services for the British army.

———. *The Collected Works of Florence Nightingale.* Ed. Lynn McDonald. 10 vols. published of planned 16 vols. Ontario: Wilfrid Laurier University Press, 2001–. This will be the definitive collection of Nightingale's writings; ten volumes are available.

Russell, William Howard. *Dispatches from the Crimea 1854–1856.* Ed. Nicolas Bentley. London: Deutsch, 1966. A meaningful collection of dispatches by a noted journalist of the period.

Spilsbury, Julian. *The Thin Red Line: An Eyewitness History of the Crimean War.* London: Weidenfeld and Nicolson, 2005. Consists of personal narratives of participants in the war.

Secondary Sources

Arnold, Guy. *Historical Dictionary of the Crimean War.* Lanham, MD: Scarecrow Press, 2002. An excellent reference on the war that is reliable and comprehensive.

Baumgart, Winfried. *The Crimean War, 1853–1856.* London: Arnold, 2002. A very good history of the war that considers the clash between modern technology in war and the tactics of an earlier age.

Blake, R. L. V. *The Crimean War.* Barnsley, U.K.: Pen and Sword, 2006; originally published in 1971. A general history of the war that is reliable and readable.

Bridge, F. R., and Roger Bullen. *The Great Powers and the European States System 1814–1914.* Harlow, U.K.: Pearson Longman, 2005. The section on the Crimean War concludes that the war was a crisis of the European order and shook the confidence of many noncombatants.

Conacher, J. B. *Britain and the Crimea, 1855–56: Problems of War and Peace.* New York: St. Martin's Press, 1987. A seminal study of the war and associated issues by a noted historian.

Edgerton, Robert. *Death or Glory: The Legacy of the Crimean War.* New York: Basic Books, 2000. Examines the reforms that resulted in the military and in diplomacy after the war.

Fletcher, Ian, and Natalia Ishchenko. *The Crimean War: A Clash of Empires.* Staplehurst, U.K.: Spellmount, 2004. An important study of the geopolitical significance of the war.

Goldfrank, David M. *The Origins of the Crimean War.* New York: Longman, 1994. A very worthwhile scholarly study that focuses on the Anglo-Russian rivalry at mid-century.

Hibbert, Christopher. *The Destruction of Lord Raglan: A Tragedy of the Crimean War, 1854–1855.* Harmondsworth, U.K.: Viking, 1984; originally published in 1961. A good study of Raglan's failures and their impact on him and others.

Judd, Denis. *The Crimean War.* London: Hart-Davis/MacGibbon, 1975. A good, reliable, and readable history of the war that provides a solid introduction.

Keller, Ulrich. *The Ultimate Spectacle: A Visual History of the Crimean War.* Amsterdam: Gordon and Breach, 2001. A very interesting and useful assemblage of photographs, illustrations, and maps.

Lambert, Andrew D. *The Crimean War: British Grand Strategy, 1853–56.* Manchester, U.K.: Manchester University Press, 1990. A seminal study that focuses on British global strategy and the place of the Crimean War in its geopolitical values.

———— and Stephen Badsey. *The Crimean War.* Dover, NH: A. Sutton, 1994. This book focuses on the coverage of the war by journalists and their experiences.

Massie, Alastair. *The National Army Museum Book of the Crimean War: The Untold Stories.* London: Sidgwick and Jackson, 2004. Includes information on sources, campaigns, and personal narratives—all from the British perspective.

Pemberton, William Baring. *Battles of the Crimean War.* New York: Macmillan, 1962. A very good and reliable military history of the war.

Ponting, Clive. *The Crimean War.* London: Chatto and Windus, 2004. A reliable and well-written comprehensive history of the war by a noted historian.

Puryear, Vernon John. *England, Russia, and the Straits Question.* Hamden, CT: Archon Books, 1965; originally published in 1931. Examines the war as an element in the larger issue of the Straits that dominated Anglo-Russian relations during the nineteenth century.

Royce, Simon. *The Crimean War and Its Place in European Economic History.* London: University of London Press, 2001. An economic historian's interpretation of the war as a major point of contention and lynchpin in understanding great-power relations during the nineteenth century.

Royle, Trevor. *Crimea: The Great Crimean War, 1854–1856.* New York: Palgrave/Macmillan, 2000. An accurate and readable history of the war.

Saab, Anne P. *The Origins of the Crimean Alliance.* Charlottesville: University of Virginia, 1977. A very good monograph on the evolution of the anti-Russian coalition.

Schroeder, Paul W. *Austria, Great Britain, and the Crimean War: The Destruction of the European Concert.* Ithaca, NY: Cornell University Press, 1972. An interpretation of the war that is centered on its disruption of the system that the Austrian Foreign Minister Metternich established after the defeat of Napoleon.

Sweetman, John. *War and Administration: The Significance of the Crimean War for the British Army.* Edinburgh: Scottish Academic Press, 1984. At best the performance of the British army in the Crimean War was questionable—the Russians were worst. The reforms of the British army that came about during the decades after the war were needed but were slow to be realized.

————. *The Crimean War.* Chicago: Fitzroy Dearborn, 2001. A reliable and comprehensive history of the war.

Temperley, Harold W. *England and the Near East: The Crimea.* Hamden, CT: Archon Books, 1964. An excellent study by a preeminent historian who viewed the war in the context of larger historical issues and forces.

Troubetzkoy, Alexis G. *A Brief History of the Crimean War: The Causes and Consequences of a Medieval Conflict Fought in a Modern Age*. New York: Carroll and Graf, 2006. A useful and seminal study of the war with a very good bibliography.

Wetzel, David. *The Crimean War: A Diplomatic History*. East European Monographs, no. 193. New York: Columbia University Press, 1985. A scholarly and well-argued study of the diplomacy related to the war.

World Wide Web

"Crimean War." http://www.armysearch.mod.uk/query.html?charset=iso-8859-1&col=armyweb&qt=crimea. Provides links to ten Web sites related to the Crimean War.

"Roger Fenton's Letters from the Crimea." http://rogerfenton.dmu.ac.uk/. An important collection of letters by a major photographer of the war.

"The Battle of the Alma." http://www.britishbattles.com/crimean-war/alma.htm. An excellent account of the British and French victory over the Russians at Alma on September 20, 1854. Included are one battlefield map and 25 illustrations.

"The Battle of Balaclava." http://www.britishbattles.com/crimean-war/balaclava.htm. A very good description of the Charge of the Light Brigade and other aspects of this British offensive on October 25, 1854, that resulted in no substantive advantage to either side. Included are a battlefield map, four photographs, and 29 illustrations.

"The Battle of Inkerman." http://www.britishbattles.com/crimean-war/inkerman.htm. A useful and detailed account of the British and French victory over the Russians on November 5, 1854. Included are a battlefield map, two photographs, and 13 illustrations.

"The Crimean War." http://www.bookrags.com/wiki/Crimean_War. A very good introduction to the war that includes a bibliography, one map, and ten illustrations.

"The Siege of Sevastopol." http://www.britishbattles.com/crimean-war/sevastopol.htm. A very good description of the allied siege of Sevastopol (September 1854–September 1855). Included are a map of the siege, seven photographs, and 13 illustrations.

Multimedia Sources

"Charge of the Light Brigade." Warner Home Video, 2007; original film release, 1936. DVD. Directed by Michael Curtiz; written by Michel Jacoby and Rowland Leigh. An early dramatic rendering of the charge and the war.

"Charge of the Light Brigade." MGM/UA Home Video, 2001; original film release, 1968. DVD. Directed by Tony Richardson; written by Charles Wood. Based on the poem by Alfred Lord Tennyson, this is a dramatic film on the infamous charge.

"Crimea—The First Modern War." Military History Podcast/2006. http://www .militaryhistorypodcast.blogspot.com/2006/04/crimea-first-modern -war.html. A critical introduction to the Crimean War.

"Crimean War." History Podcast/2007. http://www.learnoutloud.com/Podcast -Directory/History/Military-History/Military-History/Podcast/18822. A lecture on the Crimean War by Jason Watts Mon.

"Roger Fenton—Crimean War Photographs." Library of Congress. http://www .lcweb2.loc.gov/pp/ftncnwhtml/ftncnwback.html. An excellent collection of relevant photographs by one of the preeminent photographers of the period.

49. Nien Rebellion (1851–1868)

The Nien (*Nian*) movement was established in northern China by Zhang Lexing (1810–1863) during the 1840s as an instrument for expressing criticism of the Qing/Manchu regime. The government was viewed as inept and detached from the interests and conditions of its peoples. In 1851 a massive flood resulted in extensive loss of life and property. Although the government started a recovery effort, Lexing condemned it as inadequate and uncaring. Beijing's resources were being stretched by the costs associated with containing the Tai'ping rebellion and the Opium Wars with Great Britain. In 1855 another flood occurred and the government was paralyzed because of these other concerns. Zhang Lexing initiated military actions against the government and scored victories during the first year of hostilities. Government forces counterattacked in 1856 and retook much of what had been captured the previous year. Zhang Lexing was killed in 1863. Nien forces came under Tai'ping leadership and resumed offensive operations in 1865. However, the Qing/Manchu government decided to purchase massive quantities of Western arms and artillery. The result was the defeat of the Nien army and movement by 1868. However, the costs of suppressing the Nien Rebellion resulted in a significant loss of government manpower and treasure. The Qing/Manchu government was collapsing under the weight of mounting opposition from within and outside of China.

TERM PAPER SUGGESTIONS

1. Write a term paper on the origins of the Nien Rebellion. What was the objective of the revolt?

2. Develop a paper on the development of the Nien Rebellion? Did the Nien forces fail to become allies with the T'ai Ping rebels? Why?

3. Write a paper in which you evaluate the leadership of Zhang Lexing, the founder of the Nien Movement.

4. Write a term paper on the consequences of the Rebellion. Did anything change as a result of the massive loss of life?

ALTERNATIVE TERM PAPER SUGGESTIONS

1. Develop a podcast in which you interview Zhang Lexing on his rationale for the Nien Rebellion.

2. Develop a hyperlink map of locations during the 1850s and 1860s in which you indicate all of the regions involved in conflict and the early successes of the Nien forces. Also provide a narrative in which the Nien Rebellion is considered in light of all of the other actions against the Qing/Manchu government.

3. Develop an iMovie in which Nien soldiers explain why they were participating in the Rebellion.

SUGGESTED SOURCES

Primary Sources

Scarth, John. *Twelve Years in China: The People, the Rebels, and the Mandarins, by a British Resident.* Wilmington, DE: Scholarly Resources, 1972; originally published in 1860. Scarth's memoir includes extensive information on the movement that should be very useful.

Tĕng, Ssu-yu, and John King Fairbank. *China's Response to the West: A Documentary Survey, 1839–1923.* Cambridge, MA: Harvard University Press, 2006. Includes translations of 65 documents, some of which relate to the Rebellion and its aftermath.

Secondary Sources

Chiang, Siang-tseh. *The Nien Rebellion.* Seattle: University of Washington Press, 1954. Still a standard on the Nien Rebellion—solid scholarship and well written.

Chien-Nung, Li, and J. Ingalls. *Political History of China, 1840–1928.* Trans. Ssu-Yu-Teng and J. Ingalls. Stanford, CA: Stanford University Press,

1956. Provides a solid introduction to the movement with the context of Chinese political thinking and the mounting fear of foreign culture.

Fairbank, John King. *The Great Chinese Revolution 1800–1985.* New York: Harper, 1987. The classic history by the preeminent twentieth-century American historian of China that includes information on the movement.

Fenby, Jonathan. *Modern China: The Fall and Rise of a Great Power, 1850 to the Present.* New York: Ecco, 2008. Includes information on the Nien Rebellion and the other disruptions that China experienced during the same period.

Grasso, June M., Jay Corrin, and Michael Kort. *Modernization and Revolution in China: From the Opium Wars to World Power.* 3rd ed. Armonk, NY: M. E. Sharpe, 2004. An excellent and reliable study that includes data on the rebellion.

Gray, Jack. *Rebellions and Revolutions: China from the 1800s to 2000.* 2nd ed. New York: Oxford University Press, 2003. A worthwhile study of the forces of change in China—both internal and external—during the nineteenth and twentieth centuries.

Joes, Anthony James. *Resisting Rebellion: The History and Politics of Counterinsurgency.* Lexington: University Press of Kentucky, 2004. Includes insights on the multiple methods that government can utilize in confronting internal rebellions—Nien Rebellion.

Leung, Edwin, ed. *Historical Dictionary of Revolutionary China, 1839–1976.* Westport, CT: Greenwood Press, 1992. Excellent reference work that includes information on the Nien Rebellion and parallel movements such as the T'ai Ping Rebellion and the Moslem revolts in China.

Perry, Elizabeth. *Rebels and Revolutionaries in Northern China, 1845–1945.* Stanford, CA: Stanford University Press, 1980. Excellent resource that includes extensive information on the Nien Rebellion and the government's response to it.

———. *Chinese Perspectives on the Nien Rebellion.* Armonk, NY: M. E. Sharpe, 1981. An essential resource for all students working on this topic. This thoughtful study may lead to new research topics.

Schoppa, R. Keith. *The Columbia Guide to Modern Chinese History.* New York: Columbia University Press, 2000. An indispensable resource for studying any topic in modern Chinese history.

Tamura, Eileen, Linda K. Menton, Noren W. Lush, Francis K. C. Tsui, and Warren Cohen. *China: Understanding Its Past.* Honolulu: University of Hawaii Press, 1997. Includes some introductory materials on the Nien Rebellion that may be useful.

Têng, Ssu-yu. *Some New Light on the Nien Movement and Its Effect on the Fall of the Manchu Dynasty.* Hong Kong: Department of Chinese, University of

Hong Kong, 1968. An analysis of the movement and the rebellion by the preeminent authority on the subject.

————. *The Nien Army and Their Guerrilla Warfare, 1851–1868*. Westport, CT: Greenwood Press, 1984; reprint of the 1961 edition. The best work on the military aspects of the Rebellion.

Wang, Ke-wen. *Modern China: An Encyclopedia of History, Culture, and Nationalism*. Bristol, PA: Taylor & Francis, 1998. An excellent resource on all aspects of Chinese history.

World Wide Web

"Nian Rebellion." http://www.infoplease.com/ce6/history/A0835557.html. Provides information on the rebellion and links to several related sites.

"Nien Rebellion." http://www.encyclopedia.com/doc/1E1-X-NienRebe.html. Provides links to articles from several reliable reference works.

"Nien Rebellion, China, 1853–1868." http://www.ibiblio.org/chinesehistory/contents/03pol/c03s12.html#Nien%20Rebellion%201853-1868. A very good description of the rebellion in the context of the other problems that Manchu China was experiencing at the same time.

"Nien Rebellion in China, 1853–1868." http://www.onwar.com/aced/data/charlie/china1853.htm. Provides a succinct but accurate description of the rebellion.

Multimedia Sources

"Qing Dynasty." http://encarta.msn.com/medias_761557160/Qing_Dynasty.html. Includes 11 images, one of which is a very good map of China in the nineteenth century, as well as some other images that relate to the Nien Rebellion.

"Timeline on Chinese History." http://www.timelines.info/history/empires_and_civilizations/chinese_dynasties/qing_(ch'ing)_(manchu)/. Includes Nien and Moslem rebellions and the attempts at reform in late nineteenth-century China.

50. Eureka Stockade (1854)

The battle of the Eureka Stockade in Australia on December 3, 1854, which resulted in more than two dozen deaths and many injured, can be viewed as the suppression of a gold miners' revolt against the management and bureaucracy that supervised the mining. In fact, this incident resulted from more than three years of dispute between the miners and officials over the political and economic rights of the workers. In the fall of 1854 tensions mounted as the miners became more vocal and organized, and in November, the Ballarat Reform League was established to advance the workers' rights. In many ways, the Ballarat movement resembled the English Chartist cause that advocated universal male suffrage, secret ballot, redistribution of electoral districts based on population, and abolition of discriminatory taxes and fees, such as those imposed on the miners. Support for the Ballarat movement expanded rapidly. More than 200 Americans joined the cause, and the Victorian government in Australia viewed it as a rebellion. The political crisis was transformed into violent action when the government launched an offensive against those in the stockade during the early hours of December 3, 1854. The brutality of the assault has become a legend. More than a hundred miners were captured and 13 were held for trial. The accused enjoyed overwhelming public support and all were acquitted. Further, before the close of 1855, most of the Ballarat demands had been enacted and its leaders became influential in Victoria's government. The Eureka Stockade is a pivotal moment in Australian history.

TERM PAPER SUGGESTIONS

1. What were the political and economic tensions that resulted in the violence at the Eureka Stockade in 1854?

2. Write a paper on the impact of the English Chartists movement on the miners and the Ballarat Reform League.

3. Develop a paper on the role that the American contingent played in the Eureka Stockade incident. Why were these foreign volunteers there?

4. For a brief period of time on December 3, 1854, the violence at the Eureka Stockade resembled a "killing field." What accounted for the intensity of violence? What was the public reaction to the slaughter?

5. Write a paper on the emergence of the Eureka Stockade as a legend in Australian history.

ALTERNATIVE TERM PAPER SUGGESTIONS

1. Develop a podcast on why you as an American volunteer at the stockade sympathized with the miners. What attracted you to their cause?

2. As a newspaper correspondent at the incident, develop a blog on the incident and the subsequent public outcry and judicial proceedings.

SUGGESTED SOURCES

Primary Sources

Blyton, Enid. *The Eureka Stockade: Original Eyewitness Account.* Sydney, Australia: Pan/Macmillan, 1999. A useful account with commentary on the actions involved in the Eureka Stockade incident.

Carboni, Raffaello. *The Eureka Stockade.* London: Echo Library, 2007. This is the classic memoir of the incident by an Italian revolutionary who participated in the event. This is the required primary source.

Secondary Sources

Butler, Richard. *Eureka Stockade.* Sydney: Angus and Robertson Publishers/HarperCollins, 1983. This is a readable and reliable history of the incident and its importance in Australian history.

Harvey Jack. *Eureka Rediscovered: In Search of the Site of the Historic Stockade.* Victoria, Australia: University of Ballarat Press, 1994. An important account of the archaeological survey of the incident site.

Hernon, Ian. *Blood in the Sand: More Forgotten Wars of the Nineteenth Century.* Stroud: Sutton, 2001. A chapter on the Eureka Stockade is a reliable introduction.

Hocking, Geoff. *Eureka Stockade: A Pictorial History.* Scoresby, Australia: Five Mile Press, 2004. This is an excellent resource that provides numerous photographs of the site from a multitude of directions and is a valuable visual in gathering a clearer image of Ballarat.

Lawson, Henry. *Selected Works.* Edited and introduced by Lyle Blair. East Lansing: Michigan State University Press, 1957. This volume includes three versions of "The Eureka Stockade" poem. These poems provide an insight into the place of the incident in Australian national culture.

Molony, John Neyton. *Eureka.* Carlton South, Australia: Melbourne University Press, 2001. A scholarly account of the Eureka Stockade incident with documentation, maps, bibliography.

O'Brien, Bob. *Massacre at Eureka—The Untold Story.* Victoria, Australia: Australian Scholarly Publications, 1992. O'Brien argued that most of the Australians killed at Eureka were massacred by the British after the close of the conflict.

O'Grady, Desmond. *Stages of the Revolutions: A Biography of Eureka Stockade's Raffaello Carboni.* Victoria, Australia: Hardie Grant Books, 2004. This is the best biography of Carboni that is currently available. It is reliable and readable.

Schreuder, Deryck, and Stuart Ward, eds. *Australia's Empire.* New York: Oxford University Press, 2008. This volume includes a series of scholarly essays that includes the Eureka Stockade and its place in Australian history.

Smith, Neil C. *Soldiers Bleed Too—the Redcoats at the Eureka Stockade 1854.* Melbourne, Australia: Mostly Unsung Military History and Research and Publications, 2004. Focused on the service of the British 12th and 40th Regiments who served during the Eureka Miners' Rebellion in December 1854, with biographical and service detail of over 300 Redcoats who participated

World Wide Web

"Defending Victoria Website." http://users.netconnect.com.au/~ianmac/ eureka.html. A useful site with links and commentary on new titles and research projects.

"Eureka." http://www.ballarat.com/eurekastockade.htm. An excellent Web site on the incident, with text and reproductions of paintings.

"The Affair at Eureka." http://www.ballarat.com/eurekaffair.htm. This is an excerpt from Jack Harvey's *Eureka Rediscovered: In Search of the Site of the Historic Stockade.*

Multimedia Sources

"Ballarat Site of the 'Eureka Stockade' Shortly after the Fight." A print of the drawing/sketch by S. T. Gill. Giclee print. Emmeryville, CA: Art.com, n.d. This drawing is the standard visual representation of the incident.

Blyton, Enid. "Roy Darling: Eureka the Stockade Song." Sydney: Pan, 1999. A children's book with music that provides readers with an early introduction into the history of the incident and its importance.

Eureka Stockade. Ealing Studios, 1949. VHS. Directed by Harry Watt. A popular postwar film that commemorated the incident and emphasized Australian nationalist identity.

Eureka Stockade. Thorn EMI, 1984. VHS. Directed by Rod Hardy. Dramatic film based on the Eureka stockade incident.

Haylen, Leslie. *Blood on the Wattie: A Play of the Eureka Stockade.* Sydney, Australia: Angus and Robertson, 1948. Part of the post-World War II Australian national renaissance that was performed throughout the country.

51. Second Opium War (1856–1860)

During the 1850s Great Britain, France, and the United States expanded their interests in trading in China. They sought preferential agreements with the Qing government of China. Britain, fearing that their position might be weakened, demanded that the Chinese reopen the Treaty of Nanking for renegotiation. They sought access to all Chinese markets and demanded that they enjoy a most-favored nation position through exemption from duties, a preeminent position for the British Ambassador, and an unrestricted market for the sale of opium in China. France and the United States also demanded concessions from the Chinese. An incident on a ship named the *Arrow* (October 8, 1856) was manipulated by the British and French, and they announced that a state of war existed with China. The war was known as the Second Opium War or the Arrow War. From the outset, China was at a significant disadvantage because of the Tai'ping Rebellion. British and French forces defeated the Qing government's forces but were unable to force China to accept a dictated settlement in 1858. The war continued for another two years during which the British and French increased their armies. They attacked Beijing and forced a change in regime. The Convention of Peking (Beijing) was concluded on October 18, 1860. Britain and France attained their objectives, and the British expanded their markets and had unrestricted control over the opium trade in China.

TERM PAPER SUGGESTIONS

1. Develop a paper in which you compare the British, French, and American ambitions in China during the mid-1850s.
2. Write a paper on the *Arrow* incident. How was this manipulated by the British into a *causa belli*?
3. Develop a paper on the Chinese prosecution of the war and how they resisted the dictated peace in 1858.
4. Write a paper on the terms and impact of the Convention of Peking (Beijing.)

ALTERNATIVE TERM PAPER SUGGESTIONS

1. Develop a podcast in which the Chinese leaders analyzed the British and French motives for involvement in this war.
2. As a young intellectual nationalist in China during the 1850s, you are appalled at the European penetration of Chinese life and the inability of the

Chinese government to successfully rebel it. Develop a blog that reflects your views.

3. Develop an iMovie in which the British, French, and Chinese representatives present their arguments for the Convention of Peking (Beijing.)

SUGGESTED SOURCES

Primary Sources

Loch, Henry. *Personal Narrative of Occurrences During Lord Elgin's Second Embassy to China 1860.* London: J. Murray, 1869. Also available as an e-book at http://www.archive.org/details/personalnarrativ00loch rich. An important and useful primary source that provides insights on the closing year of the war and its impact on the British position in China.

Morse, Hosea Ballou, ed. *In the Days of the Taipings: Being the Recollections of Ting Kienchang, otherwise Meisun, sometime Scoutmaster and Captain in the ever-victorious army and Interpreter-in-chief to General Ward and General Gordon.* San Francisco: Chinese Materials Center, 1974. A valuable resource that includes information on the Tai'ping Rebellion and the background and causes for the Arrow War.

Secondary Sources

Bartle, G. F. "Sir John Bowring and the Arrow War in China." *Bulletin of the John Rylands Library* 43, no. 2 (1961): 293–316. An excellent scholarly article on Bowring's role in the conflict and after.

Beeching, Jack. *The Chinese Opium Wars.* New York: Harvest Books, 1977. A very good resource on both of the Opium Wars.

Bonner-Smith, D., and Esmond W. Lumley. *The Second China War.* London: Naval Records Society, 1944. A reliable, interesting, and critical study of the Arrow War that should be useful to many students.

Coston, W. C. *Great Britain and China, 1833–1860.* London: Oxford University Press, 1968; originally published in 1937. Very worthwhile but dated study that includes extensive information on both of the Opium Wars.

Faught, C. Brad. *Gordon: Victorian Hero.* Washington, DC: Potomac Books, 2008. A good introduction to Gordon's life, including his experiences in China.

Grasso, June M., Jay Corrin, and Michael Kort. *Modernization and Revolution in China: From the Opium Wars to World Power.* 3rd ed. Armonk, NY: M. E. Sharpe, 2004. An excellent and reliable study that includes data on the Opium Wars.

Gray, Jack. *Rebellions and Revolutions: China from the 1800s to 2000.* 2nd ed. New York: Oxford University Press, 2003. A worthwhile study of the forces of change in China—both internal and external—during the nineteenth and twentieth centuries.

Hanes, William Travis, and Frank Sanello. *Opium Wars: The Addiction of One Empire and the Corruption of Another.* Naperville, IL: Sourcebooks, 2002. A very good reference for the Opium Wars that should be consulted by students working on this topic.

Hevia, James L. *English Lessons: The Pedagogy of Imperialism in Nineteenth Century China.* Durham, NC: Duke University Press, 2003. Includes information on the Opium Wars and other British actions in China.

Holt, Edgar. *The Opium Wars in China.* New York: Putnam, 1964. Reliable and well-written study of both of the Opium Wars. It considers the impact on both China and Britain and the resulting relationship.

Janin, Hunt. *The India-China Opium Trade in the Nineteenth Century.* Jefferson, NC: McFarland, 1999. Includes information on the two Anglo-Chinese Opium Wars.

Olson, James Stuart, and Robert Shadle, eds. *Historical Dictionary of the British Empire.* Westport, CT: Greenwood Press, 1996. Includes information on the Treaties of Tientsin that concluded the war.

Roberts, S. H. *History of the French Colonial Policy, 1870–1925.* 2 vols. London: P. S. King and Son, 1929. An excellent resource that includes some primary materials and is very good on the situation in China after the Arrow War.

Schoppa, R. Keith. *The Columbia Guide to Modern Chinese History.* New York: Columbia University Press, 2000. An indispensable resource for studying any topic in modern Chinese history.

Wakeman, Frederic E. *Strangers at the Gate: Social Disorder in South China, 1839–1862.* Berkeley: University of California Press, 1966. An examination of the internal social, economic, and political conditions in China from the beginning of the First Opium War to the 1860s.

Wong, J. W. *Deadly Dreams: Opium, Imperialism, and the Arrow War (1856–1860) in China.* Cambridge Studies in Chinese History, Literature, and Institutions. Cambridge, U.K.: Cambridge University Press, 1998. A scholarly analysis of the issues and policies that contributed to the outbreak and prosecution of the Arrow War.

World Wide Web

"Charles George Gordon." http://www.bambooweb.com/articles/c/h/Charles _George_Gordon.html. A good biographical sketch of Gordon, including information on his activities in China.

"Charles George Gordon (1833–1885): A Brief Biography." http://www.usp .nus.edu.sg/victorian/history/empire/gordon/bio1.html. Useful introduction to Gordon and his work in China.

"England and China: The Opium Wars, 1839–1860." http://www.victorianweb .org/history/empire/opiumwars/opiumwars1.html. Provides extensive information on both of the Anglo-Chinese Opium Wars.

"Second Opium War, 1856–1860." http://www.onwar.com/aced/nation/cat/ china/fopium1856.htm. Provides statistical data on the combatants.

"Second Opium War." http://www.bambooweb.com/articles/s/e/Second _Opium_War.html. Provides good, extensive, detailed information.

"Second Opium War, Overview." http://militaryhistory.about.com/od/battleswars1800s/p/secondopiumwar.htm. A useful statement that provides an introduction to the war.

"The Second Opium War." http://www.koreanhistoryproject.org/Ket/C19/ E1905.htm. A very extensive description of the war that includes a useful map.

"The Second Opium War, 1856–1860." http://www.howardscott.net/4/Shameen _A_Colonial_Heritage/Files/Documentation/Second_Opium_War.pdf. Provides a solid introduction to the war and includes comments on the extent of foreign involvement.

"The Taiping Rebellion and the Second Opium War." http://www.fsmitha.com/ h3/h38china.htm. Provides reliable information on the rebellion and the war.

Multimedia Source

"The Arrow War." BBC Radio-4. *This Scepterd Isle* series. Includes statement, timeline, and links to traditional and multimedia sites.

52. Sepoy Mutiny (1857–1858)

In April 1857 Indian units of the British Bengal Army refused to accept the cartridges that were required for their new Enfield rifles because it was believed that the cartridges, which needed to have their protective covers bitten off, were protected by grease from swine and cattle. Both Muslim and Hindu soldiers refused to comply with these orders because the use of pork violated their religious principles and, second, they were generally dissatisfied with their treatment by British officers. They were arrested and, on May 10, 1857, other soldiers mutinied in Meerut and killed their British officers. While this incident may explain the outbreak of the violence, it became quite apparent that many who fought against the British thought that they were fighting for much more—for their independence. The level of violence used by both sides was extreme; the battles at Delhi, Cawnpore, and Lucknow involved war atrocities. The British, under the leadership of Sir Colin Campbell and Sir Hugh Rose, prevailed, and the mutiny was concluded with the fall of Gwalior on June 20, 1858. The most important outcome of the mutiny was the disestablishment of the British East India Company and its control over India. India became a Crown Colony under the direct control of the British government—a situation that lasted for the next 90 years. Another result was the transformation of the "mutiny" into an image of national resistance against the British who had transformed Indian culture forever.

TERM PAPER SUGGESTIONS

1. Write a term paper on the outbreak and early weeks of the Sepoy Mutiny. Was the mutiny a reaction against the cartridges for the Enfield rifle or did it embody other factors?
2. Develop a paper on the British response to the mutiny during 1857 and 1858.
3. What impact did the mutiny have on the geopolitical situation in South Asia during the remainder of the nineteenth century?
4. Develop a term paper on the issue of whether the mutiny enjoyed a high level of public support in India.

ALTERNATIVE TERM PAPER SUGGESTIONS

1. After the mutiny, two correspondents, one British and one Indian (both supportive of their respective sides), meet to discuss the impact of the mutiny on India and its future. Develop a podcast of that discussion utilizing both contemporary and scholarly sources.
2. Develop a 3–5 minute iMovie on the immediate outbreak of the mutiny in 1857.
3. Develop a blog among British soldiers in India and their friends and parents during the military operations associated with the mutiny.
4. Develop a Web site on the mutiny that includes detailed maps of the military operations during 1857 and 1858.

SUGGESTED SOURCES

Primary Sources

Bloomfield, David, ed.. *Lahore to Lucknow: The Indian Mutiny Journal of Arthur Moffat Lang.* London: L. Cooper, 1992. A valuable personal account of the mutiny that includes bibliographic references.

Bourchier, George. *Eight Months' Campaign against the Bengal Sepoy Army, During the Mutiny of 1857.* Chestnut Hill, MA: Adamant Media, 2005. A detailed account of British military operations by Colonel Bourchier of the British Bengal Horse Artillery.

Duberly, Frances Isabelle. *Suppression of Mutiny, 1857–1858.* New Delhi: Sirjana Press, 1974; initially published in 1859. Some firsthand experiences are recorded in this account.

Dunlop, Robert Henry. *Service and Adventure with the Khakee Ressiah: or, Meerut volunteer horse, during the mutinies of 1857–58.* Allahabad, India: Legend Publications, 1974. An account of this unit by a participant.

Edwards, William. *Personal Adventures during the Indian Rebellion in Rochilcund, Futtehghur, and Oude.* 4th ed. Allahabad, India: Legend Publications, 1974. Personal memoir on engagements in these three areas.

Harrrison, A. T., ed. *The Graham Indian Mutiny Papers.* With an historiographical essay by T. G. Fraser. Belfast: Public Record Office of Northern Ireland, 1980. Includes sources and personal narratives of British participants in the mutiny.

Knollys, Henry, ed. *Incidents in the Sepoy War: 1857–58: Compiled from the Private Journals of General Sir Hope Grant.* Chestnut Hill, MA: Adamant Media, 2002; reprint of the 1873 edition. An important source on detailed military developments from the perspective of James Hope Grant.

Littlewood, Arthur, ed. *Indian Mutiny and Beyond: The Letters of Robert Shebbeare.* Barnsley, U.K.: Pen and Sword Military, 2007. The letters of a participant who later received the Victoria Cross.

Majendie, Vivian Dering. *Up Among the Pandies: or, A Year's Service in India.* Allahabad, India: Legend Publications, 1974; reprint of the 1859 edition. An eyewitness account of the Sepoy Mutiny.

Malcolm, Thomas. *Barracks and Battlefield in India, or, The Experiences of a Soldier of the 10th Foot (North Lincoln) in the Sikh Wars and Sepoy Mutiny.* 2nd ed. Ed. Caesar Caine. Lahore: Patiata Languages Department/Punjab University, 1971; originally published in 1891. An account of military actions by a participant that provides insights on the attitudes of British troops during the war.

Malleson, George Bruce. *The Indian Mutiny of 1857.* Delhi: Datta Book Centre, 1977; originally published in 1871. This is an important memoir written by Colonel Malleson who fought during the mutiny.

Maude, Francis Cornwallis, and John W. Sherer. *Memories of the Mutiny: Volume 1*. Chestnut Hill, MA: Adamant Media, 2001; reprint of 1894 edition. Valuable personal recollections by participants.

Prichard, Iltudus Thomas. *The Mutinies in Rajpootana: Being a Personal Narrative of the Mutiny at Nusseerabad, with subsequent residence at Jodhpore and journey across the desert into Sind, together with an account of the outbreak at Neemuch and mutiny of the Jodhpore Legion at Erinpoora and attack on Mount Aboo*. Ajmer, India: Shabd Sanchar, 1976; first published in 1860. A history of the conflict by a former member of the Bengal Army; this work includes many printed primary sources.

Sherer, John Walter. *Daily Life during the Indian Mutiny, Personal Experiences of 1857*. Allahabad, India: Legend Publications, 1974; first published in 1898. Recollections by a British eyewitness who served as a British Collector at Fatehpur during the mutiny.

Roberts, Frederick S. (1st Earl; Field Marshal Lord Roberts of Kandahar). *Letters Written during the Indian Mutiny*. New Delhi: Lal Publishers, 1979; reprint of the 1924 edition. An important resource for those who are doing research on the military aspects of the mutiny.

———. *An Eye Witness Account of the Indian Mutiny*. Delhi: Mittal Publications, 1983; originally published in 1898. A well-written and obviously pro-British account of the mutiny by a leading participant.

Vibart, Edward Daniel Hamilton. *The Sepoy Mutiny as seen by a Subaltern: From Delhi to Lucknow*. New York: Charles Scribner's Sons, 1898. A reliable account by a junior officer who served in combat during the war.

Ward, Andrew. *Our Bones Are Scattered: The Cawnpore Massacre and the Indian Mutiny of 1857*. New York: Henry Holt, 1996. A primary account of one of the most unfortunate incidents associated with the mutiny.

Wilberforce, Reginald Garton. *An Unrecorded Chapter of the Indian Mutiny: Being the Personal Reminiscences of Reginald G. Wilberforce, late 52nd Light Infantry compiled from a diary and letters written on the spot*. Gurgaon, India: Academic Press, 1976; originally published in 1894. A fascinating and authoritative account by a military participant.

Secondary Sources

Cave-Browne, J. *The Punjab and Delhi in 1857: Being a Narrative of the Measures by which the Punjab was saved and Delhi recovered during the Indian Mutiny*. 2 vols. Lahore: Patiata Languages Department/Punjab University, 1970; originally published in 1861. An unabashed pro-British interpretation of the mutiny and its aftermath by a contemporary writer/journalist.

Cosens, F. R., and Charles Wallace. *Fatehgarh and the Mutiny.* Karachi: Indus Publications, 1978. A scholarly study of localized activities during the mutiny.

Embree, Ainslie Thomas, ed. *1857 in India: Mutiny or War of Independence?* Boston: D. C. Heath, 1963. A valuable but dated work that includes contemporary and scholarly interpretations of the mutiny.

Dalrymple, William. *The Last Mughal: The Fall of a Dynasty, Delhi, 1857.* New York: Vintage, 2008. A well-written and well-documented history of the fall of Bahadur Shah II, Delhi's last Mughal ruler.

David, Saul. *The Indian Mutiny 1857.* New York: Penguin, 2002. Perhaps the best comprehensive history of the mutiny that is readily available.

———. "Greased Cartridges and the Great Mutiny of 1857: A Pretext to Rebel or the Final Straw?" In *War and Society in Colonial India, 1807–1945.* Ed. Kaushik Roy. Oxford in India Readings/Themes in Indian History. New York: Oxford University Press, 2005. An examination of the immediate outbreak of the mutiny by one of its foremost scholars.

Heathcote, T. A. *Mutiny and Insurgency in India, 1857–58: The British Army in a Bloody Civil War.* Barnsley, U.K.: Pen and Sword Military, 2007. A reliable and readable history of the Mutiny interpreted as a civil war.

Herbert, Christopher. *War of No Pity: The Indian Mutiny and Victorian Trauma.* Princeton, NJ: Princeton University Press, 2008. A very important study of the Mutiny in the context of Victorian culture and values.

Hodge, Carl Cavanaugh, ed. *Encyclopedia of the Age of Imperialism, 1800–1914.* 2 vols. Westport, CT: Greenwood Press, 2007. This is an excellent resource on all aspects of European imperialism during the nineteenth century, including the Sepoy Mutiny.

Kaye, John William. *A History of the Sepoy War in India, 1857–1858.* 2 vols. Chestnut Hill, MA: Adamant Media, 2004; reprint of the 1874 edition. Still a good history by a contemporary who worked for the East India Company.

Kinsley, D. A. *They Fight Like Devils: Stories from Lucknow during the Great Indian Mutiny.* New York: Sarpedon, 2001. Based on primary sources—personal recollections and memoirs.

Majumdar, Ramesh C. *The Sepoy Mutiny and the Revolt of 1857.* 2nd ed. Calcutta: Firma K. L. Mukhopadhyay, 1963. An interesting scholarly examination of the mutiny from an Indian perspective.

Palmer, Julian Arthur. *The Mutiny Outbreak at Meerut in 1857.* Cambridge South Asian Studies, no. 2. Cambridge, U.K.: Cambridge University Press, 1966. A detailed and scholarly account of the events in Meerut during the mutiny—reliable.

Rawling, F. W. *The Rebellion in India, 1857.* New York: Cambridge University Press, 1977. A comprehensive study on the origins of the British presence in India up to and including the Sepoy Mutiny. This is still a very good source.

Robinson, Jane. *Angels of Albion: Women of the Indian Mutiny.* New York: Viking, 1996. An unusual study of the role of women during the mutiny that may provoke additional topics for papers.

Spilsbury, Julian. *The Indian Mutiny.* London: Weidenfeld and Nicolson, 2007. A very reliable and comprehensive introduction to the mutiny.

Srivastava, M. P. *The Indian Mutiny, 1857.* Allahabad, India: Chugh, 1979. This history is centered on the role of the Allahabad Division during the mutiny.

Tisdall, E. E. P. *Mrs. Duberty's Campaigns: An Englishwoman's Experiences in the Crimean War and Indian Mutiny.* London: Jarrolds, 1963. An interesting account of Frances I. Duberty's encounters during the Sepoy Mutiny that provides a needed feminist view.

Taylor, P. J. O. *A Companion to the "Indian Mutiny" of 1857.* New York: Oxford University Press, 1996. An invaluable encyclopedic guide to the Sepoy Mutiny.

———. *What Really Happened During the Mutiny: A Day-by-Day Account of the Major Events of 1857–1859 in India.* New York: Oxford University Press, 1997. An authoritative detailed timeline of the mutiny.

Watson, Bruce. *The Great Indian Mutiny: Colin Campbell and the Campaign at Lucknow.* New York: Praeger, 1991. A very good history centered on the exploits of Baron Clyde (Colin Campbell.)

Wilkinson-Latham, Christopher. *The Indian Mutiny.* Oxford: Osprey Publishing, 1977. A short but valuable introductory history of the Mutiny.

World Wide Web

"1857: The First Challenge." http://www.tribuneindia.com/2007/20070510/index.htm. The 150th anniversary (2007) supplement to *The Tribune* (India) in which the history of the mutiny is provided.

"Timeline of the Mutiny." http://nielsenhayden.com/makinglight/archives/006442.html. A very useful resource for all doing research on the mutiny.

Internet archive. http://www.archive.org/search.php?query=subject%3A%22India%20–%20History%20Sepoy%20Rebellion%2C%201857-1858%22. Has extensive links.

Multimedia Sources

Alur, Bhanumurthy. *1857—The Beginning.* 2008. Documentary that emphasizes the impact of the mutiny on the development of Indian nationalism.

Derrien, Marie-Louise, and Marc Ferro. *The Road to Indian Independence.*
    Princeton, NJ: Films for the Humanities, 1993. VHS. Educational film
    argues that the Sepoy Mutiny was the basis for increased British power
    in India and, at the same time, a motivation for later Indian nationalist
    movements.

Misra, Amaresh. *1857: Ek Safarnama.* April 2008. Dramatic play. Sympathetic to
    the rebels, this play focused on the role of the common people—farmers
    and artisans during the mutiny.

Rising: The Ballad of Mangal Pandey. 2005). Directed by Ketan Mehta. Film that
    celebrates the Indian commitment to freedom and their role in the
    mutiny.

53. Irish Republican Brotherhood Is Established (1858)

Throughout the nineteenth century, Irish nationalists, motivated by the
historical antipathy toward England and the emergence of nationalist
movements in Europe, worked to overturn the Act of Union of 1801,
which incorporated Ireland into the United Kingdom. During the Revolutions of 1848, Irish insurgents James Stephens (1824–1901) and John
O'Mahony (1816–1877) led an unsuccessful rebellion against the British
in Ireland. During the 1850s Irish nationalists avoided arrest, attained
support from Irish émigré communities in the United States and Europe,
and recognized that their cause required an effective structure that would
support their efforts to gain independence from Britain. On March 17,
1868, James Stephens established the Irish Republican Brotherhood to
provide such a structure that could unify the dispersed Irish population
and to raise the necessary resources to end British control of their country.
The Irish Republican Brotherhood established a network of contacts
throughout the world and took on the name of the "Fenians." During
its early decades, the Irish Republican Brotherhood enjoyed more external
support than within Ireland itself. The tenant farmers and the Roman
Catholic Church denounced the use of violence and feared the response
of the British government. Stephens established the *Irish People,* a publication that supported radical action in the name of independence. The
Irish Republican Brotherhood and its affiliates continued to agitate mili-
tantly against the British throughout the remaining decades of the

century, but the establishment of an independent Ireland was not attained until after the First World War.

TERM PAPER SUGGESTIONS

1. Develop a term paper on the role that James Stephens played in the establishment of the Irish Republican Brotherhood.
2. Write a paper on the rationale and the momentum that led to the establishment of the Irish Republican Brotherhood in 1858.
3. Develop a paper on the Irish opposition to the Irish Republican Brotherhood. How extensive and significant was this level of internal resistance?
4. Write a paper on the role of the Irish diaspora on the organization and early history of the Irish Republican Brotherhood.

ALTERNATIVE TERM PAPER SUGGESTIONS

1. Develop a 4–5 minute podcast in which Stephens and his colleagues formulate their plans and articulate their aspirations for the new Irish Republican Brotherhood.
2. As a Dublin youth, you are attracted to the "national cause." Develop a blog on the meetings that you have attended with Stephens and others on organizing the Irish Republican Brotherhood—be sure to provide your reflections on alternatives that might have been considered.
3. Develop a 4 minute iMovie in which British leaders discuss how they are going to confront the threat imposed by the Irish Republican Brotherhood.

SUGGESTED SOURCES

Primary Sources

Clarke, Kathleen. *Revolutionary Woman: My Fight for Ireland's Freedom.* Dublin: O'Brien Press, 1997. A useful memoir that includes extensive information on the Irish Republican Brotherhood.

Denieffe, Joseph. *A Personal Narrative of the Irish Revolutionary Brotherhood.* New York: Gael Publishing, 1906. A participant's recollections that should be useful in many student papers.

Devoy, John. *Michael Davitt: From the "Gaelic American."* Ed. Carla King and W. J McCormack. Dublin: University College Dublin, 2008. An important memoir of Devoy's long relationship with Davitt, a major figure in the Irish Republican Brotherhood.

O'Leary, John. *Recollections of Fenians and Fenianism.* 2 vols. London: Downey, 1896. A very useful primary source that should be consulted.

Parnell, Charles Stewart. *The Repeal of the Union Conspiracy: or, Mr. Parnell, M.P., and the Irish Republican Brotherhood.* London: William Ridgway, 1886. The e-book is available at http://books.google.com/books?id=AFU NAAAAYAAJ&dq=Parnell,+Charles+Stewart.+The+Repeal+of +the+Union+Conspiracy:+or,+Mr.+Parnell,+M.P.,+and+the+Irish +Republican+Brotherhood&source=gbs_summary_s&cad=0. Irish leader Parnell's memoir of his contacts with the Irish Republican Brotherhood should be of interest to many students.

Rossa, Jeremiah O'Donovan. *Rossa's Recollections, 1838 to 1898.* New York: Mariner's Harbor, 1898. A very important memoir by a prominent Irish nationalist.

Ryan, Mark F. *Fenian Memories.* Ed. T. F. O'Sullivan. Dublin: M. H. Gill and Son, 1945. A useful memoir that includes extensive information on the Irish Republican Brotherhood.

Sheehan, Patrick Augustine. *The Graves of Kilmorna: A Story of '67.* New York: Longmans, Green, 1918. A personal recollection of the land revolt of 1867 in which the Irish Republican Brotherhood was involved.

Secondary Sources

Bew, Paul. *Land and the National Question in Ireland, 1858–82.* Atlantic Heights, NJ: Humanities Press, 1979. A scholarly account that includes extensive information on the impact of the Irish Republican Brotherhood on Irish politics.

Comerford, R. V. *The Fenians in Context: Irish Politics and Society, 1848–82.* Rev. ed. Dublin: Wolfhound Press, 1998; originally published in 1985. The earlier sections of this book should be useful on the Brotherhood.

Connolly, S. J. *The Oxford Companion to Irish History.* 2nd ed. New York: Oxford University Press, 2007. A very useful reference that most students should use.

Kee, Robert. *The Green Flag: A History of Irish Nationalism.* New York: Penguin, 2001. A general work that includes information on the establishment of the Irish Republican Brotherhood.

Kelly, M. J. *The Fenian Ideal and Irish Nationalism, 1882–1916.* Woodbridge, U.K.: Boydell, 2006. Includes information on the Irish Republican Brotherhood at the close of the nineteenth century.

Lyons, F. S. L. *Ireland since the Famine.* London: Fontana, 1973. A general history that provides a useful introduction to the Irish Republican Brotherhood.

McGee, Owen. *The IRB: The Irish Republican Brotherhood from the Land League to Sinn Féin.* Dublin: Four Courts Press, 2005. A very important study that will be useful to almost all students working on this topic.

Moody, T. W., ed. *The Fenian Movement.* Cork: Mercier Press, 1968. A series of essays on various aspects of Fenian history.

Ó Broin, León. *Revolutionary Underground: The Story of the Irish Republican Brotherhood, 1858–1924.* Dublin: Gill and Macmillan, 1976. An excellent history by a prominent historian that should be consulted by students working on the Irish Republican Brotherhood.

Power, Patrick C., and Sean Duffy. *Timetables of Irish History.* New York: Black Dog and Leventhal, 2001. A useful tool that provides detailed chronology.

Quinlivan, Patrick, and Paul Rose. *The Fenians in England, 1865–1872: A Sense of Insecurity.* London: J. Calder, 1982. Includes data on the Irish militant plans and activities in England.

Ramon, Marta. *A Provisional Dictator: James Stephens and the Fenian Movement.* Dublin: University College Dublin, 2008. An important study of Stephens and his impact on Irish nationalism.

Regan, Stephen, ed. *Irish Writing: An Anthology of Irish Literature in English, 1789–1939.* New York: Oxford University Press, 2008. Includes useful literary works that are representative of the Irish national tradition that developed in the nineteenth century.

World Wide Web

"1850–1909: Parnell, Gladstone and the Battle for Home Rule." http://news.bbc.co.uk/2/hi/events/northern_ireland/history/60767.stm. Provides a reliable introduction to the influence that the Irish nationalists had on the formulation of Liberal policy.

"Irish Republican Brotherhood." http://www.bbc.co.uk/history/british/easterrising/profiles/po17.shtml. A very good introduction to the history of the Irish Republican Brotherhood.

"Irish Republican Brotherhood." http://www.ucd.ie/archives/html/collections/irb.html. Includes a reliable introduction to the Irish Republican Brotherhood and other sites.

"Irish Republican Brotherhood." http://www.triskelle.eu/history/irishrep brotherhood.php. An introduction to the Irish Republican Brotherhood.

"Irish Republican Brotherhood." http://www.nationmaster.com/encyclopedia/Irish-Republican-Brotherhood. A reliable and useful introduction.

"Irish Republican Brotherhood." http://www.experiencefestival.com/irish _republican_brotherhood/articleindex. An introduction and bibliography.

Multimedia Source

"The Irish Question" (May 9, 2006). BBC-4 Audio. http://www.bbc.co.uk/radio4/history/empire/episodes/episode_62.shtml. A segment of the *Empire* series that includes information on the Irish Republican Brotherhood, the land issue, and the impact of Charles Parnell.

54. Discovery of the Source of the Nile (1858–1871)

During the mid-nineteenth century, explorers and geographic societies throughout Western Europe experienced a renewed interest in locating the source (headwaters) of the Nile River. Since antiquity the Nile had been charted and traveled south to Khartoum in the Sudan where two large rivers met to form the Nile River. However, little was known about the sources of these rivers. The larger White Nile appeared to have its source in the higher elevations hundreds of miles south-southwest of Khartoum, while the smaller Blue Nile approached Khartoum from the southeast. During the 1850s and 1860s British explorers Richard F. Burton (1821–1890), John Hanning Speke (1827–1864), James Augustus Grant (1827–1892), Samuel Baker (1821–1892), David Livingstone (1813–1873), and the American/British journalist-explorer Henry Morton Stanley (1841–1904) seized the imagination of the public with their exploits in search of the White Nile. While an expedition by Speke and Burton in 1858 reached Lake Victoria, Speke alone announced that it was the source of the White Nile. Speke's assertion would later be proved when Stanley circumnavigated Lake Victoria in 1871. The Blue Nile would first be traversed by an American-Norwegian expedition in 1902.

TERM PAPER SUGGESTIONS

1. Write a paper in which you compare the achievements of Burton and Speke in discovering the headwaters of the Nile. Why were they such rivals?

2. Develop a paper on the expeditions and significance of the discoveries of Samuel Baker.

3. David Livingstone was a missionary explorer who has retained an aura of mystery for more than a century. Write a paper that focuses on his aspirations in Africa and his relationship with the native Africans.

4. Write a paper on the impact of Stanley's discoveries in Africa. How did he get there? Did Africa transform Stanley's life?

5. Develop a paper on the impact of the discovery of the sources of the White Nile on European imperialism during the last decades of the nineteenth century.

ALTERNATIVE TERM PAPER SUGGESTIONS

1. Develop a podcast in which you interview separately Burton and Speke about their 1858 expedition.

2. As an African aide to Livingstone, you agree to accompany Stanley on his trip around Lake Victoria. Develop a blog on that trip. Comment on Stanley's character and leadership.

3. Develop an iMovie in which you interview Stanley after his return to Britain.

4. Sam and Florence Baker were important explorers in East Africa. Develop a podcast in which you interview them late in life as they reflect on their African experiences.

SUGGESTED SOURCES

Primary Sources

Baker, Samuel W. *The Nile Tributaries of Abyssina, and the Sword Hunters of the Hamran Arabs.* Philadelphia: J. B. Lippincott, 1868. Baker's well-written and authoritative memoir of his travels in Ethiopia searching for the source of the Nile.

Burton, Isabel. *The Life of Captain Sir Richard F. Burton.* Boston: Longwood Press, 1977; originally published in 1893. Biography written by Burton's widow who used extensive primary materials in her book.

Burton, Richard Francis. *The Search for the Source of the Nile. . . .* London: Roxburghe Club, 1999. Burton's recollections of his experiences while searching for the Nile.

Burton, Richard Francis, and James MacQueen. *The Nile Basin and Captain Speke's Discovery of the Source of the Nile.* New York: Da Capo Press, 1967. Includes memoirs of both Burton and Speke about their discoveries while searching for the headwaters of the Nile.

Hayes, Arthur John. *The Source of the Blue Nile: A Record of a Journey through the Sudan to Lake Tsana in Western Abyssinia, and of the Return to Egypt by the Valley of the Nile. . . .* Chestnut Hill, MA: Elibron/Adamant Media, 2003; originally published in 1905. An explorer's reminiscences of his search for the source of the Blue Nile.

Johnston, Harry Hamilton. *The Nile Quest: A Record of the Exploration of the Nile and Its Basin*. London: A. Rivers, 1905. Includes both primary and secondary materials.

Speke, John Hanning. *Journal of the Discovery of the Source of the Nile*. Eugene, OR: Wipf and Stock, 2007. Speke's *Journal* needs to be read by students working on this topic.

————. *What Led to the Discovery of the Nile*. Edinburgh: William Blackwood and Sons, 1864. A personal defense by Speke of his work in Africa.

———— and James Augustus Grant. *The Discovery of the Source of the Nile*. Exeter: Star, 2006. A reprint of an earlier work by Speke and Grant.

Stanley, Henry Morton. *Through the Dark Continent: Or, The Sources of the Nile, around the Great Lakes of Equatorial Africa, and down the Livingstone River to the Atlantic Ocean*. 2 vols. Chestnut Hill, MA: Elibron/Adamant Media, 2000; originally published in 1878. Perhaps the best primary source on this topic—well written and authoritative, by the most tireless and successful of the explorers.

Secondary Sources

Burne, Glenn S. *Richard F. Burton*. Boston: Twayne, 1985. A literary biography of Burton with extensive information on his work in Africa.

Camochan, W. B. *The Sad Story of Burton, Speke, and the Nile, or, Was John Hanning Speke a Cad?: Looking at the Evidence*. Stanford, CA: Stanford General Books, 2006. A polemic that raises numerous questions about Speke and others.

Cohen, Daniel. *Henry Stanley and the Quest for the Source of the Nile*. New York: M. Evans, 1985. An introductory biography of Stanley and his achievements in Africa.

Guadalupi, Gianni. *The Discovery of the Nile*. New York: Stewart, Tabori & Chang, 1997. Provides information on nineteenth-century travels and includes drawings, paintings, maps, and charts.

Hall, Richard Seymour. *Lovers on the Nile: The Incredible African Journeys of Sam and Florence Baker*. New York: Random House, 1980. A very good account of the Bakers' lives and achievements in Africa.

Jeal, Tim. *Stanley, The Impossible Life of Africa's Greatest Explorer*. New York: Faber and Faber, 2007. This is the best biography on Stanley—a must read for a student who is researching his life and achievements.

————. *Livingstone*. London: Pimlico, 1993. An excellent biography of the missionary explorer.

Kennedy, Dane Keith. *The Highly Civilized Man: Richard Burton and the Victorian World.* Cambridge, MA: Harvard University Press, 2005. Perhaps the best scholarly biography of Burton.

Lovell, Mary S. *A Rage to Live.* New York: Little, Brown, 1998. An excellent biography of the Bakers.

Middleton, Dorothy. *Baker of the Nile.* Tempe, AZ: Falcon Press, 1949. A good biography of Samuel Baker and his role as an explorer of the Nile.

Moorehead, Alan. *The Blue Nile.* Rev. ed. New York: Harper and Row, 1972. An exceptionally well written and researched study of the exploration of the Blue Nile in Ethiopia.

———. *The White Nile.* North Salem, NY: Adventure Library, 1995. A classic that needs to be read by all who are beginning their research on this topic.

Posnansky, Merrick, ed. *The Nile Quest: Centenary Essays and Catalogue.* Kampala: Uganda Museum, 1962. A collection of essays on a wide range of issues related to the search for the headwaters of the Nile.

Shipman, Pat. *To the Heart of the Nile: Lady Florence Baker and the Exploration of Central Africa.* New York: William Morrow, 2004. The best biography of Florence Baker and her work in Africa.

Stisted, Georgiana M. *The True Life of Captain Sir Richard F. Burton.* New York: Appleton, 1897. A sympathetic biography written by Burton's niece with the approval of the Burton family.

World Wide Web

"Exploration and Discovery." http://www.oldandsold.com/articles35/19th-century-16.shtml. Provides extensive information on the explorers who searched for the sources of the Nile.

"Journal of the Discovery of the Source of the Nile." http://findarticles.com/p/articles/mi_m1058/is_5_119/ai_84054094/pg_5. Focused on Speke's journal—a useful paragraph.

"Mystery of the Nile." http://www.nilefilm.com/p_history.htm. Includes a section on the nineteenth-century explorers and their achievements.

"Nile, A Quest for Its Source." http://myweb.tiscali.co.uk/kenanderson/histemp/nilesource1.html. A comprehensive Web page on the topic with maps, photographs, and additional links.

"Quest for the Source of the Nile." http://uk.geocities.com/ticketyboo13/index.html. A very good site with information and links to other Web pages.

"White Nile." http://www.nationmaster.com/encyclopedia/White-Nile. Introductory information on the search for the sources of the White Nile.

Multimedia Sources

The Arab World Reference Book. Multi-Media, 2000. CD-Rom. Includes material on the search for the Nile, including maps and photographs.

Biography—Stanley and Livingstone. A&E Entertainment, 2006. DVD. A documentary on the explorers that includes information on the Nile.

Forbidden Territory: Stanley's Search for Livingstone. Platinum, 1997. DVD. Includes information on the discovery of the sources of the Nile.

Great Adventurers: David Livingstone—Journey to the Heart of Africa. Kultur Video, 2006. DVD. A documentary on Livingstone's life, discoveries, and work.

The Mountains of the Moon. Artisan Entertainment, 1989. DVD. Directed by Bob Rafelson. A dramatic film about the discovery of the Nile.

Source of the Nile, Game of African Exploration in the 19th Century. Avalon Hill, 1980. An historically accurate board game in which the board serves as a map of the headwaters of the Nile.

55. Charles Darwin's *The Origin of Species* Is Published (1859)

In 1859 Charles Darwin published his revolutionary work, *The Origin of Species.* It included his scientific argument for natural selection. Darwin was born in 1809 into a family of naturalists. Between 1831 and 1836, Darwin served as a naturalist assigned to *H. M. S. Beagle.* His service on that ship that traveled the world provided the defining experiences of his life. It was on the *Beagle* that Darwin began to formulate his ideas on natural selection. During the 1840s and 1850s Darwin worked slowly on his book and finally published in 1859 when he feared that others would publish similar theories prior to him. Darwin argued that animals with better survival traits would continue to exist—others would disappear because they could not adapt to changes in the environment. The impact of Darwin's concept of evolution was comparable to the heliocentric theory on science and on humanity's understanding of itself.

Darwin's basic concepts were later applied by Herbert Spencer and others in the formulation of "Social Darwinism." Darwin had little or nothing to do with these applications of his scientific thesis.

TERM PAPER SUGGESTIONS

1. Develop a term paper on Darwin's development of *The Origin of Species.*

2. Write a paper on the reception of Darwin's *The Origin of Species.*

3. Using primary sources, develop a paper on Darwin's reluctance to publish and his competition with others who were threatening to publish similar works before him.

4. Write a paper on the popular acceptance of Darwin's view on natural selection during the last half of the nineteenth century.

5. Write a paper on the opposition that Darwinian ideas received from fundamentalists—Christian and non-Christian—who remained staunch advocates of creationism.

ALTERNATIVE TERM PAPER SUGGESTIONS

1. You are the navigator of *H. M. S. Beagle* during its trip around the world. Report in a blog your observations of the young Charles Darwin and his ideas—especially after the visit to the Galapagos Islands.

2. Develop a podcast of a conversation between Thomas Henry Huxley and Charles Darwin as they reflect on the public reception to *The Origin of Species.*

3. Charles Darwin was a very private person, but he recognized the need to communicate his ideas clearly and precisely. Develop an iMovie that is 3–4 minutes in length in which Darwin clarifies what he maintains and what has been attributed falsely to him.

4. Create an iMovie of a debate between Thomas Henry Huxley and a creationist in which they advanced their respective positions on the content, meaning, and value of Darwin's thoughts.

SUGGESTED SOURCES

Primary Sources

Beer, Gavin de, ed. *Autobiographies/Charles Darwin, Thomas Henry Huxley.* New York: Oxford University Press, 1983. Includes excerpts from the two autobiographies and related information on *The Origin of Species.*

Darwin, Charles. *On the Origins of the Species by Means of Natural Selection.* Ed. Joseph Carroll. Orchard Park, NY: Broadview Press, 2003. A scholarly edition with introduction and commentary.

———. *The Origin of Species: A Variorum Text.* Ed. Morse Peckham. Philadelphia: University of Pennsylvania Press, 2006; originally published in 1959. The Peckham edition is still one of the best available.

———. *The Beagle Record: Selections from the Original Pictorial Records and Written Accounts of the Voyage of H. M. S. Beagle.* Ed. Richard Darwin

Keynes. New York: Cambridge University Press, 1979. Excellent selection of segments of this work with a useful introduction.

———. *Diary of the Voyage of H. M. S. Beagle.* Ed. Nora Barlow. New York: New York University Press, 1987. A very comprehensive edition with a good introduction.

———. *Charles Darwin's Letters: A Selection 1825–1859.* Ed. Frederick Burkhardt. New York: University of Cambridge, 1996. Burkhardt's selection of Darwin's letters is excellent and captures the anxious process that Darwin experienced prior to publication.

———. *The Darwin Reader.* Ed. Mark Ridley. 2nd ed. New York: Norton, 1996. An excellent resource with many important primary sources.

———. *The Foundations of the "Origin of Species": Two Essays Written in 1842 and 1844.* New York: New York University Press, 1987. Important preliminary essays in which Darwin's direction is evident.

———. *The Works of Charles Darwin.* Ed. Paul H. Barrett and R. B. Freeman. New York: New York University Press, 1987. A reliable and scholarly edition of many of Darwin's writings.

———. *The Essential Darwin.* Ed. Robert Jastrow; selections and commentary by Kenneth A. Korey. Boston: Little, Brown, 1984. A classic and most useful collection of Darwin's writings and commentaries.

———. *The Correspondence of Charles Darwin.* Ed. Frederick Burkhardt and Sydney Smith. 15 vols. Cambridge, U.K.: Cambridge University Press, 1985. Perhaps the most important and comprehensive collection of Darwin's letters ever published.

———. *The Red Notebook of Charles Darwin.* Ed. Sandra Herbert. Ithaca, NY: Cornell University Press, 1979. An important but seldom referenced work by Darwin.

Secondary Sources

Aydon, Cyril. *Charles Darwin.* London: Constable, 2002. A reliable and well-written general biography of Darwin.

Barrett, Paul H., Donald J. Weinshank, and Timothy T. Gottleber. *A Concordance to Darwin's "Origin of Species."* Ithaca, NY: Cornell University Press, 1981. This is a serious volume for serious and able students who are reading *The Origin of Species.*

Barzun, Jacques. *Darwin, Marx, Wagner: Critique of a Heritage.* Rev. 2nd ed. Garden City, NY: Doubleday, 1958. A marvelous and provocative comparative study that should be consulted.

Bowler, Peter J. *Charles Darwin: The Man and His Influence.* Oxford: Blackwell, 1990. A very good introduction to Darwin's place in history.

Bowlby, John. *Charles Darwin: A New Life.* New York: W. W. Norton, 1991. A very good biography that is based on primary sources that are not frequently used.

Browne, E. Janet. *Charles Darwin: A Biography.* New York: Knopf, 1995. A very good biography of Darwin for the general educated reader.

Contosta, David. *Rebel Giants: The Revolutionary Lives of Abraham Lincoln and Charles Darwin.* Amherst, NY: Prometheus Books, 2008. A seminal study on the parallel lives of Lincoln and Darwin by an important historian.

Desmond, Adrian, James Moore, and Janet Browne. *Charles Darwin.* New York: Oxford University Press, 2007. Three of the foremost authorities on Darwin collaborated on this biographical study that emphasizes the significance of his work and life.

Francis, Keith. *Charles Darwin and "The Origin of Species."* Westport, CT: Greenwood Press, 2007. A perceptive study of Darwin and his major opus, how he wrote it, and what it achieved.

Freeman, R. B. *Charles Darwin, A Companion.* Hamden, CT: Archon Books, 1978. Very useful for all term papers on Darwin.

Himmelfarb, Gertrude. *Darwin and the Darwinian Revolution.* Chicago: I. R. Dee, 1996. Perhaps the most significant analysis of Darwin and his impact by one of the most brilliant historical minds of our age.

Hodge, Jonathan, and Gregory Radick, eds. *The Cambridge Companion to Darwin.* New York: Cambridge University Press, 2003. A substantive book that includes a multitude of approaches to Darwin and Darwinism.

Lewens, Tim. *Darwin.* New York: Routledge, 2007. A very good introduction to Darwin and his thoughts and their impact on cultural history.

Quammen, David. *The Reluctant Mr. Darwin: An Intimate Portrait of Charles Darwin and the Making of His Theory of Evolution.* New York: Atlas Books/Norton, 2006. A very perceptive and fascinating study of Darwin's personality and its impact on his work and the communication of his ideas to the world.

Ruse, Michael. *Charles Darwin.* Malden, MA: Blackwell, 2008. Includes a comprehensive chapter on *The Origin of Species* and extensive bibliography.

World Wide Web

"Charles Darwin." http://www.victorianweb.org/science/darwin/index.html. A good introduction to Darwinism and the responses to his theories on the Victorian Web.

"Chronology of Life of Charles Darwin." http://www.victorianweb.org/science/darwin/darwin_chron.html. A useful timeline on Darwin's life.

"The Complete Work of Charles Darwin Online." http://www.darwin-online.
org.uk/. Comprehensive resource on Darwin sponsored and maintained
by Cambridge University.

Multimedia Sources

Darwin, Charles. *The Origin of Species.* Tantor Media, 2006. Audiobook, CD.
Narrated by David Case. An excellent reading of Darwin's masterpiece.

————. *The Voyage of the Beagle.* Recorded Books, 1994. Audiobook, Audio
Cassette, or MP3 Digital Download. Narrated by David Case. Case's
reading is nothing less than superb.

Evolution. Co-production of the WGBH/NOVA Science Unit and Clear Sky
Productions, 2001. DVD. An excellent four-part video recording that
includes a relevant section on the publication of *The Origin of Species*
and its impact on nineteenth-century thought.

Great Books: "Origin of Species." Discovery Education, 2006. DVD. A documentary on Darwin's book and a very good introduction to Darwinian
thought and its impact.

"Origin of Species": Beyond Genesis. Discovery Channel Video, 1993. VHS.
A documentary on Darwin's book.

"Origin of Species": Was Darwin Right? AiG Distributor, 2006. DVD. A documentary in which Terry Mortenson examines Darwin's claims and concludes that good science confirms the theological explanation of the
emergence of mankind—a fundamentalist response.

Quammen, David. *The Reluctant Mr. Darwin.* Audio Partners Publishing, 2006.
Audiobook, CD. Narrated by Grover Gardner. A quality reading of an
important new book on Darwin and his ideas.

Venable, Alan. *Charles Darwin, The Man Who Looked at Life.* Don Johnston,
2007. MP3 Digital Download Audiobook. A worthwhile examination
of Darwin, his methodology, and his conclusions.

56. Self-Strengthening Movement, Manchu, China (1860–1890)

Between the 1830s and early 1860s China had witnessed the First and
Second Opium Wars and the devastating Tai'ping Rebellion—all of these
experiences had their roots in European culture and all resulted in the
humiliation of China, which appeared powerless to resist the foreign
intruders and ideologies. Determined to restore their power and prestige,

the Manchu leaders of China launched a reform program in the early 1860s. It was known as the Self-Strengthening Movement. This movement consisted of two distinct elements: first, there would be an effort to learn Western technology, business methods, and languages so that the Chinese would be able to contend with the Europeans and Americans; and, second, the traditional Chinese moral values and customs in the administration of the government needed to be restored. Moral Chinese leaders were needed to confront the decadent (selfish and aggressive) Westerners who were bent on exploiting China. Conservative Chinese supported this aspect of the movement. They wanted to see the reemergence of the Chinese *chŭn tzu* (the superior leader) who was morally superior and, thus, a worthy leader. After nearly 30 years of effort, the Self-Strengthening Movement failed primarily because of China's inability to enforce reforms throughout its huge, already-centralized government. While some reformers instituted changes, the machinery of the state was entrenched in the past. The result was frustration and a wave of xenophobia that manifested itself in the 1890s.

TERM PAPER SUGGESTIONS

1. Write a paper focused on the origins of the Self-Strengthening Movement.
2. Develop a paper on the Chinese program designed to learn Western technology, business practices, and languages.
3. Write a paper on the rise of neo-Confucianism that constituted the second element of the movement. What differences existed among the conservatives and the moderates on this issue?
4. Develop a paper on the reasons for the failure of the Self-Strengthening Movement.

ALTERNATIVE TERM PAPER SUGGESTIONS

1. Wang T'ao (1828–1897) was a radical reformer who wanted to westernize all aspects of Chinese life. In a podcast interview Wang T'ao about his vision for a new China.
2. Develop an iMovie in which the leaders of the Manchu government review China's place in the world and its experiences in the mid-nineteenth century, and determine to launch the Self-Strengthening Movement.
3. As a recorder of the progress of the movement, maintain a blog from the 1870s to the early 1890s.

SUGGESTED SOURCES

Primary Sources

Chang Chih-tung. *China's Only Hope: An Appeal.* Trans. Samuel I. Woodbridge. New York: Fleming H. Revell, 1900. A memoir by a participant in the movement.

De Bary, William Theodore, Irene Bloom, and Joseph Adler, eds. *Sources of Chinese Tradition.* 2nd ed. 2 vols. New York: Columbia University Press, 2000. Includes primary materials on the movement.

Ebrey, Patricia Buckley, ed. *Chinese Civilization: A Sourcebook.* 2nd ed. New York: Free Press, 1993. Provides insights on the movement as well as related materials.

Giquel, Prosper. *A Journal of the Chinese Civil War, 1864.* Ed. Steven A. Leibo. Honolulu: University of Hawaii Press, 1985. A critical memoir by a leading advocate of change in China.

Snyder, Anthony, and Sherri West, eds. *Readings in Global History.* Vol. II. Rev. 2nd ed. Dubuque, IA: Kendall-Hunt, 1997. Includes primary materials that may be of use to students working on this topic.

Secondary Sources

Chien-Nung, Li, and J. Ingalls. *Political History of China, 1840–1928.* Trans. Ssu-Yu-Teng and J. Ingalls. Stanford, CA: Stanford University Press, 1956. Provides a solid introduction to the movement with the context of Chinese political thinking and the mounting fear of foreign culture.

Cohen, Paul A. *Between Tradition and Modernity: Wang T'ao and Reform in Late Ch'ing China.* Harvard East Asian Monographs, no. 133. Cambridge, MA: Harvard University Press, 1987. A meaningful scholarly study that includes extensive information on the reform movement.

Elman, Benjamin A., and Alexander Woodside, eds. *Education and Society in Late Imperial China, 1600–1900.* Studies on China No. 19. Berkeley: University of California Press, 1994. Integrates the development of education in China with the political and economic history of the nation.

Fairbank, John King. *The Great Chinese Revolution 1800–1985.* New York: Harper, 1987. A very important study by a leading American historian of China.

———. *The United States and China.* Cambridge, MA: Harvard University Press, 1983. Also available as an e-book at http://books.google.com/books?id=QCTvjaScEzYC. Includes data on American-Chinese relations during the period of the movement.

Grasso, June M., Jay Corrin, and Michael Kort. *Modernization and Revolution in China: From the Opium Wars to World Power.* 3rd ed. Armonk, NY: M. E. Sharpe, 2004. An excellent and reliable study that includes data on the rebellion.

Gray, Jack. *Rebellions and Revolutions: China from the 1800s to 2000.* 2nd ed. New York: Oxford University Press, 2003. A worthwhile study of the forces of change in China—both internal and external—during the nineteenth and twentieth centuries.

Hsu, Immanuel C. Y. *The Rise of Modern China.* 6th ed. New York: Oxford University Press, 1999. Good introduction to the movement and its impact on China.

Kim, Ki Hang. *Japanese Perspectives on China's Early Modernization: The Self-Strengthening Movement, 1860–1895, A Bibliographical Survey.* Ann Arbor: University of Michigan Press, 1974. While dated, this volume provides an excellent review of Japanese thinking on the movement.

Lee, Thomas B. K., ed. *Modern History of China and Japan.* New York: MSS Information, 1972. Includes scholarly essays that provide information on the Self-Strengthening Movement and comparisons between China and Japan in their efforts to modernize.

Leibo, Steven A. *A French Adviser to Imperial China: The Dilemma of Prosper Giquel.* Ann Arbor, MI: University Microfilms, 1982. An intriguing study of a Westerner in service to the Manchus during the movement.

———. *Transferring Technology to China: Prosper Giquel and the Self-Strengthening Movement.* Berkeley: University of California Press, 1985. An excellent study that should be consulted by all students working on this topic.

Pong, David. *Shen Pao-chen and China's Modernization in the Nineteenth Century.* Cambridge, U.K.: Cambridge University Press, 2003. Pong's scholarly work is essential for all students developing papers on the movement.

Schoppa, R. Keith. *The Columbia Guide to Modern Chinese History.* New York: Columbia University Press, 2000. An indispensable resource for studying any topic in modern Chinese history.

Shaughnessy, Edward L. *China: Empire and Civilization.* New York: Oxford University Press, 2000. A very good history that includes information on the movement.

Wakeman, Frederic E. *Strangers at the Gate: Social Disorder in South China, 1839–1862.* Berkeley: University of California Press, 1966. An examination of the internal social, economic, and political conditions in China from the beginning of the First Opium War to the T'ai Ping Rebellion and the Second Opium War.

Wright, David Curtis. *The History of China.* Westport, CT: Greenwood Press, 2001. Also available as an e-book at http://books.google.com/books ?id=Mot11Al5DNMC. An excellent general history of China that includes reliable data on the movement.

Zhao, Suishen. *A Nation-state by Construction: Dynamics of Modern Chinese Nationalism.* Stanford, CA: Stanford University Press, 2004. Connects Chinese identity with modernization.

World Wide Web

"Ch'iag China, Self-Strengthening." http://wsu.edu/~dee/CHING/SELF.HTM. Provides an excellent introduction to the movement.

"China, The Self-Strengthening Movement." http://www.workmall.com/ wfb2001/china/china_history_the_self_strengthening_movement.html. A reliable introduction to the movement with links to other sites.

"Protestant Missionaries and the Self-strengthening Movement in China." http://www.socyberty.com/History/Protestant-Missionaries-and-the -Self-strengthening-Movement-in-China.92225. An interesting and recent article by Andrew Sean Murphy that emphasizes the role of Prot-estant ministers in the Self-Strengthening Movement.

"Self-Strengthening Movement." http://www.encyclopedia.com/doc/1O48 -SelfStrengtheningMovement.html. Includes a brief introduction to the movement and its significance.

"Self-Strengthening Movement." http://www.onpedia.com/encyclopedia/Self -Strengthening-Movement. A very good article on the movement with multiple links to participants.

"The Self-Strengthening Movement." http://countrystudies.us/china/17.htm. Provides a comprehensive statement on the movement and its failure.

Multimedia Source

"Quing Dynasty." http://encarta.msn.com/encyclopedia_761557160_3/qing _dynasty.html. Includes 11 items on the dynasty, including a very good map and some items related to the Self-Strengthening Movement.

57. Social Democratic Party Is Founded in Germany (1863–1890)

The founding of the Social Democratic Party in Germany came about from two distinct but related developments. In 1863 Ferdinand Lassalle

(1825–1864) established the General German Workers' Association. Four years later August Bebel (1840–1913) and Wilhelm Liebknecht (1826–1900) founded the Social Democratic Workers' Party of Germany. In 1875 the two groups merged at the Gotha Congress and created the Socialist Workers' Party of Germany; in 1890 it became the Social Democratic Party (SPD). This Marxist party was designed to alter the relationship between those who governed and those who were being governed. It identified with the exploited workers against those who owned land and businesses and with those who shared a Marxist vision of the future—a classless society. During the late 1880s Edward Bernstein (1850–1932) emerged as a new leader and advanced a revisionist position on the attainment of power. He abandoned the Marxist requirement for revolutionary action and argued for an evolutionary approach—working within the increasingly democratic German political system. The SPD supported the German Emperor and his government in foreign policy, especially when that policy advanced anti-Russian positions. By 1912 the SPD was the strongest political party in Germany.

TERM PAPER SUGGESTIONS

1. Write a paper in which you compare the impact of Lassalle, Liebknecht, and Bebel on the early development of the Social Democratic Party.

2. Develop a term paper that addresses the reception of the Social Democratic Party and its Marxist agenda in Germany. Was it successful? Why?

3. Under the leadership of Edward Bernstein, the SPD moved clearly to evolutionary rather than revolutionary tactics to bring change to Germany. They accepted the movement of democracy and were confident in the inevitable success of their cause. Write a paper on this shift and Bernstein's role in it.

4. Write a paper based on the SPD's electoral results in Germany from the 1870s to 1900. Was the party more successful in certain regions? What about the demographic distinction between urban and rural voters?

5. Write a paper on the position of the SPD in 1900. Did it appear that the moderate evolutionary approach was prevailing?

ALTERNATIVE TERM PAPER SUGGESTIONS

1. Develop a podcast in which you interview Liebknecht and Bernstein on their hopes for the SPD. Where do they agree and disagree?

2. Develop an iMovie of the significant proceedings at the Gotha Congress.

3. Develop a podcast on the Erfurt Program of 1891—was it more radical than the positions taken at the Gotha Congress in 1875?

SUGGESTED SOURCES

Primary Sources

Bernstein, Edward. *Ferdinand Lassalle as a Social Reformer.* London: Swan Sonnenschein, 1893. Available online at http://www.marxists.org/reference/archive/bernstein/works/1893/lassalle/index.htm. A sympathetic account by a younger associate in the socialist movement that includes some primary materials.

Lassalle, Ferdinand. *The Working Man's Programme.* Trans. Edward Peters. New York: The Modern Press, 1884. Available as an e-book at http://books.google.com/books?id=jAnvxDwjIYgC. One of the founder's major works that advances the socialist ideals and agenda.

Marxists' Internet Archive. *Wilhelm Liebknecht.* http://www.marxists.org/archive/liebknecht-w/index.htm. This outstanding archive provides 19 primary sources written by Liebknecht between 1881 and 1901 and a biography.

————. *August Bebel.* http://www.marxists.org/archive/bebel/index.htm. Includes the text of Bebel's *Woman and Socialism* and 14 other writings, including his *Reminiscences* (1911).

Petz, William A., ed. *Wilhelm Liebknecht and German Social Democracy.* Trans. Erich Hahn. Westport, CT: Greenwood Press, 1994. Includes some excerpts of primary materials relating to Liebknecht's role during the early years of the Social Democratic Party.

Secondary Sources

Brandes, Georg. *Ferdinand Lassalle.* Chestnut Hill, MA: Elibrion/Adamant Media, 2001. Also available as an e-book at http://books.google.com/books?id=jTC_1mATZIYC. A biased but still worthwhile biography of Lassalle by the left-wing Danish literary critic Georg Brandes.

Dominick, Raymond H. *Wilhelm Liebknecht and the Founding of the Social Democratic Party.* Chapel Hill: University of North Carolina Press, 1982. Dominick's study remains the best analysis of Liebknecht's role in the establishment of the SPD.

Evans, Richard J. *Proletarians and Politics: Socialism, Protest, and the Working Class in Germany before the First World War.* New York: St. Martin's Press, 1990. An excellent study that considers the condition and politicalization of the German industrial works and their allegiance to the SPD.

Fisher, Lars. *The Socialist Response to Antisemitism in Imperial Germany.* Cambridge, U.K.: Cambridge University Press, 2007. An important study that includes information on the SPD's handling of anti-Semitism during the late nineteenth and early twentieth centuries.

Fletcher, Roger, ed. *Bernstein to Brandt: A Short History of German Social Democracy.* London: E. Arnold, 1987. The introductory chapter provides information on the founding of the Social Democratic Party and the movement toward evolutionary change.

Hunt, Karen. *Equivocal Feminists: The Social Democratic Federation and the Woman Question, 1884–1911.* Cambridge, U.K.: Cambridge University Press, 2002. A recent study on the complexities associated with the socialist's position on women's rights.

Lopes, Anne, and Gary Roth. *Men's Feminism: August Bebel and the German Socialist Movement.* Amherst, NY: Humanity Books, 2000. A scholarly study of Bebel, his views on feminism and women's rights, and the response of men to these views.

Maehl, William Harvey. *August Bebel: Shadow Emperor of the German Workers.* Philadelphia: American Philosophical Society, 1980. An absorbing study of Bebel and his enduring influence on the German working class during the late nineteenth century.

Potthoff, Heinrich, and Susanne Miller, eds. *A History of German Social Democracy from 1848 to the Present.* Trans. J. A. Underwood. New York: Berg/St. Martin's, 1986. A classic and comprehensive study that should be useful to all students working on this topic.

Reinhard, Richard W. *Crippled from Birth: German Social Democracy, 1844–1870.* Ames: Iowa State University Press, 1969. A critical analysis of the origins of Social Democracy and the obstacles that it confronted.

Roth, Guenther. *The Social Democrats in Imperial Germany: A Study in Working-Class Isolation and National Integration.* Totowa, NJ: Bedminster Press, 1963. A study of the growth of the SPD into the largest political party in Germany prior to the First World War.

Schultz, Hans-Joachim. *German Socialist Literature, 1860–1914: Predicaments of Criticism.* Columbia, SC: Camden House, 1993. Focuses on the intellectual and literary factors that emerged within German socialism.

Steger, Manfred B. *The Quest for Evolutionary Socialism: Eduard Bernstein and Social Democracy.* New York: Cambridge University Press, 1997. Perhaps the best study of Bernstein and his success in moving the SPD into the mainstream of German political life.

Weikart, Richard. *Socialist Darwinism: Evolution in German Socialist Thought from Marx to Bernstein.* San Francisco: International Scholars

Publications, 1999. Traces the movement from revolutionary to evolutionary tactics with the organizational structure of the SPD.

World Wide Web

"Ferdinand August Bebel." http://www.1911encyclopedia.org/Ferdinand _August_Bebel. An extensive biographical statement on Bebel and his role in the founding of the Social Democratic Party in Germany.

"Ferdinand Lassalle." http://www.1911encyclopedia.org/Ferdinand_Lassalle. A comprehensive statement on Lassalle's life and work.

"Wilhelm Liebknecht." http://www.1911encyclopedia.org/Wilhelm_Liebknecht. An introduction to Liebknecht life and his role in founding and developing the Social Democratic Party.

"Wilhelm Liebknecht." http://www.answers.com/topic/wilhelm-liebknecht. A collection of biographical statements from British, American, and German sources.

Multimedia Sources

"Timeline on Wilhelm Liebknecht." http://www.google.com/archivesearch ?hl=en&q=Wilhelm+Liebknecht&um=1&ie=UTF-8&scoring=t&sa =X&oi=timeline_result&resnum=11&ct=title. A very useful resource that provides a convenient chronological review of Liebknecht's life and achievements.

"Wilhelm Liebknecht." http://www.britannica.com/EBchecked/topic/339864/ Wilhelm-Liebknecht. Includes a photograph of Liebknecht.

"Wilhelm Liebknecht." http://www.encyclopedia.com/topic/Wilhelm _Liebknecht.aspx. Includes three photographs of Liebknecht.

58. *Syllabus of Errors* Is Issued (1864)

In 1864 Pope Pius IX, who served as pontiff from 1846 to 1878, issued a Papal Encyclical (*Quanta cura*) with an appended document known as the *Syllabus of Errors.* In the *Syllabus* Pius IX denounced as heretical to Catholicism most of the ideas that were current throughout Western culture—secularism, modernism, rationalism, and so forth. Pius IX came to the papacy as a liberal reformer but was transformed into a reactionary by the Revolutions of 1848 when he was forced to flee Rome. He was only reinstated as leader of the Papal States with the assistance of French troops. By the 1860s Pius IX was distancing the Papacy from the leadership of the national governments through a series of statements and appointments that resulted in identifying the Papacy with the distant past. To many secular leaders, the Roman Church was becoming increasingly irrelevant and marginalized. Therefore, while astounded with the breadth and depth of Pius IX's denunciation of the nineteenth-century world, European political leaders did not expend much effort in responding to it. The *Syllabus of Errors* was issued after several years of development within the Vatican. Catholic leaders believed that the triumph of secularism would result in the loss of many souls and that they had an obligation to make a clear statement on the perils of modernism. The *Syllabus of Errors* consisted of ten sections that identified false values, defined acceptable ideas, and specified errors that could lead to the loss of salvation: Pantheism, Naturalism, and Absolute Rationalism; Moderate Rationalism; Indifferentism, Latitudinarianism; Socialism, Communism, Secret Societies, Biblical Societies, Clerico-Liberal Societies; Errors Concerning the Church and Her Rights; Errors about Civil Society, considered both in itself and in its relation to the Church; Errors Concerning Natural and Christian Ethics; Errors Concerning Christian Marriage; Errors Regarding the Civil Power of the Sovereign Pontiff; and Errors Having Reference to Modern Liberalism.

TERM PAPER SUGGESTIONS

1. Develop a paper in which you focus on Pius IX's rationale for developing and distributing the *Syllabus of Errors*.
2. Write a paper in which the contents of the *Syllabus of Errors* are analyzed.
3. Develop a paper on the Roman Catholic response to the *Syllabus of Errors*—be sure to include the Catholic response that was critical of Pius IX.
4. Write a paper on the reaction of the European governments and the liberal community to the *Syllabus of Errors*.

ALTERNATIVE TERM PAPER SUGGESTIONS

1. Develop a 4–5 minute iMovie in which the English Catholic leadership evaluates the substance and significance of the *Syllabus of Errors*.
2. Develop a podcast in which Pius IX and his principal aides consider the consequences of the publication of the *Syllabus of Errors*.

3. As an American priest assigned to the Vatican, you are perplexed over some aspects of the *Syllabus of Errors.* Develop a blog with your family in Boston, expressing your concerns.

SUGGESTED SOURCES

Primary Sources

Cassidy, John F. *Personal Reminiscences of Pope Pius IX: A Tribute of Esteem and Love to the Memory of the Saintly and Glorious Pontiff.* Whitefish, MT: Kessinger Publishing, 2008; originally published in 1880. A worthwhile but obviously favorably biased memoir by a colleague of Pius IX.

Hull, Robert R., ed. *Dogmatic Canons and Decrees of the Council of Trent, Vatican Council I, Plus the Decree on the Immaculate Conception and the Syllabus of Errors.* Rockford, IL: Tan Books and Publishers, 1977. Very good translations of the critical documents published by Pius IX.

Gladstone, William. *Speeches of Pope Pius IX.* Whitefish, MT: Kessinger Publishing, 2007. An interesting collection of papal pronouncements assembled by a Protestant British politician.

Pius IX, Pope. *Encyclical: Quanta Cura & The Syllabus of Errors.* Kansas City, MO: Angelus Press, 2006. Complete text of the *Syllabus of Errors* along with notes.

"The Syllabus of Errors." http://www.ewtn.com/library/PAPALDOC/P9 SYLL.HTM. The contents of the document are presented in a comprehensible manner.

"The Syllabus of Errors." http://www.dailycatholic.org/syllabus.htm. Its contents with limited notes.

"The Syllabus of Errors Condemned by Pius IX." http://www.papalencyclicals.net/Pius09/p9syll.htm. A very good summary and text of the *Syllabus of Errors.*

Secondary Sources

Bury, J. B. *History of the Papacy in the 19th Century: Liberty and Authority in the Roman Catholic Church.* Ed. R. H. Murray. New York: Schocken Books, 1964. A classic criticism of the *Syllabus,* the First Vatican Council, and Pius IX.

Chiron, Yves. *Pope Pius IX: The Man and the Myth.* Kansas City, MO: Angelus Press, 2005. A generally sympathetic biography that includes a chapter on the *Syllabus of Errors.*

De Mattei, Roberto. *Pius IX.* Trans. John Laughland. Herefordshire, U.K.: Gracewing, 2004. A very good, critical scholarly account of Pius IX's life and times.

Gladstone, William E. *The Life and Pontificate of Pope Pius IX.* Ithaca, NY: Cornell University Library, 1878; reproduced digitally. Gladstone's biography deserves to be considered. It is biased but, in many ways, well-argued.

Hales, Edward Elton Y. *Pio Nono, A Study in European Politics and Religion in the Nineteenth Century.* London: Eyre and Spottiswoode, 1954. An excellent biography of Pius IX that is very useful for any paper on *The Syllabus of Errors.*

Hull, Robert R. *The Syllabus of Errors of Pope Pius IX: The Scourge of Liberalism.* Huntington, IN: Our Sunday Visitor Press, 1926. A defense of Pius IX and the *Syllabus.*

Jagodits, Ernest. *Prisoner of the Vatican: A Story of Pope Pius IX.* Notre Dame, IN: Dujarie Press, 1962. A Catholic interpretation of Pius IX and his pontificate.

McElrath, Damian. *The Syllabus of Pius IX, Some Reactions in England.* Louvain: Bibliothèque de l'université, 1964. A relevant and useful scholarly work on British public and private reactions to the publication of the *Syllabus of Errors.*

Mills, Alexius. *The Life of Pope Pius IX.* London: D. Lane, 1877. An old but still useful biography that contains interesting information on the personal life of Pius IX.

Monk of St. Augustines. *The Syllabus for the People: A Review of the Propositions Condemned by His Holiness Pope Pius IX, with text of the Condemned List.* Whitefish, MT: Kessinger Publishing, 2007; originally published in 1875. A defense and amplification of the ideas advanced in the *Syllabus of Errors.*

Nielsen, Fredrik. *The History of the Papacy in the XIXth Century.* 2nd ed. Ed. and trans. Arthur James Mason. London: John Murray, 1906. A scholarly and useful history of the papacy with sections on Pius IX and the *Syllabus of Errors.*

Noll, Mark A. *Turning Points: Decisive Moments in the History of Christianity.* 2nd ed. Grand Rapids, MI: Baker Academic, 2001. An evangelical historian's interpretation on Pius IX and the *Syllabus of Errors.*

O'Reilly, Bernard. *A Life of Pius IX Down to the Episcopal Jubilee of 1877.* New York: P. F. Collier, 1877. A very reliable and sympathetic biography of Pius IX.

Shea, John Gilmary. *The Life of Pope Pius IX and the Great Events in the History of the Church During His Pontificate.* Whitefish, MT: Kessinger Publishing, 2008; originally published in 1877. The classic Catholic biography of Pius IX, it is sympathetic on almost all aspects of his life.

Thornton, Francis B. *Cross Upon Cross: The Life of Pope Pius IX.* New York: Benziger Brothers, 1955. A sympathetic biography of Pius IX.

Wallace, Lillian Parker. *The Papacy and European Diplomacy, 1869–1878.* Chapel Hill: University of North Carolina Press, 1948. A scholarly examination of Pius IX's diplomatic relations with the European states during the establishment of the Kingdom of Italy. It is very useful.

Washburn, Henry Bradford. *Men of Conviction.* New York: Charles Scribner's Sons, 1931. The final chapter in this well-written book is an analysis of Pius IX's life and work.

Williams, John Herbert. *Pope Pius IX.* London: Sands, 1920. A Catholic interpretation of Pius IX's life.

World Wide Web

"Encyclicals and Writings of Pope Pius IX." http://www.piustheninth.com/appendix.htm. A thorough and accurate listing of the published works of Pius IX.

"Letter of John Henry Newman to the Duke of York on the *Syllabus of Errors.*" http://www.newmanreader.org/works/anglicans/volume2/gladstone/section7.html. An important commentary on the *Syllabus of Errors* by a prominent British contemporary

"Pius IX." http://atheism.about.com/library/glossary/western/bldef_piusix.htm. A good introduction to the life of Pope Pius IX.

"Pius IX (Giovanni Maria Mastai-Ferretti, 1792–1878)." http://www.ohiou.edu/~Chastain/ip/piusix.htm. A good biography of Pius IX on the Ohio University Web site.

"The Syllabus of Pius IX." http://www.newadvent.org/cathen/14368b.htm. A very good summary of the encyclical, its origins, and significance.

Multimedia Source

"Bishop Richard Williamson on *The Syllabus of Errors.*" http://www.youtube.com/watch?v=F2LO97E7ycg. Seven-part defense of the *Syllabus,* from a conference on June 8, 2008, Stockholm, Sweden.

59. Paraguayan War (1864–1870)

During the 1860s tensions mounted in South America between Paraguay and three of its neighbors, Argentina, Brazil, and Uruguay. While Uruguay experienced political civil war and economic and social weakness and instability, Paraguay, under the leadership of its dictator, Francisco Solano López (1827–1870), strove to be recognized as comparable to these three states. In response, Argentina and Brazil were anxious about Paraguay's intentions. The war, also called the War of the Triple Alliance, began when Argentina and Brazil allied themselves with the rebels in Uruguay and the Uruguayan government sought the assistance of Paraguay. López invaded a section of Brazil in the fall of 1864 and then Argentina in 1865. The Triple Alliance (Argentina, Brazil, and the Uruguayan rebels) was formed in May 1865 to counter Paraguay. Within a year Paraguayan forces were defeated on land and sea in devastating losses, and Argentinean, Brazilian, and Uruguayan forces invaded Paraguay. In addition to the losses that resulted from the military actions, many thousands died from diseases that were not controlled. By 1868 much of Paraguay and its capital, Asunción, were occupied by the allied forces; however, the struggle continued until López was killed on March 1, 1870. The impact of the war was devastating to all of the participants, especially Paraguay, which experienced more than 300,000 casualties while the allies suffered about 100,000 casualties. Paraguay was isolated after the war and never achieved the political or economic recognition that it sought.

TERM PAPER SUGGESTIONS

1. López had great ambitions for Paraguay and himself but appeared to have little understanding of the geopolitical situation that he confronted. Develop a term paper on López's plans for his country and his actions during 1864.

2. Write a term paper on the internal political crisis in Uruguay and how that contributed to the outbreak of the War of the Triple Alliance.

3. Develop a paper in which you compare and contrast the prosecution of the war by both sides.

4. The human toll of this war was staggering, especially when comparing the losses with the total populations at that time. Analyze the impact of the war on all of the participants and the region.

ALTERNATIVE TERM PAPER SUGGESTIONS

1. As López became involved in Uruguayan affairs, Pedro II of Brazil and others became increasingly concerned with his intentions. Develop a 4–5 minute podcast in which Brazilian and Argentinean leaders reflected on Paraguayan motives and actions that led to the outbreak of the war.

2. Many Paraguayan youths were attracted to López's ambitious plans for Paraguay in the 1860s. Imagine yourself one of these and develop a blog that consists of your diary entries during 1864 and 1865, recording and reflecting on the developments in the war.

3. The war is over in 1870 and it is time to take an account of its costs and impact. Develop an iMovie in which you interview survivors on both sides.

SUGGESTED SOURCES

Primary Sources

Burton, Richard Francis. *Letters from the Battlefield of Paraguay.* London: Tinsley Brothers, 1870. A valuable collection of personal letters from a partici- pant in the war.

Codman, John. *Ten Months in Brazil with Notes on the Paraguayan War.* White- fish, MT: Kessinger, 2008; originally published in 1872. A memoir of a participant who supported the Brazilians during the struggle.

Garcia, Manuel. *Paraguay and the Alliance against the Tyrant Francisco Solano Lopez: General Remarks, Reliable Documents.* New York: Hallett and Breen, 1869. An important contemporary account that held López per- sonally responsible for the tragedies that emerged from the war.

Hutchinson, Thomas Joseph. *The Paraná: With Incidents of the Paraguayan War, and South American Recollections, from 1861 to 1868.* London: Edward Stanford, 1868. Available as an e-book at http://books.google.com/ books?id=elYCAAAAYAAJ&dq=Hutchinson,+Thomas+Joseph.+The +Paran%C3%A1:+with+incidents+of+the+Paraguayan+War,+and +South+American+Recollections,+from+1861+to+1868&source=gbs _summary_s&cad=0. Includes personal reflections and remembrances that should be valuable to many students.

Lidgerwood, William Van. *Paraguay Difficulties: Letter from the Secretary of State, Transmitting a Copy of the Dispatch of February Last.* Washington: U.S. Government Printing Office, 1869. Within the context of the American perception of dominance in the Western Hemisphere, this let- ter may be useful to students who are working on papers involving the combatant nations and other states.

Mastermann, George Frederick. *Seven Eventful Years in Paraguay: A Narrative of Personal Experiences Amongst the Paraguayans.* 2nd ed. London: S. Low, Son and Marston, 1870. Mastermann was a captive who was released. While much of this volume constitutes primary material, some sections were not based on firsthand information.

United States Congress, House Committee on Foreign Affairs. *Report of the Committee on Foreign Affairs, on the Memorial of Porter C. Bliss and*

George F. Mastermann, in Relation to Their Imprisonment in Paraguay. Washington, DC: U.S. House of Representatives, 1870. Generally, a reliable account of the experiences of Bliss and Mastermann in Paraguay; they were American citizens who were imprisoned in Paraguay during the war.

Washburn, Charles A. *The History of the Paraguay War, with Notes of Personal Observations, and Reminiscences of Diplomacy under Difficulties.* New York: AMS Press, 1973; originally published in 1871. A useful memoir by a retired diplomat.

Secondary Sources

Bethell, Leslie. *The Paraguayan War: History and Historiography.* London: Institute of Latin American Studies, University of London, 1996. An excellent review of the primary and secondary source materials available on the war.

Box, Pelham Horton. *The Origins of the Paraguayan War, With Bibliography.* Urbana: University of Illinois Press, 1929. An old but still excellent and useful scholarly study of the causes of the Paraguayan War.

Cunningham-Graham, Robert. *Portrait of a Dictator: Francisco Solano Lopez (Paraguay, 1865–1870).* London: William Heinemann, 1933. An important biography of López that should be useful to many students.

Diego, Abente. "The War of the Triple Alliance." *Latin American Research Review* XXII, no. 2 (1987): 47–69. An excellent history of the war by an established scholar.

Dominguez, Jorge I. *Latin America's International Relations and Their Domestic Consequences: War and Peace, Dependence and Autonomy.* New York: Routledge, 1994. Includes references to the Paraguayan war that may stimulate new term paper ideas.

Hooker, Terry. *The Paraguayan War: Armies of the Nineteenth Century—The Americas.* Mineral Point, WI: Foundry Books, 2008. Perhaps the best military history of the war.

Kohn, Roger. *Weep, Grey Bird, Weep: The Paraguayan War 1864–1870.* Bloomington, IN: AuthorHouse, 2008. A history of the war from the perspective of a Paraguayan couple. It is sympathetic to the Paraguayan people on their sufferings caused by the war.

Kolinski, Charles J. *Independence or Death! The Story of the Paraguayan War.* Gainesville: University of Florida Press, 1965. A readable and reliable history of the war that should be available in most large libraries.

Leuchars, Chris. *To the Bitter End: Paraguay and the War of the Triple Alliance.* Westport, CT: Greenwood Press, 2002. A comprehensive and valuable history of the war that is well documented and includes a useful bibliography.

Michigan Historical Society. *The Paraguayan Question.* Ann Arbor: University of Michigan Library, 2005. This pamphlet includes information on the war and the place of Paraguay in nineteenth-century Latin American affairs.

Phelps, Gilbert. *Tragedy of Paraguay.* New York: St. Martin's Press, 1975. A well-written analysis of the impact of the war on the region and its people.

Saeger, James Schofield. *Francisco Solano López and the Ruination of Paraguay: Honor and Egocentricism.* Lanham, MD: Rowman and Littlefield, 2007. An excellent study that indicts López as being personally accountable for the war and its horrors.

Scheina, Robert L. *Latin America's War. Volume I: The Age of the Caudillo, 1791–1899.* Dulles, VA: Potomac Books, 2003. An important book by a prominent scholar that includes excellent information on the Paraguayan War.

Schumway, Nicolas. *The Invention of Argentina.* Berkeley: University of California, 1991. This accurate and reliable scholarly study includes extensive information on the Argentinean involvement in the Paraguayan War.

Thompson, Jorge. *The War in Paraguay, With a Historical Sketch of the Country and Its People and Notes upon the Military Engineering of the War.* London: Longmans, Green, 1869. A contemporary's analysis of the causes and progress of the war.

Whigham, Thomas. *The Paraguayan War.* Lincoln: University of Nebraska Press, 2002. An excellent scholarly study of all aspects of the war.

———— and Hendrik Kraay, eds. *I Die with My Country: Perspectives on the Paraguayan War, 1864–1870.* Lincoln: University of Nebraska Press, 2004. A series of useful essays on aspects of the Paraguayan War.

World Wide Web

"The Paraguayan War." http://www.erroluys.com/ParaguayanWar.htm. A description of aspects of the war between November 1864 and June 1865.

"The War of the Triple Alliance." http://countrystudies.us/paraguay/11.htm. A good introduction to the war, with some statistical information provided.

"War of the Triple Alliance 1864–1870." http://www.onwar.com/aced/data/tango/triple1864.htm. A fact-filled statement on the war that serves as a very good introduction.

Multimedia Source

Cerro Cora. IMDb Pro, 1978. DVD. Directed by Guillermo Vera; in Spanish, with English subtitles. Dramatic film that portrays Francisco Solano López as a hero.

60. Passage of the British North America Act (Constitution Act), Canada (1867)

The British North America Act of 1867 established a federal, self-governing union in Canada and initiated the process that would lead to extended centralized government during the years ahead. This Act, which established the Dominion of Canada, has been referred to as the Constitution Act or, more frequently, as the BNA Act. The draft text for the British North America Act was developed by a Canadian constitutional committee that convened in Quebec in 1864. The draft that was developed was presented to the British government and passed without any modifications in 1867. Queen Victoria enacted the measure when she signed it on July 1, 1867. This Act has been amended and expanded by 19 subsequent acts that were adopted between 1871 and 1975. Full Canadian independence over their affairs was achieved in 1982.

The rationale for the British North America Act of 1867 was complex and involved both internal and external factors. Supporters of a centralized Canadian government feared the rebellious tradition that had been evident in the rebellions in Upper and Lower Canada and the autonomy that the Métis (racially mixed residents of the western provinces) wanted. In addition, Canadians feared a potential invasion by the United States after the close of the American Civil War. The Act of Union of 1841 reflected the division of Anglo and French Canadians and attempted to develop a structure that would sustain the peace and provide for economic and political growth. By the 1860s Canada had been transformed by the impact of railroads and canals in the east. The population was expanding rapidly and tensions against the central government were beginning to mount. It was in this environment that the British North America Act of 1867 was developed and adopted. The BNA Act provided for a federal system with a distribution of powers among the branches of government; modeled on Britain, it is a parliamentary system. Specific sections of the Act address criminal law, the judicial system, property, civil and language rights, and other areas of common concern.

TERM PAPER SUGGESTIONS

1. Write a paper on the background and causes for the adoption of the British North America Act of 1867.

2. Develop a paper on the constitutional impact of the British North America Act (1867) on Canadian history.

3. Develop a paper in which you present an analysis of the British North America Act (1867).

ALTERNATIVE TERM PAPER SUGGESTIONS

1. Develop a 4–5 minute podcast on the deliberations of the Canadian committee that developed a draft of the British North America Act. Be sure to include the views of dissenters.

2. Develop an iMovie on the reception of the news of the passage of the British North America Act by French Canadians.

3. As a young English-speaking Canadian in Toronto in 1867, develop a blog that reflects your aspirations and concerns for the new Canada as established by the British North America Act.

SUGGESTED SOURCES

Primary Sources

Fieldhouse, David, and Frederick Madden, eds. *Settler Self-Government 1840–1900: The Development of Representative and Responsible Government, Select Documents on the Constitutional History of the British Empire and Commonwealth.* Westport, CT: Greenwood Press, 1990. An excellent resource that includes data on the tensions between Upper and Lower Canada and eastern and western Canada on government structures and processes.

Loranger, T. J. J. *Letters Upon the Interpretation of the Federal Constitution known as the British North America Act (1867).* Halifax, Nova Scotia: Morning-Chronicle, 1884. An important collection of Loranger's letters on the impact of the Act on Canadian national unity.

Samuels, H. Raymond. *Selected Canadian Constitutional Documents: British North America Acts, 1867, 1886, 1907, 1960 and the Statue of Westminster 19931 in the Original Presentation: Unannotated.* Toronto: The Agora Cosmopolitan, 2002. A comprehensive collection of primary source documents on Canadian constitutional and political development.

Secondary Sources

Anonymous. *The British North America Act, 1867.* Lenox, MA: Hard Press, 2006. A description of the Act with comments by contemporaries.

Bourinot, John George. *A Manual of the Constitutional History of Canada from the Earliest Period to 1901; . . . Including the British North America Act of 1867, a Digest of Judicial . . . on the Working of Parliamentary Government.* Toronto: Coop, Clark, 1901. An informative and still useful introduction to the passage of the British North America Act of 1867.

Buckner, Philip, ed. *Canada and the British Empire.* New York: Oxford University Press, 2008. This is an outstanding resource that is focused on Canada's place and image within the British Empire. It includes chapters on nineteenth-century Canadian history and the movement to and the impact of the British North America Act.

Driedger, Elmer A., ed. *The British North America Acts 1867 to 1975.* Ottawa: Canadian Justice Department, 1976. Provides useful commentary on the 1867 Act and its impact.

Hassard, Albert Richard. *Canadian Constitutional History and Law.* Whitefish, MT: Kessinger, 2008; originally published in 1900. An old but still reliable standard history of Canadian constitutional history including a major section on the British North America Act of 1867.

Lefroy, A. H. F. *Canada's Federal System: Being a Treatise on Canadian Constitutional Law Under the British North America Act.* Clarek, NJ: Lawbook Exchange, 2006. The definitive legal study on the Act and its impact on Canadian history.

McConnell, William H. *Commentary on the British North America Act.* Toronto: Macmillan, 1977. Includes contemporary and later commentaries on the Act and its meaning in Canadian history.

Martin, Ged. *Britain and the Origins of Canadian Confederation, 1837–1867.* Vancouver: University of British Columbia Press, 1995. Includes a major chapter on the passage and provisions of the British North America Act.

Morton, W. L. *The West and Confederation, 1857–1871.* Ottawa: Canadian Historical Association, 1968. A short but useful monograph that includes the impact of the Act on western Canada.

Riddell, William Renwick. *Some Origins of "The British North America Act, 1867."* Ottawa: Royal Society of Canada, 1917. Provides information on the background and causes for the British North America Act.

Westra, Johan G. *Confederation in Canada: A Study of the British North America Act.* Toronto: National Union of Christian Schools, 1976. A general history of the constitutional evolution of Canada.

World Wide Web

"British North America Act, 1867: Document." http://www.thecanadian encyclopedia.com/index.cfm?PgNm=TCE&Params=A1ARTA00

10015. Provides a selected text of the most important provisions of the Act.

"Constitution Act, 1867." http://www.thecanadianencyclopedia.com/index.cfm ?PgNm=TCE&Params=A1ARTA0001873. Provides a history of the Act that was renamed the Constitution Act.

"Constitution Act, 1867." http://www.solon.org/Constitutions/Canada/ English/ca_1867.html. An excellent text of the Act with notes.

"Province of Canada, 1841–67." http://www.thecanadianencyclopedia.com/ index.cfm?PgNm=TCE&Params=A1ARTA0006530. Addresses the development of Canadian politics from the uprisings in Lower and Upper Canada during the 1830s to the passage of the British North America Act in 1867.

Multimedia Sources

"British North America Act, 1867." Encyclopedia Britannica, 2007. Audio/ Video. www.britannica.com/EBchecked/topic/80310/British-North -America-Act. Provides an introduction to the Act and its significance.

"Confederation and Expansion (How History Works?)." Audio/Video, 2003. http://history.howstuffworks.com/canadian-history/history-of-canada5. htm. A brief introduction to the impact of the provisions of the British North America Act of 1867.

61. Red River Rebellion in Canada (1869–1870)

Following the establishment of the Canadian Confederation in 1867, tensions mounted between the Métis (French-speaking mixed-breed people) and the Canadian government when the latter proceeded to incorporate the recently acquired Rupert's Land under its authority. Rupert's Land had been acquired recently from the Hudson's Bay Company. The government indicated that it intended to establish an English-speaking society that was modeled on local communities in Ontario. The Métis refused to comply and established a provisional government—this was the initial act of rebellion. The Métis were led by Louis Riel who was an advocate of French-speaking institutions and the rights of the Catholic Church. While efforts were made to resolve the crisis, events, such as Riel's execution of Thomas Scott, led to general outrage in Ontario and demands for suppression of the French/Catholic Métis. An army was formed and sent to the West. Its arrival pressured the Métis to reach an accommodation, as they were unprepared to confront a fully equipped military force. The resistance collapsed and Manitoba was established as a new province in the Confederation. Riel fled to Montana (he was exiled formally in 1875). The Red River Rebellion resulted from a cultural conflict that was to be reignited in 1885 in the North-West Rebellion.

TERM PAPER SUGGESTIONS

1. Write a paper on the causes and outbreak of the Red River Rebellion.
2. Develop a paper on the actions associated with the rebellion and its suppression.
3. Write a paper in which you discuss the emergence of the Métis and their role in the rebellion.
4. Develop a term paper in which you connect the results of the Red River Rebellion with the origins and outbreak of the North-West Rebellion in 1885.
5. Write a paper in which you discuss and analyze the detailed aspirations of the rebels.
6. Develop a paper on the role of the Catholic Church and its leaders in the rebellion.

ALTERNATIVE TERM PAPER SUGGESTIONS

1. In a podcast format, interview the rebel leader, Louis Riel. What motivated him? What did he hope to achieve?
2. Develop a Web site on the rebellion in which you include a detailed map of the war, and information on the causes, participants, and consequences of the Red River Rebellion.
3. Develop an iMovie in which you are a correspondent with the Métis and follow them in their efforts during the rebellion.
4. Develop a blog on your experiences in the rebellion as a member of the Royal Canadian Mounted Police.

SUGGESTED SOURCES

Primary Sources

Bumsted, J. M., ed. *Reporting the Resistance: Alexander Begg and Joseph Hargrave on the Red River Resistance.* Winnipeg: University of Manitoba Press, 2003. Includes correspondence by the two journalists and other source materials.

Crissey, Forrest. *The Young Newspaper Scout. An Interesting Narrative of a Boy's Adventures in the Northwest during the Riel Rebellion.* 2 vols. Chicago: W. B. Conkey, 1895. Available as an e-book through American Libraries, Internet Archive, http://www.archive.org/details/youngnewspapersc00cris. A useful narrative of recollections by an eyewitness who was a teen during the rebellion.

Huyshe, George Lightfoot. *The Red River Expedition.* London and New York: Macmillan, 1871. Available as an e-book through Canadian Libraries, Internet Archive, http://www.archive.org/details/redriverexpediti00huys. A memoir of the rebellion by a British army officer.

MacBeth, R. G. *The Making of the Canadian West; Being the Reminiscences of an Eye-Witness.* Toronto: Coles Publishing, 1973; originally published in 1898. MacBeth's recollections constitute a major primary source on the rebellion.

MacDougall, William, Francis Hincks, and Joseph Howe. *The Red River Rebellion: Eight Letters to Hon. Joseph Howe, Secretary of States for the Provinces, Etc., in Reply to an Official Pamphlet.* Ottawa: Hunter, Rose, 1870. Available as an e-book through Google Book Search, http://www.books.google.com/ books?id=sqpLVqWa8H4C&dq=Sources+on+Red+River+Rebellion. MacDougall was a major participant in the rebellion, and these letters are important resources in understanding anti-Riel sentiment.

McDougall, John. *In the Days of the Red River Rebellion: Life and Adventure in the Far West of Canada (1868–1872).* Edmonton: University of Alberta Press, 1983; originally published in 1911. Available as an e-book through Canadian Libraries, Internet Archive, http://www.archive.org/ details/indaysofredriver00mcdouoft. A useful eyewitness account of much that occurred during the rebellion.

O'Donnell, John H. *Manitoba as I Saw It, from 1869 to Date, with Flash-lights on the First Riel Rebellion.* Toronto: Musson, 1909. Available as an e-book through American Libraries, Internet Archive, http://www.archive.org/ details/manitobaasisawit00odon. An eyewitness account that includes select recollections.

Stanley, G. F. G., ed. *The Collected Writings of Louis Riel/Les Ecrits complets de Louis Riel.* 5 vols. Edmonton, Alberta: University of Alberta Press, 1985. The definitive collection of Riel's works.

Secondary Sources

Begg, A. *The Creation of Manitoba or a History of the Red River Troubles.* Toronto: Hunter Rose, 1871. A history of the rebellion that is critical of Riel and the Métis.

Bowsfield, Hartwell. *Louis Riel: Rebel of the Western Frontier or Victim of Politics and Prejudice?* Toronto: Copp Clark, 1969. Presents alternative sources and interpretations on Riel, and is a very useful resource for term papers.

Buckner, Philip. *Canada and the British Empire.* Oxford History of the British Empire Companion. New York: Oxford University Press, 2008. An outstanding comprehensive history that provides a solid introduction to most aspects of Canadian history and a very good bibliography.

Bumsted, J. M. *The Red River Rebellion.* Toronto: Watson and Dwyer, 1996. An excellent history by a recognized authority.

Giraud, Marcel. *The Métis in the Canadian West.* Lincoln: University of Nebraska Press, 1986. A very useful introduction to the Métis, their values, and role on the rebellions.

Flanagan, Thomas. *Louis "David" Riel: Prophet of the New World.* Rev. ed. Toronto: University of Toronto Press, 1996. A scholarly and readable study based on primary sources that emphasizes the impact of religion on Riel's political ideology.

Howard, James H. *The Canadian Sioux.* Lincoln: University of Nebraska Press, 1984. An excellent history of the Canadian Sioux—includes data on their impact in the Riel rebellions.

Howard, Joseph Kinsey. *Strange Empire: A Narrative of the Northwest.* Westport, CT: Greenwood Press, 1974. Focused on Louis Riel's role in the rebellion, this is a reliable resource.

Kreutzweiser, Erwin E. *The Red River Insurrection: Its Causes and Events.* Gardenvale, Quebec: Garden City Press, 1939. A well-organized and presented history of the Red River Rebellion that provides an excellent introduction.

Morice, A. G. *A Critical History of the Red River Insurrection.* Winnipeg, Manitoba: Canadian Publishers, 1935. A history that is sympathetic to Riel and the Métis but is still useful.

Oppen, William A. *The Riel Rebellions: A Cartographic History.* Toronto: University of Toronto Press, 1980. A very important and useful book that examines the geopolitical significance of the Red River and North-West Rebellions.

Pannekoek, Frits. *A Snug Little Flock: The Social Origins of the Riel Resistance of 1869–70.* Toronto: J. Gordon Shillingford, 1998. An important scholarly study that provides insightful comments on the Métis society and its impact in the Red River Rebellion.

Peel, Bruce Braden. *Early Printing in the Red River Settlement 1859–1870: And its effect on the Riel Rebellion.* Winnipeg, Manitoba: Peguis, 1974. Highly specialized and valuable study of the impact of the press on the development of the revolutionary opposition.

Siggins, Maggie. *Riel: A Life of Revolution.* Toronto: HarperCollins, 1994. A very good and useful biography of Riel and the values and ideas that motivated his leadership in the Red River and North-West Rebellions.

Stanley, George F. *The Birth of Western Canada: A History of the Riel Rebellions.* Toronto: University of Toronto Press, 1960. Examines the impact of the Red River and Riel rebellions on the development of western Canada, and includes useful maps by C. C. J. Bond.

———. *Louis Riel.* Toronto: McGraw-Hill Ryerson, 1963. An excellent biography of Riel that is comprehensive and well-documented.

———. *Toil and Trouble: Military Expeditions to Red River.* Toronto: Dundurn Press, 1989. A very good account of the government's suppression of the rebellion.

World Wide Web

"*Canadian Illustrated News* and the Red River Rebellion." http://www.collectionscanada.gc.ca/cin.026019-204-e.html. A review of the coverage of the rebellion included in the *Canadian Illustrated News* by Sean Sullivan, which includes copies of some of the illustrations.

"Métis." http://www.thecanadianencyclopedia.com/index.cfm?PgNm=TCE&Params=A1ARTA0005259. An excellent introduction by Jennifer S. H. Brown to the Métis (mixed-blood natives and Europeans) and their role in the rebellion.

"MétisNet, A Handbook of Métis Facts." http://www.saskschools.ca/~mandelassash/newsite/metisfacts/metisfactsa.html. See the section on the "Red River Resistance."

"Rebellion/Settlement Timeline." http://timelinks.merlin.mb.ca/ourcommunity/History/1869-1870.htm. Valuable and useful detailed timeline on the rebellion.

"Red River Expeditionary Force, 1870–1877." http://www.rootsweb.ancestry.com/~canmil/riel/rrefint.htm?cj=1&o_xid=0001091115&o_lid=0001091115. Data on the composition of the force that suppressed the rebellion.

"Red River Rebellion." http://www.thecanadianencyclopedia.com/index.cfm?PgNm=TCE&Params=A1ARTA0006727. A very good introduction to the history of the rebellion by J. M. Bumsted.

"Red River Resistance." http://www.mhs.mb.ca/docs/mb_history/29/redriverresistance.shtml. An account of the rebellion on the Web site of the Manitoba Historical Society that includes five photographs and two maps.

"The Red River Rebellions." http://www.iigs.org/newsletter/9811news/metis.htm.en. An account of the Red River and North-West Rebellions by Robert A. Bonnar that focused on Riel and his aspirations.

"Selkirk Settlement and the Creation of Manitoba." http://www.canadiana.org/
citm/themes/pioneers/pioneers5_e.html. Includes documents on the
Red River Rebellion.

Multimedia Sources

"Map of the District of Assiniboia 1812–1870" and copy of a portrait of
"Louis Riel." http://encarta.msn.com/media_461539957_761588467
_-1_1/Louis_Riel.html. The map is very useful and accurate.

"Red River Rising." http://www.canadianheritage.ca/galleries/warsbattles
rebellions0600.htm#Red%20River%20Rising. Includes one photograph of the First Ontario Rifles and a copy of a proclamation about
the rebellion.

Rethinking Riel. Online video series produced by the Canadian Broadcasting
Company, 2004, CBC Archives. http://archives.cbc.ca/society/native
_issues/topics/1482-9912/. Very useful source on Riel's character and
his life as a rebel.

62. Opening of the Suez Canal (1869)

With the revolution in transportation that resulted from the Industrial
Revolution and the development of an industrial economy, the development of an Egyptian canal connecting the Mediterranean Sea with the
Gulf of Suez on the Red Sea (and then on to the Indian Ocean) was
advanced by French engineers led by Ferdinand de Lesseps (1805–
1894). The original design for the canal was developed by Alois Negrelli
(1799–1858), an Austrian engineer. During the Crimean War (1854–
1856), de Lesseps obtained a charter to organize a company to build such
a canal. The *Compagnie Universelle du Canal Maritime de Suez* was
formed late in 1858 and began to raise the necessary capital. Shares in
the *Compagnie* sold rapidly in France but not in other countries. Construction required 11 years with more than 25,000 forced laborers and
extensive cost overruns. The canal opened on November 17, 1869. During its initial decade, two unexpected developments occurred with the
Suez Canal. First, the anticipated increase in world trade did not materi-
alize, and, second, Britain, which did not support the project and, at the
same time, feared French expansionist intentions in East Africa and South
Asia, gained a significant financial holding in the canal as a result of Prime
Minister Benjamin Disraeli's acquisition of the shares of Isma'il Pasha.

By 1882 British troops were deployed to protect the canal. The British position was ratified by the Convention of Constantinople in 1888.

TERM PAPER SUGGESTIONS

1. Write a paper on the engineering, financial, and diplomatic arrangements that were necessary to support the construction of the Suez Canal.

2. Develop a paper in which you evaluate the significance of the Suez Canal on European diplomacy and world trade during the nineteenth century.

3. Construct a paper on the crisis that led to the British acquiring a substantial interest in the Suez Canal. What were the immediate results of that action?

4. Write a paper on the impact of the Suez Canal project on the Egyptian people.

ALTERNATIVE TERM PAPER SUGGESTIONS

1. As an engineer on the Suez Canal project, develop a blog on the most significant milestones in the construction of the canal.

2. Develop an iMovie about the weekend in which Disraeli managed to gain Britain an interest in the Suez Canal.

3. Develop a 4–5 minute podcast in which French financial, political, and engineering leaders consider the potential pitfalls in undertaking the construction of the Suez Canal.

SUGGESTED SOURCES

Primary Sources

"Consolidation of Egypt's Debts, 1876." http://www.nationalarchives.gov.uk/battles/egypt/popup/consolidation.htm. A copy of the British commitment to assume Egypt's debts for exchange of a controlling interest in the Suez Canal.

Disraeli, Benjamin. *Selected Speeches of Benjamin Disraeli*. Whitefish, MT: Kessinger Publishing, 2004. A collection of most of Disraeli's most important public statements, including his defense on acquiring the Suez Canal.

Harlow, Barbara, and Mia Carter, eds. *Archives of Empire: Volume I, From the East India Company to the Suez Canal*. Durham, NC: Duke University Press, 2003. Includes useful documents related to the Suez Canal project and British interest in it.

Gillard, David, ed. *British Documents on Foreign Affairs: Reports and Paper from the Foreign Office Confidential Print. Part I, From the Mid-Nineteenth*

Century to the First World War. Series B. The Near and Middle East, 1856–1914. 20 vols. Frederick, MD: University Publications of America, 1984ff. Excellent primary sources in Volume 8 on the Ottoman Empire in North Africa, the Suez Canal, Red Sea, and Tunisian problems, 1859–1882.

Lesseps, Ferdinand de. *Recollections of Forty Years.* Trans. C. B. Pitman. 2 vols. London: Chapman and Hall, 1887. Essential for an understanding of the scope and complexity of the Suez Canal project.

Secondary Sources

Avram, Benno. *The Evolution of the Suez Canal Status from 1869 up to 1956, A Historico-Juridical Study.* Ambilly: Coopérative "Les Presses de Savoie," 1958. The early sections of this study should be useful to many students writing term papers on Suez.

Balfour, Patrick. *Between Two Seas: The Creation of the Suez Canal.* New York: William Morrow, 1968. A very good and readable history of the planning and construction of the Suez Canal.

Blake, Robert. *Disraeli.* New York: St. Martin's Press, 1967. Still the best single-volume biography of Disraeli, which includes very useful information on Disraeli's takeover of the canal.

Bradford, Sarah. *Disraeli.* New York: Stein and Day, 1983. A very good and readable biography of Disraeli, which includes information on the British *coup* in gaining control of the Suez Canal.

Buckle, William F., and George E. Monypenny. *The Life of Benjamin Disraeli, Earl of Beaconsfield.* 6 vols. London: Macmillan, 1914. A marvelous biography that includes both secondary and some printed primary materials on Disraeli's acquisition of the Suez Canal.

Davidson, Frank P., and Kathleen L. Brooke. *Building the World: An Encyclopedia of the Great Engineering Projects in History.* Westport, CT: Greenwood Press, 2006. An excellent work that includes information on the construction of the Suez Canal.

Everett, Suzanne. *Disraeli and the Suez Canal.* New York: Historical Times, 1975. A useful account of the British takeover of the canal.

Farnie, D. A. *East and West of Suez, The Suez Canal in History, 1854–1956.* Oxford: Clarendon Press, 1969. The earlier sections of this book should be useful for many student papers.

Ferguson, Bill. *The House of Rothschild.* 2 vols. Rev. ed. London: Penguin, 2000. Includes information on the Rothschild loans that supported Disraeli's move to acquire the canal.

Ferguson, Niall. *Empire: The Rise and Demise of the British World Order and the Lessons of Global Power.* New York: Basic Books, 2004. An important, seminal study that includes data and analysis on the British acquisition of Suez.

Hallberg, Charles W. *The Suez Canal, Its History and Diplomatic Importance.* New York: Octogan Books, 1974; originally published in 1931. A very good and useful work that includes material on the geopolitical significance of the Suez Canal.

Karabell, Zachary. *Parting the Desert: The Creation of the Suez Canal.* New York: A. A. Knopf, 2003. A good history of the construction of the canal and its impact on nineteenth-century history.

Marlowe, John. *The Making of the Suez Canal.* London: Cresset, 1964. A reliable and useful account of the construction of the canal.

Roberts, Frank Harold. *Egypt and the Suez Canal.* Washington, DC: Smithsonian Institution, 1943. An important work on the Suez Canal and its impact on Egyptian history.

Schonfield, Hugh Joseph. *The Suez Canal in Peace and War, 1869–1969.* Rev. ed. Coral Cables: University of Miami Press, 1969. A scholarly examination of the geopolitical significance of the Suez Canal during its first century.

Siegfried, André. *Suez and Panama.* Trans. Henry H. and Doris Hemming. New York: Harcourt, Brace, 1940. A very worthwhile comparative study of the two canals and their impact on the world.

Wilson, Arnold Talbot. *Suez Canal, Its Past, Present, and Future.* London: Oxford University Press, 1933. A dated but still useful work on the canal. The earlier chapters should be important for some student papers.

World Wide Web

"Construction of the Suez Canal." http://www.historywiz.com/galleries/suezconstruction.htm. Includes an illustration of the construction project.

"Suez Canal." http://www.britannica.com/EBchecked/topic/571673/Suez-Canal#tab=active~checked%2Citems~checked&title=Suez%20Canal%20-%20Britannica%20Online%20Encyclopedia. Includes information on the history of the canal and a map.

"The Suez Canal." http://www.steam-ship-sudan.com/en/history/the-suez-canal.asp. A good introduction on the early history of the Suez Canal in the nineteenth century.

Multimedia Sources

Modern Marvels—Suez Canal. A&E Home Video/History Channel, 2006. DVD. A very good presentation on the planning, construction, and early history of the Suez Canal.

"The Egyptian Crisis and Arabi Pasha." BBC Radio 4, 2006. Audio. http://www .bbc.co.uk/radio4/history/empire/episodes/episode_63.shtml. A segment of the *Empire* series that includes information on Suez and its immediate impact on the region.

63. Ultramontanism in Quebec (1869–1877)

After the passage of the British North America Act in 1867 that created a unified Canadian dominion, French-Canadian Catholics in Quebec became increasingly concerned about the survival of their identity, their faith, and their language. They did not support the separation of church and state and argued that they needed to support their language and religion as one. This conservative approach—known as ultramontanism—paralleled the right-wing philosophy of the Roman Catholic Church under Pope Pius IX. In 1864 Pius IX issued the *Syllabus of Errors* that denounced modernism, statism, liberalism, socialism, communism, and many other trends of the era. In the First Vatican Council (1870–1871), Pius IX succeeded in gaining enough support for the doctrine of papal infallibility. Ultramontanism in Quebec opposed liberal, democratic progress and espoused a partnership of the Catholic Church and the Quebec government. It also opposed the advances of feminism. The leader of the ultramontanists in Quebec was Archbishop Ignace Bourget (1799–1885). A staunch advocate of Church rights, Bourget was an activist who opposed reforms in New Brunswick and earlier had lent support to the rebels during the rebellion in Upper Canada in 1838. Bourget and his successors sent more than 150 priests to Europe for training. While the ultramontanists enjoyed the immediate support of a large part of the population of Quebec, the movement was sustained largely through the efforts of the Catholic Church. That cadre of clerics and their successors dominated French-Canadian life the next century and contributed to the development of separatist sentiments and the notion of Quebec nationalism.

TERM PAPER SUGGESTIONS

1. Write a paper on the underlying values and fears of the ultramontanist community in Quebec after the passage of the British North America Act.

2. Develop a paper on the impact of Archbishop Ignace Bourget on life in Quebec during the late nineteenth century.

3. Write a paper on the following question: was ultramontanism a positive or negative force on the cultural history of Quebec?

ALTERNATIVE TERM PAPER SUGGESTIONS

1. As an ambitious youth in Montreal in 1880, you find that your freedoms and options are restricted by the ultramontanist culture of that time. Develop a blog that expresses your understanding of the origins of this movement and its impact on you.

2. Develop a podcast in which Bourget and his colleagues discuss the reasons why they believe that the ultramontanist movement is beneficial for Quebec.

3. Create a 4–5 minute iMovie in which you interview liberal critics of Bourget and his grip on the culture of Quebec.

SUGGESTED SOURCES

Primary Source

Cook, Ramsay. *French-Canadian Nationalism: An Anthology.* Toronto: Macmillan, 1969. Provides some primary materials that may be useful to some students.

Secondary Sources

Bernier, Gerald. *The Shaping of Québec Politics and Society: Colonialism, Power, and the Transition to Capitalism in the 19th Century.* Bristol, PA: Taylor and Francis, 1992. Includes information on the significant role of the Roman Catholic Church in nineteenth-century Quebec.

Bothwell, Robert. *Canada and Quebec: One Country, Two Histories.* Rev. ed. Vancouver: University of British Columbia Press, 1998. Provides an introduction to the impact of ultramontanism in Quebec.

Choquette, Robert. *Canada's Religions: An Historical Introduction.* Ottawa: University of Ottawa Press, 2004. Includes valuable information on ultramontanism in Quebec and the influence of the Roman Catholic hierarchy in French Canadian life.

Dickinson, John A. *A Short of Quebec.* 4th ed. Montreal: McGill-Queen's University Press, 2008. An adequate introduction to ultramontanism in Quebec.

Gougeon, Gilles. *A History of Quebec Nationalism.* Halifax: Lorimer, 1994. Includes information on the early influence of ultramontanism on French Canadian identity.

Henderson, Ailsa. *Hierachies of Belonging: National Identity and Political Culture in Scotland and Quebec.* Montreal: McGill-Queen's University Press, 2007. Includes insights into recent nationalist movements and the forces that shaped them.

Linteau, Paul-André, René Durocher, Jean-Claude Robert, and Robert Chodos. *Quebec: A History 1867–1929.* Halifiax: Lorimer, 1983. A very good general history of Quebec that includes considerable information on ultramontanism.

Little, John Irvine. *Nationalism, Capitalism, and Colonization in Nineteenth Century Quebec: The Upper St. Francis District.* Kingston, Ontario: McGill-Queen's University Press, 1989. Includes data on ultramontanist influence in this district.

Mann, Susan. *The Dream of Nation: A Social and Intellectual History of Quebec.* 2nd ed. Montreal: McGill-Queen's University Press, 2002. An excellent study that considers ultramontanism and its impact on Quebec's culture.

World Wide Web

"Ignace Bourget." http://www.newadvent.org/cathen/02721a.htm. Provides a detailed biographical statement on Bourget.

"Ignace Bourget." http://oce.catholic.com/index.php?title=Ignace_Bourget. An introduction to Bourget's life.

"Jules-Paul Tardivil." http://www.biographi.ca/009004-119.01-e.php?&id_nbr=7096&&PHPSESSID=vgi92ao1f4vtevh2s81391k9s3. A comprehensive account of Tradavil's life as an active advocate of ultramontanist positions during the late nineteenth and early twentieth centuries.

"The Roman Catholic Church and Quebec." http://faculty.marianopolis.edu/c.belanger/quebechistory/readings/church.htm. A very informative and reliable account by Claude Bélanger of Marianopolis College on the role of the Church in Quebec history.

"Ultramontane Nationalism: 1840–1960." http://faculty.marianopolis.edu/c.belanger/quebechistory/events/natpart3.htm. A detailed historical introduction to the movement by Claude Bélanger (Marianopolis College).

Multimedia Sources

French and Colonial Quebec. Schlessinger Media, 1998. DVD/VHS. A brief
    video on life in early Quebec.
"Pictures of Ignace Bourget Monument." http://www.webshots.com/search
    ?query=Bishop+Ignace+Bourget+monument. Provides several photo-
    graphs of the monument and the central cathedral.

64. Ten Years' War (1868–1878)

The Ten Years' War was the first of three conflicts that in the end resulted
in Cuba's independence from Spain. From the outset, the struggle was
associated with the slavery issue. During the 1860s the gap between economic and social conditions of the Spanish minority and the majority
of Cuban people became acute and led to the establishment of
revolutionary committees. The Spanish did not respond for calls for
reform and on October 10, 1868, Carlos Manuel de Céspedes (1819–
1874) freed his slaves and declared Cuban independence. These actions
started the Ten Years' War. After a shaky start, the revolution gained
momentum and had more than 10,000 supporters by the end of October.
Throughout the war both sides enjoyed victories and defeats—both were
ravaged by yellow fever. The Spaniards resorted to attacking the families
of the rebels, and they followed this with a policy of extermination in
which thousands of innocents were killed. Those actions resulted in
international condemnation but Spain persisted. It was not until the outbreak of the Third Carlist War in Spain in 1872 that Spanish resources
and interests were diverted back home. By 1876 both sides were
exhausted and wanted the war to end. After protracted negotiations and
discussions within each camp, the Pact of Zanjón was signed on February
10, 1878, and the peace became a reality on May 28, 1878, when the last
rebel leaders signed the agreement. Cuba was still under Spanish control,
but the slaves were freed (1880) and land reforms were implemented.

TERM PAPER SUGGESTIONS

1. Write a paper on the causes for the outbreak of the Ten Years' War. Be sure to
   include comments on the slavery issue.
2. Develop a paper on the development of the war between 1868 and 1878.

3. Write a paper in which you develop an analysis of the Pact of Zanjón.

4. Write a paper on this question: why were the Spanish successful in suppressing Cuban independence efforts throughout most of the nineteenth century?

ALTERNATIVE TERM PAPER SUGGESTIONS

1. Develop a podcast in which you interview Carlos Manuel de Céspedes on his views on slavery and an independent Cuba.

2. Develop an iMovie on the negotiations that led to the Pact of Zanjón.

3. Develop a blog of your experiences during the war as a rebel soldier.

SUGGESTED SOURCES

Primary Sources

Arango, Napoleon. *The Cuban Rebellion, Its History, Government, Resources.* Washington: Government Printing Office, 1870. Includes an important address by General Arango.

Bramosio, José Silverio. *Spain and Cuba: The Geneva Pamphlet on the Relations between Spain and Cuba: Preceded by an Explanation of the Interest which the American People Have in the Solution of the Cuban Difficulty.* New York: Appleton, 1876. An important analysis on the war in Cuba and the interests of the United States and its people in it.

Carpenter, Matthew H. *Neutrality between Spain and Cuba: The Spanish Gunboats.* Washington: Congressional Globe Office, 1869. A critique of Spanish practices that were viewed as provocative.

Chomsky, Aviva. *The Cuba Reader: History, Culture, Politics.* Durham, NC: Duke University Press, 2003. A resource that students should refer to if working on any aspect of Cuban history.

Clark, James Hyde. *Cuba and the Fight for Freedom, A Powerful and Thrilling History of the "Queen of the Antilles," the Oppression of the Spanish Government, the Insurrection of 1868 and the Compromise of 1878 ....* Philadelphia: Globe Bible Publishing, 1896. A sympathetic account of the Cuban situation by an observer of the struggle.

O'Kelly, James J. *The Mambi-land: or Adventures of Herald Correspondent in Cuba.* Philadelphia: J. B. Lippincott, 1874. A journalist eyewitness account of activities in Cuba.

Ryan, John George. *Life and Adventures of Gen. W. A. C. Ryan, the Cuban Martyr: Captured on the Steamer Virginius and murdered by the Spaniards at Santiago, November 4, 1873.* New York: Scully, 1876. A pro-Cuban biography by a contemporary observer of the struggle with Spain.

Valdés-Dominguez, Fermin. *Tragedy in Havana: November 27, 1871.* Ed. and trans. Consuelo E. Stebbins. Gainesville: University Press of Florida, 2000. A worthwhile primary source that students working on this topic will want to consult.

Secondary Sources

Bethell, Leslie. *Cuba: A Short History.* New York: Cambridge University Press, 1993. A reliable introduction that includes accurate information on the Ten Years' War.

Bradford, Richard H. *The Virginius Affair.* Boulder: Colorado Associated University Press, 1980. A scholarly history of a significant naval incident that occurred during the war.

Casanovas, Joan. *Bread, or Bullets!: Urban Labor and Spanish Colonialism in Cuba, 1850–1898.* Pittsburgh: University of Pittsburgh Press, 1998. A solid and useful study that focuses on the clash between the Cuban proletariat and the Spanish colonial regime.

Doscal, Paul J. *Cuba Libre: A Brief History of Cuba.* Wheeling, IL: Harlan Davidson, 2006. Provides a good introduction to the Ten Years' War.

Ferrer, Ada. *Insurgent Cuba: Race, Nation, and Revolution, 1868–1898.* Chapel Hill: University of North Carolina Press, 1999. Ferrer inserts race as a substantive factor in its own right—that separated the Cuban people from their Spanish governors.

Foner, Philip. *History of Cuba and Its Relations with the United States.* 2 vols. New York: International Publishers, 1963. An excellent history of Cuban-American relations with extensive information on the Ten Years' War.

Gallenga, Antonio Carlo Napoleone. *The Pearl of the Antilles.* London: Chapman and Hall, 1873. A contemporary's commentary on Cuban history with information on the origins and early development of the Ten Years' War.

Gott, Richard. *Cuba: A New History.* New Haven, CT: Yale University Press, 2005. Provides a very good introduction to the war.

Martinez-Fernandez, Luis, D. H. Figueredo, Louis A. Perez, and Luis Gonzalez, eds. *Encyclopedia of Cuba: People, History, Culture.* Westport, CT: Greenwood Press, 2003. An excellent reference work that should be useful to all students working this topic.

Johnson, Willis Fletcher. *The History of Cuba.* New York: B. F. Buck, 1920. Still a useful history with considerable information on the Ten Years' War.

Ponce de León, Néstor. *The Book of Blood: An Authentic Record of the Policy Adopted by Modern Spain to Put an End to the War for the Independence of Cuba, (October 1868 to December 1870).* Trans. M. M. Zarzamendi.

New York: M. M. Zarzamendi, 1871. A contemporary writer's useful
account of the first two years of the Ten Years' War.

Prados-Torreira, Teresa. *Mambisas: Rebel Women in Nineteenth-Century Cuba.*
Gainesville: University Press of Florida, 2005. Includes information on
the role of women during the Ten Years' War.

Quesada, Gonzalo de, and Henry Davenport Northrop. *The War in Cuba.*
Whitefish, MT: Kessinger, 2004; originally published in 1896. Includes
information on the Ten Years' War and the rebellion that broke in the
1890s. This was written to gain support for the Cuban insurgency
against Spain.

Robinson, Albert G. *Cuba, Old and New.* Charleston, SC: BiblioBazaar, 2008.
Provides a useful introduction to the war.

Schmidt-Nowara, Christopher. *The Conquest of History: Spanish Colonialism and
National Histories in the Nineteenth Century.* Pittsburgh: University of Pittsburgh Press, 2006. Very good on the imperial-national Latin American
conflicts including the Ten Years' War.

Staten, Clifford L. *The History of Cuba.* New York: Palgrave Macmillan, 2005.
Includes information on the Ten Years' War.

Suchicki, Jaime. *Cuba: From Columbus to Castro and Beyond.* 5th ed. Dulles, VA:
Potomac Books, 2002. A comprehensive history of Cuba that includes
data on the war.

World Wide Web

"1868–1878: The Ten Years War in Cuba." http://www.pbs.org/crucible/
tl1.html. A very useful statement on the war with links to other Web
sites.

"Ten Years' War." http://www.answers.com/topic/ten-years-war. A good introduction to the war with links to relevant sites.

"Ten Year War (1868–1878)." http://www.historyofcuba.com/history/funfacts/
tenyear.htm. A brief introduction to the war.

"Ten Years War, 1868–1878." http://www.encyclopedia.com/doc/1E1
-TenYears.html. A good introduction to this phase of the Cuban struggle
for independence.

"Ten Years of War in Cuba; Almost Continuous Fighting There Between 1868 and
1878. The Declaration of Independence Spanish Authorities Unprepared
for the Formidable Movement that Followed—Guerilla Warfare Waged
by Cubans. II." http://query.nytimes.com/gst/abstract.html?res
=980DE5DC1E30E333A25751C2A96F9C94649ED7CF. An article in
The New York Times (September 22, 1895) from a series on the Cuban
situation.

Multimedia Source

Armas, Mayda de. *Pages of Cuban History/Páginas de la historia de Cuba.* (CD-ROM.) Madrid: Leon Press, 1998. A useful collection of documents, illustrations, photographs, and other materials on a CD.

65. Meiji Restoration (1868–1912)

For more than 300 years after its initial contact with Westerners during the sixteenth century (when three Portuguese sailors washed ashore after a shipwreck), Japan pursued a deliberate and careful policy of isolationism from the West and other cultures. In 1854 an American delegation was received, and within a decade the Japanese leaders of the new Meiji period (1868–1912) became convinced that they needed to westernize their country so that it would be able to sustain its independence. They feared not only the possibility of becoming a target for Western imperialism but also saw the opportunity for Japan to be able to forge a sphere of influence for itself in East Asia. The implementation of this vision resulted in internal conflicts, such as Saigō Takamori's rebellion against the government in 1877. Nonetheless, the policy of westernizing Japan prevailed and substantive changes were implemented through political reforms, the emergence of political parties, changes in religious developments and state ideology, the economy, diplomacy, and the military. By the end of the century, Japan had a constitution (1889), developed an imposing modern military establishment on Western lines, and embarked on the policy of expansion in Korea. These processes of westernization remained in place until the defeat of Japan (1945) in the Second World War.

TERM PAPER SUGGESTIONS

1. What was the rationale for the Meiji leaders in westernizing Japan during the late nineteenth century?
2. Discuss the resistance to the westernization of Japan. Describe the role of Saigō Takamori in the resistance.
3. The westernization of Meiji Japan was led by a ruling elite. Describe the components that constituted this elite and consider its disruptions as the nation moved to implement the Western model during the 1870s.

4. Many scholars consider the Meiji Constitution (1889) to be the most significant political achievement of the era. Describe the origins, structure, and impact of this Constitution.

5. An outgrowth of the westernization process was the emergence of political parties in Meiji Japan. Discuss the motivation behind the establishment of the Jiyūtō and Kaishintō parties.

6. What impact did the westernization of Japan have on Japanese religious beliefs, traditions, and structures?

7. Consider the impact of the Meiji era on facilitating the emergence of Japan as a world political and economic force today.

ALTERNATIVE TERM PAPER SUGGESTIONS

1. Develop a podcast in which Japanese leaders consider the advantages and disadvantages of "westernizing" their society.

2. Develop an iMovie on the deliberations that resulted in the Meiji Constitution.

3. Develop a podcast in which you cover Takamori's rebellion.

SUGGESTED SOURCES

Primary Sources

Cobbing, Andrew. *The Japanese Discovery of Victorian Britain: Early Travel Encounters.* Richmond, U.K.: Japan Library, 1998. Significant and meaningful excerpts from letters, diaries, and memoirs by Japanese are included.

Gubbins, J. H. *The Progress of Japan, 1853–1871.* New York: AMS Press, 1971. Twenty-four primary sources are provided as appendices to this volume. They range from the American-Japanese Treaty of 1854 to documents on the last days of the Shōgunate, and the Shōgun's resignation in the wake of the westernization of Japan.

Meiji Japan Through Contemporary Sources. Compil. the Centre for East Asian Cultural Studies. 3 vols. Tokyo and London: [no imprint], 1969–1972. These volumes constitute an outstanding selection of primary materials on the Meiji era and the westernization of Japan.

Sources of Japanese Tradition. Compil. Ryusaku Tsunoda, William Theodore de Bary, and Donald Keene. 2 vols. New York: Columbia University Press, 1964. An older but very useful collection of primary materials that can be found in most academic and larger public libraries.

Steele, M. William. *Alternative Narratives in Modern Japanese History.* London and New York: RoutledgeCurzon, 2003. Steele's historiographical study provides insights and sources on nineteenth- and twentieth-century Japanese history.

Secondary Sources

Akamatsu, Paul. *Meiji 1868: Revolution and Counter-Revolution in Japan.* London: Allen and Unwin, 1972. Still a very useful introduction to the struggle to modernize Japan. A very good bibliography is appended to the text.

Avakian, Monique. *The Meiji Restoration and the Rise of Modern Japan.* Englewood Cliffs, NJ: Silver Burdett Press, 1991. A very readable and reliable introduction to the Meiji era and the modernization of Japan that is strong on political, economic, and social issues.

Bodie, Bertrand. *The Imported State: The Westernization of the Political Order.* Trans. Claudia Royal. Stanford: Stanford University Press, 2000. An important study that emphasizes the impact of Western practices and procedures on Japanese politics at the national and regional levels.

Chang, Richard T. *Historians and Meiji Statesmen.* Gainesville: University of Florida Press, 1970. Chang's historiographical study on the varying interpretations of Meiji political and diplomatic leaders remains unsurpassed in its scope and quality.

French, Calvin L. *Shiba Kokan: Artist, Innovator, and Pioneer in the Westernization of Japan.* New York: Columbia University Press for Studies of the East Asia Institute, 1974. French's study of Shiba Kokan is a classic in understanding the westernization of Japan through the life and values of one individual.

Huffman, James L. *Creating a Public: People and Press in Meiji Japan.* Honolulu: University of Hawaii Press, 1997. A provocative and worthwhile study on print communications and the emergence of a Japanese "public" that identified with the Western movement and the unity of their country.

Jansen, Marius B. *The Emergence of Meiji Japan.* New York: Cambridge University Press, 1995. A standard introduction to Meiji Japan and the westernization movement that is a solid and comprehensive study.

Keene, Donald. *Emperor of Japan: Meiji and His World, 1852–1912.* New ed. New York: Columbia University Press, 2005. The most recent and reliable study of Meiji and his impact on Japan. A very good bibliography is provided.

Kornicki, Peter, ed. *Meiji Japan: Political, Economic and Social History: Volume 1.* London: Routledge, 1998. This is the first volume of three in a comprehensive scholarly history that consists of a series of essays by prominent authorities on Japanese history.

Lone, Stewart. *Army, Empire, and Politics in Meiji Japan: The Three Careers of General Katsura Tarō.* New York: St. Martin's Press, 2000. An interesting study of Meiji Japan focused on the career of Katsura Tarō that is very worthwhile for students studying the emergence of Japanese expansion in East Asia.

Low, Morris. *Building a Modern Japan: Science, Technology, and Medicine in the Meiji Era and Beyond.* London: Palgrave Macmillan, 2005. This is an excellent study on the impact of westernization on the new Japanese concept of progress and its application to science, technology, and medicine.

Miller, J. Scott. *Adaptations of Western Literature in Meiji Japan.* London: Palgrave Macmillan, 2001. For students pursuing topics on the transformation of Japanese literature during the Meiji era, Miller's study is indispensable.

Westney, D. Eleanor. *Imitation and Innovation: The Transfer of Western Organization Patterns in Meiji Japan.* [n.p.]: iUniverse.com, 2000. A scholarly examination on the process and impact of Western organizational structures and practices in Meiji Japan. This is a self-published online book.

Wilson, George M. *Patriots and Redeemers in Japan: Motives in the Meiji Restoration.* Chicago: University of Chicago Press, 1991. Wilson examines the basis and various rationale that emerged in the struggle to westernize Japan during the Meiji period.

World Wide Web

"Japan as World Power." http://afe.easia.columbia.edu/japan/japanworkbook/modernhist/meiji.html. The online "Contemporary Japan: A Teaching Workbook" is an excellent reliable source of information on the westernization of Japan. Provocative questions are included after each section in this source from Columbia University.

"Meiji Japan." http://www.fordham.edu/halsall/eastasia/eastasiasbook.html #Japan%20as%20a%20World%20Power. This Web page from the Internet East Asia History Sourcebook (Fordham University) constitutes a reliable and extensive source on Japanese history, including the Meiji period.

"Meiji Restoration." http://www.britannica.com/ebc/article-9051827. A general and useful introduction to the Meiji and the issue of westernization in Japan.

Multimedia Sources

The Last Samurai. Warner Home Video, 2003. Directed by Edward Zwick. This is a dramatic rendering of the struggle to defend the Samurai tradition against the westernization of Japan during the 1870s.

Mishima: A Life in Four Chapters. Warner Home Video, 2001 [original film, 1985]. Directed by Paul Schrader. English narration by Roy Scheider. A film on the life of Yukio Mishima, Japan's most famous writer after the Second World War. Mishima committed suicide after his unsuccessful attempts to reverse the westernization of Japan.

66. Unification of Italy (1870)

During the decades after the defeat of Napoleon and the subsequent Congress of Vienna, a nationalist movement emerged among the Italians that was directed at the unification of the nation. The nationalists refused to accept the restoration of the multitude of independent states in Italy that was supported and "guaranteed" by the major powers. During the revolutionary years 1820 and 1830, Italian nationalists attempted to overthrow the existing system but were defeated. Nonetheless, Italian nationalism gained increasing support among the people and was espoused by leaders such as Giuseppe Mazzini and Vincenzo Gioberti, who emerged to challenge the old order. Mazzini founded the "Young Italy" movement, and Gioberti envisioned a unified Italy under the pope. Even liberal Pope Pius IX entertained reform ideas until the "Revolutions of 1848" broke and endangered Rome. Pius IX was transformed by his forced flight from Rome and became one of the most reactionary pontiffs of the modern period. During the 1850s Camillo Cavour, Prime Minister to King Victor Emmanuel II of Sardinia, introduced a wide range of liberal reforms in Sardinia. The path to unification was now clear—the *Risorgimento* would be realized from above, through the Kingdom of Sardinia with assistance from a new brand of post-Mazzini Italian nationalists, such as Giuseppe Garibaldi. Cavour developed a close relationship with Emperor Napoleon III during and after the Crimean War so that France would support the expulsion of Austria from the northern Italian areas of Venetia and Lombardy. War broke out in 1859 and, after some diplomatic intrigue and betrayal, resulted in Lombardy being added to Sardinia. In December 1859 four Italian states—Tuscany, Parma, Modena, and

Legations (parts of the old Papal States)—formed the United Provinces of Central Italy and approached Sardinia to annex them. During the 1860s Garibaldi's forces invaded the Kingdom of the Two Sicilies and overthrew King Ferdinand II. The Kingdom of Italy was proclaimed under King Victor Emmanuel II on March 17, 1861—Rome was to be the capital. In 1866 the Sardinians supported Bismarck in the German Civil War and received Venetia. Finally, during the Franco-Prussian War with its French protection withdrawn, Rome and the remnants of the Papal States were seized and added to Italy in the fall of 1870.

TERM PAPER SUGGESTIONS

1. Develop a paper on Cavour's role in the unification of Italy. Was he always/ ever an Italian nationalist?

2. What impact did Napoleon III and France have on the process of Italian unification?

3. Write a paper on the transformation of Pope Pius IX from a "liberal" pontiff to a "reactionary" who opposed the formation of the Italian state.

4. Was the unification of Italy inevitable? Why or why not?

5. Compare and contrast the impact of Napoleon III and Bismarck on the process of Italian unification.

ALTERNATIVE TERM PAPER SUGGESTIONS

1. You are a merchant in Milan during the 1850s. In a blog, state your position/ concerns about the unification movement.

2. It is 1861 and you are an 18-year-old woman in Rome witnessing the transformation of your society. Develop a blog in which you identify yourself as a supporter of liberal nationalism or the status quo and justify your position.

SUGGESTED SOURCES

Primary Sources

"Documents of Italian Unification, 1846–61." http://teacher.sduhsd.k12.ca.us/ mmontgomery/world_history/nationalism/it_unification.htm. Includes primary materials by Cavour, Mazzini, Garibaldi, and others.

Garibaldi, Giuseppe. *My Life.* Trans. Stephen Parkin. London: Hesperus Press, 2004. A useful and exciting primary source by perhaps the most zealous Italian nationalist of the era.

"Modern History Sourcebook: Documents of Italian Unification, 1846–1861." http://www.fordham.edu/halsall/mod/1861italianunif.html. Provides a range of useful primary materials on Italian unification.

Secondary Sources

Beales, Derek E., and Eugenio Biagini. *The Risorgimento and the Unification of Italy.* 2nd ed. New York: Longman, 2002. This important and valuable study focuses on the cultural underpinnings that shaped and support the expansion of Italian nationalism and movement toward unification.

Davis, John A., ed. *Italy in the Nineteenth Century.* New York: Oxford University Press, 2000. A volume of scholarly essays including reliable pieces on Mazzini, Cavour, and Garibaldi.

Gooch, John. *The Unification of Italy.* London: Routledge, 2001. An excellent introduction to the development of the Italian nation-state with an analysis of its significance in the nineteenth century.

Morrogh, Michael. *The Unification of Italy.* New York: Palgrave Macmillan, 2003. An introduction to the documents that were critical in the unification process provides the focus for this book.

Pearce, Robert, and Andrina Stiles. *The Unification of Italy 1815–70.* London: Hodder and Stoughton, 2006. A solid introduction to the complex issues and values of the period as they moved toward Italian unification.

Riall, Lucy. *Sicily and the Unification of Italy: Liberal Policy and Local Power.* New York: Oxford University Press, 1998. An important study on the role that Sicily and its people played in the establishment of Italy.

———. *Garibaldi: Invention of a Hero.* New Haven, CT: Yale University Press, 2007. A reliable and readable biography of Garibaldi and the cultivation of his legend.

Scirocco, Alfonso. *Garibaldi: Citizen of the World.* Trans. Allan Cameron. Princeton, NJ: Princeton University Press, 2007. The best biography of Garibaldi that is currently available.

World Wide Web

"Historical Background Maps—The Unification of Italy." Valente and DiRenzo Web site, at http://www.roangelo.net/valente/garibald.html. Includes a valuable map tracing the Garibaldi route from Genoa to Naples.

"Italian Unification." http://www.amitm.com/thecon/lesson6.html. Provides a limited number of valuable sources such as maps, images, documents, and caricatures on Italian unification.

"Italian Unification Timeline." http://www.timelines.info/history/ages_and _periods/the_age_of_liberalism/nation_building/italian_unification/.

Provides a useful timeline of the major events in the history of Italian unification.

"Joseph Mazzini, *The Duties of Man* (1844)." In the Hanover Historical Texts Project, Hanover College, http://history.hanover.edu/project.html. Excerpts from this important work by Mazzini.

Multimedia Source

The Leopard. 20th Century Fox, 1963. DVD. Directed by Luchino Visconti. Dramatic film based on the novel *The Leopard* by Giuseppe Di Lampedusa. Set in Sicily during the turbulent 1860s, *The Leopard* centers on the later years of Prince Salina, a local aristocrat with extensive land holdings, and the challenges that he confronts with the approaching shifts of political structure.

67. Tientsin Massacre (1870)

The Tientsin Massacre of June 1870 reflected the mounting resentment against developing foreign influence in China as well as the specific opposition to the presence and influence of Christian missionaries in Chinese society. In the late spring 1870 rumors circulated among the Chinese in Tientsin that children and others had been kidnapped by the French Catholic missionary nuns who were attempting to fill their orphanages and schools. Although most of the children in the orphanage appeared to have been orphaned or abandoned, some families and others may have been paid for children. Some of the most vehement anti-Western Chinese contended that the "Catholic women" were using witchcraft to attract children. As a result of waves of diseases that hit the Tientsin area, the number of deaths among the children increased during the first half of 1870. Tensions between the xenophobic Chinese and the Westerners were aggravated on June 18, 1870, when an alleged kidnapper was arrested. He revealed that he had sold children to the housekeeper at the orphanage. This was interpreted by the Chinese that the employee had served as an agent of the Catholic missionaries in acquiring the children. Tensions mounted and reached a high point on June 21 when the French Consul Henri Fontanier became embroiled in an argument with a Chinese magistrate. Fontanier ordered that his guard fire on the magistrate and others. The Chinese retaliated and killed Fontanier, his guards, 21 Westerners (including some nuns), and about 40 Chinese who had converted to Catholicism. The French, with the support of the Vatican, responded by sending a squadron of ships to Tientsin and demanded that the Chinese punish those responsible and pay reparations. Over the next several months the Chinese executed 16 Chinese who were involved and agreed to pay reparations. However, the cultural tensions that exploded at the Tientsin Massacre remained evident in Chinese-Western relations for the remainder of the nineteenth century.

TERM PAPER SUGGESTIONS

1. Write a paper on the background of Sino-Western relations that contributed to the Tientsin Massacre.
2. Develop a paper on the immediate causes and development of the massacre on June 21, 1870.
3. Was the Tientsin incident symptomatic of Chinese-Western relations at this time in Chinese history? Why would the Chinese allow such cultural interventions?
4. Develop a paper on the impact that the Tientsin Massacre had on Chinese-Western relations.
5. Was Christianity a real threat to native Chinese religions or was the combination of Christianity and Western material culture the real threat?

ALTERNATIVE TERM PAPER SUGGESTIONS

1. Develop a 3 minute iMovie on the events of June 19, 1870, in Tientsin—be sure that the script accurately reflects the sentiments of both the Westerners and the local Chinese.
2. You are a young French nun working in the orphanage in Tientsin in 1870 who survives the troubles. Develop a blog on the mounting tensions, the Tientsin Massacre, and its consequences.
3. As an 18-year-old Chinese son of a wealthy Tientsin merchant, you are attracted by the mysterious Christians and their concept of God and the afterlife. Your parents give you a choice—remain loyal to them and traditional Chinese culture or be an outcast from the family because of your Christian commitment. Write a blog to reveal your feelings.

SUGGESTED SOURCES

Primary Sources

Allen, Tamar. *Miss Tamar Allen's narrative of the Tientsin Massacre in China, during which so many Christians and foreigners were ruthlessly butchered by the Chinese . . . and her own miraculous escape . . . .* Philadelphia: C. W. Alexander, 1870. A brief, dramatic, and important account of the massacre by a survivor.

Tĕng, Ssu-yu, and John King Fairbank. *China's Response to the West: A Documentary Survey, 1839–1923.* Cambridge, MA: Harvard University Press, 2006. An important compendium of documents including some that relate directly to the Tientsin massacre.

Staff of the *"North-China Herald." A Retrospect of Political and Commercial Affairs in China During the Five Years 1868 to 1872.* Chestnut Hill, MA: Adamant Media Corporation, 2001. This is a reprint of the 1873 edition that consisted of a series of articles, including those having to do with the massacre.

Secondary Sources

Barend, J. ter Haar. *Telling Stories: Witchcraft and Scapegoating in Chinese History.* Leiden: Brill, 2006. In a lengthy chapter on "Westerners as Scapegoats," Barend provides an analysis of the Tientsin Massacre focused on internal Chinese difficulties.

Cohen, Paul A. *China and Christianity: The Missionary Movement and the Growth of Chinese Anti-Foreignism, 1860–1870.* Cambridge, MA: Harvard University Press, 1963. A very good history of the impact of Christian missionaries in China during this period. It places the Tientsin Massacre in context of being a threat to Chinese nationalist identity.

Fairbank, John King. "Patterns behind the Tientsin Massacre." *Harvard Journal of Asiatic Studies* 20, no. 3/4 (1957): 480–511. Still the best explanation for the massacre by one of the foremost American historians of China.

Hsu, Immanuel C. Y. *The Rise of Modern China.* New York: Oxford University Press, 1999. A very solid and dependable resource on Chinese history including the Tientsin massacre and its consequences.

Michie, Alexander. *The Englishman in China during the Victorian Era: Volume 2.* Chestnut Hill, MA: Adamant Media Corporation, 2001. A reprint of an important book by a contemporary observer of English interests in China during the second half of the nineteenth century.

Seagrave, Sterling. *Dragon Lady: The Life and Legend of the Last Empress of China.* New York: Vintage, 1993. A readable and reliable biography of a vehement defender of Chinese culture and autonomy.

Weightman, Barbara A. *Dragons and Tigers: A Geography of South, East, and Southeast Asia.* New York: Wiley, 2005. This valuable interdisciplinary study provides regional and national perspectives on the rise of China and Japan during the modern era.

World Wide Web

"Background to the Boxer Rebellion." Modern History Sourcebook, Fordham University, Paul Halsall. http://www.fordham.edu/halsall/mod/1900Fei-boxers.html. Fei Ch'i-hao (Chinese Christian) describes the background that led to the rebellion, including the anti-Christian atrocities in Tientsin.

Forbes, William. *An Account of the Tientsin Massacre.* Shanghai: [n.p.], 1870. http://janus.lib.cam.ac.uk/db/node.xsp?id=EAD%2FGBR%2F0012%2FMS%20JM%2FMS.JM%2FA8%2F121%2F14. An important contemporary description of the massacre, in the Jardine Matheson Archive.

"Internet Guide to Chinese History." Ed. Hanno Lecher Sinological Institute, Leiden University, Netherlands. http://sun.sino.uni-heidelberg.de/igcs/ighist.htm. This is an outstanding resource with links to many resources.

"Sir Thomas Francis Wade (1818–1895)." http://www.lib.cam.ac.uk/mulu/wadebio.html. A biography of the British diplomat who negotiated a settlement following the Tientsin Massacre.

"Tianjin [Tientsin] Massacre." http://www.encyklopedia.a300.pl/Tianjin_Massacre.html. An introductory essay on the massacre.

"Tientsin Massacre." http://www.britannica.com/EBchecked/topic/595356/Tientsin-Massacre#tab=active~checked%2Citems~checked&title=Tientsin%20Massacre%20–%20Britannica%20Online%20Encyclopedia. A brief account with links to additional information.

"Tientsin Massacre in China 1870." http://www.onwar.com/aced/data/charlie/china1870.htm. A brief account of the massacre and its consequences.

Multimedia Source

"James Hudson Taylor." http://www.learnoutloud.com/Catalog/Religion-and-Spirituality/Christianity/Hudson-Taylor-Sermons/15636. Podcast on Taylor, an English Methodist missionary in China from the 1850s through the period of the Tientsin Massacre.

68. Unification of Germany (1871)

The establishment of the German Empire in January 1871 resulted from a series of events and a shift in perspective that followed the Revolutions of 1848. While most of the revolutions failed, the Prussian government recognized that the confederation of German states in the north was no longer effective and that support for a unified German state (without Austria) had gained momentum. The Austrian-Prussian rivalry over the future of central Europe and the "German world" had been evident for more than a century—since the Great War of the Mid-Eighteenth Century. Austria supported the concept of a "large" Germany under its dominance. Prussia envisioned a "Small" Germany that excluded Austria and the many non-German peoples that were part of the Austrian Empire. In 1862, Otto von Bismarck was appointed minister-president of Prussia during the midst of an internal Prussian political crisis between the "lower" house of the assembly and the monarch. Bismarck was interested in defending and developing a strong Prussia that would dominate north-central Europe. In 1864, Prussia was involved in a controversy with Denmark over the status of the duchies of Schleswig and Holstein. Bismarck entered an alliance with Austria and went to war against Denmark. After this brief and successful war, the Austrians and Prussians entered into a complex sharing arrangement that was designed to fail. By 1866, the German Civil War (between Austria and Prussia) broke out. Most of the members of the Confederation supported Austria, and the emerging Italian state was allied with Prussia. The Prussia military scored a convincing victory over the Austrians, and Prussia was generous with the Austrians at the peace negotiations. In 1867 Prussia supported the development of the North German Confederation with which it was closely affiliated. During the next three years Bismarck followed a foreign policy that was focused on Prussian interests; however, support for the establishment of a unified Germany gained a significant following. The issue of who should serve as the next Spanish monarch contributed to the development of a crisis between Prussia and France. The policies and diplomacy of the French Emperor Napoleon III proved inept, and Bismarck took full advantage of every opportunity. War broke out between Prussia and France in the summer of 1870. From the outset, it was a disaster for France. French forces were defeated at Sedan in September and Paris was surrounded. Napoleon III's government collapsed and was replaced by the Third French Republic in 1871. The brief experiment with communism failed when the Paris Commune was defeated by French forces. In the midst of these disorders, the German Empire was proclaimed in January 1871 when the south German states were incorporated into the new Second Reich. While the Prussian king—the future Kaiser William I of Germany—was the technical head of state, Bismarck was the architect of the new unified Germany.

TERM PAPER SUGGESTIONS

1. Some historians have considered Bismarck an opportunist. Appraising the realities of the European scene, he looked for ways to advance his goal of an expanded and secure Prussia. Develop a paper on how Bismarck utilized the Italian nationalist movement to contribute to victory in the war with Austria.

2. Write a term paper on the internal support and opposition that Bismarck encountered in Prussia during the unification process.

3. Selecting either the decade of the 1850s or the 1860s, write a paper on the comparative strength and influence of Prussia and Austria in Central Europe.

4. Historians have maintained that in many ways the German people were more motivated by the notion of nationalism than Bismarck. Write a paper on the development of German national identity among the people in Prussia and elsewhere.

5. For more than a century Austria and Prussia were rivals for hegemony in Central Europe. Why did Prussia prevail and Austria fail?

ALTERNATIVE TERM PAPER SUGGESTIONS

1. As an independent journalist in Bavaria, develop a blog on Bismarck's defeat of Austria in 1866 and the question of the inevitably of the absorption of Bavaria into the new developing German state.

2. As a French intellectual you witnessed the defeat of your country in the Franco-Prussian War and the proclamation of the German Empire at Versailles. Develop an audio podcast to the French nation on the meaning of this defeat and the establishment of the new Germany.

3. Develop a 3 minute iMovie in which William I and Bismarck in either 1867 or the spring of 1870 discuss the advantages and disadvantages of a unified Germany under Prussian leadership.

4. Develop a blog in which advocates and opponents of German nationalism discuss the movement toward unification in the late 1860s.

5. Create a Web site on the diplomacy involved in German unification. Include a series of political maps tracking the development, photographs and artistic renderings of important events, and battlefield maps.

SUGGESTED SOURCES

Primary Sources

Butler, A. J., ed. *The Memoirs, being the Reflections and Reminiscences of Otto, Prince von Bismarck, written and dictated by himself after his retirement from office.* New York: H. Fertig, 1966. A useful volume in which Bismarck justifies his policies and actions.

Gorman, Michael, ed. *The Unification of Germany—Documents.* Cambridge, U.K.: Cambridge University Press, 1989. An extremely useful and relevant collection of primary materials on German unification.

Hauterive, Ernest d', ed. *The Second Empire and Its Downfall: The Correspondence of the Emperor Napoleon III and His Cousin Prince Napoleon.* Trans. Herbert Wilson. New York: George H. Doran, 1927. A useful collection of letters that include information on the impact of the process of German unification on France.

Lord, Robert H. *The Origins of the War of 1870. New Documents from the German Archives.* Cambridge, MA: Harvard University Press, 1924. An old but outstanding volume of primary sources on the background and outbreak of the Franco-Prussian War.

Moltke, Helmuth Graf von. *Strategy: Its Theory and Application: The Wars for German Unification, 1866–1871.* Westport, CT: Greenwood Press, 1971. This is an excellent primary source by the Prussian field commander during the Austro-Prussian and Franco-Prussian Wars.

Schoenfield, Hermann, ed. *Bismarck's Speeches and Letters.* New York: D. Appleton, 1905. A highly edited but still useful collection of Bismarck's papers, many relating to the unification of Germany.

Secondary Sources

Abrams, Lynn. *Bismarck and the German Empire, 1871–1918.* London and New York: Routledge, 2006. A new and important book that begins with a chapter on the new German Empire in 1871.

Bucholz, Arden. *Moltke and the German Wars, 1864–1871.* New York: Palgrave, 2001. This is an outstanding account of Marshal Helmuth Graf von Moltke's leadership of Prussian forces during the Schleswig-Holstein War, the Austro-Prussian War, and the Franco-Prussian War.

Carr, William. *The Origins of the Wars of German Unification.* London: Longman, 1991. A readable and mostly reliable account of the origins of wars that contributed to the unification of Germany.

Darmstaedter, Friedrich. *Bismarck and the Creation of the Second Reich.* Piscataway, NJ: Transaction Publishers, 2008. A worthwhile and insightful volume on Bismarck's role in the establishment of the German Empire.

Dumke, Rolf H. *German Economic Unification in the 19th Century: The Political Economy of the Zollverein.* Munich: Institut für Volkswirtschaftslehre, Universität der Bundeswehr München, 1994. Dumke emphasizes the evolution of German unification as a consequence of the economic integration that developed throughout the century prior to the establishment of the German state.

Farmer, Alan, and Andrina Stiles. *The Unification of Germany 1815–1919.* 3rd ed. London: Hodder Murray, 2007. This standard work provides a broad look at the rise of German nationalism and its manifestation in the new German Empire.

Förster, Stig, and Jörg Nagler, eds. *On the Road to Total War: The American Civil War and the German Wars of Unification, 1861–1871.* Washington, DC: German Historical Institute, 1997. In this volume of essays the editors focused on the transformation of the prosecution of war that emerged during the decade of the American and German Civil Wars.

Geiss, Imanuel. *The Question of German Unification: 1806–1996.* Trans. Fred Bridgham. New York: Routledge, 1997. Geiss examines the historical force of German nationalism in Central Europe as it expressed itself during the nineteenth and twentieth centuries.

Hamerow, Theodore. *The Social Foundations of German Unification, 1858–1871.* 2 vols. Princeton, NJ: Princeton University Press, 1969–1972. Hamerow's study is still the most comprehensive and well-documented study of the economic and social conditions in northern central Europe during the decade that led to the establishment of the German Empire.

Howard, Michael Eliot. *The Franco-Prussian War: The German Invasion of France, 1870–1871.* London and New York: Routledge, 2001. A reliable and readable account of the German defeat of France and the subsequent establishment of the German Empire.

Leman, Katherine Anne. *Bismarck.* New York: Pearson Longman, 2004. A scholarly and useful study that demonstrates a command of the sources and provides good documentation.

Pape, Walter, ed. *1870/71–1989/90: German Unifications and the Change of Literary Discourse.* Berlin and New York: W. de Gruyter, 1993. An insightful and provocative comparison of the two unifications of Germany that is focused on an examination of the political and national literatures of the periods.

Pflanze, Otto. *Bismarck and the Development of Germany: The Period of Unification, 1815–1871.* Princeton, NJ: Princeton University Press, 1990. This is volume one of a three-volume study on Bismarck and Germany. It remains as the standard on the subject. Pflanze's scholarship reflects his mastery of the primary sources and his in-depth knowledge of the nineteenth-century German world.

———. *The Unification of Germany, 1848–1871*. Melbourne, FL: Krieger, 1979. In this valuable collection of excerpts from sources, Pflanze compares interpretations on German unification.

Showalter, Dennis E. *The Wars of German Unification*. London: Arnold, 2004. Mostly focused on the German Civil War and the Franco-Prussian Wars, this book demonstrates Bismarck's use of war in realizing his aspirations of an expanded Prussia.

Ullrich, Volker. *Bismarck, Life and Times*. London: Haus Publishers, 2008. This is a revisionist biography of Bismarck that attempts to discard the interpretations that have been advanced during the past 50 years. Volker's thesis is advanced in the light of the recent reunification of Germany in 1989–1991.

Wawro, Geoffrey. *The Austro-Prussian War: Austria's War with Prussia and Italy in 1866*. New York: Cambridge University Press, 1996. The best book on the Austro-Prussian War.

———. *The Franco-Prussian War: The German Conquest of France in 1870–1871*. Cambridge and New York: Cambridge University Press, 2003. An excellent source on the military history of the Franco-Prussian War.

World Wide Web

Bismarck, Otto von. *Memoirs*. http://history.hanover.edu/project.html. Excerpts from Bismarck's memoirs in the Hanover Historical Texts Project, Hanover College.

"Documents of German Unification, 1848–1871." http://www.fordham.edu/halsall/mod/germanunification.html. Included in these useful documents assembled by Paul Halsall for Fordham University's "Modern History Sourcebook" are excerpts from the following: Johann Gustav Droysen's *Speech to the Frankfurt Assembly* (1848); King Friedrich Wilhelm IV's *Proclamation of 1849;* Bismarck's *Letter to Minister von Manteuffel* (1856); Field Marshal Helmuth con Moltke's *1866*; and *The Imperial Proclamation* (1871).

"Franco-Prussian War." www.onwar.com/aced/data/foxtrot/franceprussia1870.htm. Provides some statistical data on the war that ended with German unification.

"German Unification under Bismarck." www.zum.de/whkmla/region/germany/bismarck.html. A reliable history of German unification movement from the revolutions of 1848 through the defeat of France and the proclamation of the German Empire in 1871.

"The Unification Era." www.geocities.com/Athens/Rhodes/6916/unification
.htm. A general introduction to the phases in the development of
German unification under Bismarck's direction.

Multimedia Sources

Anderson, Margaret. "The 2nd Reich." Podcast. Berkeley: University of California, 2007. http://www.learnoutloud.com/Podcast-Directory/History/
European-History/The-Rise-and-Fall-of-the-Second-Reich-Podcast/
24264. A university lecture on the history of the Second Reich with a
solid and fascinating introduction.
Anderson, Margaret. "The Rise of Bismarck to 1866." Podcast. Berkeley: University of California, 2007. http://www.learnoutloud.com/Podcast
-Directory/History/European-History/The-Rise-and-Fall-of-the-
Second-Reich-Podcast/24264. This lecture traces the rise of Bismarck
from the Revolutions of 1848 to the German Civil War.

69. Second Ashanti War (1873–1874)

The boundary settlement (1831) in which the Pra River was recognized as
the boundary between the British protected coastal areas and the Ashanti
nation in West Africa had stood for decades. While British encroachment
into Ashanti lands continued occasionally, the peace was maintained—
that is, until 1872 when the British took the Ashanti's last access point to
the Atlantic, the coastal town of Elmina. Believing that the British were
weak, an Ashanti army crossed the Pra River in 1873 and attacked the
Fante tribe, a British ally. The British successfully defended Elmina but
the British government recognized that a much larger force was needed
to contain the Ashanti. Major General Garnet Wolseley (1833–1913)
was named as commander and additional troops were dispatched. After
diplomatic efforts failed, the British, with 4,000 men, marched on the
Ashantis. British firepower prevailed at the Battle of Amoafo (January
31, 1874) and other encounters. The war was concluded with the Treaty
of Fomena (March 14, 1874). It specified that the Ashanti were to recognize British control of Elmina, they were obliged to pay an indemnity, and
they were to abandon alliances with tribes that were hostile to the British.
After the Second Ashanti War, the British position in the region was secure
for almost a century. Other conflicts with the Ashanti occurred, but they
were not as extensive or threatening as this war.

TERM PAPER SUGGESTIONS

1. Write a paper on the background and origins of the Second Ashanti War.
2. Develop a paper on the prosecution of the war. Why were the British able to defeat the superior numbers of the Ashanti?
3. Write a paper on the terms and consequences of the Treaty of Fomena. What impact did it have on the British and Ashanti positions in West Africa?
4. Write a paper in which you analyze Wolseley's leadership during this war. Why were the explorers Henry Morton Stanley (1841–1904) and Winwood Reade (1838–1875) critical of Wolseley?

ALTERNATIVE TERM PAPER SUGGESTIONS

1. Develop a podcast in which the Ashanti leadership makes the decision to go to war with the British? Did they think that they could win? Why?
2. Develop a podcast in which British leaders decide to commit a large number of troops to suppress the Ashanti? What were their major objectives in West Africa?
3. Develop an iMovie that covers the proceedings at the Treaty of Fomena.

SUGGESTED SOURCES

Primary Sources

Blackenbury, Henry. *The Ashanti War: A Narrative Prepared from the Official Documents by Permission of Major General Sir Garnet Wolseley.* 2 vols. Uckfield, U.K.: Naval and Military Press, 2002; originally published in 1874. A very valuable primary source that is sympathetic to Wolseley and representative of Victorian values and biases.

Boyle, Frederick. *Through Fanteeland to Coomassie: A Diary of the Ashantee Expedition.* London: Chapman and Hall, 1874. Boyle was a correspondent traveling with the British army, and his diary provides useful information on the day-to-day activities of the army and its major military actions.

Henty, G. A. *The March to Coomassie.* Cave Junction, OR: Robinson Books, 2002. A very popular nineteenth-century account of the war. As a correspondent, Henty witnessed many events. His work is pro-British and imperial in tone.

Metcalfe, George Edgar. *Great Britain and Ghana, Documents of Ghana History, 1807–1957.* London: T. Nelson, 1964. This extensive collection of documents includes several on the Ashanti wars of the nineteenth century.

Prempeh I (King of Ashanti, 1870–1931). *The History of Ashanti Kings and the Whole Country Itself and other Writings.* Ed. A. Adu Boahen. Oxford: Oxford University Press, 2003. In the early sections of this book, Prempeh I provides some information about the war.

Reade, Winwood. *The Story of the Ashantee Campaign.* London: Smith, Elder, 1874. Also available as an e-book at http://books.google.com/books?id=eFMMAAAAYAAJ. Reade, a correspondent who was with the British army, was critical of Wolseley and his leadership during the war.

Stanley, Henry Morton. *Coomassie and Magdala: The Story of Two British Campaigns in Africa.* New York: Harper and Brothers, 1874. Stanley (journalist and explorer) accompanied Wolseley's force and, in this book, he expressed criticism of the British commander's leadership and methods.

Secondary Sources

Agbodeka, Francis. *African Politics and British Policy in the Gold Coast, 1868–1900.* Evanston, IL: Northwestern University Press, 1971. Provides extensive information on British ambitions in West Africa and their competitive and hostile relationship with the Ashanti.

Bond, Brian. *Victorian Military Campaigns.* New York: Praeger, 1967. In this volume see the entry on "The Ashanti Campaign, 1873–1874" by John Keegan.

Brackenbury, Henry. *The Ashanti War of 1873–74, with Maps and Plans.* London: Frank Cass, 1874. Based on the Wolseley papers, a generally accurate account that is sympathetic to the British.

Callwell, C. E. *Small Wars: Their Principles and Practices.* 3rd ed. Lincoln: University of Nebraska Press, 1996. A classic study on military history that provides information on the Ashanti Wars.

Claridge, William W. *A History of the Gold Coast and Ashanti, from the Earliest times to the Commencement of the Twentieth Century.* 2 vols. 2nd ed. New York: Barnes and Noble, 1964. An exhaustive secondary study on the Ashanti that includes information on all of the Ashanti conflicts of the nineteenth century.

Edgerton, Robert B. *The Fall of the Asante Empire: The Hundred-Year War for Africa's Gold Coast.* New York: The Free Press, 1995. A highly readable and reliable study of the collapse of the Ashanti hegemony in West Africa. Among the many factors that explain their fall were British weapons and tactics, disease, and a lack of depth in their organization.

Farwell, Byron. *The Encyclopedia of Nineteenth-Century Land Warfare: An Illustrated World View.* New York: W. W. Norton & Company, 2001. A very useful reference book that provides information on the military aspects of the Ashanti Wars.

Goldstein, Erik. *Wars and Peace Treaties, 1816–1991.* London: Routledge, 1992. A useful text that provides information on general and colonial wars (including Ashanti wars) during the nineteenth and twentieth centuries.

Lehmann, Joseph. *All Sir Garnett: A Life of Field Marshal Lord Wolseley.* London: Cape, 1964. Still the best biography of Wolseley, who served as the Victorian "utility" general in stabilizing British interests throughout the world.

Lloyd, Adam. *The Drums of Kumasi: The Story of the Ashanti Wars.* London: Longmans, 1964. A readable and reliable narrative history of the Ashanti wars of the nineteenth century.

McCarthy, Mary. *Social Change and the Growth of British Power in the Gold Coast: The Fante States, 1807–1874.* Lanham, MD: University Press of America, 1983. A scholarly study of the impact of British expansion in the Gold Coast and other areas in West Africa. While the focus is on the coastal areas, the continuing concern with the Ashantis is addressed.

McCaskie, T. C. *Asante Identities: History and Modernity in an African Village, 1850–1950.* Bloomington: Indiana University Press, 2000. A careful scholarly examination of the transformation of Ashanti life during the nineteenth and twentieth centuries.

Maxwell, Leigh. *The Ashanti Ring: Sir Garnet Wolseley's Campaigns, 1870–1882.* London: Leo Cooper in association with Secker and Warburg, 1985. Very reliable and useful source on the military aspects of the Second Ashanti War and other struggles in West Africa.

Raugh. Harold E. *The Victorians at War, 1815–1914: An Encyclopedia of British Military History.* Santa Barbara, CA: ABC-CLIO, 2004. Also available as an e-book at http://books.google.com/books?id=HvE_Pa_ZlfsC. An excellent reference tool that includes information on the Ashanti Wars of the nineteenth century.

Shillington, Kevin. *History of Africa.* New York: St. Martin's, 1996. A general text that is reliable and well organized. It provides introductory information on the Anglo-Ashanti conflicts in West Africa during the nineteenth century.

Vandervort, Bruce. *Wars of Imperial Conquest in Africa, 1830–1914.* Bloomington: Indiana University Press, 1998. Provides reliable information on the Second Ashanti War and its impact on West Africa.

Ward, William E. *A History of Ghana.* Rev. 3rd ed. London: Allen and Unwin, 1968. A standard text that provides information on the Ashanti Wars throughout the century and their impact on British interests and the other regional tribes.

Wilks, Ivor. *Asante in the Nineteenth Century: The Structure and Evolution of a Political Order.* Cambridge, U.K.: Cambridge University Press, 1975. An interesting study of the transformation of the Ashanti political system during the nineteenth century.

World Wide Web

"Ashanti Wars." http://www.heritage-history.com/www/heritage.php?R_menu=OFF&Dir=wars&FileName=wars_ashanti.php. Provides an introductory statement on this war and the British decision to provide the necessary force to suppress the Ashantis.

"Gold Coast and Ashanti." http://courses.wcupa.edu/jones/his312/lectures/brit-occ.htm#goldcoast. From West Chester University, a description of the Ashantis' impact on the Gold Coast and West Africa.

"Second Ashanti War, 1873–1874." http://www.onwar.com/aced/nation/all/asante/fasante1873.htm. Provides a very accurate statement with some detailed information on the war. Limited statistical data are also included.

Multimedia Sources

Ashanti. Tango Entertainment, 2005. DVD. A dramatic film (1979) on the Anglo-Ashanti Wars that presents these imperial conflicts in the cultural context.

"Ashanti Kingdom." http://encarta.msn.com/medias_761580620/ashanti_kingdom.html. Provides a very good map, four illustrations (including a copy of an illustration on this struggle), and a sample of traditional Ashanti music.

70. Three Emperors' League and Alliance (1873–1881)

The Three Emperors' League was an agreement between the German, Austro-Hungarian, and Russian Empires directed against the spread of republican and socialist ideas and practices in central and eastern Europe. The conservative leaders of these countries met in 1873 and resolved to sustain their political and economic philosophies and to support one another against the mounting calls for liberal reforms. The architect of the League was the German Chancellor Otto von Bismarck (1815–1898) who agreed with its principles but also wanted to tie

Austria-Hungary and Russia to the German Empire in the event that the French launched a war of revenge in response to their defeat in the Franco-Prussia War (1870–1871). The Three Emperors' League continued for five years but was weakened by Russia's reaction to the positions taken by the German Empire and Austria-Hungary at the Congress of Berlin in 1878. Rather than supporting Russia, both nations pursued their own agendas. Austria-Hungary expanded its interests in the Balkans, and Germany appeared to support the British who defeated Russian plans for access to the Straits and the Eastern Mediterranean and for the establishment of a large Bulgaria that would be a satellite of Russia. In 1881, realizing that Austria-Hungary and Germany had entered into a new agreement (terms unknown), the Russians sought to renew the League. The result was the Three Emperors' Alliance of 1881, which did not involve a hard commitment of forces; rather, it continued the ideological affiliation of the earlier arrangement. In 1886 Russia failed to renew its membership in this alliance because of its increased anxiety over the closeness of the Austro-Hungarian and German relationship.

TERM PAPER SUGGESTIONS

1. Write a paper on the meeting of the Russian, German, and Austro-Hungarian leaders in 1873 and the resulting Three Emperors' League.

2. Develop a paper in which you consider and analyze the place of the Three Emperors' League in Bismarck's German diplomacy.

3. Write a paper on the collapse of the Three Emperors' League at the Congress of Berlin. Why did Russia no longer trust the Germans and the Austro-Hungarians?

4. Write a term paper on why Russia disengaged itself from the Three Emperors' Alliance in 1886.

5. Write a paper in which you evaluate the ideological origins of the League and the nationalist policies of its members.

ALTERNATIVE TERM PAPER SUGGESTIONS

1. Develop a podcast in which you interview Bismarck in later life about the purposes for German involvement in the Three Emperors' League and Alliance.

2. Develop an iMovie in which the three leaders, meeting in 1873, discuss their fears about republicanism and socialism and the need to suppress such notions in their countries.

3. As a mid-level Russian diplomat during this period, develop a blog on your experiences and thoughts on the usefulness of the Three Emperors' League from the Russian perspective.

SUGGESTED SOURCES

Primary Sources

Bismarck, Otto von. *The Memoirs, Being the Reflections and Reminiscences of Otto, Prince von Bismarck, written and dictated by himself after his retirement from office.* 2 vols. Translated under the supervision of A. J. Butler. New York: H. Fertig, 1966. Includes comments and evaluative remarks on the Three Emperors' League and Alliance by its creator.

———. *Bismarck's Speeches and Letters.* Ed. Hermann Schoenfeld. New York: D. Appleton, 1905. Useful primary materials that include data on the interrelationships between Germany, Austria-Hungary, and Russia.

Hamerow, Theodore S., ed. *The Age of Bismarck: Documents and Interpretations.* New York: Harper and Row, 1973. A very useful collection of primary sources and excerpts from significant secondary sources on Bismarck's diplomatic and political agendas.

"Primary Documents: Three Emperors' League, 18 June 1881." http://www.firstworldwar.com/source/threeemperorsleague.htm. A copy of the text of the agreement with an introduction and a photograph.

Saburov, Petr A. *The Saburov Memoirs: or Bismarck and Russia, Being Fresh Light on the League of the Three Emperors, 1881.* Trans. James Simpson. New York: Macmillan, 1929. The Russian perspective on the alliance and the relationships with Germany and Austria-Hungary.

"The Three Emperors' League." http://wwi.lib.byu.edu/index.php/The_Three_Emperors%27_League. Another copy of the agreement signed on June 18, 1881, which renewed the League and transformed it into a more formal alliance.

"The Three Emperors' League, June 18, 1881." http://avalon.law.yale.edu/19th_century/empleagu.asp. A certified copy of the alliance provided by the Yale University School of Law.

William I. *The Correspondence of William I and Bismarck, with Other Letters from and to Prince Bismarck.* 2 vols. Trans. J. A. Ford. New York: F. A. Stokes, 1903. Also available as an e-book at http://www.archive.org/stream/correspondenceof02bismuoft/correspondenceof02bismuoft_djvu.txt. Includes information on the origins of the Three Emperors' League and what the Germans hoped that it would achieve.

Secondary Sources

Abrams, Lynn. *Bismarck and the German Empire, 1871–1918.* New York: Routledge, 1995. Includes data on Bismarck's changing aspirations for the League.

Andrassy, Jules. *Bismarck, Andrassy, and Their Successors.* San Antonio, TX: Simon Publications, 2001; originally published in 1927. An excellent study by the son of the Austrian foreign minister who was a partner in the development of the Three Emperors' League.

Bagdasarian, Nicolas Der. *The Austro-German Rapproachement, 1870–1879.* Rutherford, NJ: Fairleigh Dickinson University Press, 1975. A scholarly study of Bismarck's success in renewing normal relations with Austria-Hungary after the German Civil War of 1866.

Crankshaw, Edward. *Bismarck.* New York: Penguin, 1983. A reliable and well-written biography of the German Chancellor—includes data on the League and the Alliance.

Decsy, Janos. *Prime Minister Gyula Andrassy's Influence on Habsburg Foreign Policy.* East European Monographs, no. 52. New York: Columbia University Press, 1979. An excellent scholarly work that includes Andrassy's impact on the Three Emperors' League and Alliance.

Eyck, Erich. *Bismarck and the German Empire.* New York: W. W. Norton, 1964. Still a classic in studying Bismarck's role in German history—including his diplomacy and the Three Emperors' League.

Feuchtwanger, E. J. *Bismarck.* London: Routledge, 2002. This study includes a section on Bismarck as the preeminent statesman of the era, and provides insights on Bismarck's rationale for the Three Emperors' League and Alliance.

Fuller, Joseph Vincent. *Bismarck's Diplomacy at its Zenith.* Harvard Historical Studies, v. 26. Cambridge, MA: Harvard University Press, 1922. Also available as an e-book at http://www.archive.org/stream/jamesspruntstudi17nortuoft/jamesspruntstudi17nortuoft_djvu.txt. Fuller's classic study on Bismarck is sympathetic and includes extensive information on the Three Emperors' League.

Glenny, Misha. *The Balkans: Nationalism, War, and The Great Powers, 1804–1999.* London: Penguin, 1999. A very important study on the Balkans that includes information on connecting Bismarck's diplomacy with the collapse of order prior to the First World War.

Hildebrand, Klaus. *German Foreign Policy from Bismarck to Adenauer: The Limits of Statecraft.* Trans. Louise Wilmot. London: Unwin Hyman, 1989. An examination of the intent and skill that Bismarck brought to diplomacy during the 1870s and 1880s.

Kissinger, Henry. *Diplomacy.* New York: Simon and Schuster, 1995. An important study by a scholar and diplomat who specialized in nineteenth-century diplomatic history, which includes data on Bismarck and the League.

Palmer, Alan. *Twilight of the Habsburgs: The Life and Times of Emperor Francis Joseph.* New York: Atlantic Monthly Press, 1997. The best biography of the Austro-Hungarian emperor in English—includes data on the Three Emperors' League and Alliance.

Rupp, George H. *A Wavering Friendship: Russia and Austria, 1876–1878.* Cambridge, MA: Harvard University Press, 1941. Still a standard on the collapse of Russian-Austrian relations over their conflicting ambitions in the Balkans, which weakened the Three Emperors' League.

Simpson, William. *The Second Reich: Germany, 1871–1918.* Cambridge, U.K.: Cambridge University Press, 1995. A very good political history that includes valuable information on the League and Bismarck's diplomacy.

Ullrich, Volker. *Bismarck: The Iron Chancellor.* Trans. Timothy Beech. London: Haus, 2008. A new biography of Bismarck that includes data on his leadership of European diplomacy and the establishment of the Three Emperors' League.

Waller, Bruce. *Bismarck at the Crossroads: The Reorientation of German Foreign Policy after the Congress of Berlin, 1878–1880.* London: Athlone, 1974. With the rifts between Austria and Russia and Russia and Germany that emerged in 1878, Bismarck had to reorient German diplomacy while attempting to salvage the Three Emperors' League.

Williamson, D. G. *Bismarck and Germany, 1862–1890.* 2nd ed. New York: Longman, 1998. Includes useful data on the League and the Alliance.

World Wide Web

"Three Emperors' League." http://www.infoplease.com/ce6/history/A0848607.html. An introduction to the League with additional links to other relevant sites.

"Three Emperors' League." http://www.answers.com/topic/league-of-the-three-emperors. A comprehensive Web site that includes an excerpt from *The Russian Encyclopedia* in addition to others. Many links to relevant sites are provided.

Multimedia Sources

"Austria-Hungary." http://encarta.msn.com/medias_761579967/Austria-Hungary.html. Includes a very useful map that focuses on the centrality of Austria-Hungary in the Three Emperors's League, as well as a photograph of a late nineteenth-century painting.

"*Dreikaiserbund.*" http://encyclopedia.farlex.com/_/viewer.aspx?path=hut &name=1823n049.jpg. A caricature of Bismarck's manipulation of the League and its leaders.

"Three Emperors' League." http://www.encyclopedia.com/doc/1E1 -ThreeEmp.html. Includes three photographs of participants and explanatory text.

71. Founding of Arya Samaj Movement (1875)

During the years after the British suppression of the Sepoy Mutiny (1857–1858), India came under direct British control. Britain began a process of transforming India into a Western society. Resistance to this cultural change emerged quickly and from varying quarters. In the early 1870s Swami Dayananda (1824–1883) initiated a period of study of the current state of Hindu society. This led to the establishment on a Hindu reform movement, Arya Samaj, which was based upon the absolute truth of the Vedas, the ancient sacred texts of Hinduism. Dayananda advanced his proposals at Varanasi in 1875 when he promulgated the "Light of Truth." With the disappearance of Vedic schools, he relied on popularizing his beliefs through a continuing series of public statements. After some initial disappointments, an Arya Samaj (orthodox Hindu education and worship center) was established in Bombay. The movement grew rapidly and contributed to sustaining the Indian/Hindu identity during an era of extensive British intervention in the life of Indian society. While the Arya Samajs were established throughout the world and rejuvenated the Vedas, they also had an impact on many prominent Indian leaders including Mahatma Gandhi (1869–1948) during the late nineteenth and early twentieth centuries.

TERM PAPER SUGGESTIONS

1. Write a paper on the state of Indian religious culture during the early 1870s. Why were the Vedic schools disappearing?

2. Develop a paper of Dayananda's philosophy of religion. In what ways did it support traditional Indian values?

3. Write a paper on the difficulties that Dayananda experienced in establishing the first Arya Samaj.

ALTERNATIVE TERM PAPER SUGGESTIONS

1. Develop a podcast in which Dayananda discusses his beliefs with the leaders in Bombay.

2. Develop an iMovie in which Dayananda is interviewed and explains his failure at Ahmedabad.

3. As the leader of an Arya Samaj during the 1890s, write a blog as a reflection on the progress of the movement to that time.

SUGGESTED SOURCES

Primary Sources

Dayananda, Sarasvati, Swami. *Autobiography of Dayanand Saraswati.* Ed. K. C. Yadav. 2nd rev. ed. New Delhi: Manohar, 1978. The essential primary source for understanding the Arya Samaj movement and its impact on India.

Rai, Laipat. *A History of the Arya Samaj: An Account of Its Origins, Doctrines and Activities with a Biographical Sketch of the Founder.* Ed. Ram Sharma. Bombay: Orient Longmans, 1967; originally published in 1914. Includes some primary materials that may be useful to students who are working on this topic.

Secondary Sources

Arya, Anupama. *Religion and Politics in India: A Study of the Role of Arya Samaj.* Delhi: K. K. Publications, 2001. A very good study that links the religious values of Arya Samaj with the Indian independence movement and later politics.

Dua, Veena. *The Arya Samaj in Punjab Politics.* New Delhi: Picus Books, 1999. A relevant study of the impact of Arya Samaj on Punjab political development and history.

Griswold, Harvey. *The Problem of the Arya Samaj.* Calcutta: [n.p.], 1901; originally published in 1892. Griswold considers the impact of the movement on the westernization process.

Gupta, Shiv Kumar. *Arya Samaj and the Raj, 1875–1920.* New Delhi: Gitanjali Publishing House, 1991. A very good history of the movement's impact on the British imperial administration of India.

Jones, Kenneth W. *The Arya Samaj in the Punjab, A Study of Social Reform and Religious Revivalism, 1877–1902.* Microbook. Ann Arbor: University Microfilms, 1966. A useful scholarly study of Arya Samaj's impact in Punjab that demonstrates the depth of its power.

Llewellyn, J. S. *The Arya Samaj as a Fundamentalist Movement: A Study in Comparative Fundamentalism.* New Delhi: Manohar Publishers, 1993. Very worthwhile study of the reactionary aspects of the Arya Samaj in its defense of chastity, honor, and other similar Vedic values.

Pandey, Dhanpati. *The Arya Samaj and Indian Nationalism, 1875–1920.* New Delhi: S. Chand, 1972. This is a very important book in gaining an understanding of the interrelationship of the movement with Indian nationalism.

Pareek, Radhey Shyam. *Contribution of Arya Samaj in the Making of Modern India, 1875–1947.* New Delhi: Sarvadeshik Arya Pratinidhi Sabha, 1973. Another significant study that connects Arya Samaj with the Indian nationalist movement.

Saxena, Gulshan Swarup. *Arya Samaj Movement in India, 1875–1947.* Delhi: South Asia Books, 1990. An excellent study of the movement within Indian society and life.

Sharma, J. B. *Arya Samaj and Regeneration of India.* New Delhi: Commonwealth Publishers, 1990. J. B. Sharma's work should be read by students who wish to understand Arya Samaj's impact on Indian identity.

———. *The Arya Samaj and Its Impact on Contemporary India in the Nineteenth Century.* Una, India: Institute of Public Administration, 1960. This should be read by students who wish to understand Arya Samaj's impact on Indian identity.

Sharma, Satish Kumar. *Social Movements and Social Change: A Study of Arya Samaj and Untouchables in Punjab.* Delhi: B. R. Publishing, 1985. A book that should be read along with Dua's work listed here. It is provocative and worthwhile.

Shastri, Vaidyanath. *The Arya Samaj, Its Cult and Creed.* 2nd ed. New Delhi: Sarvadeshik Arya Pratiniidhi Sabha, 1967. An introduction to Arya Samaj that may be useful.

Upadhyaya, Ganga Prasad. *The Origin, Scope and Mission of Arya Samaj.* Allahabad: Arya Samaj, 1940. A good resource that provides basic information.

Yadav, Kripal, and Krishan Singh Arya. *Arya Samaj and the Freedom Movement.* New Delhi: Manohar, 1988. Another scholarly study that connects the movement with the nationalist cause.

World Wide Web

"Arya Samaj." http://www.britannica.com/EBchecked/topic/37454/Arya-Samaj. Provides a brief introduction to the movement.

"Arya Samaj." http://aryasamaj.forumwise.com/. The Web site of the Arya Samaj forum provides multiple links that may be useful.

"Arya Samaj." http://www.answers.com/topic/arya-samaj. Useful description of the founding of the movement.

"Arya Samaj." http://www.encarta.sg/encyclopedia_761571990/Arya _Samaj.html. A brief but good introduction to Arya Samaj.

"Dayananda's Arya Samaj: The 19th-century Firebrand's Crusade to Revive the Vedas, Reform Hinduism and Win Social Justice for All Continues to Impact India." http://www.encyclopedia.com/doc/1P1-79274557.html. This article from *Hinduism Today* includes information on the founding of Arya Samaj.

"Dayananda Sarasvati." http://www.encarta.sg/encyclopedia_761570053/ Dayananda_Sarasvati.html. A useful biography and information on the tenets of Arya Simaj.

Multimedia Source

"Ten Principles of Aryan Samja." http://www.youtube.com/watch?v=0dQg00T -oaY. A video presentation of the ten basic principles that were articulated in 1875.

72. Congress of Berlin (1878)

A diplomatic crisis with the potential of war between Russia and Great Britain broke in the spring of 1878 when the terms of the Treaty of San Stephano were revealed. The crisis had its origins in the Russo-Turkish War of 1877–1878 that was caused by Russian ambitions in the Balkans, alleged Turkish atrocities against Christians, and the continuing decline of the Ottoman Empire. After holding the Russian forces for several months, Turkish resistance collapsed and the Russians imposed the terms of the Treaty of San Stephano in March 1878. The major points of concern were the establishment of a "large" Bulgarian state (which would be allied to Russia) and Russian naval access to the Mediterranean Sea. British Prime Minister Benjamin Disraeli and his foreign secretary, Lord Salisbury, denounced the arrangement and stated that it was not acceptable. A squadron of British ships were sent to the Sea of Marmara. The German Chancellor Otto von Bismarck, fearing that a European war would break out, offered to mediate the differences between Britain and Russia. Other nations also expressed their interests. Reluctantly, the Russians concurred and the Congress of Berlin convened on June 13, 1878. The British has secured three arrangements with the Austro-Hungarian

Empire, the Russian Empire, and the Ottoman Empire. After Disraeli threatened to walk away from the Congress, terms were reached. The Russians gained a "small" Bulgaria, and the independent principalities of Serbia, Macedonia, and Romania were recognized. Britain acquired Cyprus and succeeded in keeping Russia out of the Mediterranean. However, the Russians were outraged by Bismarck's lack of support and the German-Russian relationship was strained. In the Balkans, the Congress of Berlin failed to stifle the developing Austro-Russian rivalry and the struggles caused by ethnic differences, such as the Greece-Turkish dispute.

TERM PAPER SUGGESTIONS

1. Develop a paper on how and why the strategies and interests of Imperial Russia and Great Britain collided in 1878.
2. Write a paper on the secret pre-Congress negotiations or alliances that Disraeli and Salisbury concluded contributed to predetermining the outcomes.
3. Was Bismarck an honest broker at the Congress? Was he outmaneuvered by Disraeli?
4. By the end of the Congress, the Russians felt betrayed by Bismarck. Why?
5. Develop a paper on the impact of the crisis of 1878 on the development of the Eastern/Balkan question during the late nineteenth and early twentieth century. Was it a "defining moment" among the great powers that clarified the struggle between the Austro-Hungarian Empire and the Russian Empire for hegemony in the Balkans?

ALTERNATIVE TERM PAPER SUGGESTIONS

1. Develop a 3 minute iMovie on the crisis of the Congress—Disraeli's threat to walk out and take the next train to the West.
2. Create a podcast on how the Russian diplomats reacted to British dominance of the agenda at the Congress.
3. Italy was represented at the Congress by Count Corti and Count De Launay. Develop a blog of dispatches that they might have sent to Rome on the month-long Congress of Berlin.
4. The Russians won the war with Turkey but thought that they had been denied the spoils of their victory. From the perspective of either a Viennese or a Moscow journalist, write a detailed op-ed piece on whether this perception was correct.

5. Develop two maps of the Balkans—one prior to the Congress and the other reflecting its terms—provide annotated notes on the changes, and comment on their geopolitical significance.

SUGGESTED SOURCES

Primary Sources

Smith, Paul, ed. *Lord Salisbury on Politics: A Selection from His Articles in the "Quarterly Review," 1860–1883.* Cambridge, U.K.: Cambridge University Press, 1972. Provides valuable insights into Salisbury's developing foreign policy positions that served Disraeli and him well from 1874 to 1880.

Swartz, Helen M., and Marvin Swartz, eds. *Disraeli's Reminiscences.* New York: Stein and Day, 1976. A highly selective but useful source on Disraeli's public and private comments.

Secondary Sources

Abrams, Lynn. *Bismarck and the German Empire, 1871–1918.* London and New York: Routledge, 2006. A new and important book that begins with a chapter on the new German Empire in 1871.

Beeler, John Francis. *British Naval Policy in the Gladstone-Disraeli Era, 1866–1880.* Stanford, CA: Stanford University Press, 1997. A reliable study that examines British interest in denying Russia access to the Mediterranean, which was a significant factor in the Anglo-Russian crisis of 1877–1878.

Blake, Robert. *Disraeli.* New York: St. Martin's Press, 1967. Still one of the most reliable biographies of Disraeli—an important resource on the Congress of Berlin.

———— and Hugh Cecil, eds. *Salisbury, the Man and His Policies.* New York: St. Martin's Press, 1987. While primarily centered on Salisbury as prime minister, this book is useful on the Congress of Berlin and the Eastern Question.

Durman, Karel. *The Time of the Thunderer: Mikhail Katkov, Russian Nationalist Extremism and the Failure of the Bismarckian system, 1871–1887.* East European monographs, no. 237. New York: Columbia University Press, 1988. A fascinating and worthwhile study that focuses on the unanticipated consequences of Bismarck's policies, including those at the Congress of Berlin.

Jelavich, Barbara. *Russia's Balkan Entanglements, 1806–1914.* Cambridge, U.K.: Cambridge University Press, 1991. An excellent study of Russian policies and actions in the Balkans that contributed to the Anglo-Turkish War, 1877–1878.

Kent, Marian, ed. *The Great Powers and the End of the Ottoman Empire.* London: Frank Cass, 1995. Provides insights into the power politics that contributed to the crisis that preceded the Congress.

Kiraly, Bela K., and Gale Stokes, eds. *Insurrections, Wars, and the Eastern Crisis of the 1870s.* East European Monographs, no. 197. New York: Columbia University Press, 1985. Includes a series of essays that cover many aspects of the causes, development, and consequences of the crisis.

Leman, Katherine Anne. *Bismarck.* New York: Pearson Longman, 2004. A scholarly and useful study that demonstrates a command of the sources and includes good documentation.

Medlicott, William Norton. *The Congress of Berlin and After: A Diplomatic History of the Near Eastern Settlement, 1878–1880.* 2nd ed. London: Frank Cass, 1963. Still the standard on the history of the Congress of Berlin.

Milojković-Djurić, Jelena. *The Eastern Question and the Voices of Reason: Austria-Hungary, Russia, and the Balkan States 1875–1908.* East European Monographs, no. 592. New York: Columbia University Press, 2002. An innovative study based on primary sources that is for the advanced student.

Steele, David. *Lord Salisbury: A Political Biography.* London: UCL, 1999. One of the best Salisbury biographies available. It is excellent on the Disraeli-Salisbury relationship and is a good introduction to the crisis of 1877–1878.

Swartz, Marvin. *The Politics of British Foreign Policy in the Era of Disraeli and Gladstone.* New York: St. Martin's Press, 1985. A scholarly study that examines the similarities and differences in foreign policy that were pursued by Disraeli and Gladstone.

Taylor, Robert. *Lord Salisbury.* London: Lane, 1975. A reliable political biography of the British foreign secretary and, later, prime minister, this provides a useful introduction to Salisbury's role at the Congress of Berlin.

Waller, Bruce. *Bismarck at the Crossroads: The Reorientation of German Foreign Policy after the Congress of Berlin, 1878–1880.* London: Athlone Press of the University of London, 1974. A scholarly study of the impact of the Congress of Berlin on German foreign policy—especially toward Russia.

World Wide Web

"Berlin Congress." www.lahana.org/blog/Congress%20of%20Berlin.htm. A reliable but brief introduction accompanied by a valuable map.

"Berlin Treaty." www.unet.com.mk/mian/berlin.htm. Focuses on the period from March through June 1878.

Bismarck, Otto von. *Memoirs.* Available at http://history.hanover.edu/
project.html. Excerpts from Bismarck's memoirs in the Hanover Historical Texts Project, Hanover College.
"Congress of Berlin, 1878." www.factmonster.com/ce6/history/A0807198
.html. A general introduction to the causes and consequences of the
Congress.
"Congress of Berlin, 1878." www.serbianunity.net/culture/history/berlin78/
index.html. An important site sponsored by the Serbian Unity network
that advances the Serbian interpretation of the Congress and provides
extensive commentary and links.
"Europe after the Congress of Berlin 1878." www.wwnorton.com/college/history/
ralph/resource/32europe.htm. A very good map indicating the impact of
the Congress on Eastern Europe and the Eastern Mediterranean.

Multimedia Sources

Bismarck. Bayerischer Rundfunk, 1990. DVD. Directed by Tom Toelle. West
German miniseries.
Disraeli. BBC, 1978. DVD/VHS. Starring Ian McShane as British Prime Minister
Benjamin Disraeli, this BBC-produced miniseries won critical acclaim for
its historical accuracy and the quality of the production.
Fall of Eagles. BBC, 1974; available in the United States in 2006. DVD/VHS.
This 13-part BBC dramatization of the collapse of the Romanovs, the
Habsburgs, and the Hohenzollerns includes episodes that focus on the
unification of Germany.

73. Second Afghan War (1878–1880)

During the late 1870s Great Britain became wary of Russian expansion in
eastern Europe, the Mediterranean, and central and south Asia. Prime
Minister Benjamin Disraeli and his foreign secretary, Lord Salisbury, curtailed the Russians in the European sector through the Congress of Berlin
in the summer of 1878. In Asia the British feared that Russia planned to
threaten India by gaining an advantageous position in Afghanistan. Disraeli's government determined that Afghanistan must be a British sphere
of influence; it needed to protect the Khyber Pass and its access to India.
A small Russian force was present in Kabul in 1878, and the British
demanded that they be allowed to send in a small force. The Afghan
leader, Sher Ali, refused. In spite of the Russian withdrawal, the British

invaded Afghanistan on November 22, 1878, with a force of more than 35,000 troops. After a few military encounters, the British forced Sher Ali to step down and replaced him with another local leader who ceded the Khyber Pass to Great Britain. The next phase of this war started in September 1879 when the members of the British mission in Kabul were killed by a mob. A British army expelled the insurgents from Kabul but then found themselves confronted by a major uprising. The British abandoned Kabul and seized Kandahar. In 1881 British forces withdrew. Afghanistan was governed by tribal leaders for several decades. In the Anglo-Russian Entente of 1907, Russia recognized that Afghanistan was a British sphere of influence.

TERM PAPER SUGGESTIONS

1. During the nineteenth and early twentieth century, Britain was involved in three wars in Afghanistan. What was the rationale for this policy and why did Britain enter into the Second Afghan War?

2. Write a paper on the consequences of the Second Afghan War. What changed as a result of the war?

3. Develop a term paper on the major or defining moments of the Second Afghan War.

4. Write a paper on the background and causes of the Second Afghan War from both the British and Afghan perspectives.

ALTERNATIVE TERM PAPER SUGGESTIONS

1. Assume that you are son of an Afghan tribal chief who fought and died in the First Anglo-Afghan War. Now you are confronted with the decision to fight in the Second Anglo-Afghan War. Write a blog on the issues and motivating forces that impact your decision and explain your decision.

2. Develop a 5 minute podcast as a journalist for *The Daily Mail*, a London newspaper, assigned to the British army. Your report consists of monthly dispatches on the progress of the conflict.

3. Develop a Web site that includes maps with an accompanying narrative on the Afghan strategy and tactics during the war.

4. Develop an iMovie (2–3 minutes) in which you provide two or three "from the front" reports on the Second Afghan War for the BBC.

SUGGESTED SOURCES

Primary Sources

Ashe, John. *Soldiers and Others That I have Known*. London: Herbert Jenkins, 1925. Includes personal recollections of several significant participants of the Second Anglo-Afghan War.

Creagh, O'Moore. *The Autobiography of General Sir O'Moore Creagh*. London: Hutchinson, 1924. A valuable account by a leading officer during the war.

Hamilton, Ian. *Listening to the Drums*. London: Faber and Faber, 1944. A worthwhile memoir of his life fighting colonial and general wars by a major British military leader.

Howard, Francis. *Reminiscences, 1848–1890*. London: John Murray, 1924. Sir Francis Howard's memoir of his military career including his role during the Second Afghan War.

Robertson, Charles Gray. *Kurum, Kabul, and Kandahar, Being a Brief Record of Impressions in these Campaigns under General Roberts*. Chestnut Hill, MA: Adamant Media/Elibron, 2003; reprint of 1881 edition. While this is a "brief" account, it is outstanding in its accuracy and depth of understanding on the significance of the war.

Trousdale, William, ed. *War in Afghanistan, 1879–1880: The Personal Diary of Major General Sir Charles Metcalfe Macgregor*. Detroit: Wayne State University Press, 1985. An excellent edition of Macgregor's diary as a leader of British forces during the war. It is valuable on British tactics.

Warburton, Robert. *Eighteen Years in the Khyber: 1879–1898*. Chestnut Hill, MA: Adamant Media/Elibron, 2002; reprint of the 1900 edition. Warburton's memoir provides a perspective of a long-term British resident on the India-Afghan border.

Secondary Sources

Anderson, J. H. *The Afghan War 1878–1880*. London: R. J. Leach, 1991; reprint of 1905 edition. A dated but still useful history of the war with many extensive quotations from primary sources.

Argyll, George Douglas Campbell. *The Eastern Question from the Treaty of Paris 1856 to the Treaty of Berlin 1878 and to the Second Afghan War*. Chestnut Hill, MA: Adamant Media, 2001; reprint of the 1879 edition. An old but durable study by a reputable contemporary scholar who places the war in the context of east-west relations during the second half of the nineteenth century.

Dockerty, Paddy. *The Khyber Pass: A History of Empire and Invasion.* Somerville, MA: Union Square Press, 2008. Includes a good survey of the Second Afghan War.

Forbes, Archibald. *Britain in Afghanistan: The Second Afghan War 1878–80.* London: Leonaur, Ltd., 2007. An excellent, readable, and reliable history of the Second Afghan War.

Heathcote, Tony. *The Afghan Wars: 1839–1919.* London: The History Press, 2007. A scholarly examination of the causes and development of the Afghan wars from 1839 through the Versailles Peace Conference of 1919.

Hensman, Howard. *The Afghan War of 1879–89.* London: W. H. Allen, 1881. An old but useful detailed account of the war with ten maps.

James, Lawrence. *The Rise and Fall of the British Empire.* New York: St. Martin's, 1994. A reliable standard text that places the specific incidents in British imperial history in the context of the sweep of British imperialism as an historical force and includes a very good bibliography.

Meyer, Karl E., and Shareen Blair Brysac. *Tournament of Shadows: The Great Game and the Race for Empire in Central Asia.* Washington, DC: Counterpoint, 1999. In this outstanding study, the mutiny is considered as an incident in the long Anglo-Russian rivalry in South Asia.

Richards, D. S. *The Savage Frontier, A History of the Anglo-Afghan Wars.* London: Macmillan, 1990. A reliable study based on primary and secondary sources with photographs of important locations and individuals.

Robson, Brian. *The Road to Kabul: The Second Afghan War, 1878 to 1881.* Stroud, U.K.: Spellmount, 2003. This is the most scholarly analysis of the Second Afghan War. Using primary accounts—memoirs and many unpublished private sources—Robson provides an excellent history of the war that almost bankrupted the Indian Colonial Government.

World Wide Web

"Battle of Ali Masjid" (November 21, 1878). http://www.britishbattles.com/second-afghan-war/ali-masjid.htm. A detailed account of this battle between British/Indian forces under Lieutenant General Sir Sam Browne and Afghan and tribal troops under Gholam Hyder Khan that occurred near the western end of the Khyber Pass. Also included are area and battlefield maps, one photograph, and 12 illustrations.

"Battle of Peiwar Kotal" (December 2, 1878). http://www.britishbattles.com/second-afghan-war/peiwar-kotal.htm. A reliable account of a British/Indian victory over Afghan troops in the Kurrum Valley between

Afghanistan and India. Included are area and battlefield maps, as well as nine illustrations.

"Battle of Futtehabad" (April 2, 1879). http://www.britishbattles.com/second-afghan-war/futtehabad.htm. A detailed description of the British/Indian victory over Afghan tribesmen in northeastern Afghanistan. Included are area and battlefield maps, as well as six illustrations.

"Battle of Charasiab" (October 6, 1879). http://www.britishbattles.com/second-afghan-war/charasiab.htm. A brief but reliable account of the British/Indian victory over Afghan forces led by Nek Mohammed Khan in the region south of Kabul. Also included are area and battlefield maps and 11 illustrations.

"Battle of Kabul" (December 23, 1879). http://www.britishbattles.com/second-afghan-war/kabul-1879.htm. An adequate description of the victory of Major General Sir Frederick Roberts over the Afghan forces led by Mohammed Jan. Included are area and battlefield maps and nine illustrations.

"Battle of Ahmed Khel" (April 19, 1880). http://www.britishbattles.com/second-afghan-war/ahmed-khel.htm. A solid narrative on the British/Indian victory over Afghan tribal forces even though the victors were outnumbered by more than two to one. Included are area and battlefield maps, one photograph, and six illustrations.

"Battle of Maiwand" (July 27, 1880). http://www.britishbattles.com/second-afghan-war/maiwand.htm. An account of the Afghan victory over the British/Indian army. Also included are area and battlefield maps, three photographs, and ten illustrations.

"Battle of Baba Wali" (September 1, 1880). http://www.britishbattles.com/second-afghan-war/kandahar.htm. A description of Lieutenant General Sir Frederick Roberts's march to Kandahar and the subsequent and decisive British/Indian victory at Baba Wali and the Treaty of Gandamark. Included are area and battlefield maps, one photograph, and 12 illustrations.

"The Second Anglo-Afghan War 1878–1880." http://www.garenewing.co.uk/angloafghanwar/index.php. An excellent and comprehensive Web site on all aspects of the war.

Multimedia Sources

"Map Room." http://www.garenewing.co.uk/angloafghanwar/waroffice/maproom.php. Provides four excellent maps on the Second Afghan War.

"Second Anglo-Afghan War." http://ca.encarta.msn.com/media_1481505989/second_anglo-afghan_war.html. A rare photograph of a British camp in Afghanistan during this war.

74. Anglo-Zulu War (1878–1879)

During the nineteenth century the Zulus were a dominant clan within the Nguni tribe in South Africa. As the Boers and British colonized South Africa, they came into conflict with the Zulus, who were independent and prided themselves on their military strength. Violent raids and skirmishes occurred increasingly during the 1870s. Diplomatic settlements were short-lived and showed no promise of enduring peace. In 1878 three incidents occurred between the Zulus and British subjects. The British held the Zulu king Cetshwayo responsible and issued an ultimatum December 11, 1878, which was a humiliation and challenged Zulu independence. Cetshwayo failed to respond and the British launched an invasion of Zululand in January 1879. The Zulus defeated the British at Isandlwana but were repelled by a smaller force at Rorke's Drift. The British government was embarrassed by the defeat and "minimized" it when informing the British public. During the spring and early summer, the British launched a second offensive that was more successful. Fully reinforced and with superior firepower, the British scored a major victory over the Zulus at the Battle of Ulundi on July 4, 1879. Cetshwayo was captured and later restored to limited power. While the Zulus rose up on several occasions after 1879, they no longer constituted a meaningful threat to the British position in South Africa. The Zulu War of 1879 has been interpreted by many scholars to be a "last stand" when a native African tribe defeated a British force but ultimately was defeated itself by European imperialism.

TERM PAPER SUGGESTIONS

1. Develop a paper on the origins of the Zulu War of 1879.
2. Write a paper on the prosecution of the war. Did the Zulus ever have a real opportunity to win this war?
3. Write a paper on the impact of the Zulu war on Britain's role in South Africa. Was the Zulu war a natural preface to the later Boer War? Were British ambitions and intent consistent?
4. Why did the British prevail at Rorke's Drift? Was this the turning point of the war?
5. Compare and contrast the Zulu and British leadership during the war.

ALTERNATIVE TERM PAPER SUGGESTIONS

1. Develop a 3–5 minute iMovie focused on the British government's reaction to the Zulu victory at Isandlwhana. How did this major defeat fit the British image of these natives as inferior beings?

2. As an intelligent Zulu warrior, you are fighting the British to maintain the independence and the power of your kingdom. By the end of 1879 your forces have been defeated. Write a blog on how your worldview has changed.

3. As a British survivor of Rorke's Drift, write a blog detailing your assessment of the Zulu nation.

4. Develop a 3–5 minute podcast in which you play the part of a foreign correspondent who observed the battle of Isandlwhana from a safe distance.

SUGGESTED SOURCES

Primary Sources

Moodie, D. C. F. *Zulu: 1879: The Anglo Zulu War of 1879 from Contemporary Sources: First Hand Accounts, Interviews, Dispatches, Official Documents and Newspaper Reports.* London: Leonaur, Ltd., 2006. A reliable and indispensable source of primary materials on the Anglo-Zulu war.

Norris-Newman, Charles L. *In Zululand with the British Army: The Anglo-Zulu War of 1879 through the First-hand Experiences of a Special Correspondent.* London: Leonaur, Ltd., 2006. A very valuable and reliable primary account of the Zulu war by a correspondent attached to Lord Chelmsford's army. Norris-Newman's decision to remain with the staff saved him from being a victim of the Zulu warriors at Isandlwhana.

Secondary Sources

Austin, Ronald James. *Australian Illustrated Encyclopedia of the Zulu and Boer Wars.* McCrae, Victoria, Australia: Slouch Hat Publications, 1999. An excellent and authoritative resource on the involvement of Australians in the Zulu war.

Bancroft, James W. *Rorke's Drift: The Heroic Bastion—Zulu War, 1879.* 2nd rev. ed. Staplehurst, U.K.: Spellmount Publishers, Ltd., 1990. Based on primary and secondary sources, this is a solid introduction to the Battle of Rorke's Drift.

Castle, Ian. *British Infantryman in South Africa 1877–1881: The Anglo-Zulu and Transvaal Wars.* Oxford: Osprey Publishing, 2003. Focused on the performance of the infantry during the war, this volume provides rare insights into the lives of those who were involved in direct combat.

————. *Zulu Wars: Volunteers, Irregulars and Auxiliaries (Men-at-arms).* Oxford: Osprey Publishing, 2003. Generally a pro-British account of the role of the white colonists in these colonial struggles in Africa.

Colenso, Frances E., and Edward Durnford. *Colenso and Durnford's Zulu War.* London: Leonaur, 2008. A new edition of a contemporary history of the Zulu War. Frances Colenso was the daughter of the Bishop of Zululand and Edward Durnford's brother died in the battle of Isandlwhana. While the bias is obvious, the descriptions of events and people are nonetheless valuable.

David, Saul. *Zulu: The Heroism and Tragedy of the Zulu War of 1879.* London: Penguin, 2005. A reliable account of victory and defeat on January 22, 1879, and the mishandling of these events by the British government.

Edgerton, Robert. *Like Lions They Fought: The Zulu War and the Last Black Empire in South Africa.* New York: Ballantine Books, 1989. A readable account that is sympathetic to the Zulus.

Giese, Toby. *The Men of the 24th: The Zulu War of 1879.* Kansas City, MO: Toby Giese, 1987. A history of the performance of the 24th regiment during the war.

Greaves, Adrian. *Rorke's Drift.* London: Cassell/Orion, 2002. A popular history of the battle, it is reliable and readable.

————. *Redcoats and Zulus: Thrilling Tales from the 1879 War.* Barnsley, Yorkshire, U.K.: Leo Cooper, Ltd./Pen and Sword, 2004. A very good volume of seldom-recorded incidents in the war by one of the war's most reliable authorities.

————. *Crossing the Buffalo: The Zulu War of 1879.* London: Weidenfeld and Nicolson/Orion, 2005. The best general account that is readily available.

————. *Who's Who in the Anglo Zulu War 1879.* Barnsley, Yorkshire, U.K.: Pen and Sword Military, 2006. An indispensable guide to the many personalities involved in the war

James, Lawrence. *The Rise and Fall of the British Empire.* New York: St. Martin's, 1994. A reliable standard text that places the specific incidents in British imperial history in the context of the sweep of British imperialism as an historical force and includes a very good bibliography.

Knight, Ian. *The National Army Museum Book of the Zulu War.* London: Pan/Macmillan, 2004. An excellent history of the Zulu War of 1879 based largely on the archives of the National Army Museum.

————. *British Fortifications in Zululand 1879.* Oxford: Osprey Publishing, 2005. A review of the extensive fortification system that the British constructed in their outpost networks during the Zulu war.

————. *The Zulu War 1879.* Oxford: Osprey Publishing, 2003. Knight argues that the Zulu War of 1879 was the end of Zulu power. The British victory was followed by the breakup of the Zulu kingdom and the subjugation of the tribe to British authority.

———. *Isandlwana 1879: The Great Zulu Victory.* Oxford: Osprey Publishing, 2002. A thorough and reliable account of this Zulu victory over British forces.

———. *The Anatomy of the Zulu Army: From Shaka to Cetshwayo, 1818–79.* New ed. Newbury, U.K.: Greenhill Books, 1999. A scholarly examination of the structure, strategies, and tactics of the Zulu armies.

Laband, John. *The Rise and Fall of the Zulu Nation.* Minneapolis: Arms and Armour, 1995. An excellent history that covers the swipe of Zulu history through the nineteenth century and beyond.

———. *Kingdom and Colony at War: Sixteen Studies on the Anglo-Zulu War of 1879.* Scottsville, South Africa: University of KwaZulu-Natal Press, 1990. A rather sophisticated collection of essays on aspects of the Zulu War that are often overlooked, including diplomatic initiatives and Zulu strategic and tactical plans and values.

———. *Kingdom in Crisis: The Zulu Response to the British Invasion of 1879.* Barnsley, Yorkshire, U.K.: Pen and Sword Military, 2007. This seminal study of the impact of imperialism on a native civilization provides an analysis of how the Zulus reacted to the British invasion and an explanation of why the Zulu response failed.

Latham, Christopher Wilkinson. *Uniforms and Weapons of the Zulu Wars.* London: Batsford, 1978. A valuable volume for those interested in regimental and battlefield histories.

Lock, Ron, and Peter Quantrill. *Zulu Victory: The Epic of Isandlwana and the Cover-Up.* Newbury, U.K.: Greenhill, 2002. Focused on the actions of the British government to conceal the depth of the defeat from the British populace.

McBride, Angus. *The Zulu Wars (Men-at-arms).* Oxford: Osprey Publishing, 1992. A good volume on the military aspects of the conflict.

Morris, Donald R. *The Washing of the Spears: The Rise and Fall of the Zulu Nation.* Cambridge, MA: Da Capo Press, 1998. From the perspective of the Zulus, this study provides valuable alternative insights and interpretations on the impact of the Zulu War of 1879.

Omer-Cooper, J. D. *The Zulu Aftermath: A Nineteenth Century Revolution in Bantu Africa.* Evansville, IL: Northwestern University Press, 1972. Still a valuable resource in considering the impact of the defeat of the Zulus on the development of South African history.

Rattray, David. *David Rattray's Guidebook to the Anglo-Zulu War Battlefields.* Barnsley, Yorkshire, U.K.: Pen and Sword Books, Ltd., 2002. This is an accurate and highly illustrated book by an authority who owns and operates a lodge on the battlefields.

World Wide Web

"Battle of Isandlwana" (January 22, 1879). http://www.britishbattles.com/zulu
-war/isandlwana.htm. An account of the Zulu destruction of a 1,200
man British force that includes a battlefield map, four photographs,
and 13 illustrations.

"Battle of Rorke's Drift" (January 22, 1879). http://www.britishbattles.com/
zulu-war/rorkes-drift.htm. A detailed description of the British victory
over Zulu forces under Prince Dabulamanzi kaMapande that includes a
battlefield map, three photographs, and 12 illustrations.

"Battle of Khambula" (March 29, 1879). http://www.britishbattles.com/zulu
-war/khambula.htm. An account of the British victory over the Zulus
even though they were outnumbered ten to one, which includes a battlefield map, one photograph, and five illustrations.

"Battle of Gingindlovu" (April 2, 1879). http://www.britishbattles.com/zulu
-war/gingindlovu.htm. A description of the British victory over the Zulus.
Included are a battlefield map, three photographs, and six illustrations.

"Battle of Ulundi" (July 4, 1879). http://www.britishbattles.com/zulu-war/
ulundi.htm. An account of the last major battle in the Zulu war in which
the British routed the Zulu forces and caused the Zulus to surrender.
A battlefield map and 14 illustrations are included.

Multimedia Sources

History of Warfare: Zulu Wars, 1879. Cromwell Productions, 2007. DVD/VHS.
Narrated by Robert Powell. This documentary film is a reliable introduction to the Anglo-Zulu War of 1879.

Zulu. MGM Studio, 1964. VHS/DVD. Directed by Cy Endfield. An excellent
dramatization of the Battle of Rorke's Drift.

Zulu Dawn. Tango Entertainment Studio, 1979. VHS/ DVD. Directed by
Douglas Hickox. A "prequel" to *Zulu,* which focuses on the defeat of
the British at Isandlwana.

Zulu Wars: Shaka-King of the Zulu/Blood River/Red Coat Black Blood. Good
Times Video, 2003. DVD. In three parts. Historically accurate docu-
mentaries on three aspects of the Zulu wars of the nineteenth century.

75. Panama Canal and the French (1878–1899)

After their success in building the Suez Canal, French engineers and financial
and political leaders began to consider a canal through Central America

connecting the Atlantic and Pacific Oceans. French engineering was considered the finest in the world and Ferdinand de Lesseps (1805–1894) its leading advocate. He had a career in diplomacy and had achieved renown for his Suez achievement. In 1875 he expressed interest in building the canal, and a route through the Isthmus of Panama, the northern part of Columbia, was identified as the most desirable. The Columbian government supported the project and, after of years of preparations, French engineers employed by the *Compagnie Universelle du Canal Interoceanique* arrived in Colon, Columbia, in January 1881 to launch the construction project. For the next eight years, vast financial and human resources were used to make progress on the canal. In 1888 the corruption with the firm and its financial and political supporters was revealed in the Panama Scandal that shocked France and weakened and jeopardized the Third French Republic. The *Compagnie Universelle du Canal Interoceanique* collapsed in early February 1889, and all construction was suspended in May 1889. During the next few years, more than 150 officials were involved in the scandal, mostly for taking bribes, and de Lesseps was charged, found guilty, and required to pay a fine. In 1894 a new company was established and work was resumed. While planning, site surveying, and equipment maintenance were continued, progress was very slow. After the Panamanian revolution and the involvement of the United States, the project was turned over to the Americans in 1904. The Panama Canal opened in 1912.

TERM PAPER SUGGESTIONS

1. Write a paper on the background and origins of the French plan to build the Panama Canal.

2. Develop a paper on the causes and consequences of the Panama Canal Scandal in France.

3. Write a paper on Columbian/Panamanian support for the French canal and the impact of the failure of the project on its local supporters.

4. Develop a paper on the role of Ferdinand de Lesseps on the French effort to build the Panama Canal.

5. Write a paper on how the Panama Scandal was transformed into an anti-Semitic propaganda event.

ALTERNATIVE TERM PAPER SUGGESTIONS

1. Develop an iMovie as a journalist for newspaper *Le Figaro* investigating the developing Panama Scandal.

2. Develop a podcast in which Ferdinand de Lesseps announces his involvement and support for the French construction of the Panama Canal. Be sure to include information on the rationale for the route, a projected time frame, and the requirements of the project.

3. As an investor in the Panama Canal project, you are outraged when work is halted because of a lack of funds. Through a blog with friends in Lyons, relay information about the unfolding crisis in Paris.

SUGGESTED SOURCES

Primary Sources

"Dr. Cornelius Herz." http://hansard.millbanksystems.com/commons/1894/aug/14/dr-cornelius-herz. Includes a report in the House of Commons on the condition of Cornelius Herz, one of the principals involved in the French Panama Scandal during the 1890s.

Lesseps, Ferdinand de. *Recollections of Forty Years.* Trans. C. B. Pitman. 2 vols. London: Chapman and Hall, 1887. A valuable resource for understanding French interests in developing a canal across the Isthmus of Panama.

Secondary Sources

Anguizola, G. A. *Philippe Bunau-Varilla: The Man Behind the Panama Canal.* Chicago: Nelson-Hall, 1980. A very good biography of the Panama Canal's most forceful advocate. He was involved in both the French and American projects.

Davidson, Frank P., and Kathleen L. Brooke. *Building the World: An Encyclopedia of the Great Engineering Projects in History.* Westport, CT: Greenwood Press, 2006. A standard and reliable resource that includes valuable information on the early years of the Panama Canal project.

Fortescue, William. *Third Republic in France: Conflicts and Continuities.* London and New York: Routledge, 2000. Useful on the Panama Scandal and corruption of several political and financial leaders.

Gildea, Robert. *France, 1870–1914.* 2nd ed. London: Longman, 1996. Provides a very good introduction to the Panama project and the scandal that ensued.

Harding, Robert C. *The History of Panama.* Westport, CT: Greenwood Press, 2006. An excellent resource on the French canal project and its failure on Panama.

Jankowski, Paul. *Shades of Indignation: Political Scandals in France, Past and Present.* New York: Berghahn, 2007. Very good resource on the Panama Scandal and the collapse of the financial support for the canal.

Keller, Ulrich. *The Building of the Panama Canal in Historic Photographs.* Minoela, NY: Dover Publications, 1984. Includes a few photographs and maps on the French project.

Mayeur, Jean-Marie and Madeleine. *The Third Republic from Its Origins to the Great War, 1871–1914.* Trans. J. R. Foster. Cambridge, U.K.: Cambridge University Press, 1988. Includes an excellent section on the French interest and plans for the canal and the scandal.

McCullough, David. *The Path Between the Seas: The Creation of the Panama Canal 1870–1914.* New York: Simon and Schuster, 2004. A very readable and well-researched study that includes information on the failed French effort.

Parker, Matthew. *Panama Fever: The Epic Story of One of the Greatest Human Achievements of All Times—The Building of the Panama Canal.* Garden City, NY: Doubleday, 2008. A very good general history of the Panama Canal, includes data on French plans and their failure.

Rodriquez, José Carlos. *The Panama Canal: Its History, Its Political Aspects, and Financial Difficulties.* London: Low, Marston, Searle and Rivington, 1885. A contemporary account that addresses the manifold concerns in building the canal.

Siegfried, André. *Suez and Panama.* Trans. Henry H. and Doris Hemming. New York: Harcourt, Brace, 1940. A very good comparative study on the construction of the two canals—this may provide several term paper ideas.

Sowerwine, Charles. *France Since 1870.* Basingstoke: Palgrave, 2001. Includes a good introduction to the scandals that plagued the Third French Republic, including the Panama Scandal.

Tombs, Robert. *Nationhood and Nationalism in France: From Boulangism to the Great War, 1889–1919.* London: Routledge, 1992. The early chapters in this book should be valuable for understanding the forces that contributed to the failure of the French Panama Canal project.

Vizetelly, Ernest A. *Republican France, 1870–1912: Her Presidents, Statesmen, Policy, Vicissitudes, and Social Life.* Chestnut Hill, MA: Elibiron/Adamant Media, 2004. A reprint that includes data on the Panama Scandal.

World Wide Web

"Anti-Semitism in France During the Period 1870–1914, the Panama Canal Scandal, and the Dreyfus Affairs." http://www.blacksacademy.net/content/3444.html. Provides information on the origins of the Panama Scandal, which resulted in the collapse of funding for the project.

"Foreign Affairs, Panama and the Canal, Construction Begins in 1904." http://www.u-s-history.com/pages/h932.html. Includes information on the French plans for the canal.

"History of Count Ferdinand de Lesseps and the Panama Canal." http://www.ared.com/history.htm. Reliable resource on de Lesseps and his failed attempt to build the Panama Canal.

"Panama Canal History Documents and Prints." http://www.canalmuseum.com/documents/panamacanalhistory014.htm. Includes rare photographs and illustrations of the French work on the canal.

"The Great Adventure of Panama." http://net.lib.byu.edu/estu/wwi/comment/Panama/PanamaTC.htm. An account of the German efforts against France and the United States in Panama by Philippe Bunau-Varilla, Former Chief Engineer of the French Panama Canal Company (1886–1886) and First Minister Plenipotentiary and Envoy Extraordinary of the Republic of Panama to Washington (1903–1904).

"The Panama Scandal." http://www.historyhome.co.uk/europe/3rd-rep.htm#panama. Provides an introduction to the Panama Scandal.

Multimedia Sources

A Man, A Plan, A Canal—Panama. Nova/WGBH-Boston, 2004. DVD. Directed by Carl Charlson; narrated by David McCullough. Includes information and scenes of the failed French initiative to build the canal.

Modern Marvels—Panama Canal. A&E Home Video/History Channel, 2004. DVD. Includes data on the French plan and efforts.

76. War of the Pacific (1879–1884)

The War of the Pacific was a conflict between Chile and the allies Bolivia and Peru over mineral-rich land in the Atacama Desert. Scientific advances had identified new applications for the mineral saltpeter and for guano (the excrement from seabirds, bats, and seals, which is used in gunpowder and fertilizer). The Atacama region held vast deposits of both. Not only were these Latin American states involved, but the conflict took on international dimensions when the United Kingdom, United States, and Spain advanced aggressive policies in which they or their citizens would have claims to these minerals. After several years of mounting tensions during the mid-1870s, the crisis intensified in the fall of 1878 and, in the spring of 1879, Chile declared war on Bolivia and Peru on April 5,

1879. This war involved naval and land campaigns and in both Chile, after some difficult battles, prevailed. The war ended with Chilean victories and a peace that was costly to Bolivia and Peru. Under the terms of the Treaty of Ancón, Chile acquired extensive land from Peru on an intermediate basis. In a separate agreement Bolivia was forced to give up its coastal territories on the Pacific—this resulted in Bolivia becoming a landlocked country. The strategic consequences of the War of the Pacific resulted in the continuing rise of Chile as a preeminent political, military, and economic power, interrupted the ascendancy of Peru, and greatly diminished the image of Bolivia.

TERM PAPER SUGGESTIONS

1. Write a term paper on the background and outbreak of the War of the Pacific.
2. Compare and contrast the leadership, strategy, and tactics used by the opposing armies during the War of the Pacific.
3. Did the United Kingdom support Chile in its war with Bolivia and Peru?
4. Write a paper in which you assess the impact of the war on the region and on the three participants.

ALTERNATIVE TERM PAPER SUGGESTIONS

1. Develop a 5 minute podcast in which representatives of the Chilean government meet with British and Chilean business leaders prior to the war to discuss the potential wealth that could be extracted from the Atacama region.
2. Develop an iMovie in which a journalist interviews the leaders of Chile, Bolivia, and Peru after the war to gain their impressions on the struggle.
3. As a Bolivian residing in the coastal region prior to the war, you find that your world (property rights, social position, etc.) has been adversely affected by the war when your government surrendered your region to Chile. Write a blog on your life and prospects before and after this war.

SUGGESTED SOURCES

Primary Sources

Acland, William Allison Dyke. *Six Weeks with the Chilian Army: Being a Short Account of a March from Pisco to Lurilon and the attack on Lima.* Wellington: Melanesian Mission, 1881. A valuable primary source by an eyewitness on the military aspects during this brief period of time.

Boyd, Robert Nelson. *Chili: Sketches and Chili and the Chilians During the War 1879–1880*. London: W. H. Allen, 1881. A contemporary's account of the war with several important primary sources imbedded in the text.

Lisle, Gerard de, ed. *Royal Navy and the Peruvian-Chilean War 1879–1881: The Rudolf de Lisle's Diaries and Watercolors*. Barnsley, U.K.: Pen and Sword, 2008. De Lisle's diaries and watercolors provide information on the role and placement of the British navy during the war.

Secondary Sources

Farcau, Bruce W. *The Ten Cents War: Chile, Peru, and Bolivia in the War of the Pacific*. Westport, CT: Praeger, 2000. A very good, general history of the war with an excellent bibliography.

Markham, Clements R. *The War between Peru and Chile, 1879–1882*. London: Sampson Low, Marston, Searle and Rivington, 1882. A contemporary secondary account of the struggle that may be useful to some students.

Meigs, John Forsyth. *The War in South America*. Princeton, NJ: D. Van Nostrand, 1879. Another contemporary secondary account that may be useful to students who are studying these types of sources as the topic for their paper.

Sater, William F. *Chile and the War of the Pacific*. Lincoln: University of Nebraska, 1986. Emphasizes Chile's successful participation in the War of the Pacific.

———. *Andean Tragedy: Fighting the War of the Pacific, 1879–1884*. Lincoln: University of Nebraska Press, 2007. A very good history of the impact of the war on the people, the combatants, and their long-term relationships.

Scheima, Robert L. *Latin America's Wars*. 2 vols. Charleston, SC: Potomac Books, 2003. Includes extensive information on the War of the Pacific.

World Wide Web

"The Pacific War of 1879–1884." http://www.zum.de/whkmla/military/19cen/pacwar187984.html. A very good resource with many useful links.

"The Pacific War of 1879–1884/Chile-Peruvian War." http://www.casah istoria.net/Chile.htm#Military_conflict. A comprehensive review of the war that includes many links.

"War of the Pacific." http://www.encyclopedia.com/doc/1E1-Pacific.html. A good introduction to the scope of the war that includes several illustrations.

"War of the Pacific." http://www.globalsecurity.org/military/ops/war-of-the
-pacific.htm. Good summary, with emphasis on military actions.

"War of the Pacific, 1879–1883." http://countrystudies.us/chile/15.htm.
Emphasis is on Chile's role in the war.

"War of the Pacific, 1879–1883." http://www.onwar.com/aced/data/papa/
pacific1879.htm. A good summary of the war that includes statistics on
the casualties that resulted.

"War of the Pacific, 1879–1883, Chile versus Bolivia and Peru." http://warofthe
pacific.com/. An entire Web site dedicated to the war, which includes
copies of illustrations, photographs, maps, and many links to other
sources—students should make use of this site.

Multimedia Source

"Chile." http://encarta.msn.com/encyclopedia_761572974_9/chile.html.
Includes 55 multimedia items, several related to the war, and also includes
a very useful interactive map that covers the region involved in the war.

77. Scramble for Africa (1880s–1890s)

The Scramble for Africa by European powers dominated the last quarter
of the nineteenth century. Whether initiated by King Leopold II of
Belgium with his seizure of the Congo or by French and German claims
and advances in southern Africa, the historic independence of millions of
Africans was curtailed by European imperialists' ambitions. European
interest in southern Africa was based on economic, political, and diplomatic considerations. Religious motivations were secondary, and even
the missionaries held little or no respect for native religious values and
practices. The "Scramble" resulted in an immediate European diplomatic crisis that was addressed at the Berlin Conference on Africa in
1884–1885. Enduring animosity between the British and Germans can
be traced to their differences in East and West Africa where the British
felt they had a historic claim and viewed German intervention as con-
trary to their interest. The British also thought that the Germans might
have been pursuing an alliance with the Boers who were becoming a serious problem for the British and their plan to dominate southern and
eastern Africa. Some scholars have argued that the "Scramble for Africa"
not only resulted in the loss of native political independence but also
endangered native African cultures.

TERM PAPER SUGGESTIONS

1. Write a paper on the background and outbreak of the "Scramble for Africa."
2. Develop a paper on the impact of the "Scramble for Africa" on the relationships among the European powers.
3. What was the "New Imperialism"? Did it have any impact on the "Scramble for Africa"?
4. Write a paper in which you focus on the impact of the "Scramble" on the native populations.
5. Did the "Scramble for Africa" constitute cultural genocide?

ALTERNATIVE TERM PAPER SUGGESTIONS

1. Create a Web site that describes through a series of annotated maps the transformation of Africa south of the Sahara from 1870 through 1900.
2. Develop a podcast on an imaginary conversation between British, Belgium, and German diplomats on the advantages of acquiring control of land in southern Africa.
3. As a native African in the Congo, create a blog that focuses on how the Congo has changed since its seizure by King Leopold II of Belgium.

SUGGESTED SOURCES

Primary Sources

Brooke-Smith, Robin, ed. *The Scramble for Africa: Documents and Debates.* London: Palgrave Macmillan, 1987. Provides essential documents and other materials that outline the varying interpretations on European imperialism in Africa.

Chamberlain, Muriel Evelyn. *The Scramble for Africa.* 2nd ed. New York: Longman, 1999. Includes a collection of useful primary documents and other sources.

Harlow, Barbara, ed. *Archives of Empire: Volume 2. The Scramble for Africa.* Durham, NC: Duke University Press, 2003. An excellent collection of documents on European imperialism in Africa.

Secondary Sources

Axelson, Eric. *Portugal and the Scramble for Africa, 1875–1891.* Johannesburg: Witwatersrand University Press, 1967. A very solid account of Portuguese involvement in Angola and elsewhere during this turbulent period.

Betts, Raymond F. *The Scramble for Africa: Causes and Dimension of Empire.* 2nd ed. Lexington, MA: Heath, 1972. A valuable but dated introduction to the interpretations on the scramble for Africa from contemporaries to later scholars.

Chamberlain, Muriel Evelyn. *The Scramble for Africa.* 2nd ed. New York: Longman, 1999. An excellent introduction to all aspects of the scramble for Africa.

Coupland, Reginald. *The Exploitation of East Africa, 1856–1890: The Slave Trade and the Scramble.* London: Faber and Faber, 1939. A worthwhile examination of the relationship between the remnants of the slave trade and the European rush for territory during the 1880s and 1890s.

Erlich, Haggal. *Ras Alula and the Scramble for Africa: A Political Biography: Ethiopia and Eritrea 1875–1897.* Lawrenceville, NJ: Red Sea Press, 1996. Focused on the Ethiopian leader Ras Alula, this study examines the issues associated with East African independent states during the Scramble for Africa.

Hochschild, Adam. *King Leopold's Ghost: A Story of Greed, Terror, and Heroism in Colinial Africa.* New York: Mariner Books, 1999. A important book of the Belgian king's "rape" of the Congo and those who resisted.

Hodge, Carl Cavanaugh, ed. *Encyclopedia of the Age of Imperialism, 1800–1914.* 2 vols. Westport, CT: Greenwood Press, 2007. This is an excellent resource on all aspects of European imperialism during the nineteenth century, including the Scramble for Africa.

Lewis, David Levering. *The Race to Fashoda: European Colonialism and African Resistance in the Scramble for Africa.* New York: Weidenfeld and Nicolson, 1987. Marvelous book by a preeminent American scholar that provides provocative insights into the African reception to European imperialism.

Meredith, Martin. *Diamonds, Gold, and War: The British, the Boers, and the Making of South Africa.* New York: Public Affairs, 2007. An excellent study of the British-Boer impact on South Africa and their conflicts during the 1880s and 1890s.

Nutting, Anthony. *Scramble for Africa, The Great Trek to the Boer War.* London: Constable, 1970. Focused on southern Africa, Nutting's book is still worthwhile and reliable.

Oliver, Roland A. *Sir Harry Johnston and the Scramble for Africa.* London: Chatto and Windus, 1957. An old but reliable account of Johnston's role in this period of European imperial expansion.

Pakenham, Thomas. *The Scramble for Africa, 1876–1912.* New York: Random House, 1991. Very good and readily available, Pakenham's study is a critical examination of the European seizure of Africa.

Schreuder, D. M. *The Scramble for Southern Africa, 1877–1895: The Politics of Partition Reappraised.* Cambridge, U.K.: Cambridge University Press, 1980. A scholarly work on the Scramble with a focus on the British-Boer ambitions and conflicts.

Shorter, Aylward. *Cross and Flag in Africa: The "White Fathers" During the Colonial Scramble (1892–1914).* Maryknoll, NY: Orbis Books, 2006. An interesting study of the role of missionaries during the era of European colonialism in Africa.

Thomas, Antony. *Rhodes, the Race for Africa.* London: London Bridge, 1997. A very readable and reliable study of the life of Cecil Rhodes (1853–1902), South African statesman and financier, and his impact on Africa during the late nineteenth century.

Vandervert, Bruce. *Wars of Imperial Conquest in Africa, 1830–1914.* Bloomington: Indiana University Press, 1998. In the chapters devoted to the Scramble for Africa, Vandervert excels in his analysis of the European seizure of the continent during the last quarter of the nineteenth century.

World Wide Web

"Africa, South of the Sahara." http://www-sul.stanford.edu/depts/ssrg/africa/history/hisprimary.html. A valuable Web site maintained by Stanford University that provides access to primary and secondary sources—including those related to the Scramble for Africa.

"Internet African History Sourcebook." http://www.fordham.edu/halsall/africa/africasbook.html. Produced by Fordham University under the direction of Paul Halsall, this site provides numerous sources and Web sites on the Scramble for Africa. It is an essential source for many term papers.

"Missionary Travels and Researches in South Africa by David Livingstone." http://www.gutenberg.org/ebooks/1039. Web site of the Project Gutenberg Library Archive Foundation that provides links to the e-book and other sources.

Weintraub, Stanley. "The Scramble for Africa." http://www.pbs.org/empires/victoria/history/scramble.html. Introductory text for "Empires: Queen Victoria's Empire."

Multimedia Sources

"Scramble for Africa Cartoons." http://www.cartoonstock.com/vintage/directory/s/scramble_for_africa.asp. Contemporary cartoons and caricatures on the Scramble for Africa.

Empires: Queen Victoria's Empire. PBS Video, 2001. DVD. Directed by Paul
    Burgess. An award-winning documentary that provides an excellent sur-
    vey of the Scramble for Africa.
"The Magnificent African Cake," episode in *Africa: A Voyage of Discovery.* Writ-
    ten and presented by Basil Davidson, University of California. Home
    Vision, 1984. VHS. The Scramble for Africa is discussed at the begin-
    ning of this video, which is based on archival and other sources. It is
    filmed on site in Africa.
"Military History Podcast," by George Hageman. http://www.learnoutloud.com/
    Podcast-Directory/History/Military-History/Military-History-Podcast/
    18822. Focuses on the territorial adjustments that resulted from the Berlin
    Conference.
"Scramble for Africa," an excerpt from *The African Safari.* http://video.aol.com/
    video-detail/the-african-safari-clip-3-the-european-scramble-for-africa/
    3515633784. Brief film that advances a critical interpretation of the
    impact of European expansion.

78. First Boer War (1880–1881)

Relations between the British and the Boers in South Africa were strained
throughout the nineteenth century. To avoid the British, the Boers
migrated to the area of the Transvaal during the Great Trek in 1837–
1838. However, the British continued to encroach upon Boer territory.
British expansion was due to its historic interest in controlling South
Africa, the discovery of vast diamond deposits, and the New Imperialism
advanced by Prime Minister Benjamin Disraeli in the early 1870s. In the
late 1870s the British and Boers confronted a common enemy, a revital-
ized and militant Zulu nation. The Boers were outraged when the British
announced their annexation of the Transvaal. However, the Boers needed
the British to protect them from the Zulus. Shortly after the defeat of the
Zulus in 1879, tensions mounted between the Boers and the British and
led to an Anglo-Boer war between December 16, 1880, and March 23,
1881. The Boers did not have a regular army but, through their knowledge of the terrain, outstanding horsemanship, and talents as sharpshoot-
ers, they gained the initiative during the early months of this brief
struggle. The Boers defeated the British in the most significant battle in
the war—at Majuba Hill on February 26, 1881. However, by the late
winter, British power was evident and the many sieges that the Boers

had laid were lifted. The British did not wish to expend the necessary force and funds that would be necessary to suppress the Boers. On March 6, 1881, both sides agreed to a truce that led to a peace treaty on March 23, 1881. Under the new peace, the Boers were to have self-government in the Transvaal under British supervision. The Boers agreed that they were under Queen Victoria's rule. In October 1881, the British army withdrew from the Transvaal. The discovery of gold later in the decade aggravated Anglo-Boer relations, which deteriorated steadily and led to the outbreak of the Boer War in 1899.

TERM PAPER SUGGESTIONS

1. Develop a paper on the background and causes for the revolt.
2. Write a paper on the progress of the revolt—include the military operations, public sentiment, and immediate outcomes.
3. Develop a paper on the consequences of the Transvaal Revolt and consider whether they contributed to the continued tensions between the Boers and the British and whether they were factors in the outbreak of the Boer War in 1899.
4. Write a paper in which you compare and contrast the leadership of the Boers and the British during this struggle.
5. Develop a paper on how the revolt and its development was received by the major European powers—what impact did it have on the "Scramble for Africa"?

ALTERNATIVE TERM PAPER SUGGESTIONS

1. Develop a podcast on the outbreak of the revolt that includes interviews with the Boer and British leadership as they consider the deteriorating situation.
2. Develop a 4–5 minute iMovie in which the opposing sides deliberate the end of hostilities and begin to negotiate the peace.
3. Create a blog on the war—its causes, development, and impact—from the perspective of an 18-year-old Boer or British combat soldier.
4. Develop a chat-room correspondence between a Boer grandmother and her grandson who is fighting in the war. The grandmother was involved in the Great Trek of 1837–1838 in which the Boers resettled to avoid conflict with the British.

SUGGESTED SOURCES

Primary Sources

Bellairs, Sir William. *The Transvaal War, 1880–1881*. Ed. Lady Blanche Bellairs. Chestnut Hill, MA: Elibron/Adamant, 2005; originally published in 1885. Valuable recollections by a major British participant in the war.

Butler, Lt-Gen. Sir William. *Sir William Butler: An Autobiography.* 2nd ed. New York: Charles Scribner's Sons, 1913. The sections on the Transvaal War are very useful.

Butterfield, P. H., ed. *War and Peace in South Africa 1879–1881: The Writings of Philip Anstruther and Edward Essex.* Melville, SF: Scripta Africana, 1986–1989. Very useful source on the origins and development of the Transvaal War.

Carter, Thomas Fortescue. *A Narrative of the Boer War: Its Causes and Results.* London: J. C. Jutta, 1896. A perceptive memoir that raised numerous questions about Anglo-Boer relations.

Creswicke, L. *South Africa and the Transvaal War.* 6 vols. Edinburgh: T. C. and E. C. Jack, 1900. Volume 1 is available as an e-book through the Gutenberg Project at http://www.archive.org/details/southafricatrans01cres. Contains useful information on the Transvaal War, and includes excerpts from many primary sources.

Emery, F. *Marching over Africa: Letters from Victorian Soldiers.* London: Hodder & Stoughton, 1986. A very useful collection that includes letters on the Transvaal Revolt and the Boer War.

Hart-Synnot, B. M., ed. *The Letters of Major-General Fitzroy Hart-Synnot.* London: E. Arnold, 1912. A very important and worthwhile collection of letters that refer to several South African campaigns by British forces.

Martineau, J. *The Life and Correspondence of the Right Hon. Sir Bartle Frere, Bart.* London: J. Murray, 1895. Includes relevant primary material on the Transvaal Revolt.

Norris-Newman, C. L. *With the Boers in the Transvaal and Orange Free State in 1880–1.* London: Allen and Company, 1882. Very good on the impact of the revolt on the Boers and their aspirations.

Preston, A., ed. *Sir Garnet Wolseley's South African Journal 1879–80: Zululand/ Transvaal: Military Campaigns/Cetwayo/Sekukhuni/Negotiations with Boer Committee.* Cape Town: A. A. Balkema, 1973. Includes firsthand information on the Zulu War and the Transvaal Revolt.

Throup, David, ed. *British Documents on Foreign Affairs: Reports and Papers from the Foreign Office Confidential Print. Part 1: From the Mid-Nineteenth Century to the First World War. Series G, Africa, 1848–1914.* 25 vols. Bethesda, MD: University Publications of America, 1995. Excellent resource of primary documents. Volumes 4 and 5 include material on the Transvaal Rebellion of 1880–1881.

Secondary Sources

Barthorp, M. *The Anglo-Boer Wars: The British and the Afrikaners 1815–1902.* London: Blanford Press, 1987. A scholarly account of the continuing tensions between the British and the Boers throughout the nineteenth century.

Brinton, Wilfred. *History of the British Regiments in South Africa, 1795–1895.* Cape Town: University of Cape Town, 1977. Reliable study on the units involved in the Transvaal Revolt.

Duxbury, G. R. *David and Goliath: The First War of Independence, 1880–1881.* Johannesburg: South African Museum of Military History, 1981. A well-written and well-argued account of the Transvaal Revolt that is sympathetic to the Boers.

Haggard, Henry Rider. *The Last Boer War.* London: Kegan Paul, Trench Trübner, 1899. Also available as an e-book at http://books.google.com/books?hl=en&id=pYccAAAAMAAJ&dq=Haggard,+Henry+Rider.+The+Last+Boer+War.+London:+1899.&printsec=frontcover&source=web&ots=wdgj6FzlCP&sig=WCobFmuDrLwbkPvjTjJ0chRVHmY&sa=X&oi=book_result&resnum=2&ct=result#PPR3,M1. A pro-British study of the Transvaal Revolt that is reliable on most issues.

Haythornthwaite, P. J. *The Colonial Wars Source Book.* London: Greenhill Books, 2000. An outstanding reference book that includes information and bibliography on the Anglo-Boer wars.

Knight, I. *Boer Wars 1836–1898.* London: Osprey, 1996. A very reliable account of the Anglo-Boer military conflicts in South Africa.

Laband, John. *The Transvaal Rebellion: The First Boer War, 1880–1881.* Harlow, U.K.: Pearson/Longman, 2005. The best comprehensive history of the war, based on primary and secondary sources and very well-documented.

Lehmann, Joseph H. *The First Boer.* London: Jonathan Cape, 1972. A reliable and well-documented study of the rebellion and its aftermath.

Nixon, John. *The Complete Story of the Transvaal.* Cape Town: Struik, 1972. Includes accurate information on the revolt and its significance.

Smith, I. R. *The Origins of the South African War 1899–1902.* New York: Longman, 1996. Smith refers to the Transvaal Revolt and its impact as a major factor in the origins of the Boer War that broke out in 1899.

Vandervort, B. *Wars of Imperial Conquest in Africa 1830–1914.* London: Arnold, 1998. A very reliable, scholarly account of European imperial actions in Africa, including the Transvaal Revolt.

Winsloe, R. W. C. *Siege of Potchefstroom (First Boer War, 1880–1881).* Uckfield, U.K.: Naval and Military Press, 2005. The best account of this important siege during the Transvaal Revolt.

World Wide Web

"Battle of Laing's Nek." http://www.britishbattles.com/first-boer-war/laings-nek .htm. An accurate and detailed account of the Boer victory at Laing's Nek on January 28, 1881, which includes a battlefield map and four illustrations.

"Battle of Majuba Hill." http://www.britishbattles.com/first-boer-war/majuba-hill .htm. A useful account of the great Boer victory at Majuba Hill on February 27, 1881, that includes a battlefield map, one photograph, and three illustrations.

Creswicke, Louis. *South Africa and the Transvaal War.* London: T. C. & E. C. Jack, 1907; digitized by the New York Public Library, 2007. http://www.books.google.com/books?hl=en&id=N2cLAAAAYAAJ&dq =Transvaal+War&printse. Still a worthwhile study that provides detailed information. Also available through Project Gutenberg at http://www .gutenberg.org/etext/26198.

Gough Palmer, M. "The Besieged Towns of the First Boer War, 1880–1881." http://www.samilitaryhistory.org/vol052mg.html. Produced by the South African Military History Society, this site includes accurate information on the sieges of Lydenburg, Marabastad Fort, Rustenburg, Standerton, and Wakkerstroom, along with one illustration.

"The First Anglo-Boer War (Transvaal War), Causes." http://www.sahistory .org.za/pages/governance-projects/anglo-boer-wars/anglo-boer-war1i .htm. A useful introduction to the causes of the war that includes three photographs and two illustrations.

"The First Anglo-Boer War (Transvaal War), The War." http://www.sahistory .org.za/pages/governance-projects/anglo-boer-wars/anglo-boer-war1 ii.htm. A general introduction to the war that includes one map and one illustration.

"The First Anglo-Boer War (Transvaal War), Effects." http://www.sahistory .org.za/pages/governance-projects/anglo-boer-wars/anglo-boer-war1 iii.htm. Includes information on the Pretoria Convention and the consequences of the war.

McCullough, Joseph Allan. "The First Boer War, The Anglo-Boer War of 1881." http://georgian-victorian-britain.suite101.com/article.cfm/the_first _boer_war. Provides an introduction to the war and its consequences.

"Nourse's Horse at Elandsfontein Ridge, 16 January 1881." http://www
.samilitaryhistory.org/vol052hk.html. Very good on the unit's performance in this battle.

Multimedia Source

Lee, Christopher. *This Sceptred Isle: Empire.* Audio CD, 1999. Narrated by Juliet
Stevenson. Includes information and commentary on the Transvaal
Revolt and other aspects of British imperial activities in South Africa.

79. Sino-French War (1883–1885)

During the early 1880s the French continued their expansion in South Asia
and targeted Tonkin (today's northern Vietnam) as the next major area in
Southeast Asia that would come under French control. In May 1883
Vietnamese forces under the Chinese adventurer Liu Yongfu (1837–1917)
were encouraged by Chinese leaders to attack the French force in Hanoi.
In the subsequent Battle of Paper Bridge (May 19, 1883), the French were
defeated. France responded by sending additional naval and army units to
Vietnam. China, which viewed itself as a protector of the Vietnamese, pro-
tested this expansion of French forces. Sino-French negotiations failed to
resolve the crisis, and the French launched a war against China on August
23, 1884, with the Battle of Fuzhou during which the Chinese fleet was
destroyed. During this relatively brief war, the Chinese and their Vietnamese allies won several battles but, in the end, the French prevailed. A preliminary peace was enacted in April 1885 and finalized by the Treaty of
Hué in June 1885. The terms paved the way for the French to announce
the establishment of French Indo-China in 1887 that included Tonkin,
Cambodia, and the Mekong Delta; Laos was added in 1893. From the outset, French public opinion indicated that it did not think that this imperial
venture warranted the human and financial costs that were incurred. The
French remained in Indo-China until 1954 when they were defeated by a
Vietnamese nationalist insurrection.

TERM PAPER SUGGESTIONS

1. Write a paper on French imperial ambitions in Southeast Asia. Why did they
   seek to expand their authority into Tonkin?

2. Develop a paper on the resistance to the French that was mounted by Liu Yongfu and his Black Flag Army.

3. Write a paper focused on the military engagements during the Sino-French War.

4. Write a paper in response to the following question: why did China involve itself in this war with the French?

5. Write a paper on the expansion of French authority in Indo-China that resulted from this war.

ALTERNATIVE TERM PAPER SUGGESTIONS

1. Develop an iMovie in which the French leaders consider their next steps after the defeat at the Battle of Paper Bridge.

2. Develop a podcast in which you interview Liu Yongfu on his plans to resist French incursion into Tonkin.

3. As a 20-year-old recruit in the Black Flag Army, you are committed to keeping the French from extending their influence in your country. Write letters to your parents during the war in which you discuss your ideas and experiences.

SUGGESTED SOURCES

Primary Sources

Scott, James George. *France and Tongking: A Narrative of the Campaign of 1884 and the Occupation of Further India.* London: T. F. Unwin, 1885. Includes extensive excerpts from primary sources.

Staunton, Sidney Augustus. *The War in Tong-king: Why the French Are in Tong-king and What They Are Doing There.* New Haven, CT: Human Relations Area Files, 1951; originally published in 1884. A brief (45-page) tract by a respected contemporary in which French expansion in Southeast Asia is explained.

Secondary Sources

Buttinger, Joseph. *Vietnam: A Political History.* New York: Praeger, 1968. Provides some useful information on the developing French presence in Vietnam during the 1880s.

Chan, Ming K., and John D. Young. *Precarious Balance: Hong Kong Between China and Britain, 1842–1992.* Armonk, NY: M. E. Sharpe, 1994. A very good study that includes information on French encroachment in Vietnam and the Chinese and British reaction to it.

Chere, Lewis M. *Great Britain and the Sino-French War: The Problems of an Involved Neutral, 1883–1885*. Ogden, UT: Western Conference of the Association for Asian Studies, 1978. Excellent study by a recognized authority on the war that focuses on the complex British reaction to the French action in Tonkin.

———. *The Diplomacy of the Sino-French War (1883–1885)*. Notre Dame, IN: Cross Cultural Publications, 1989. The best publication in English on the diplomacy associated with the war.

Chien-Nung, Li, and J. Ingalls. *Political History of China, 1840–1928*. Trans. Ssu-Yu-Teng and J. Ingalls. Stanford, CA: Stanford University Press, 1956. A scholarly and reliable study that includes information on the war and its impact on Sino-Franco relations.

Eastman, Lloyd E. *Throne and Mandarins: China's Search for a Policy during the Sino-French Controversy, 1880–1885*. Cambridge, MA: Harvard University Press, 1967. A fascinating study of China's reaction to the French incursion and its difficulty in formulating a comprehensive policy regarding the mounting European imperial activity in Southeast Asia.

Elleman, B. *Modern Chinese Warfare, 1795–1989*. New York: Routledge, 2001. Includes information on the performance of Chinese forces during the war with France.

Hsieh, Pei-Chih. *Diplomacy of the Sino-French War, 1883–1885*. Philadelphia: University of Pennsylvania Press, 1968. A useful scholarly work on the diplomacy related to the war.

Immanuel, C. Y. Hsu. *The Rise of Modern China*. 6th ed. New York: Oxford University Press, 2000. Includes data on the Sino-French War that provide an accurate introduction to the war.

Neiss, P. *The Sino-Vietnamese Border Demarcation, 1885–1887*. Trans. Walter E. J. Tips. Bangkok: White Lotus Press, 1998. A study of the postwar settlement between France and China.

World Wide Web

"Battle of Foochow (Fuzhou), Sino-French War, 1884." http://www.geocities.com/Athens/Agora/8088/FoochowB.html. Includes extensive information on the battle, a very good map, and drawings of all of the ships that were involved.

"Causes of the Sino-French War." http://warandgame.wordpress.com/2007/08/22/causes-of-the-sino-french-war/. Provides an excellent analysis of the causes for the war and additional links, including a bibliography.

"Li Hongzhang." http://www.encyclopedia.com/doc/1B1-370227.html. Provides information on the hapless Chinese leader who opposed the French.

"Sino-French War." http://www.answers.com/topic/sino-french-war. A good introduction to the war with additional links.

"Sino-French War." http://www.bookrags.com/research/sino-french-war-ema -05/. A well-written history with a good bibliography.

"Sino-French War." http://www.absoluteastronomy.com/topics/Sino-French _War. Provides information on the war and related links.

"Sino-French War." https://www.amazines.com/Sino-French_War_related.html. Provides relevant data and links to other sites.

"Sino-French War 1884–1885." http://www.onwar.com/aced/nation/cat/china/ fsinofrench1884.htm. Provides statistical data on the numbers involved in the war, including casualties.

Multimedia Source

"Story from the Sino-French War." http://ocw.mit.edu/ans7870/21f/21f.027/ throwing_off_asia_01/2000_161_l.html. Includes a marvelous rendering of a battle during the war.

80. Berlin Conference (1884–1885)

During the early 1880s the European powers became extremely interested in Africa and began to extend their visions and ambitions of empire. This is sometimes referred to as "The Scramble for Africa." This interest in Africa was caused by the steady flow of new information that was coming from explorers, especially Henry Morton Stanley and Pierre de Brazza. While the traditional colonial powers (Great Britain, France, and Portugal) found themselves involved in occasional disputes as a result of imperial expansion, new European powers (Germany, Italy, Belgium, and others) manifested their own ambitions in Africa. The immediate factor that led the Portuguese to approach the German Chancellor Otto von Bismarck to call for an international meeting was a conflict over the Congo. Bismarck, who wanted to limit Britain's power, concurred and convened the Berlin Conference (also known as the Congo Conference) on November 15, 1884. Representatives from Austria-Hungary, Belgium, Denmark, France, Great Britain, Italy, the Netherlands, Portugal, Russia, Spain, Sweden-Norway, the Ottoman Empire, and the United States convened. While the United States sent a representative, it did not participate in the conference. The resulting agreement, known as the General Act, was signed on February 26, 1885. The most significant element in this Act was the "Principle of Effectivity," which required European powers to have a real (military and economic) presence in any areas that they claim. Simple declarations of a claim to a territory (a British technique) would no longer be recognized as valid. Other provisions included the recognition of the Free State of the Congo as the property of the Belgian King Léopold II, the establishment of free trade zones in the Congo basin and along the Niger and Congo Rivers, no slave trade, and a notification protocol for future claims. Within a decade after the Berlin Conference, Africa, south of the equator, was divided completely among the European powers.

TERM PAPER SUGGESTIONS

1. Write a paper on Bismarck's goals for the Berlin Conference. Did he achieve them?

2. Develop a paper on the issues and concerns on the "Principle of Effectivity" that was addressed at the Conference.

3. How did the Berlin Conference address the lingering problem of slavery and slave trade in Africa?

4. Some argue that economics determined the agenda and outcomes of the Berlin Conference. Consider this interpretation in a paper that balances the pros and cons on this issue.

5. Write a paper on the impact of the Berlin Conference on the diplomatic relations between Germany and Great Britain.

ALTERNATIVE TERM PAPER SUGGESTIONS

1. As a representative of Leopold II of Belgium, create a blog of diplomatic dispatches with him about how successful you were at the Berlin Conference.

2. Develop a radio podcast consisting of reports on the opening of the Berlin Conference, an interim report on its progress, and a wrap-up after the closure of the meeting.

SUGGESTED SOURCES

Primary Sources

Bismarck, Otto von. *Memoirs* (excerpts) in the Hanover Historical Texts Project, Hanover College. http://history.hanover.edu/texts/bis.html. Useful resource that includes many excerpts from the *Memoirs* over Bismarck's long career.

"Dr. Carl Peters (1856–1918) on German Colonial Policy, 1885." PSM-Data, from *Colonial-Political Correspondence,* 1st year, Berlin, May 16, 1885. http://www.zum.de/psm/imperialismus/peters1e.php3. This is a very good summary of German policy at the conference by an advocate of German colonialism.

Medlicott, W. N., and Dorothy K. Coveney, eds. *Bismarck and Europe.* New York: St. Martin's Press, 1972. Provides primary sources and commentaries on Bismarck and his relationship with European leaders, and includes colonial issues and conflicts.

Pinto-Duschinsky, Michael. *The Political Thought of Lord Salisbury.* London: Constable, 1967. In addition to the author's interpretation of the British Conservative leader Lord Salisbury's political thinking, this volume includes two noteworthy sections: "Published Writings of Lord Salisbury" and "Speeches of Lord Salisbury."

"The Berlin Conference: The General Act of February 26, 1885." John Jay College of Criminal Justice, City University of New York, Joseph V. O'Brien. http://www.web.jjay.cuny.edu/~jobrien/reference/ob45. html. A reliable text of the final document that emerged from the Berlin Conference.

Secondary Sources

Abrams, Lynn. *Bismarck and the German Empire, 1871–1918.* London and New York: Routledge, 1995. An excellent account of Bismarck's role in German affairs to 1890 (including a worthwhile section on the Berlin Conference, 1884–1885) and his legacy through the end of the First World War.

Aydelotte, William Osgood. *Bismarck and British Colonial Policy: The Problem of South West Africa.* New York: Octagon Books, 1974. Aydelotte's study is an important contribution in developing an understanding of Bismarck's transition to a reluctant imperialist during the 1880s.

Blij, H. J. de, and Peter O. Muller. *Geography: Realms, Regions, and Concepts.* New York: Wiley, 2005. This is an excellent study of geopolitics and includes a section on the Berlin Conference on Africa.

Chamberlain, M. E. *The Scramble for Africa.* Hong Kong: Longman, 1974. A standard that is a well-written and reliable panorama of the European seizure of colonies during the last decades of the nineteenth century and that includes an account of the Berlin Conference.

Edgerton, Robert B. *The Troubled Heart of Africa: A History of the Congo.* New York: St. Martin's Press, 2002. Well-researched study that includes the rule of Belgium in the Congo and the events that preceded the Berlin African Conference.

Eyck, Erich. *Bismarck and the German Empire.* London: Allen and Unwin, 1950. A great narrative history of Bismarck's life and impact on German history, which views the Berlin Conference as a major factor in reorienting German and British foreign policies.

Hochschild, Adam. *King Leopold's Ghost.* New York: Mariner Books, 1999. Focused on the Belgian legacy, Hochschild's study includes valuable information on the Berlin Conference on Africa.

Jenkins, Roy. *Gladstone.* New York: Random House, 2002. A sympathetic and readable biography of the four-time British Prime Minister William Gladstone. The anti-imperialist Gladstone found himself defending traditional imperial policies.

Mommsen, Wolfgang J., Stig Forster, and Ronald Robinson, eds. *Bismarck, Europe, and Africa: The Berlin African Conference 1884–1885 and the Onset of Partition.* New York: Oxford University Press, 1989. A critical book in researching the Conference. These essays require a general knowledge of the Conference.

Petringa, Maria. *Brazza, A Life for Africa.* Bloomington, IN: AuthorHouse, 2006. The best biography in English of the Belgian explorer Pierre de Brazza.

Steele, E. Day. *Lord Salisbury: A Political Biography.* London: Routledge, 2001. Perhaps the best single-volume biography of the Conservative British prime minister and foreign policy expert of the era.

Waller, Bruce. *Bismarck at the Crossroads: The Reorientation of German Foreign Policy after the Congress of Berlin, 1878–1880.* London: Athlone Press, 1974. The sections in the volume that treat the 1880s are important for the Berlin African Conference of 1884–1885. Waller provides insights into Bismarck's thoughts at that time and how he viewed imperialism within the context of German national interests.

———. *Bismarck.* Oxford: Blackwell, 1997. A solid biography by a recognized authority.

Williamson, D. G. *Bismarck and Germany, 1862–1890.* New York: Longman, 1998. A dependable and useful history that includes detailed information on Bismarck's intentions at the Berlin African Conference.

World Wide Web

Rosenberg, Matt. "Berlin Conference of 1884–1885 to Divide Africa, the Colonization of the Continent by European Powers." http://www.geography .about.com/cs/politicalgeog/a/berlinconference.htm. A useful account of the Conference.

"The Conference of Berlin (1884–1885)." Open Door Web Site, Shirley Burchill, Nigel Hughes, Richard Gale, Peter Prince, and Keith Woodall, 2007. http://www.saburchill.com/history/chapters/empires/0054.html. Another account of the Conference that is accurate.

Multimedia Sources

Watts, Jason. "Colonization of Africa." Podcast, 2007. http://www.learnut loud.com/Podcast-Directory/History/World-History/History -Podcast/ 6768. A good introduction to the issues associated with the colonization of Africa in the nineteenth century and the concerns that led to the Berlin Conference in 1884.

Empires: Queen Victoria's Empire. PBS Video, 2001. DVD. Narrated by Donald Sutherland. This video documentary examines the evolution of the British Empire during Queen Victoria's reign (1837–1902). British political rivalries as well as the impact on the native populations are considered.

81. Pandjeh Incident (1884)

During most of the nineteenth century, tensions flared between Great Britain and Russia over Afghanistan and access to South Asia. Britain wanted to block any Russian moves against India, and Russia was interested in expanding its authority along the Persian (now Iranian) and Afghanistan borders. In 1884 these tensions exploded with the Pandjeh incident. Pandjeh was a remote area in Afghanistan that held geopolitical significance because it was one of the gateways to India. During the early 1880s, Russia gained Persian support for a new border that resulted in Russia gaining territory that confronted the Pandjeh. In 1884 in response to this Russian claim, Afghanistan with British support occupied the Pandjeh, and the potential for a major conflict between Russia and Britain was raised. The opposing parties agreed that a commission would attempt to resolve the points of contention. In 1887, the commission concluded that Russia had a valid claim because of the ethnicity of its residents and the agreement with Persia. While Britain agreed to comply with the commission's conclusions, tensions, at a reduced level, between Russia and Britain continued until Russia (in the Anglo-Russian Entente of 1907) agreed that Afghanistan was a British sphere of influence.

TERM PAPER SUGGESTIONS

1. Develop a paper on the causes for the Pandjeh incident. Why were Russia and Britain rivals in South Asia?
2. Write a term paper on the immediate and long-term impact of the Pandjeh incident on Anglo-Russian relations.
3. Was war between Britain and Russia likely over the Pandjeh incident?
4. Write a term paper on the Pandjeh incident as representative of a continuing nineteenth-century geopolitical problem over access to India.

ALTERNATIVE TERM PAPER SUGGESTIONS

1. Develop a podcast of the negotiations between the British and Russian representatives at the commission meeting that resolved the Pandjeh crisis.
2. Create an iMovie of a British Cabinet meeting in which Prime Minister William Gladstone leads the discussion on the formulation of British strategy in response to the Pandjeh incident.
3. Write a blog as a Russian journalist on the unfolding Pandjeh incident.

SUGGESTED SOURCES

Primary Sources

Evans, Martin. *The Great Game: Britain and Russia in Central Asia.* London: Routledge, 2003. A compendium of scores of nineteenth-century sources—many of them primary—on the struggle for hegemony in Central Asia.

Gladstone, William E. *Bulgarian Horrors and Russia in Turkistan: With Other Tracts.* Chestnut Hill, MA: Elibron/Adamant Media, 2005. Provides insights into Gladstone's views on Russia, India, and imperialism.

Secondary Sources

Avery, P., G. R. G. Hambly, and C. Melville, eds. *The Cambridge History of Iran. Volume 7: From Nadir Shah to the Islamic Republic.* Cambridge, U.K.: Cambridge University Press, 1991. An authoritative resource on the Persian concerns over the Anglo-Russian dispute.

Clements, Frank A. *Conflict in Afghanistan: A Historical Encyclopedia.* Santa Barbara, CA: ABC-CLIO, 2003. An excellent resource on many personalities and issues associated with the incident.

Drage, Geoffrey. *Russian Affairs.* London: John Murray, 1904. A contemporary account of Russian ambitions in the region.

Green, Rose Louise. *Persia and the Defense of India, 1884–1892.* London: Athalone Press, 1959. Includes extensive information on the incident and a solid bibliography.

Isserman, Maurice, and Stewart Weaver. *Fallen Giants: A History of Himalayan Mountaineering from the Age of Empire to the Age of Extremes.* New Haven, CT: Yale University Press, 2008. Includes information on the Anglo-Russia conflict.

Johnson, R. A. "The Panjdeh Incident, 1885." *The Journal of the British Records Association* XXXIV, no. 100 (April 1999): 28–48. Excellent summary and analysis of the Pandjeh incident.

Kochanski, Halik. *Sir Garnet Wolseley: Victorian Hero.* London: Hambledon Press, 1969. An impressive biography on Wolseley who served as the British military's utility general throughout the world.

Lee, Stephen. *Gladstone and Disraeli.* London: Routledge, 2005. A comparative study of many issues, including their foreign policy with Russia.

Olson, James S., and Robert Shadle. *Historical Dictionary of the British Empire.* Westport, CT: Greenwood Press, 1996. A valuable resource on many aspects of the Anglo-Russian struggle.

Rasanayagam, Angelo. *Afghanistan: A Modern History.* London: I. B. Tauris, 2005. Provides an adequate introduction.

Sykes, Peter. *The Right Honorable Sir Mortimer Durand: A Biography.* Whitefish, MT: Kessinger, 2006. A worthwhile biography of a British leader associated with the Russian problem.

World Wide Web

"Frederick Sleigh Roberts, Field Marshal Lord Roberts of Kandahar." http://www.pinetreeweb.com/roberts-bio.htm. Accurate introduction to the life of the leading British commander in the region.

"Frederick Temple Hamilton-Temple-Blackwood, 1st Marquess of Dufferin and Ava." http://www.answers.com/topic/frederick-hamilton-temple-blackwood-1st-marquess-of-dufferin-and-ava. Biography of British leader against Russia.

"Garnet Wolseley." http://www.newworldencyclopedia.org/entry/Garnet_Wolseley. Reliable biographical information on the British general.

"Lord Dufferin." http://www.nationmaster.com/encyclopedia/Lord-Dufferin. Provides an introductory biography of the prominent British leader.

Multimedia Source

"Only His Play." http://www.cartoonstock.com/vintage/directory/w/wolf.asp. An 1884 British editorial cartoon that quotes Prime Minister William Gladstone in denouncing Russia for its expansionist policies.

82. Gaelic Revival in Ireland (1884)

Throughout the nineteenth century, Irish dissidents, who opposed British domination and control and sought nothing less than Irish independence, became increasingly active and established organizations to advance their cause. In the 1840s the Young Ireland movement published *The Nation* to publish the works of Irish writers as well as to advance the nationalist political agenda. In 1858 the Irish Republican Brotherhood was established to unite all Irish throughout the world in support of Irish independence and identity. In 1877 the Society for the Preservation of the Irish Language was established. These efforts predated the earlier calls for Irish Home Rule and contributed to the Gaelic Revival that constituted a dominant cultural force in Ireland during the 1880s and 1890s. The Gaelic Revival was a movement that advanced all aspects of Irish culture—music, literature, theatre, language, history, sports, and other aspects of Irish heritage—and opposed connections with the English. A central component of the Gaelic Revival was the Gaelic Athletic Association that was established in 1884 by Michael Cusack (1847–1906). Its approach to the Gaelic Revival was to restore all aspects of Irish sport and to make these activities—hurling and jumping—dominant in Irish life. The Irish were to refrain from English sports such as cricket and rugby. Another element in the Gaelic Revival was the Gaelic League, which was established in 1893. The Gaelic League emphasized the need to restore Irish (Gaelic) as the sole language of the country. While the Gaelic League was dominated by Catholics, involvement was open to all Irish, including Protestants. By the end of the nineteenth century the movement had published a newspaper (*Claideamdh Solius*), organized local and regional fairs, established Gaelic schools, and coordinated an annual Irish national festival. The impact of the Gaelic Revival was significant and contributed to the public development of the Irish identity.

TERM PAPER SUGGESTIONS

1. Write a paper on Michael Cusack's vision for the Gaelic Athletic Association and his achievements.

2. The Gaelic Revival was a significant development in advancing the cause of Irish nationalism during the late nineteenth century. Develop a paper on

how the components of the Revival were connected with the militant Fenians and the Irish political leadership.

3. Develop a term paper on the establishment and achievements of the Gaelic League.
4. Write a paper on the development of Irish literature during the Gaelic Revival of the 1880s or the 1890s.

ALTERNATIVE TERM PAPER SUGGESTIONS

1. Develop a 4–5 minute podcast in which Michael Cusack holds a press conference to announce the establishment of the Gaelic Athletic Association—be sure to include a question and answer segment.
2. As a mayor of a small Irish town of 1,200 on the west coast of the island, you are interested in extending the Gaelic Revival to your community. Develop a blog on your mayoral agenda based on successful events elsewhere.
3. Develop an iMovie in which the planners of the annual Irish festival explain their rationale for the events that they propose to advance the Gaelic identity.

SUGGESTED SOURCES

Primary Sources

Duffy, Charles Gavan, George Sigerson, and Douglas Hyde. *The Revival of Irish Literature.* New York: Lemma, 1973. An important collection of works by some of the leading writers of the Gaelic Revival.

Hyde, Douglas. *Douglas Hyde and the Revival of the Irish Language.* 2nd ed. London: n.p., 1910. This work constitutes Hyde's testimony for the need to resurrect the Gaelic language.

O'Grady, Standish James. *The History of Ireland: The Heroic Period.* New York: Lemma, 1970; originally published in 1878. O'Grady was a leader of the Gaelic Revival but he was not much of an historian. He believed that he need not be concerned with objectivity and that he was free to use his imagination when writing Irish history.

———. *To the Leaders of Our Working People.* Ed. Edward A. Hagan. Dublin: University College Dublin Press, 2002. O'Grady stresses the importance of Irish cultural unity among all those living on the island.

Secondary Sources

Bhroiméil, Úna Ni. *Building Irish Identity in America, 1870–1915: The Gaelic Revival.* Dublin: Four Courts, 2003. This important book stresses the connection between the origins of the Gaelic Revival in Ireland and its impact on Irish Americans.

Connolly, S. J. *The Oxford Companion to Irish History.* 2nd ed. New York: Oxford University Press, 2007. This very useful volume should be used by most students in the development of term papers on the Gaelic Revival.

Daly, Dominic. *The Young Douglas Hyde: The Dawn of the Irish Revolution and Renaissance, 1874–1893.* Totowa, NJ: Rowman and Littlefield, 1974. Daly's study of Hyde constitutes excellent scholarship and should be referred to by all students researching Hyde.

Dunleavy, Janet E., and G. W. Dunleavy. *Douglas Hyde: A Maker of Modern Ireland.* Berkeley: University of California Press, 1991. An excellent biography with extensive information on the Gaelic Revival.

Gibbons, Luke. *Gaelic Gothic: Race, Colonization and Irish Culture.* Galway, Ireland: Arlen House, 2004. A very good study of complex issues that were associated with the Gaelic Revival.

Hutchinson, John. *The Dynamics of Cultural Nationalism: The Gaelic Revival and the Creation of the Irish Nation State.* London: Allen and Unwin in association with the London School of Economics and Political Science, 1987. Available as an e-book at http://www.questia.com/library/book/ the-dynamics-of-cultural-nationalism-the-gaelic-revival-and-the -creation-of-the-irish-nation-state-by-john-hutchinson.jsp. An essential resource for all students working on this topic.

Kee, Robert. *The Green Flag: A History of Irish Nationalism.* New York: Penguin, 2001. Includes information on the Gaelic Revival and its impact on the nationalist movement.

Legg, Marie-Louise. *Newspapers and Nationalism: The Irish Provincial Press, 1850–1892.* Dublin: Four Courts Press, 1999. Includes considerable information on the Gaelic Revival and its popularity.

McMahon, Timothy G. *Grand Opportunity: The Gaelic Revival and Irish Society, 1893–1910.* Syracuse, NY: Syracuse University Press, 2008. A comprehensive, scholarly, and readable study of the revival.

O'Leary, Philip. *The Prose Literature of the Gaelic Revival, 1881–1921: Ideology and Innovation.* University Park: Pennsylvania State University Press, 1994. An integrated scholarly study combining literature, politics, and Irish nationalism that provides numerous potential topics for term papers.

Regan, Stephen, ed. *Irish Writing: An Anthology of Irish Literature in English, 1789–1939.* New York: Oxford University Press, 2008. Includes writings by participants in the Gaelic Revival and commentary.

World Wide Web

"Blasket Island Writers." http://www.novelguide.com/a/discover/eich_01/eich_01_00039.html. An online resource on the works of some of the writers of the Gaelic Revival.

"Douglas Hyde." http://www.answers.com/topic/douglas-hyde. A very good introduction to Hyde and his involvement with the Revival.

"Douglas Hyde." http://www.encyclopedia.com/doc/1E1-Hyde-Dou.html. Includes a brief biography and four illustrations that may be useful.

"Early Gaelic Revival." http://www.nationmaster.com/encyclopedia/Gaelic-Revival. A very good introduction to the emergence of the Gaelic Revival.

"Gaelic Revival." http://www.michealscully.com/thegaelicrevival.htm. A good introduction with links to other sites.

Multimedia Sources

"Gaelic Revival, In Our Times." BBC 4, 2008. Audio Podcast. http://www.bbc.co.uk/radio4/history/inourtime/inourtime_haveyoursay.shtml. Includes commentary on the Gaelic Revival as social history.

"Irish History Part 1." http://www.youtube.com/watch?v=YUOgvrjQygs. Includes photographs and film excerpts of some of the leaders of the Gaelic Revival.

83. Third Burmese War (1885)

The Third Burmese War was the final conflict between Burma and Great Britain during the nineteenth century and resulted in Burma being absorbed into the British Empire. During the 1880s Britain became concerned with the expanding French presence in Southeast Asia and monitored carefully the border disputes between Burma and the French in Indo-China. During 1884, Anglo-French relations were strained and threats were exchanged, after which the French backed down. Shortly thereafter, a Burmese court levied a fine against an Indian company for illegal business practices that circumvented Burmese taxes. Britain joined the company in denouncing the decision and, on October 22, 1885, Britain sent an ultimatum to Burma. The British demands extended well beyond the court decision and constituted a clear statement of British intentions to eliminate the last vestiges of independent Burma. For example, one of the demands required that Britain would control the foreign policy and decisions of Burma. Burma refused to comply. Within a few months the Burmese were defeated. Mandalay was occupied and, on January 1, 1886, Britain declared the annexation of Burma into the British Empire. During the next four years the British extended their control throughout the country and eliminated the small pockets of resistance that emerged.

TERM PAPER SUGGESTIONS

1. Write a paper on the origins of the Third Burmese War. Was the Second Burmese War related to the beginning of this struggle?
2. Develop a paper in which you analyze British and French imperial policies in Southeast Asia. What were their colonial aims?
3. Write a paper on the prosecution of the Third Burmese War.

ALTERNATIVE TERM PAPER SUGGESTIONS

1. Develop a podcast in which the British develop their strategy in confronting the Burmese with the ultimatum.
2. As an officer serving in the British army in Burma, create a blog on the Third Burmese War.
3. Develop an iMovie in which the British develop their plans for the postwar pacification program in Burma.

SUGGESTED SOURCES

Primary Sources

Great Britain. *British Documents on Foreign Affairs: Reports and Papers from the Foreign Office Confidential Print. Part I, From the mid-nineteenth century to the First World War. Series E, Asia, 1860–1914*. Ed. Ian Nish. 30 vols. Frederick, MD: University Publications of America, 1989ff. See volume 26 for information and documents on the Third Burmese War.

Marks, John Ebenezer. *Forty Years in Burma*. Ed. W. C. B. Purser. London: Hutchinson, 1917. The personal recollections of a missionary who served many years in Burma, which include the Third Burmese War.

Thatcher, Mary, ed. *Cambridge South Asian Archive: Record of the British Period in South Asia Relating to India, Pakistan, Ceylon, Burma, Nepal, and Afghanistan Held in the Centre of South Asian Studies, University of Cambridge*. London: Mansell, 1973. A directory of primary sources, many of which can now be located online.

Secondary Sources

Bečka, Jan. *Historical Dictionary of Myanmar.* Metuchen, NJ: Scarecrow Press, 1995. A very reliable and useful reference work that includes information on the Burmese wars.

Blackburn, Terence R. *The British Humiliation of Burma.* Bangkok: Orchid Press, 2000. A critical assessment of the British domination of Burma during the nineteenth and twentieth centuries that includes information on the Third Burmese War.

Ghosh, Parimal. *Brave Men of the Hills: Resistance and Rebellion in Burma, 1825–1932.* Honolulu: University of Hawaii Press, 2000. A scholarly study of the Burmese resistance movement against foreign intervention.

Hack, Karl, and Tobias Rettig, eds. *Colonial Armies in Southeast Asia.* Routledge Studies in the Modern History of Asia, no. 33. London: Routledge, 2006. Includes an essay on the British in Burma by Robert Taylor that may be useful. The maps are quite good.

Hall, Daniel G. *Europe and Burma: A Study of European Relations with Burma to the Annexation of Thibaw's Kingdom, 1886.* New York: Oxford University Press, 1945. A scholarly account of Burma's unfortunate relationships with the European states prior to its collapse.

Harvey, Godfrey E. *British Rule in Burma, 1824–1942.* London: Faber and Faber, 1946. A useful study of the British governance in Burma that includes information on all of the Anglo-Burmese wars.

Htin Aung, U. *The Striken Peacock: Anglo-Burmese Relations, 1752–1948.* The Hague: M. Nijhoff, 1965. A critical analysis of Britain's role in Burma that includes information on the Anglo-Burmese wars.

James, Lawrence. *The Rise and Fall of the British Empire.* New York: St. Martin's, 1994. Provides reliable information on the Anglo-Burmese wars.

Jones, Martin D. W. "The War of Lost Footsteps: A Re-assessment of the Third Burmese War, 1885–1886." *Bulletin of the Military Historical Society* XL (1989): 36–40. A standard source on the Third Burmese War that should be available through most databases.

Keeton, Charles Lee. *King Thebaw and the Ecological Rape of Burma: The Political and Commercial Struggle between British India and French Indo-China in Burma, 1878–1886.* Delhi: Manohar, 1974. A seminal study that may prove useful in identifying a unique term paper project on this topic.

Nisbet, John. *Burma under British Rule—and Before.* Westminster: A. Constable, 1901. A dated but useful work that is sympathetic to the British actions in Burma.

Raugh, Harold E. *The Victorians at War, 1815–1914: An Encyclopedia of British Military History.* Santa Barbara, CA: ABC-CLIO, 2004.

An excellent reference work that should be useful to those working on this topic.

Seekins, Donald M. *Historical Dictionary of Burma.* Lanham, MD: Scarecrow, 2006. Most students will want to refer to this reference book that includes extensive information on the Anglo-Burmese wars.

Stewart, Anthony. *The Pagoda War: Lord Dufferin and the Fall of the Kingdom of Ava, 1885–6.* London: Faber, 1972. A fascinating study of Dufferin, who annexed northern Burma in 1886.

Trager, Helen Gibson. *Burma Through Alien Eyes: Missionary Views of the Burmese in the Nineteenth Century.* New York: Praeger, 1966. Using the accounts of missionaries, Trager presents a vivid and distinctive interpretation of Burmese attitudes during the nineteenth century.

Wheeler, James T. *A Short History of India and the Frontier States of Afghanistan, Nipal, and Burma.* London: Macmillan, 1894. An old but still useful study that includes information on the Anglo-Burmese wars.

World Wide Web

"The Third Burmese War, 1885." http://www.zum.de/whkmla/military/imperialism/burmesewar3.html. Provides a comprehensive introduction to the war with some additional links.

"The Third Burmese War, 1885–1887." http://www.somerset.gov.uk/archives/sli/3burmese.htm. A very good Web site on the war, with links.

"Third Anglo-Burmese War, 1885–1890." http://www.onwar.com/aced/chrono/c1800s/yr85/fburma1885.htm. Provides statistics on the populations and the troop commitments and casualties during the war.

"Third Burmese War." http://www.indopedia.org/Third_Burmese_War.html. An interesting description of the war from an Indian source.

"Third Burmese War." http://www.experiencefestival.com/third_burmese_war_-_the_war. Provides a list of Web articles on the war.

Multimedia Source

"Multimedia: British Empire." http://encarta.msn.com/media_701766307_761566125_-1_1/British_Empire.html. Includes ten maps and photographs, two of which relate to Burma.

84. North-West Rebellion (1885)

The Red River Rebellion of 1869–1870 in Canada failed to address the needs and complaints of the French-speaking white settlers, the Métis (interracials), and the native Indians in the great plains of Canada. Conditions grew more desperate during the 1870s when crops failed and starvation became a reality. At the same time, the investment in the Canadian railroad system continued and the Canadian government became interested in extending its authority in the region west of Ontario. Louis Riel (1844–1885), leader of the Métis, who had fled Canada after the failure of the Red River Rebellion, returned to the region and, in 1884, organized an effort to pass a Revolutionary Bill of Rights that would guarantee Métis property rights, the standing of the Catholic Church, and fundamental freedoms and limited autonomy to the native settlers of the area. Riel established a provisional government with himself as its leader and named Gabriel Dumont as the leader of its military forces. The Canadian government responded rapidly and organized a military force that eventually grew to 5,000 armed men. Several skirmishes and battles occurred, which resulted in the loss of about 100 lives on both sides. The rebellion ended at the Battle of Loon Lake on June 3, 1885. Riel was captured and charged with treason and executed on November 10, 1885. The Métis and native Indians were suppressed and found themselves with very limited freedoms. These conditions continued well into the twentieth century.

TERM PAPER SUGGESTIONS

1. Develop a paper on the general background and outbreak of the North-West Rebellion.
2. Write a paper on the suppression of the North-West Rebellion.
3. Construct a term paper on the consequences of the North-West Rebellion on Canada and Canadian identity.
4. Write a paper on the Métis people and their role in the rebellion and the impact of its failure on them.

ALTERNATIVE TERM PAPER SUGGESTIONS

1. Develop a podcast that consists of Louis Riel's explanation for the rationale for the Rebellion.
2. Develop an iMovie in which Riel's trial is covered as a televised news broadcast.
3. Develop a Web page focused on the geopolitical challenges that were confronted in suppressing the Rebellion.

4. You are the teenage child of Métis parents who supported the Rebellion. Create a postwar blog of your parents' views and how they handled the outcome.

SUGGESTED SOURCES

Primary Sources

Boulton, Charles A. *I Fought Riel: A Military Memoir.* Ed. Heather Robertson. Halifax, Nova Scotia: J. Lorimer, 1985. This is Boulton's memoir. He was one of Riel's most dedicated enemies and later served in the Canadian Senate.

Canadian Parliament. *Epitome of Parliamentary Documents in Connection with the North-West Rebellion 1885.* Ottawa: Maclean, Roger, 1886. A collection of important documents on the North-West Rebellion that should be useful for most term papers. It is still available in many libraries.

Denison, G. T. *Soldiering in Canada.* Whitefish, MT: Kessinger, 2006; originally published in 1900. A memoir by a participant in the North-West Rebellion.

Dumont, Gabriel. *Gabiel Dumont's Account of the North West Rebellion, 1885.* Ottawa: Canadian Historical Association, 1950. A primary account by a significant participant who was a leader of the Métis rebellion in 1885.

Flanagan, Thomas, ed. *Diaries of Louis Riel.* Edmonton: Hurtig, 1982. An excellent, reliable, and fascinating source by the leader of the rebellion.

Kennedy, Howard Angus. *The North-West Rebellion.* Canadian History Readers Series. Toronto: Ryerson Press, 1928. Provides excerpts from primary sources as well as a secondary account of the Rebellion.

Laurie, J. Wimburn. *Report of Major General Laurie: Commanding Base and Line of Communication upon Matters in Connection with the Suppression of the Rebellion in the North-West Territories in 1885.* Ottawa: Maclean, Roger, 1887. Laurie's report on the military defeat of the rebels is vivid and mostly reliable.

Macleod, Roderick C. *The Reminiscences of a Bungle by One of the Bunglers: And Two Other Northwest Rebellion Diaries.* Edmonton: University of Alberta Press, 1983. Highly descriptive diaries by three of the participants involved in the suppression of the rebellion.

Morton, Desmond, and Reginald Herbert Roy, eds. *Telegrams of the North-West Campaign, 1885.* Toronto: Chaplain Society, 1972. An important resource in determining the sequence of events and the communication trail.

Stanley, G. F. G., ed. *The Collected Writings of Louis Riel/Les Ecrits complets de Louis Riel.* 5 vols. Edmonton: University of Alberta Press, 1985. A critical primary source on Riel and his rebellions.

Secondary Sources

Acorn, Milton, George Bowering, and Lorna Crozier. *No Feather, No Ink: After Riel.* Saskatoon, Saskatchewan: Thistledown Press, 1985. An interesting study on the issue of Canadian identity after the collapse of Riel's rebellion.

Anderson, Frank, and Robert Allan. *The Riel Rebellion 1885.* Santa Barbara, CA: Frontier Publishing, 1984. A fact-filled introduction to the North-West Rebellion.

Beal, Bob, and Rod Macleod. *Prairie Fire: The 1885 North-West Rebellion.* Toronto: McClelland and Sons, 1994. An exciting and authoritative examination of the rebellion and its aftermath.

Boulton, Charles Arkell. *Reminiscences of the North-West Rebellions.* Toronto: Davis & Henderson/Grip, 1886. A very important memoir by a major participant in the rebellion.

Bowsfield, Hartwell. *Louis Riel: Rebel of the Western Frontier or Victim of Politics and Prejudice?* Toronto: Copp Clark, 1969. Presents alternative sources and interpretations on Riel, and is a very useful resource for term papers.

Braz, Albert. *The False Traitor: Louis Riel in Canadian Culture.* Toronto: University of Toronto Press, 2003. This important study examines the interpretations of Riel that have emerged in Canadian culture and historiography.

Brown, Wayne F. *Steele's Scouts: Samuel Benfield Steele and the North-West Rebellion.* Victoria, British Columbia: Heritage House, 2001. A narrative description of a military unit involved in the rebellion.

Buckner, Philip. *Canada and the British Empire; Oxford History of the British Empire Companion.* New York: Oxford University Press, 2008. An outstanding comprehensive history that provides a solid introduction to most aspects of Canadian history and a very good bibliography.

Bumsted, J. M. *Louis Riel v. Canada: The Making of a Rebel.* Winnipeg, Manitoba: Great Plains Publications, 2001. A very important study by a recognized authority that is very good, particularly on the background and causes for the rebellion.

Burt, A. L. *The Romance of the Prairie Provinces.* Toronto: Gage, 1930. A well-written introduction to the rebellion and life in central Canada during the second half of the nineteenth century.

Cameron, William Bleasdell. *The War Trail of Big Bear: Being the Story of the Connection of Big Bear and Other Cree Indian Chiefs and their Followers with the North-West Rebellion of 1885, the Frog Lake Massacre and Events Leading Up to and Following it.* London: Duckworth, 1927. A worthwhile and useful history of the role and impact of natives in the rebellion. It includes information on the impact of Canadian expansion and politics on the native population.

Carol, Lindon. *Gatling Guns at the North West Rebellion.* Rev. ed. Edmonton: Shorthorn Press, 1999. A very good account on the impact of new technology on the rebellion.

Clink, W. L. *Battleford Beleaguered, 1885: The Story of the Riel Uprising from the Columns of "The Saskatchewan Herald."* Regina: University of Calgary Press, 1985. Includes significant excerpts from the *Herald* as it covered the rebellion in 1885.

Flanagan, Thomas. *Louis "David" Riel: Prophet of the New World.* Rev. ed. Toronto: University of Toronto Press, 1996. A scholarly and readable study based on primary sources that emphasizes the impact of religion on Riel's political ideology.

———. *Riel and the Rebellion: 1885 Reconsidered.* 2nd ed. Toronto: University of Toronto Press, 2000. Flanagan (University of Calgary) argues that Riel was a rather destructive figure in Canadian history.

Flanagan, Thomas, and Claude Rocan. *Rebellion in the North-West.* Toronto: Grolier, 1984. A very good history of the North-West Rebellion that should be available in many libraries.

Hathorn, Ramon. *Images of Louis Riel in Canadian Culture.* Lewiston, NY: Edwin Mellen Press, 1992. A scholarly examination of Louis Riel and his place in nineteenth-century Canadian history and memory. This is a comprehensive work that takes into consideration opposing interpretations of Riel.

Howard, Joseph K. *Strange Empire: Louis Riel and the Métis People.* Toronto: J. Lewis and Samuel, 1974. Howard's study is an important contribution to Riel and Métis historical literature and suggests that the rather simplistic interpretations of the interrelationship of the two are misguided.

Lamb, R. E. *Thunder in the North: Conflict over the Riel Risings, 1870–1885.* New York: Pageant Press, 1957. A useful introduction to both the Red River and North-West Rebellions.

MacBeth, R. G. *The Making of the Canadian West: Being the Reminiscences of an Eye-Witness.* Coles Canadiana Collection. Toronto: Coles Publishing, 1973; reprint of 1898 edition. This is a classic nationalist interpretation that has little sympathy for the rebels.

McCourt, Edward. *Revolt in the West: The Story of the Riel Rebellion.* Toronto: Macmillan, 1960. An adequate and accurate introduction to the rebellion.

Middleton, Frederick Dobson. *Suppression of the Rebellion in the North West Territories of Canada, 1885.* University of Toronto Studies: History and Economics Series, vol. 11. Toronto: University of Toronto Press, 1948.

Middleton focuses on the suppression of the revolt—Riel's trial and execution and the subsequent enforcement of Canadian rule and government.

Morton, Desmond. *The Last War Drum: The North West Campaign of 1885.* Toronto: Hakkert, 1972. A great read and a good, useful, and accurate introduction to the rebellion.

———. *Queen Versus Louis Riel.* Toronto: University of Toronto Press, 1974. Another well-written history by Morton that is focused on Riel and his trial.

Mulvany, Charles Pelham. *The History of the North-West Rebellion of 1885.* Whitefish, MT: Kessinger Publishing, 2007; reprint of 1885 edition. While very dated, Mulvany's history still provides a wealth of information and insight on the rebellion.

Needler, G. H. *Louis Riel: The Rebellion of 1885.* Toronto: Burns and MacEachern, 1957. A good introduction to Riel and his influence and defeat in the North-West Rebellion.

Oppen, William A. *Riel Rebellions: A Cartographic History.* Toronto: University of Toronto Press, 1980. A very important and useful book that examines the geopolitical significance of the Red River and North-West Rebellions.

Reid, Jennifer. *Louis Riel and the Creation of Modern Canada: Mythic Discourse and the Postcolonial State.* Albuquerque: University of New Mexico Press, 2008. Reid, a Professor at the University of Maine, Farmington, has produced a seminal study in which she examines the image and background of Riel and the rebellion in relation to Canadian identity.

Siggins, Maggie. *Riel: A Life of Revolution.* Toronto: HarperCollins, 1994. A very good and useful biography of Riel and the values and ideas that motivated his leadership in the Red River and North-West Rebellions.

Silver, A. I. *The North-West Rebellion.* Toronto: Copp Clark, 1967. This slender but important resource provides alternative interpretations and outlines the problems associated with studying the rebellion.

Stanley, George F. *The Birth of Western Canada: A History of the Riel Rebellions.* Toronto: University of Toronto Press, 1960. Examines the impact of the Red River and Riel rebellions on the development of western Canada, and includes useful maps by C. C. J. Bond.

Stewart, Sharon. *Louis Riel: Firebrand.* Montreal: XYZ Publishing, 2007. A recent and worthwhile introduction to Riel and his times.

Stonechild, Blair. *Loyal Till Death: The Indians and the Northwest Rebellion.* Saskatoon: Fifth House, 1997. A worthwhile account of the involvement of native Canadians in the 1885 rebellion.

Tolton, Gordon E. *The Rocky Mountain Rangers: Southern Alberta's Cowboy Cavalry in the North-West Rebellion 1885*. Lethbridge, Alberta: Lethbridge Historical Society, 1994. A brief but useful study of the impact of this unit during the rebellion.

———. *Prairie Warships: River Navigation in the Northwest Rebellion*. Victoria, British Columbia: Heritage House, 2007. A fascinating study of the use of steamships, ferries, and other craft during the Northwest Rebellion. Many illustrations are included.

Wallace, Jim. *A Trying Time: The North-West Mounted Police in the 1885 Rebellion*. Calgary, Alberta: Bunker to Bunker, 1998. A very solid account of the role of the police during the Riel Rebellion.

Woodcock, George. *Gabriel Dumont: The Métis Chief and His Lost World*. Edmonton: Hurtig, 1975. The best account of Dumont and his role as a Métis leader during the rebellions.

World Wide Web

"About the Northwest Rebellion of 1885." http://www3.memlane.com/gromboug/P5NWReb.htm. Includes links to Web sites about the Northwest Rebellion as well as photographs and maps.

"Louis Riel." http://www.collectionscanada.gc.ca/confederation/023001-2390 -e.html. Based on the archival materials, this biography of Riel is reliable and detailed; photographs are included.

"Louis Riel." http://www.metisnation.org/culture/Riel/home.html. Provides information on Riel and the Métis.

"Louis Riel and the North-West Rebellion." http://www.mta.ca/about_canada/ multimedia/riel/pdf/printer.pdf. Prepared by the Centre for Canadian Studies at Mount Allison University, this site is very useful.

"North-West Rebellion." http://www.collectionscanada.gc.ca/trains/kids/h32 -1030-e.html. This site is centered on the role of the Canadian Pacific Railway in the North-West Rebellion.

"North-West Rebellion." http://www.thecanadianencyclopedia.com/index.cfm? PgNm=TCE&Params=J1ARTJ0005802. Provides an accurate history of the rebellion and useful photographs.

"The Northwest Resistance." http://library.usask.ca/northwest/contents.html. Includes a database of materials focused on the 1885 resistance, a chronology, and biographies of participants.

"The Northwest Resistance 1885." http://library2.usask.ca/northwest/. A significant and excellent online resource held at the University of Saskatchewan Libraries and University Archives.

"The Red River Rebellions." http://www.iigs.org/newsletter/9811news/
    metis.htm.en. An account of the Red River and North-West Rebellions
    by Robert A. Bonnar that focuses on Riel and his aspirations.

Multimedia Sources

Gabriel Dumont and the Northwest Rebellion. A play. Toronto: Playwrights
    Co-op, 1976. A drama in which Dumont's role in the rebellion is pre-
    sented in a sympathetic manner.
"Northwest Rebellion." http://www.canadianheritage.ca/galleries/warsbattlesre-
    bellions0700.htm#North-West%20Rebellion. Includes six photographs
    of the Northwest Rebellion.
"Portrait of Louis Riel." http://encarta.msn.com/media_461569290
    _761563318_-1_1/Louis_Riel.html. A quality reproduction of the
    famous Riel portrait.
Rethinking Riel. Canadian Broadcasting Company, 2001. CBC Archives. Online
    video series. http://archives.cbc.ca/politics/provincial_territorial
    _politics/topics/1482/. Very useful source on Riel's character and his life
    as a rebel.

85. Indian National Congress Is Established (1885)

During the decades after the suppression of the Sepoy Mutiny in 1857, a
generation of Indian intellectuals and bureaucrats emerged that benefited
from British rule. While they gained social and economic power and
influence, they were also influenced by the Irish nationalist movement
and the desire to enhance Indian national and economic identity through
unifying India by using Western methods and institutions and to improve
the quality of the lives of the people. In 1883, A. O. Hume, a retired
British Colonial Office employee, suggested that the Indians establish
an organization that would realize these goals. Hume's statement was
timely because Indian intellectuals were upset with a recent ruling that
prohibited Indian judges from ruling in cases where Europeans were
being tried. In 1885 a group of Indian intellectuals and some British
reformers met and established the Indian National Congress. The prominent members of this group were Hume, Dadabhai Naoroji, and
Dinshaw Edulji Wacha. It had a very conservative agenda and was initially concerned with gaining recognition as a legitimate political voice

for moderate Indians. After 1897, under more aggressive leadership, the Indian National Congress became identified with the cause of Indian independence from Britain. Between 1897 and 1947 the Congress was the preeminent organization in leading this movement, and independence was won in 1947.

TERM PAPER SUGGESTIONS

1. Discuss the causes for the establishment of the Indian National Congress.
2. Develop a paper on the role played by A. O. Hume in the founding of the Indian National Congress. What values and experiences motivated him?
3. Write a paper on the immediate events sounding the founding of the Congress. What were its goals and objectives in 1885?
4. How successful was the Indian National Congress during its first decade—1885–1895?
5. Did the Indian National Congress serve as a model for effective representation of native peoples and ideas within the British Empire?
6. For Indians in the 1880s, were there any alternative routes to pursue racial and economic justice other than through the establishment of the Indian National Congress? If so, what were they?

ALTERNATIVE TERM PAPER SUGGESTIONS

1. As an Indian in 1885, write a blog in which you discuss whether the Indian National Congress was another surrender of Indian freedom under British rule.
2. Develop a podcast in which Indian leaders discuss the formation of the Indian National Congress.

SUGGESTED SOURCES

Primary Sources

"British Colonial India—Political and Military History." The Victorian Web. http://www.victorianweb.org/history/empire/india/history.html. Provides links to other relevant sites.
"National Archives of India." http://www.nationalarchives.nic.in/landing.htlm. This is the best source for documents and other primary materials associated with the founding of the Indian National Congress.

Zaidi, A. M., ed. *The Story of Congress Pilgrimage: Event to Event Record of Activities of the Indian National Congress from 1885 to 1985 Emanating from Official Reports of the General Secretaries.* 7 vols. New Delhi: Indian Institute of Applied Political Research, 1990. The initial volume in this series not only provides a reliable and detailed account based on official documents of the founding and initial years of the Congress but also provides valuable primary materials.

Secondary Sources

Bandhu, Deep Chand. *History of Indian National Congress 1885–2002.* New Delhi: Kalpaz Publications, 2003. A reliable and generally sympathetic history of the Indian National Congress.

Brass, Paul R., and Frances Robinson, eds. *Indian National Congress and Indian Society 1885–1985.* New Delhi: Chanakya Publications, 1987. A collection of essays that address a range of political, economic, and social issues that concerned the Indian National Congress during its first century.

Hill, John L., ed. *The Congress and Indian Nationalism: Historical Perspectives.* London: Curzon, 1991. A very solid book that consists of several essays on the Indian National Congress as it emerged as the instrument of Indian nationalism.

Kaushik, Hariah P. *Indian National Congress in England.* New Delhi: Friends Publications, 1991. A unique study of the support and criticism that the Indian National Congress encountered in England from both the immigrant sector and the British.

Roy, Kaushik, ed. *War and Society in Colonial India, 1807–1945.* New Delhi and New York: Oxford University Press, 2006. Provides a reliable and useful introduction into the origins of the Indian National Congress.

Low, D. A., ed. *The Indian National Congress: Centenary Highlights.* New Delphi and New York: Oxford University Press, 1988. A volume of seminar papers that includes contributions on Colonial Indian history from the Sepoy Mutiny of 1857 to the establishment of the Indian National Congress in 1885.

Martin, Briton. *New India, 1885. British Official Policy and the Emergence of the Indian National Congress.* Berkeley: University of California Press, 1969. An essential scholarly work on the origins of the Indian National Congress from the perspective of the British government.

Masselos, Jim, ed. *Struggling and Ruling: The Indian National Congress 1885–1985.* New Delhi: Oriental University Press, 1987. A useful history of the Congress during its first century. The initial chapter is focused on its establishment.

Mehrotra, S. R. *A History of the Indian National Congress.* Calcutta: Rupa, 2004. A solid and reliable history of the Indian National Congress.

Shepperdson, Mike, and Colin Simmons, eds. *The Indian National Congress and the Political Economy of India, 1885–1985.* Aldershot, United Kingdom: Avebury, 1988. A valuable study of the connections between the development of the Indian economy and the policies and agendas advanced by the Indian National Congress.

Singh, Igbal. *Indian National Congress: A Reconstruction, 1885–1918.* Riverdale, MD: Riverdale, 1988. Focused on the Congress from its founding through the First World War, the Indian National Congress was transformed and rendered more radical by India's obligations as a member of the British Empire.

Singh, R. P. *Education and the Indian National Congress, 1885–1947: Myths, Reality and Resolutions.* New Delhi: Scenario Publications, 1996. Singh's study remains important because it addresses the complexities associated with the politicalization of education within India's complex caste system.

Yasin, Madhvi. *Emergence of Nationalism, Congress, and Separatism.* New Delhi: Raj Publications, 1996. A study that examines the role of Frederick Temple Blackwood in the formation of the Indian National Congress, the British-Indian question, and the difficulties between the Muslims and Hindus during the colonial period.

Zaidi, A. M., ed. *The Muslim School of Congress: The Political Ideas of Muslim Congress Leaders from Mr. Badruddin Tayyabj to Maulana Abul Kalam Azad, 1885–1947.* New Delhi: Indian Institute of Applied Political Research, 1987. From the outset the Islamic voice with the Congress evoked a distinctive perspective—a good source for students studying Tayyabi.

———— and S. Zaidi, eds. *The Encyclopedia of the Indian National Congress.* 18 vols. New Delhi: S. Chand, 1976–1983. This is the most comprehensive source of information on the establishment of the Indian National Congress and the many personalities who were involved in that process.

World Wide Web

"Congress Archives, Archives of Indian National Congress." http://www.kamat.com/kalranga/freedom/congress/index.htm. This is an important source of information that is sometimes difficult to navigate.

"Internet Indian History Sourcebook." Fordham University. http://www.fordham.edu/halsall/india/indiasbook.html. This is an excellent site that provides information and sources on the emergence of the Congress from the difficult Sepoy Mutiny of 1857.

Multimedia Source

The Road to Indian Independence. Princeton: Films for the Humanities and Sciences, n.d. DVD/VHS video. This film starts with the Sepoy Mutiny in 1857 and carries the story of Indian independence until its realization in 1947. It includes commentary on the Indian National Congress and its impact on the process.

86. Irish Home Rule Established (1886)

From the Catholic Emancipation Act of 1829 it was evident that most Irish political leaders wanted more than representation in the English House of Commons. By the 1870s concerns about Ireland appeared on the agendas of the House of Commons regularly and concerned specifics such as support for state-supported churches and schools, the rights to hold lands, and the rights of tenant sharecroppers. In 1886 William Gladstone (1809–1898), leader of the Liberal Party and four-time prime minister, introduced the First Irish Home Rule Bill that would provide autonomy and self-government for Ireland *within* the United Kingdom. While most Liberal and Irish members of Parliament supported the measure, it was not passed because of the opposition of the Conservatives under Prime Minister Lord Salisbury (1830–1903) and their allies. In 1893, Prime Minister Gladstone once again advanced the proposal, which was approved by the House of Commons but defeated in the Conservative-dominated House of Lords. For two decades the issue of Ireland and Home Rule was contentious and polarized politics and society. Eventually, the measure was adopted in 1914 but not implemented because of the outbreak of the First World War. In 1920, the Government of Ireland Act set the stage for a two-state Ireland—an Irish Republic in the south and Northern Ireland as a Home Rule entity.

TERM PAPER TOPIC SUGGESTIONS

1. Develop a term paper on the background of the Anglo-Irish relationship from 1801 to 1870.

2. Write a paper on Gladstone's support of the "Home Rule" movement during the 1880s. What were his motives? What were his views of Ireland's future?

3. Develop a paper on the controversies that developed on the Irish Home Rule Bills of the 1880s and 1890s.

4. Write a paper on the aspirations of the Irish nationalist community. How did they evaluate the significance of Home Rule within the context of the larger issue of Irish independence?

ALTERNATE TERM PAPER SUGGESTIONS

1. Isaac Butt was one of the first to advance the notion of Home Rule for Ireland. Develop a podcast in which you interview Butt on his ideas and aspirations and his appraisal on what was achieved during his lifetime.

2. Develop a 4–5 minute iMovie on Gladstone's discussion on Home Rule with his Liberal Party colleagues prior to his public announcement of support.

3. As a journalist for a Dublin newspaper that supports Irish nationalism, create a blog that consists of articles dated between 1885 and 1893 in which you report on the progress of Home Rule legislation.

SUGGESTED SOURCES

Primary Sources

Arnstein, Walter. *The Past Speaks, Sources and Problems in British History.* 2nd ed. 2 vols. Lexington, MA: D. C. Heath, 1993. The second volume includes primary sources on Home Rule by Isaac Butt, Douglas Hyde, William E. Gladstone, the Marquess of Hartington, Edward Carson, and John Redmond.

Gladstone, William E. *The Speeches of the Right Hon. W. E. Gladstone: On Home Rule, Criminal Law, Welsh and Irish Nationality, National Debt, and the Queen's Reign.* London: Methuen, 1902. Excellent resource for primary materials.

———. *The Gladstone Diaries: July 1883–December 1886: With Cabinet Minutes and Prime-Ministerial Correspondence: July 1883–December 1886.* 2 vols. Ed. H. C. G. Matthew. Oxford: Clarendon Press, 1990. These two volumes provide a wealth of primary materials from Gladstone's perspective.

———. *Handbook of Home Rule: Being Articles on the Irish Question.* Charleston, SC: BiblioBazaar, 2008. Includes some of Gladstone's publications on Home Rule during the 1880s and 1890s.

Morley, John. *Recollections.* 2 vols. London: Macmillan, 1917. Memoirs by a Liberal minister who participated in the Home Rule debates.

Russell, George W., and Horace Plunkett. *The Irish Home Rule Convention: Thoughts for a Convention: A Defense of the Convention; An American Opinion.* Whitefish, MT: Kessinger, 2007. Contemporary accounts by participants in the debate on Home Rule.

Secondary Sources

Biagini, Eugenio F. *British Democracy and Irish Nationalism 1876–1906.* Cambridge, U.K.: Cambridge University Press, 2007. In this seminal study Biagini argues that the tensions caused by the Home Rule debate contributed to the radicalization of British politics in the early twentieth century.

Boyce, D. George, and Alan O'Day, eds. *Parnell in Perspective.* London: Routledge, 1991. A scholarly assessment of Irish nationalist leader Parnell and his impact on Anglo-Irish politics.

———, eds. *Ireland in Transition, 1867–1921.* London: Routledge, 2004. Includes 15 scholarly essays by established historians. Some of the essays will be useful to students working on this topic.

Hammond, John Lawrence. *Gladstone and the Irish Nation.* London: Longmans, Green, 1938. A dated but useful study on Gladstone's position on Home Rule.

Harrison, Henry. *Parnell, Joseph Chamberlain, and Mr. Garvin.* London: R. Hale, 1938. A very good account of prominent personalities who were involved in the Home Rule debate.

Jackson, Alvin. *Home Rule: An Irish History, 1800–2000.* New York: Oxford University Press, 2004. Provides a very good introduction to Irish Home Rule politics.

Morton, Grenfell. *Home Rule and the Irish Question.* New York: Longman, 1980. A worthwhile assessment of the issue with the larger matter of Irish independence.

Loughlin, James. *Gladstone, Home Rule, and the Ulster Question, 1882–1893.* Dublin: Gill and Macmillan, 1986. A very good study of the complexities associated with Home Rule.

Lubenow, William C. *Parliamentary Politics and the Home Rule Crisis: The British House of Commons in 1886.* Oxford: Clarendon Press, 1988. One of the best studies of the issue and the political machinations associated with it.

Lyons, Francis Stewart. *Charles Stewart Parnell.* New York: Oxford University Press, 1977. Very good and readable biography of Parnell.

O'Day, Alan. *Parnell and the First Home Rule Episode.* Dublin: Gill and Macmillan, 1986. Excellent study by a noted historian. If students are working on a paper related to Parnell, they will need to refer to this book.

———. *Irish Home Rule, 1867–1921.* Manchester: Manchester University Press, 1998. The best study on Home Rule that is available, and students working on Home Rule must read this book.

Peatling, Gary. *British Opinion and Irish Self-Government, 1865–1925: From Unionism to Liberal Commonwealth.* Dublin: Irish Academic Press,

2001. A seminal study that should be used by students who are studying the public debate on Home Rule.

Shannon, Richard. *Gladstone.* 2 vols. Chapel Hill: University of North Carolina Press, 1997. The second volume in this biography covers the period from 1865 to 1898 and includes valuable insights on Irish Home Rule.

Smith, Jeremy. *Britain and Ireland: From Home Rule to Independence.* New York: Longman, 2000. The "Introduction" and the "Analysis" should be useful to many students working on this topic.

Stewart, Anthony Terence. *Edward Carson.* Dublin: Gill and Macmillan, 1981. A classic study of the leader of the Ulster Unionists.

Thornley, David. *Isaac Butt and Home Rule.* Westport, CT: Greenwood Press, 1978; originally published in 1964. Excellent biography of Butt who was one of the first to advance the Home Rule proposal.

World Wide Web

"1886–1893: First and Second Home Rule Bills." http://www.wesleyjohnston .com/users/ireland/past/history/18861893.html. A good introduction to the proposals advanced by Gladstone.

"Home Rule." http://www.encyclopedia.com/topic/Home_Rule.aspx. Provides a good introduction, several illustrations, and links to other relevant sites.

"Home Rule and Ireland." http://www.historylearningsite.co.uk/home_rule _and_ireland.htm. Provides an adequate introduction to the idea of Home Rule for Ireland.

"Irish History Online." http://www.irishhistoryonline.ie/. A comprehensive research site that is sponsored by the Irish Research Council for the Humanities and Social Sciences.

"Irish History on the Web." http://larkspirit.com/history/. Includes links that are useful in studying Irish Home Rule.

Multimedia Sources

"Gladstone and Irish Home Rule." http://www.cartoonstock.com/vintage/ directory/i/irish_home_rule.asp. Provides a reproduction of a cartoon entitled "Sink or Swim" in which Gladstone is portrayed to have provided Ireland with an opportunity.

"Irish Home Rule, An Imagined Future." BBC-4, 2007. http://www.bbc.co.uk/his tory/british/victorians/home_rule_movement_10.shtml. A BBC-4 broadcast by James McConnell, as a segment in the *Empire* series, that is a very good introduction to the many facets that were involved in Irish Home Rule.

"Irish Home Rule and the Road to War." BBC-4, 2006. http://www.bbc.co.uk/ radio4/history/empire/episodes/episode_81.shtml. A BBC-4 broadcast, part of the *Empire* series (2006), that connects the late nineteenth century movement to the history of pre–World War I Britain.

87. Discovery of Gold in South Africa (1886)

The rivalry between the Boers and the British in South Africa was aggravated by the discovery of gold in 1886. In March 1886 an Australian, George Harrison (unknown birth/death), was reported to have discovered gold. Upon declaring the discovery, Harrison disappeared, but thousands of prospectors—mostly British—descended on South Africa. Among the consequences of the gold rush were the establishment of Johannesburg and the further estrangement in Anglo-Boer relations. Within a few years Cecil Rhodes (1853–1902) and others would support the Jameson Raid (1895–1896) in which British colonists launched an attack on the Boers. This was a prelude to the Boer War that started in 1899.

TERM PAPER SUGGESTIONS

1. Write a paper on the impact of the discovery of gold on Anglo-Boer relations.
2. Develop a paper on the impact of the gold rush on the native population.
3. Develop a paper on the geopolitical changes that occurred as a consequence of the discovery of gold. Include a map with a narrative that includes the founding of Johannesburg.

ALTERNATIVE TERM PAPER SUGGESTIONS

1. Develop a podcast on the British Cabinet's discussions on the significance of the discovery of gold in South Africa.
2. Develop an iMovie in which Rhodes and his associates consider their short- and long-term responses to the discovery of gold *vis-à-vis* the Boers.
3. As a prominent Boer leader, you are concerned about the ramifications of the gold strike. Write blog entries during the 1880s and early 1890s in which the level of your concern increases.

SUGGESTED SOURCES

Primary Sources

Bain, Thomas. *Report of the Recent Gold Discoveries in the Knysna Division.* n.p.: [n.pub.], 1886. A personal report on the discovery of gold.

Harlow, Barbara. *Archives of Empire.* 2 vols. Durham, NC: Duke University Press, 2003. The second volume (*Scramble for Africa*) in this collection of documents focused on the Scramble for Africa and includes items related to the discovery of gold in South Africa.

——— and Mia Carter, eds. *Imperialism and Orientalism: A Documentary Sourcebook.* New York: Wiley-Blackwell, 1999. Includes some related documents.

Secondary Sources

Attridge, Steve. *Nationalism, Imperialism and Identity in Late Victorian Culture: Civil and Military Worlds.* London: Palgrave Macmillan, 2003. Very good on the cultural response to the discovery of gold and the rush to South Africa.

Boahen, A. Adu (UNESCO). *Africa Under Colonial Domination, 1880–1935: Africa Under Colonial Domination 1880–1935.* Berkeley: University of California Press, 1990. Provides information on the gold rush and its impact on South Africa.

Chamberlain, M. E. *The Scramble for Africa.* 2nd ed. Seminar Studies in History Series. London: Longman, 1999. Includes a series of essays and documents, some related to this topic.

Horwood, Cuthbert Baring. *The Gold Deposits of the Rand.* London: C. Griffin, 1917. A description of the extent of the gold deposits and the mining operations.

Katz, Elaine M. *The White Death: Silicosis on the Witwatersrand Gold Mines 1886–1910.* Johannesburg: Witwatersrand University Press, 1994. The horrors of silicosis associated with the gold mines are described in detail.

Meredith, Martin. *Diamonds, Gold and War: The British, the Boers, and the Making of South Africa.* Jackson, TN: Public Affairs, 2007. An important book that includes extensive information on the impact of the gold rush on South African history and Anglo-Boer relations.

Nesbitt, Lewis M. *Gold Fever.* New York: Arno Press, 1974. Includes information on the South African gold rush of the 1880s.

Pakenham, Thomas. *The Scramble for Africa: White Man's Conquest of the Dark Continent from 1876 to 1912.* New York: Avon Books, 1992. A reliable source of information that includes data on the gold rush.

Rosenthal, Eric. *Gold! Gold! Gold! The Johannesburg Gold Rush.* New York: Macmillan, 1970. The best book focused on the gold rush—students working on this topic should consult this study.

Shillington, Kevin. *Encyclopedia of African History.* Boca Rotan: CRC Press, 2005. Available as an e-book at http://books.google.com/books?

id=Ftz_gtO-pngC&dq=Discovery+of+Gold+in+South+Africa +1886&source=gbs_summary_s&cad=0. An excellent resource book that includes information on this topic.

Stephens, John J. *Fuelling the Empire: South Africa's Gold and the Road to War.* New York: Wiley, 2002. A reliable study that focuses on the impact of the gold rush.

Storey, William K. *Guns, Race, and Power in Colonial South Africa.* Cambridge, U.K.: Cambridge University Press, 2008. Within the context of armaments, this study contends that the gold rush contributed to increased conflict in South Africa.

Thomas, Antony. *Rhodes: Race for Africa.* New York: St. Martin's, 1997. A very good biography of Rhodes and the development of his power based on diamonds and gold.

Thompson, Leonard. *A History of South Africa.* 3rd ed. New Haven, CT: Yale University Press, 2001. Provides an introduction to the gold rush and its consequences.

Worden, Nigel. *The Making of Modern South Africa: Conquest, Apartheid, Democracy.* 4th ed. New York: Wiley-Blackwell, 2007. Includes introductory level information on the gold rush.

World Wide Web

"Cecil Rhodes." http://www.pbs.org/empires/victoria/empire/rhodes.html. A useful biography of Rhodes.

"Discovery of Diamonds and Gold in South Africa." http://www.south-africa-tours-and-travel.com/diamonds-and-gold-in-south-africa.html. Introduction with five illustrations.

"The Discovery of Gold." http://www.britannica.com/EBchecked/topic/ 556618/southern-Africa/234073/The-discovery-of-gold. Very good introduction with an excellent map.

"Witwatersrand Gold." http://www.geoscience.org.za/content/GSSA/ GSSAWitwatersrandA.htm. Provides information on the discovery in 1886.

"Witwatersrand Gold Rush." http://www.nationmaster.com/encyclopedia/ Witwatersrand-Gold-Rush. A useful introduction on the 1886 African gold rush.

Multimedia Sources

"Cecil Rhodes and the Round Table Group." http://www.youtube.com/watch?v =9iRHbBiHuuA. Interesting video on Rhodes and his leadership in South Africa.

Rhodes: The Life and Legend of Cecil Rhodes. BBC Video, 1996. VHS. This six-part series was directed by David Drury and written by Antony Thomas. It includes a section on the gold rush and its impact in precipitating the Anglo-Boer conflict.

88. Treaty of Uccialli and the Italians in Ethiopia (1889)

Menelik II became the Emperor of Ethiopia in 1889 and extended a modernization initiative that he had previously launched. Previously, he had established Addis Ababa as the capital, begun an extensive program of public works—including road and bridge construction, built schools and health-care facilities, stabilized the currency and the economy, and attracted foreign investment to support the development of a railroad and telegraph network. Menelik welcomed the opportunity to enter into a treaty with the Italian government that controlled Eritrea. From Menelik's perspective, the Treaty of Uccialli (Wuchale) was intended to formalize the relationship between Italy and Ethiopia. The Italians viewed it as a means to expand their sphere of influence in East Africa and to establish a level of control over Ethiopia. The Treaty was written in both Italian and Amharic. At the time of the signing in 1889, it appeared that both sides thought that the document was clear and that its intent was not ambiguous. However, it soon became apparent that Article 17 of the treaty was viewed dramatically differently by the Ethiopians and the Italians. To the Ethiopians, it specified that the Italian offices would be available to Ethiopia in communicating with the rest of the world—these services were available if the Ethiopians wished to use them. The Italian text specified that the use of Italian offices was mandated. Italy declared that Ethiopia was under Italian protection, and relations between Ethiopia and Italy deteriorated. Both nations built up their arms and a war developed in the First Italo-Ethiopian War in the 1890s that resulted in the Italian defeat at the Battle of Adowa in 1896.

TERM PAPER SUGGESTIONS

1. Write a paper in which you compare the translations of the Italian and Amharic copies of the Treaty. Did the Italians intend to establish a protectorate in Ethiopia prior to the Treaty?

2. Develop a paper in which you examine the modernization of Ethiopia under Menelik II.

3. Write a paper on the decline in Italian-Ethiopian relations from the treaty to the outbreak of the First Italo-Ethiopian War.

ALTERNATIVE TERM PAPER SUGGESTIONS

1. Develop a podcast in which Menelik II is interviewed after he learns of the Italian interpretation of the Treaty.

2. As a loyal aide to Menelik II, you are involved in the negotiations on the Treaty. Write your postwar blog that attempts to present the origins of the conflict from the Ethiopian view.

3. Develop an iMovie in which the Italians consider their next steps after Menelik II rejects as out of hand any attempt to establish an Italian Protectorate over Ethiopia.

SUGGESTED SOURCES

Primary Sources

Blanc, Henri. *Narrative of Captivity in Abyssinia with some account of the Late Emperor Theodore, His Country, and People.* Charleston, SC: Biblio-Bazaar, 2005. Provides eyewitness information on Ethiopian views on European penetration of their country, prior to the Italian incursion in the 1890s.

Milkias, Paulos, and Getachew Metaferia. *The Battle of Adwa: Reflections on Ethiopia's Historic Victory Against European Colonialism.* New York: Algora Publishing, 2005. Includes excerpts from primary materials that may be useful.

Secondary Sources

Adejumobi, Saheed A. *The History of Ethiopia.* Westport, CT: Greenwood Press, 2006. An excellent general history of the country with considerable information on the Italian incursion during the 1880s.

Bahru, Zewde. *A History of Modern Ethiopia, 1855–1991.* 2nd ed. Eastern African Studies. Oxford: James Curry, 2001. A reliable and readable study of modern Ethiopia that includes data on the Ethiopian resistance to Italian imperialism.

Berkeley, G. F. H. *The Campaign of Adowa and the Rise of Menelik.* New York: Negro Universities Press, 1969. Excellent scholarly work on the victory and the leadership of Menelik II.

Boahen, A. Adu. *African Perspectives on Colonialism.* Baltimore, MD: The Johns Hopkins University Press, 1989. Includes information on Italian interest in East Africa and, in particular, Ethiopia.

Chamberlain, M. E. *The Scramble for Africa.* 2nd ed. Seminar Studies in History Series. New York: Longman, 1999. Includes some information on Italian imperial ambitions in East Africa.

Henze, Paul B. *Layers of Time: A History of Ethiopia.* New York: Palgrave Macmillan, 2004. A good general history that includes an introduction to Italo-Ethopian relations during the 1880s and 1890s.

Holmes, George, ed. *The Oxford Illustrated History of Italy.* New York: Oxford University Press, 2001. Includes data on Italian imperialism in East Africa.

Jones, A. H. M., and Elizabeth Monroe. *The History of Ethiopia.* Oxford: Clarendon Press, 1955. A dated but still useful and accessible general history that includes information on the treaty.

Marcus, Harold G. *A History of Ethiopia.* Updated ed. Berkeley: University of California Press, 2002. A very good history of the country with an excellent account of the Italian-Ethiopian crises of the 1880s and 1890s.

———. *The Life and Times of Menelik II: Ethiopia, 1844–1913.* Lawrenceville, NJ: Red Sea Press, 1995. An excellent biography of the great leader with extensive information on the treaty and the deterioration in Italian-Ethiopian relations.

Oliver, Roland. *Africa Since 1800.* 4th ed. Cambridge, U.K.: Cambridge University Press, 1994. Oliver's work is still worth reading and includes much relevant material that students will want to see.

Palumbo, Patrizia. *A Place in the Sun: Africa in Italian Colonial Culture from Post-Unification to the Present.* Berkeley: University of California Press, 2003. A scholarly study focused on Italian colonial ambitions in Africa.

Pankhurst. Richard. *The Ethiopians: A History.* Oxford: Wiley-Blackwell, 2001. A reliable history that includes data on Italian imperial ambitions in the late nineteenth century.

———. *Economic History of Ethiopia, 1800–1935.* Addis Ababa: Haile Sellassie I University Press, 1968. Provides valuable insights into the Italian interest in Ethiopia.

Pakenham, Thomas. *The Scramble for Africa: White Man's Conquest of the Dark Continent from 1876 to 1912.* New York: Avon Books, 1992. A standard work on European expansion in Africa that includes data on Italian colonialism.

Rosenfeld, C. P. *Empress Taytu and Menelik II: Ethiopia 1883–1910.* London: Ravens, 1986. An important dual biography of a significant relationship that had impact on the people of Ethiopia.

Shillington, Kevin. *Encyclopedia of African History.* London: CRC Press, 2005. An excellent and reliable reference work that should be useful to students working on this topic.

Stern, W. B. "The Treaty Background of the Italo-Ethiopian Dispute." *The American Journal of International Law* XXX (1936): 189–203. A very good article on the treaty and the confusion and manipulation associated with it.

World Wide Web

"Menelik II." http://www.infoplease.com/ce6/people/A0832671.html. A good introductory biography of the Ethiopian leader.

"Menelik II (1844–1913)." http://ethiopiamilitary.com/menelik-ii-1844-1913/. Provides information not found on other sites.

"Menelik II, Emperor of Ethiopia (1844–1913)." http://blackhistorypages.net/pages/menelikii.php. A very good account of Menelik II's role in confronting Italian imperialism.

"The Reign of Menelik II, 1889–1913." http://countrystudies.us/ethiopia/15.htm. A comprehensive statement on the impact of Menelik II on Ethiopian history.

"Treaty of Wuchale." http://www.experiencefestival.com/treaty_of_wuchale. Includes links to a range of articles on the treaty and the Italian-Ethiopian crisis.

"Treaty of Wuchale." http://www.nationmaster.com/encyclopedia/Treaty-of-Wuchale. A description of the treaty and its impact.

Multimedia Sources

"Menelik II." http://www.infoplease.com/ce6/people/A0832671.html. Includes illustrations and a map that may be useful to students.

"Treaty of Uccialli." http://www.encyclopedia.com/doc/1E1-X-Uccialli.html. Includes a map and an illustration.

89. Barings Crisis (1890)

In 1890 a financial panic occurred as a result of the near collapse of Barings, a British bank that dated back to the mid-eighteenth century. Barings had made a series of loans to Argentina which that country defaulted on because of an unanticipated financial and economic crisis. The South American crisis was connected to the Panama Scandal in France and an effort to gain control of the market in copper.

The management of Barings had gambled on succeeding in gaining control of Argentinean cooper. Its leaders had overextended the bank's capacity for debt and, when the Argentina investments failed, Barings was in crisis and ready to dissolve. The bank appealed to the Bank of England for a rescue intervention. Bank of England officials worked with Argentinean leaders to reschedule debt payments and to recast the currency. This allowed Barings to restructure its organization and finances.

TERM PAPER SUGGESTIONS

1. Write a paper on Barings-supported loans in Argentina during the 1880s. What did they hope to achieve? What were the investments based upon? Who made the decisions?
2. Develop a paper on the collapse of 1890 and the rescue plan that was developed by the Bank of England.
3. Write a paper on the impact of the crisis on the Argentinean economy.

ALTERNATIVE TERM PAPER SUGGESTIONS

1. Develop a podcast in which the leaders of Barings meet when they realize that a crisis had developed. Include their discussions on options, call money, and the commodity collapse.
2. Develop an iMovie in which the leaders of the Bank of England announce their rescue plan for Barings. What were the responsibilities that Barings had to assume? What was the role of the Argentine government in the plan?

SUGGESTED SOURCES

Primary Sources

"Barings PLC—Company History." http://www.fundinguniverse.com/company-histories/Barings-PLC-Company-History.html. Provides the official Barings statement on the crisis of 1890.

Duckenfield, Mark, Stefan Altorfer, and Benedikt Koehler, eds. *History of Financial Disasters, 1763–1995*. 3 vols. London: Pickering and Chatto, 2006. Includes primary materials on the crisis.

Wolff, Henry Drummond. *Rambling Recollections*. London: Macmillan, 1908. Personal recollections by Britain's ambassador to Spain who had first-hand information on the crisis.

Secondary Sources

Cairncross, Alec K. *Home and Foreign Investment, 1870–1913, Studies in Capital Accumulation.* Cambridge, U.K.: Cambridge University Press, 1953. Includes important information on the Barings Crisis in Argentina.

della Paolera, Gerardo, and Alan M. Taylor. *Straining at the Anchor: The Argentine Currency Board and the Search for Macroeconomic Stability, 1880–1935.* Chicago: University of Chicago Press, 2001. An important study with the credit collapse of 1890 as a focus.

Eichengreen, Barry. "The Baring Crisis in a Mexican Mirror." *International Political Science Review* 20, no. 3 (1999): 249–270. A very good article on the crisis and its impact on Mexico.

Engels, Wolfram, Armin Gutowski, and Henry C. Wallich, eds. *International Capital Movements, Debt and Monetary System.* Mainz: Hase & Koehler, 1984. Includes an essay by the late Professor Charles P. Kindleberger (Massachusetts Institute of Technology) that relates to the crisis.

Ferns, H. S. *Britain and Argentina in the Nineteenth Century.* Oxford: Clarendon Press, 1960. Includes extensive information on the Barings Crisis and its impact on both British banks and Argentine credit and economy.

———. "The Baring Crisis Revisited." *Journal of Latin American Studies* 24 (1992): 241–273. A reassessment of the crisis in light of the hundred years of financial problems since 1890.

Ford, Alec G. "Argentina and the Baring Crisis of 1890." *Oxford Economic Papers* 8, no. 2 (1956): 127–150. A most reliable and useful account of the crisis that is readily accessible.

———. *The Gold Standard, 1880–1914: Britain and Argentina.* Oxford: Clarendon Press. 1962. Includes information on the crisis and its impact on both financial systems.

Joslin, David. *A Century of Banking in Latin America; to Commemorate the Centenary in 1962 of the Bank of London & South America Limited.* New York: Oxford University Press, 1963. Includes relevant data on the Barings Crisis.

Marichal, Carlos. *A Century of Debt Crises in Latin America.* Princeton, NJ: Princeton University Press, 1989. An important study that provides an analysis of the crisis.

Meissner, Christopher M. (2005), "New World Order: Explaining the International Diffusion of the Gold Standard, 1870–1913." *Journal of International Economics* 66, no. 2 (2005): 385–406. Includes references to the Barings Crisis that may be useful to students working on this topic.

Suter, Christian. *Debt Cycles in the World Economy: Foreign Loans, Financial Crises and Debt Settlements, 1820–1990.* Boulder, CO: Westview, 1992. Provides some information on the Barings Crisis and its impact.

Williams, John H. *Argentine International Trade under Inconvertible Paper Currency, 1880–1900.* Cambridge, MA: Harvard University Press, 1920. A dated but still useful study that includes information on the Barings Crisis and its consequences.

Wirth, Max. "The Crisis of 1890." *Journal of Political Economy* 1 (1893): 214–235. A contemporary report on the crisis and its immediate impact on the world economy.

Ziegler, Philip. *The Sixth Great Power: A History of One of the Greatest of All Banking Families, the House of Barings, 1762–1929.* New York: Alfred A. Knopf, 1988. A history of Barings that includes relevant data on the crisis of 1890 and its impact on the bank, Argentina, and banking.

World Wide Web

"Argentina and the Baring Crisis of 1890." http://oep.oxfordjournals.org/cgi/content/citation/8/2/127. An article by A. G. Ford on the bond crisis of 1890.

"A Microeconomic Analysis of the Baring Crisis, 1880–1890." http://emlab.berkeley.edu/users/webfac/eichengreen/e211_fa05/211_baring.pdf.
A scholarly article by Juan Huitzi Flores in which he examines the impact of the extended market on Argentinean bonds during the 1880s and the crisis of 1890.

"Baring Crisis." http://www.encyclopedia.com/doc/1O48-Baringcrisis.html. An introductory statement on the crisis.

"The Baring Crisis and the Great Latin American Meltdown of the 1890s." http://www.crei.cat/activities/sc_conferences/31/MW_Baring%20Crisis.pdf. A scholarly article by Kris James Michener and Marc D. Weidenmier (2007) in which the impact of the crisis is considered beyond Argentina and the United Kingdom.

Multimedia Source

"Argentina." http://encarta.msn.com/encyclopedia_761556250_11/argentina.html. A multimedia site that provides information on the crisis of 1890, 75 multimedia images (some that relate), and an excellent interactive map.

90. *Rerum Novarum (On Capital and Labor)* Is Published (1891)

After the long pontificate of the reactionary Pope Pius IX (1847–1878), the more moderate Pope Leo XIII (1810–1903; reign, 1878–1903) succeeded to the papal throne. Rather than avoiding contemporary issues and concerns, Leo XIII published a series of papal encyclicals and decrees on Catholic social teaching that addressed the problems of modern society. Leo XIII's thoughts on social teaching were—to a large degree— shaped by the writings of the Bishop of Mainz, Wilhelm Emmanuel von Ketteler (1811–1877), who argued that the Catholic Church had to identify with the needs of the poor and dispossessed. Leo XIII's most important papal encyclical was *Rerum Novarum (On Capital and Labor)* (1891), in which he responded to the problems associated with the industrial economy. In particular, he was concerned with the conditions of labor and the potential for social disorder. He feared that socialism would continue to grow if the existing conditions persisted. Leo XIII argued the case for private property and the need for social justice in which the rights of labor had to be recognized and respected. The capitalists and the workers both have obligations to one another. The capitalist must provide a living wage and reasonable working conditions. The workers have an obligation to work for their wages and to respect the owner and his property. Through *Rerum Novarum* and other writings, Leo XIII repositioned the Roman Catholic Church and the Papacy so that it was viewed as a more moderate—though still conservative—force in world politics and economics.

TERM PAPER SUGGESTIONS

1. Write a paper in which you analyze the influence of Bishop von Ketteler's thoughts on Leo XIII's social consciousness.
2. Analyze the contents of *Rerum Novarum.*
3. Write a paper on the reception that *Rerum Novarum* received in Europe.

ALTERNATIVE TERM PAPER SUGGESTIONS

1. Develop a podcast in which Leo XIII discusses the core values that he wishes to state in *Rerum Novarum.*

2. Develop an iMovie in which the French and British Roman Catholic bishops react to the promulgation of *Rerum Novarum*. What are the advantages and disadvantages that they see for their Church in taking such a stance?

3. As an Italian seminarian, you welcome the proclamation of *Rerum Novarum*. Create a blog about its significance and how it will be helpful to you.

SUGGESTED SOURCES

Primary Sources

Leo XIII, Pope. *On the Condition of the Working Classes*. Chicago: Pauline Books, 2000. In addition to the copy of the official (unsigned) translation, valuable notes and commentary are included.

————. *Rerum Novarum: Encyclical Letter on the Condition of the Working Classes*. London: Catholic Truth Society, 1983. A copy of the encyclical with commentary.

————. *The Great Encyclical Letters of Pope Leo XIII*. New York: Benziger, 1903. Includes *Rerum Novarum* and all of the other encyclicals issued by Leo XIII.

————. *The Pope and the People: Select Letters and Addresses on Social Questions*. Rev. ed. London: Catholic Truth Society, 1913. Includes a multitude of documents by Leo XIII on Catholic social teaching.

"*Rerum Novarum*, Encyclical of Pope Leo XIII on Capital and Labor." http://www.vatican.va/holy_father/leo_xiii/encyclicals/documents/hf_l-xiii_enc_15051891_rerum-novarum_en.html. Official translation of the encyclical with some additional information.

"*Rerum Novarum* (On Capital and Labor)." http://www.papalencyclicals.net/Leo13/l13rerum.htm. Official translation of the encyclical.

Secondary Sources

Burton, Katherine. *Leo the Thirteenth: The First Modern Pope*. New York: D. McKay, 1962. A reliable and useful biography with extensive information on *Rerum Novarum* and its background.

Carlen, Mary C. *A Guide to the Encyclicals of the Roman Pontiffs from Leo XIII to the Present Day*. New York: H. W. Wilson, 1939. Includes this encyclical with commentary.

Clarke, Richard Henry. *The Life of His Holiness Pope Leo XIII*. Philadelphia: Ziegler, 1903. An old but very readable and reliable biography.

Corrin, Jay P. *Catholic Intellectuals and the Challenge of Democracy*. Notre Dame: University of Notre Dame Press, 2002. Includes a very good chapter on "Leo XIII and the Principles of *Rerum Novarum*."

Coppa, Frank J., ed. *The Great Popes Through History: An Encyclopedia.* Westport, CT: Greenwood Press, 2002. An excellent resource on the life and work of Leo XIII.

Furlong, Paul, and David Curtis, eds. *The Church Faces the Modern World: Rerum Novarum and Its Impact.* Scunthorpe, U.K.: Earlsgate Press, 1994. A collection of essays on the encyclical and its implications.

Hall, Arthur D. *A Life of the Pope, Leo the Thirteenth.* New York: Street and Smith, 1899. A sympathetic account of the life of Leo XIII.

Husslein, Joseph C. *The Christian Social Manifesto: An Interpretative Study of the Encyclicals Rerum Novarum and Quadragesimo Anno of Pope Leo XIII.* Rev. ed. Milwaukee: Bruce, 1939. An excellent analysis of the encyclical with extensive commentary.

McCarthy, Justin. *Pope Leo XIII.* New York: Frederick Wame, 1896. Another sympathetic and nonetheless reliable and readable biography of Leo XIII.

Molony, John. *The Worker Question: A New Historical Perspective on Rerum Novarum.* New York: HarperCollins, 1998. An analysis of the issues that motivated the encyclical and make it relevant today.

O'Byrne, Patrick Justin. *The Life and Pontificate of Pope Leo XIII.* London: Washbourne, 1903. Sympathetic but useful.

O'Reilly, Bernard. *Life of Leo XIII.* London: Sampson Low, 1903. Perhaps the best of the biographies that appeared shortly after the death of Leo XIII.

Soderini, Eduardo. *The Pontificate of Leo XIII.* Trans. Barbara Barclay Carter. London: Burns, Oates and Washbourne, 1934. A scholarly assessment of the reign of Leo XIII with considerable information on *Rerum Novarum.*

Staab, Giles. *The Dignity of Man in Modern Papal Doctrine: Leo XIII to Pius XII, 1878–1955.* Washington, DC: Catholic University of America Press, 1957. Excellent on Leo XIII and *Rerum Novarum.*

Wallace, Lillian Parker. *Leo XIII and the Rise of Socialism.* Durham, NC: Duke University Press, 1966. A scholarly assessment of Leo XIII social teachings within the context of the ascendancy of Marxist thought.

World Wide Web

"Rerum Novarum." http://www.newadvent.org/cathen/12783a.htm. Excellent narrative on the encyclical, its contents, and significance.

"Rerum Novarum." http://www.britannica.com/EBchecked/topic/498960/Rerum-Novarum. A reliable description of the encyclical and its contents.

Multimedia Sources

"Leo XIII." http://www.youtube.com/watch?v=ZCIrT5g5g3g&feature=rela
    ted. Video clip recorded in 1896. While this is in Italian, it is readily
    understood.

"Pope Leo XIII (Gioacchino Pecci 1878–1903)." http://www.youtube.com/
    watch?v=ai8DEWmZF34. Brief video of Pope Leo XIII.

"Voice of Pope Leo XIII." http://www.youtube.com/watch?v=o9Pv-UuGU
    DM&feature=related. Recorded in 1903 shortly before Leo XIII's
    death.

91. Siamese Crisis (1893)

During the last decades of the nineteenth century, Siam's (Thailand) influence in South and Southeast Asia declined as Britain and France expanded
their presence in the region. From its vantage point in India, Britain moved
east on Burma and then on to the southeast to the Malay Peninsula. During
the 1860s France moved on Indo-China—especially the Mekong Delta in
South Vietnam. From there they established a protectorate over Cambodia.
These actions were motivated by the hope to create French control over
trade with southeast China. With that in mind, the French initiated diplomatic, political, and economic activities in Laos. These developments
increased tensions between France and Siam, which viewed itself as being
surrounded by the European imperialists. The French aggravated the situation by sending ships into Siamese waters, and violent conflict broke out
in April 1893 between the French and Siamese forces in Laos. In July,
French naval forces entered Bangkok Harbor and threatened to move on
the city. Siamese resistance was not organized and collapsed by the late
summer. In October the war was over when the Siamese agreed to French
occupation of several provinces and an extensive zone along the Mekong
river. Within a year, Laos was surrendered to France.

TERM PAPER SUGGESTIONS

1. Write a paper on the causes of the Siamese Crisis of 1893.
2. Develop a paper in which you compare French and British ambitions in the
   region. What part did Siam play in these plans?
3. Write a paper on the prosecution of the Siamese-French War of 1893.
4. Develop a paper on the consequences of the war.

ALTERNATIVE TERM PAPER SUGGESTIONS

1. Develop two hyperlink maps of Siam and its environs before and after the Siamese crisis of 1893. Provide a narrative that explains all of the changes that occurred.

2. Develop a podcast in which the Siamese leadership considers its options in countering the French move on Laos. Be sure to include their evaluation of their own internal abilities to resist this encroachment.

3. Develop an iMovie in which French leaders coordinate their offensive operations in Laos and on the high seas.

SUGGESTED SOURCES

Primary Sources

Bailey, Nigel, ed. *Two Views of Siam on the Eve of the Chakri Reformation.* Arran, U.K.: Kiscadale, 1989. A very useful look into conditions in Siam prior to the crisis of 1893.

Great Britain. House of Lords Debate, September 4, 1893. "Franco-Siamese Crisis." http://hansard.millbanksystems.com/lords/1893/sep/04/the -franco-siamese-crisis. Official document on the British concerns about the Franco-Siamese crisis and its impact on British interests.

Secondary Sources

Bailey, Nigel. "The Scramble for Concessions in 1880s Siam." *Modern Asian Studies* XXXIII (1999): 513–549. A study of French and British interest in Siam prior to the 1893 crisis.

Baker, Christopher John, and Pasuk Phongpaicht. *A History of Thailand.* New York: Cambridge University Press, 2005. Includes useful information on the crisis and its aftermath.

Chula, Prince. *Lords of Life: The Paternal Monarchy of Bangkok, 1782–1932.* New York: Taplinger, 1960. A good history of the Siamese monarchy—includes information on the Siamese crisis with France in 1893.

Levy, Roger. *French Interests and Policies in the Far East.* New York: AMS Press, 1978. An excellent study that approaches the crisis from the French perspective. All students working on this topic should see this important book.

Mahajan, Sineh. *British Foreign Policy 1874–1914: The Role of India.* Bristol, PA: Taylor and Francis, 2003. A very good student of British interest in South Asia and its position during the Siamese Crisis of 1893.

St. John, Ronald Bruce, and Clive H. Schofield. *The Land Boundaries of Indochina: Cambodia, Laos and Vietnam.* Durham, U.K.: IBRU, 1998. Excellent reference source in boundary disputes and changes.

Tarling, Nichola. *Nationalism in Southeast Asia.* London: Routledge/Curzon, 2004. Includes information on the Siamese reaction to French encroachment in the 1880s and 1890s.

"The Franco-Siamese War, An Amiable Settlement." *Wanganui Herald* XXVII (August 3, 1893): 3. Contemporary newspaper article on the Siamese crisis.

Wyatt, David K. *Thailand: A Short History.* 2nd ed. New Haven, CT: Yale University Press, 2003. Provides a useful introduction to the crisis.

World Wide Web

"Anglo-French Crisis." http://www.bartleby.com/67/1406.html. Useful introduction to the crisis and its consequences.

"Franco-Siamese Relations." http://www.questia.com/PM.qst?a=o&d=7688 444. An excerpt from Graham Stuart's *French Foreign Policy from Fashoda to Serajevo* (1921).

"Franco-Siamese War 1893." http://www.onwar.com/aced/nation/tap/thailand/ffrancesiam1893.htm. A brief but fact-filled statement that may be useful as an introduction to the crisis and war.

"French Gunboat Diplomacy on Siam, 1893." http://www.geocities.com/gunboatmissionary/FrenchSiam1893.html. Includes illustration and statistics on the French ships.

"Journalists Reporting on the Franco-Siamese War, 1893." http://www.scoop-database.com/browse/by_conflicts_wars/1890s/franco-siamese_war_1893. Provides a list of the Western journalists who covered the crisis and war.

"Russia Will Support France; And China Will Lend Her Aid to Siam." http://query.nytimes.com/gst/abstract.html?res=9C05E0DB103BEF33A25 752C2A9619C94629ED7CF. An article from *The New York Times,* July 25, 1893, 5, in which the Franco-Russian entente appears to be in operation.

"Thailand History: 1500–2007. European Colonial Expansion Complicates Things." http://www.csmngt.com/Thailand_History_1511_2006.htm. Includes a useful map and information on the crisis.

"Thailand, the Crisis of 1893." http://www.workmall.com/wfb2001/thailand/thailand_history_the_crisis_of_1893.html. A comprehensive description of the crisis and its impact on South Asia.

"The Chakri Kings of Thailand—the Golden Age of Rattanakosin." http://www.tour-bangkok-legacies.com/chakri-kings.html. Through a series of links this site provides information on the nineteenth-century and early twentieth-century leaders of Siam.

Multimedia Sources

"Art of the Paknam Incident." http://commons.wikimedia.org/wiki/Image:
Art_of_Paknam_incident.jpg. French ships *Inconstant* and *Comète* under
fire in the Paknam incident, July 13,1893, during the Franco-Siamese War.

"Franco-Siamese Skirmish 1893." http://bbs.keyhole.com/ubb/showthreaded
.php?Cat=0&Board=EarthMilitary&Number=196693&fpart=1&PH
PSESSID=. Provides Google maps of the Phra Chulachomklao Fortress,
or Paknam Fort, which was completed in 1893 before it witnessed action
during the Siamese Crisis.

92. Sino-Japanese War (1894–1895)

The Sino-Japanese War (August 1, 1894–April 17, 1895) was ostensibly
fought over control of Korea but, in fact, was a struggle between China
and Japan for a dominant position in East Asia. Both nations had under-
taken modernization efforts. The "Self-Strengthening Movement" in
China was designed to cultivate Chinese power through upgrading its
influence vis à vis the reform and enhancement of its historic traditions.
Japan, on the other hand, had invested heavily in a westernization process
since the advent of the Meiji regime in 1868. The immediate cause for
the outbreak of the war was an uprising of the outlawed Tonghuk sect
in Korea against Chinese authorities. China suppressed the rebellion.
Japan sent a military force to Korea to protect the Koreans, but China
hoped that a war could be avoided through diplomacy. False confidence
in that outcome delayed the mobilization of China's military, and war
broke out on August 1, 1894, after a Chinese troop ship had been sunk.
From the very outset the Japanese prevailed in the struggle, and by the
winter Japan had scored a series of victories with no losses. The Chinese
navy suffered a devastating loss in the Battle of the Yalu in September.
The leadership of the Chinese government was overturned, and the new
government sued for peace with Japan. On April 17, 1895, the war came
to an end with the Treaty of Shimonoseki, which included the following
terms: China was forced to recognize the independence of Korea and
pay a war indemnity, Taiwan was given to Japan, and China had to grant
Japan access to several ports. Victory in the war enhanced the reputation
of Japan in the region and among the European powers. Within a decade
the Europeans would begin to assess Japan's power differently when it

defeated the Russians in the Russo-Japanese War. The weakness of China served as an invitation for additional colonial encroachments and hastened the collapse of the Chinese empire in 1911.

TERM PAPER SUGGESTIONS

1. Write a paper on the background and general causes of the Sino-Japanese War.
2. Develop a paper on the "Self-Strengthening Movement" in China. What was it intended to achieve? Was it successful?
3. Compare and contrast the military leadership of China and Japan during the Sino-Japanese War.
4. Compare and contrast the preparedness of China and Japan for this conflict.
5. What was the impact of the war on both powers?

ALTERNATIVE TERM PAPER SUGGESTIONS

1. As a member of the American State Department Far Eastern Desk, create a blog that evaluates the origins and consequences of the Sino-Japanese War on American interests in the region and comment on any adjustments that need to be made in American foreign policy.
2. You are a Korean farmer with extensive holdings. Write a blog on the meaning of this war for you and other Korean landowners.

SUGGESTED SOURCES

Primary Sources

Davids, Jules, ed. *American Diplomatic and Public Papers—The United States and China: Series III, the Sino-Japanese War to the Russo-Japanese War, 1894–1905.* Wilmington, DE: Scholarly Resources, 1981. A valuable collection of printed primary materials that focuses on America's interests and concerns in the Sino-Japanese War.

Munemitsu, Mutsu. *Kenkenroku: A Diplomatic Record of the Sino-Japanese War, 1894–95.* Ed. and trans. Gordon Mark Berger. Tokyo: University of Tokyo Press, 1995. This is a valuable and useful memoir of the war by a prominent Japanese diplomat.

Murray, John Van Antwerp. *Treaties and Agreements with and Concerning China, 1894–1919: A Collection.* 2 vols. Oxford: Oxford University Press, 1921. [Digitalized, Harvard University, 2007]. Contains most of the essential public agreements on the war.

Nish, Ian, ed. *British Documents on Foreign Affairs: Reports and Papers from the Foreign Office Confidential Print. From the Mid-Nineteenth Century to the First World War, Series E, Asia, 1860–1914.* 30 vols. Frederick, MD: University Publications of America, 1989. This indispensable set of primary documents includes a volume on the Sino-Japanese War (vol. 4) and another on the war and the Triple Intervention (vol. 5)

Secondary Sources

Chaikin, Nathan. *The Sino-Japanese War (1894–1895).* London: Art Books International, 1997. A useful study that provides an interdisciplinary approach to the war.

Dorwart, Jeffrey M. *The Pigtail War: American Involvement in the Sino-Japanese War of 1894–1895.* Amherst: University of Massachusetts Press, 1975. A study of American policy and actions during the war, which reflect the competing colonial interests of the United States and Japan.

Kajima, Morinosuke. *The Diplomacy of Japan 1894–1922.* 3 vols. Tokyo: Kajima Institute of International Peace, 1976–1980. An excellent study of Japan's expansionist foreign policy in East Asia. Useful maps have been included.

Lone, Stewart. *Japan's First Modern War: Army and Society in the Conflict with China, 1894–95.* New York: St. Martin's Press in association with Ling's College, London, 1994. This important work not only examines the war itself but also the transforming nature of the war and its impact on both societies.

Ono, Giichi. *Expenditures of the Sino-Japanese War.* Oxford: Oxford University Press, 1922. [Digitalized, University of Michigan, 2006]. Ono advances an argument that is sympathetic to Japan.

Paine, S. C. M. *The Sino-Japanese War of 1894–1895: Perceptions, Power, and Primacy.* New ed. New York: Cambridge University Press, 2003. In this important scholarly work, Paine presents a thorough examination of Japan's quick victory and the impact of that on the European view of East Asia with the dominant power being Japan. It includes useful maps and bibliography.

Worthing, Peter M. *A Military History of Modern China: From the Manchu Conquest to Tian'anmen Square.* Westport, CT: Praeger Security International, 2007. This is a very good recent study based on reliable sources. It includes a section on the Sino-Japanese War of 1894–1895.

World Wide Web

Dower, John W. "Visualizing Japan," unit of "Throwing Off Asia, Part A: Power Point on Random Sample of Sino-Japanese War." Boston, MA: Massachusetts Institute of Technology, 2006. http://ocw.mit.edu/ans7870/

21f/21f.027j/throwing_off_asia/cur_student/toa_cur_02.html. Course materials from Dower's course at the Massachusetts Institute of Technology.

"The Sino-Japanese War, 1894–1895." Web site of the Russo-Japanese War Research Society, 2002. http://www.russojapanesewar.com/chino-war.html. Offers a description of the war and some insights into its impact on the entire region of East Asia.

Wang, Jane W. "Crossroads in Sino-Japanese Relations: Exploring the Impact of Anti-Japanese Sentiment on Japanese Firms' Business Relations in China." Thesis, the Fletcher School, Tufts University, 2005. http://www.fletcher.tufts.edu/research/2005/Wang.pdf. Provides information on the Sino-Japanese War and its impact on the subsequent relationship between the two states.

Multimedia Source

Okamoto, Shumpei. *Impressions of the Front: Woodcuts of the Sino-Japanese War, 1894–95.* Philadelphia: Philadelphia Museum of Art, 1983. This is a catalog of Okamoto woodcuts from an exhibit that was held at the Philadelphia Museum of Art, April 23 to June 26, 1983.

93. Armenian Massacres (1894–1896)

During the last 25 years of the nineteenth century, the Ottoman Empire (Turkey) was viewed as "the dying man of Europe." Poorly led, financed, and organized, it was viewed as vulnerable by the Russians, Austrians, and several internal ethnic groups. During the Russo-Turkish War of 1877–1878, Russia seized Turkish land, claiming that it was defending the Christian ethnic minority. The Ottoman Sultan Abdul Hamid II (1842–1918; ruled 1876–1909) responded by calling for an Islamic revival. Within his borders, he actively persecuted Christian minorities who did not comply with his laws or indicated that they sought independence. The Armenians were the largest group of Christians within the Empire and, to Abdul Hamid II, a threat to Islam and his government. The Armenians established a resistance movement and armed themselves, but they were no match for the professional Turkish military units that were involved in the massacres. Between 1894 and 1896, there were between 100,000 and 300,000 Armenian men, women, and children slaughtered. While violence against the Armenians occurred throughout the Ottoman Empire, most of the series incidents occurred in Anatolia. The holocaust was followed by many other massacres through the next several decades. Even after the establishment of the modern Turkish state after World War I, the Armenian massacres continued. For the most part, European nations—especially Britain—condemned the atrocities but no serious actions were taken to curtail them

TERM PAPER SUGGESTIONS

1. Develop a paper on the origins and causes for the Armenian massacres of 1894–1896—who was primarily responsible?
2. Were the Armenian massacres of 1894–1896 the result of the Turkish policy of genocide against them?
3. Develop a paper on the prosecution of the massacres between 1894 and 1896.
4. Write a paper in which you analyze the British responses to the massacres.
5. Develop a paper in which you assess the consequences of the massacres.

ALTERNATIVE TERM PAPER SUGGESTIONS

1. As a member of the Armenian resistance movement, you meet frequently with colleagues to discuss plans and report on actions. Develop a 4–5 minute iMovie in which you participate in such a meeting in 1895.
2. Develop a podcast in which Sultan Abdul Hamid II explains the actions of his government against the Armenians.
3. As a member of the staff of the British Embassy in Constantinople, establish a blog on the massacres.

SUGGESTED SOURCES

Primary Sources

Harris, James Rendell, and Helen B. Harris. *Letters from the Scenes of the Recent Massacres in Armenia.* London: J. Nesbet, 1897. A highly descriptive and critical primary source that should be useful to many students.

Hodgetts, Edward Arthur. *Round About Armenia: The Record of a Journal across the Balkans through Turkey, the Caucasus and Persia.* London: Sampson Low and Marston, 1916; originally published in 1896. Personal recollections of an international traveler who came into contact with the horrors of the massacres.

Graves, Robert. *Storm Centres of the Near East: Personal Memories, 1879–1929.* London: Hutchinson, 1933. Includes significant information on the massacre at Sassun and the investigation that followed.

Kirakossian, Arman J., ed. *The Armenian Massacres, 1894–1896: British Media Testimony.* Dearborn: Armenian Research Center/University of Michigan, Dearborn, 2008. A valuable volume that consists of 49 contemporary publications, many of them primary sources, on the Armenian massacres.

————, ed. *The Armenian Massacres, 1894–1896: U.S. Media Testimony.* Detroit: Wayne State University Press, 2004. Kirakossian's comparable volume on the American media's coverage of the massacres.

Miller, Donald E., and Lorna Touryan Miller. *Survivors: An Oral History of the Armenian Genocide.* Berkeley: University of California Press, 1999. While focused mostly on the twentieth century, the introduction and initial chapter of this volume are of value on the Armenian Massacre of 1895.

"Outrages in Armenia." *London Daily Telegraph* (December 17, 1894): 5. An unattributed eyewitness account of some of the anti-Armenian actions of the Ottoman Turks.

Pierce, James Wilson, ed. *The Story of Turkey and Armenia with a Full and Accurate Account of the Recent Massacres Written by an Eye-witness. A Sketch of Clara Barton and the Red Cross.* Baltimore: R. H. Woodward, 1896. A useful primary source that is critical of the genocide.

Secondary Sources

Akcam, Taner. *A Shameful Act: The Armenian Genocide and the Question of Turkish Responsibility.* New York: Holt, 2007. Critical of the Ottoman Turks for their responsibility for the massacres.

Aslan, Kevork. *Armenia and the Armenians: From the Earliest Times until the Great War (1914).* Trans. Pierre Crabitès. Chestnut Hill, MA: Elibron/Adamant Media, 2004; originally published in 1920. Includes valuable information on the massacres of the 1890s.

Eliot, Charles. *Turkey in Europe.* 2nd ed. London: Frank Cass, 1965. Includes a series of essays, some of which address the massacres.

Filian, George H. *Armenia and Her People, or the Story of Armenia by an Armenian.* Hartford: American Publishing, 1896. A sympathetic account of the horrors perpetrated on the Armenians.

Goodwin, Jason. *Lords of the Horizons: A History of the Ottoman Empire.* London: Picador, 2003. Useful introduction to the Armenian question in Turkish history.

Greene, Frederick Davis. *Armenian Massacres, or The Sword of Mohammed . . . .* Philadelphia: American Oxford, 1896. Focuses on the anti-Christian nature of the massacres.

Hovannisian, Richard G., ed. *The Armenian People from Ancient to Modern Times.* 2 vols. New York: Palgrave Macmillan, 2004. The second volume in this set provides an excellent introduction to the Armenian Massacre of 1895.

———. *The Armenian Genocide: History, Politics, Ethics.* London: Palgrave Macmillan, 1992. This important study should be useful to most students working on this topic.

Lewy, Guenter. *The Armenian Massacres in Ottoman Turkey: A Disputed Genocide.* Salt Lake City: University of Utah Press, 2005. Presents both sides on the violence but recognizes the ultimate responsibility of the Ottoman Turks.

MacColl, Malcom. "The Constantinople Massacre and its Lesson." *Contemporary Review* LVIII (November 1895): 744–760. A contemporary's analysis of an event during the massacres in which the Turks are held accountable.

Northrop, Henry Davenport, ed. *The Mohammedan Reign of Terror in Armenia.* Philadelphia: American Oxford, 1896. A polemic condemnation of the Turks for the atrocities against the Armenians.

Terrion, Yves. *The Armenians: History of a Genocide.* Trans. R. C. Cholakian. Delmar, NY: Caravan Books, 1981. A sympathetic analysis of the massacres that the Armenians experienced in their history.

Vickery, Bess. P. *Mount Holyoke Courageous: Young Christian Women Go to the Near East, 1840–72 and Respond to the Armenian Holocaust 1872, 1895, 1915.* Rev. ed. New York: Roundtable Press, 2000. A contemporary's sympathetic account of the Armenian massacres.

World Wide Web

"Armenian Genocide." http://www.dersimsite.org/armenian.html. Provides a timeline of the 1894–1895 incidents that constituted the massacre.

"Armenian Genocide Timeline." http://www.littlearmenia.com/html/genocide/genocide_timeline.asp#1895. Places these massacres in the context of the multiple massacres that the Armenian experiences during the late nineteenth and early twentieth centuries.

"The Armenian Massacres of 1894–1897: A Bibliography." http://www.zoryaninstitute.org/Table_Of_Contents/genocide_biblio_massacres.htm. An extensive and reliable bibliography on the massacres that is divided into regional atrocities.

"The Ottoman Empire and the Armenian Genocide." http://www.armenian-genocide.org/ottoman.html. Introductory material that should be useful to many students.

Multimedia Source

Armenia: The Betrayed. BBC documentary, 2003. http://video.google.com/
videoplay?docid=-7833166317264817428. Includes a section on these
massacres within the context of the entire anti-Armenian Turkish policy.

94. Jameson Raid (1895–1896)

During the last quarter of the nineteenth century, relations between the
Boers (Europeans of Dutch ancestry who came to South Africa during
the early decades of the nineteenth century to practice their religion without persecution) and the British were aggravated primarily by British
commercial interests and the influx of British colonists in South Africa.
The extent of natural sources—both real and imagined—became a major
concern during the 1880s and 1890s when the diamond fields were discovered and exploited. Even in the Boer areas, the number of British
increased dramatically. In the 1890s the Boer government attempted to
restrict the voting rights of the *Uitlanders*—the British. In South Africa,
British policy was driven by Cecil Rhodes, quite independent of the
Colonial and Foreign Offices in London. Rhodes, who headed a quasi-
public charter company, was determined to overthrow the Boers and seize
their lands for Britain. The raid that he planned was designed to trigger a
Uitlander revolt against the Boers. Rhodes thought the incursion would
reach Johannesburg. The raid was planned for the summer of 1895 but
was delayed because of several factors. Nonetheless, Rhodes's plan was ini-
tiated by Leander Starr Jameson, a British colonial administrator for
Matabeleland, a region under British control. On December 29, 1895,
Jameson led a force of about 500 armed men across the border into the
Transvaal. As soon as Joseph Chamberlain, the British Colonial Secretary,
learned of the raid, he intervened to make it fail. The British living in the
Transvaal were urged not to aid or support Jameson and his forces.
Chamberlain feared a rapid escalation of the conflict and wanted to avoid
an unpopular war that was initiated by British citizens. Jameson's band
encountered opposition on January 1, 1896, and on the next day was
defeated by the more numerous, better equipped and led Boers. Jameson
and most of his troops were captured and transported to a prison in Pretoria. The Boers turned the prisoners over to Britain and they were taken
to London. Jameson and many of his compatriots were tried, convicted,

and given prison terms—in spite of widespread public support in England for the Raid. During 1896–1897 the native Africans revolted against the British; that revolt was suppressed by the fall of 1897. Germany sent a congratulatory note to the Boers for defeating Jameson. The Jameson Raid failed to attain its objective and resulted in increased tensions between Britain and the Boers, as well as Germany and Britain.

TERM PAPER SUGGESTIONS

1. While many British supported the Jameson Raid and called for Jameson and the others involved to be found innocent of any crime, the British Colonial Secretary Joseph Chamberlain took what appeared to be contradictory positions on the Raid. Develop a paper on Chamberlain's views and motives before and after the Jameson Raid.

2. The rivalry between the Boers and the growing number of British colonists in South Africa led ultimately to the Boer War at the end of the century. Write an analytical paper on the Jameson Raid as a defining moment in that rivalry.

3. Historians have not been kind to Cecil Rhodes and his role in South African history. Write a paper in which you either defend or denounce Rhodes's role in the Jameson Raid and as a contributor in the deterioration of Anglo-Boer relations.

4. Jameson has been criticized for being the willing and not-too-bright agent of Rhodes. Develop a paper on Jameson's character, views, and political and military abilities.

5. Was the struggle between the Boers and the British primarily economic or national?

ALTERNATIVE TERM PAPER SUGGESTIONS

1. Using online material, develop a short iMovie on the role of Cecil Rhodes in planning the Jameson Raid.

2. Imagine that you are a farmer and a member of the Boer forces that defended the Transvaal. Write a series of letters to your wife describing your experiences and views.

SUGGESTED SOURCES

Primary Sources

Garrett, Fydell Edmund. *The Story of an African Crisis: Being the Truth about the Jameson Raid and Johannesburg Revolt of 1896, Told with the Assistance of the Leading Actors in the Drama.* Chestnut Hill, MA: Adamant Media Corporation, 2001. This is a reprint of the 1897 first edition of this book (Westminster: Archibald Constable, 1897), which is a critical account of the Raid.

Schreuder, D., and J. Butler, eds. *Sir Graham Bower's Secret History of the Jameson Raid and the South African Crisis, 1895–1902.* Cape Town: Van Riebeeck Society, 2002. Provides several primary sources on the Raid and its negative impact on Anglo-Boer relations.

Throup, David, ed. *British Documents on Foreign Affairs: Reports and Papers from the Foreign Office Confidential Print, Part 1, From the Mid-Nineteenth Century to the First World War. Series G. Africa, 1848–1914.* Bethesda, MD: University Publications of America, 1995. Includes several important Colonial Office documents relating to the Raid and the complex and contradictory views of Joseph Chamberlain.

Secondary Sources

Longford, Elizabeth. *Jameson's Raid: The Prelude to the Boer War.* Chicago: Academy Chicago Publishers, 1984. A very readable and mostly reliable account of the Raid within the context of Anglo-Boer relations.

Meredith, Martin. *Diamonds, Gold, and War: The British, Boers, and the Making of South Africa.* New York: Public Affairs, 2007. An acclaimed study of the Anglo-Boer rivalry over the resources of South Africa that includes a section on Jameson's Raid.

Naval and Military Press. *The Jameson Raid.* Uckfield, East Sussex, U.K.: Naval and Military Press, 2006. An institutional history focused on the strategy and tactics associated with the Jameson Raid.

The Jameson Raid: A Centennial Retrospective. Houghton, South Africa: Brenthurst Press, 1996. A balanced and worthwhile assessment of the place of the Jameson Raid in the history of South Africa.

World Wide Web

"Jameson Raid." http:www.thehistorychannel.co.uk/site/encyclopedia/article _show/Jameson_Leander_Starr_18531917. A brief history of the Raid with links

Multimedia Sources

Kipling, Rudyard. "If." Podcast, 2005. Read by Brian Johnson. http://www .learnoutloud.com/Catalog/literature/-/If/15422. A sympathetic poem written after the Raid.

"Jameson Raid Stock Photographs and Images." Wauhesha, WI: Pubitek, Inc.
http:www.fotosearch.com/photos-images/jameson-raid.html. Photographs and artistic renderings of Jameson and Rhodes.

Rhodes. PBS, 1998. BBC miniseries. 10 hours. An acclaimed drama focusing on
Cecil Rhodes and the expansion of British interests in South Africa.

95. Publication of *The Jewish State* by Theodor Herzl (1896)

In 1986 Theodor Herzl (1860–1904) published *The Jewish State* in which
he established a political and secular argument to resolve the continuing
Jewish issue in Western societies. Herzl was a correspondent for the *Neue
Freie Presse* in Paris and was deeply moved by the anti-Jewish (anti-Zionist)
rhetoric that dominated the early years of the Dreyfus Affair in Paris. Herzl
concluded that national assimilation would not work for the Jews and that
the establishment of a new Jewish state was the only practical alternative.
Herzl hoped to create an independent Jewish state that reflected the Jewish
legacy in the light of the values of European civilization. With the publication of the English translation of *The Jewish State* Herzl emerged as the
leader of Zionism. He gained a broad and devoted following among
European Jews and many non-Jewish leaders who sympathized with the discrimination that the Jews were experiencing. After its publication, Herzl
traveled to Istanbul, London, and Egypt where he argued for the establishment of a Jewish state in Palestine. In 1897 he organized the Zionist
Congress in Basel. Through the Zionist Congress, Herzl advanced his position and attempted to unify European Jewry behind it. Before his death in
1904, Herzl published *The Old Land* in which he envisioned the future of
Zionism. Herzl's writings influenced a generation of British leaders and
had impact on the formulation of the Balfour Declaration in 1917, which
called for the establishment of an independent Jewish state in Palestine.

TERM PAPER SUGGESTIONS

1. Write a paper on the evolution of Herzl's position from being an advocate of
   assimilation to calling for an independent Jewish state.

2. Develop a paper in which you describe Herzl's idea of the Jewish state.

3. How did European Jewry respond to Herzl's proposal during the years prior
   to his death?

4. What impact did the Dreyfus affair have on Herzl?

5. What reactions to Herzl's proposal developed from the non-Jewish segments of European society?

ALTERNATIVE TERM PAPER SUGGESTIONS

1. You are a Jew living in New England in 1900 and have experienced discrimination in school and at work. In a blog, describe your reaction to Herzl's book and movement. Will you continue to work to be assimilated into American society or do you think that you should actively support the establishment of a Jewish state?

2. As an east European merchant who is dependent upon Jews for laborers and consumers, write a blog in which you discuss whether you are alarmed about Herzl's call for a Jewish state. In 1900, does it appear to be another utopian dream advanced by a reformer or is this proposal gaining support among the Jews you know?

SUGGESTED SOURCES

Primary Sources

Herzl, Theodor. *The Jewish State.* Lafayette, LA: Bnpublishing.com, 2006. A recent edition of Herzl's classic book.

———. *The Old New Land.* Berkeley: FQ Publishing/University of California Press, 2007. This is the Herzl plan for the Jewish state, a secular state that rests upon a socialist/capitalist economy and rational government.

———. *Diaries of Theodor Herzl.* Gloucester, MA: Peter Smith, 1987. Provides excerpts from Herzl's diaries that are so revealing.

———. *Theodor Herzl: Excerpts from His Diaries.* 2 vols. Kila, MT: Kessinger Publishing, 2007. Another edition of the diaries that is very useful to all students.

Rosenberger, Erwin. *Herzl and I Remember Him.* Trans. Louis Jay Herman. New York: Herzl Press, 1959. A memoir by an associate of Herzl who had access to him and his thoughts.

Secondary Sources

Beller, Steven. *Theodor Herzl and Austria: A Century Later—An Essay.* Vienna: Austrian Federal Ministry for Foreign Affairs, 2004. A useful illustrated booklet on Herzl's work and influence in Austria.

———. *Herzl.* 2nd ed. London: Peter Halban, 2004. A reliable and readable biography of Herzl that advances the standard interpretation of his impact on Zionism and the establishment of the state of Israel.

Bernard, Sir Zissman. *Theodor Herzl: Conversations with a Zionist Legend.* Manchester, U.K.: Devora, 2008. A new and very readable book on Herzl that relies on a mastery of Herzl's ideas and values.

Elon, Amos. *Herzl.* New York: Holt, Rinehart and Winston, 1975. A reliable biography of Herzl, his age, and his impact on Judaism.

Falk, Avner. *Herzl, King of the Jews: A Psychoanalytic Biography of Theodor Herzl.* Bethesda, MD: University Press of America, 1993. An important but controversial study of the life and thoughts of Theodor Herzl.

Finkelstein, Norman H. *Theodor Herzl: Architect of a Nation.* Minneapolis: Lerner Publications, 1991. An introduction to Herzl's life and impact for high school readers. Finkelstein emphasizes that Herzl was transformed from an advocate of assimilation in his development to a bold promoter of a separatist Zionism.

Greenfield, Howard. *A Promise Fulfilled: Theodor Herzl, Chaim Weizmann, David Ben-Gurin, and the Creation of the State of Israel.* New York: Harper, 2005. Greenfield interprets Herzl as a nationalist who was not religious. This is a very good introduction to Herzl's contribution to the establishment of Israel.

Kornberg, Jacques. *Theodor Herzl: From Assimilation to Zionism.* Bloomington: Indiana University Press, 1993. Kornberg examines Herzl's life from 1878 to 1896 and argues that Herzl was not motivated by the Dreyfus affair as much as he was by the experiences of his youth and his support of national self-determination.

Krämer, Gudrun. *A History of Palestine, From the Ottoman Conquest to the Founding of the State of Israel.* Princeton, NJ: Princeton University Press, 2008. This scholarly work places Herzl within the context of historical processes that pre- and postdated him.

Pawel, Ernst. *The Labyrinth of Exile: A Life of Theodor Herzl.* New York: Farrar, Straus and Giroux, 1992. Herzl is portrayed as a secular and not very agreeable nationalist who moved—somewhat reluctantly—Zionism in the direction of a democratic movement.

Peres, Shimon. *The Imaginary Voyage: With Theodor Herzl in Israel.* Hanover, NH: Zoland Books, 2000. In this work of history and fiction, Peres imagines the impact of the holocaust, the establishment of Israel, and its subsequent successes and problems on Herzl.

Robertson, Ritchie, and Edward Timms, eds. *Theodor Herzl and the Origins of Zionism.* Edinburgh: Edinburgh University Press, 1997. Includes papers that were presented at the Germanic Institute conference that was held to honor Herzl in London (1996).

Shimoni, Gideon, and Robert S. Wistrich, eds. *Theodor Herzl: Visionary of the Jewish State.* New York: Herzl Press, 1999. This volume consists of the proceedings of the Herzl conference held at Hebrew University in 1996, and it includes the papers that were presented and extensive bibliographic references.

World Wide Web

"Theodor Herzl: On the Jewish State, 1896." *Modern History Sourcebook.* Fordham University Web site. http://www.fordham.edu/halsall/mod/1896herzl.html. Provides significant excerpts from Herzl's pamphlet.

Jewish Virtual Library. http://www.jewishvirtuallibrary.org. Provides access to many of Herzl's works and commentaries by others.

Heritage: Civilization and the Jews. http://www.pbs.org/wnet/heritage. A comprehensive Web site designed to provide materials for a PBS series.

Multimedia Source

Heritage: Civilization and the Jews. PBS, 1984. DVD/VHS boxed sets. Video series introduced by William W. Hallo, Yale University. Includes information on Herzl and the early decades of the Zionist movement.

96. Battle of Adowa (1896)

The Italian interest in colonies developed later than the other European powers. Italy considered a colonial empire to be a prerequisite of great power—it wanted to be ranked with the traditional leaders of Europe and an imperial agenda was a benchmark for such status. In the 1890s the Italians launched an offensive in Ethiopia, which was still independent and very underdeveloped. This action resulted in the First Italo-Ethiopian War. In 1896 Italian forces, under the command of General Oreste Baratieri (1841–1901), found themselves running short of supplies in February, so he decided to commit his 17,700 troops to a decisive battle. The Ethiopian army of about 80,000 under Menelik II (1844–1913) met the Italians on the morning of March 1, 1896, at Adowa (Adwa). By noon the Italians had been routed with more than 7,000 killed, 3,000 captured, and 1,500 wounded; the Ethiopians suffered about 4,500 killed and 8,000 wounded. The Ethiopian victory over the Italians shocked both Europeans and Africans alike. Europeans could not understand how a primitive force could defeat a fully armed native (nonwhite) force, and Africans developed considerable respect for the Ethiopians who managed to sustain their independence. In October 1896 the

Treaty of Addis Ababa ended the war. It recognized Ethiopian independence and formalized the boundary between Ethiopia and Italian-controlled Eritrea.

TERM PAPER SUGGESTIONS

1. Develop a term paper on the background and outbreak of the First Italo-Ethiopian War.
2. Write a paper on the Battle of Adowa—what errors did the Italians make? What contributed to the Ethiopian victory?
3. Develop a paper on the consequences of the Ethiopian victory at Adowa.

ALTERNATIVE TERM PAPER SUGGESTIONS

1. Develop a podcast of a discussion among European statesmen on the meaning of the Ethiopian victory at Adowa.
2. As an aide of Menelik II you are worried about the coming battle with the well-equipped Italian army. Create a blog on the preparations for the battle of Adowa. Be sure to comment on the leadership of Menelik II.
3. Develop an iMovie on the negotiations that led to the Treaty of Addis Ababa.

SUGGESTED SOURCES

Primary Sources

Blanc, Henri. *Narrative of Captivity in Abyssinia with Some Account of the Late Emperor Theodore, His Country, and People.* Charleston, SC: BiblioBazaar, 2005. Provides eyewitness information on Ethiopian views on European penetration of their country, prior to the Italian incursion in the 1890s.

Bulatovich, Alexander. *Ethiopia Through Russia Eyes, Country in Transition 1896–1898, with the Armies of Menelik II.* West Roxbury, MA: B&R Samizdat Express, 2007; originally published in 1900. A valuable eyewitness account to the battle.

Secondary Sources

Adejumobi, Saheed A. *The History of Ethiopia.* Westport, CT: Greenwood Press, 2006. An excellent general history of the country with considerable information on the battle of Adowa.

Bahru, Zewde. *A History of Modern Ethiopia, 1855–1991.* 2nd ed. Eastern African Studies. Oxford: James Curry, 2001. A reliable and readable study of modern Ethiopia that includes data on the Ethiopian resistance and defeat of the Italians at Adowa.

Berkeley, G. F. H. *The Campaign of Adowa and the Rise of Menelik.* New York: Negro Universities Press, 1969. Excellent scholarly work on the victory and the leadership of Menelik II.

Chamberlain, M. E. *The Scramble for Africa.* 2nd ed. Seminar Studies in History Series. New York: Longman, 1999. Includes some information on Italian imperial ambitions in East Africa.

Erlich, Haggai. *Ras Alula and the Scramble for Africa: A Political Biography: Ethiopia and Eritrea 1875–1897.* Lawrenceville, NJ: Red Sea Press, 1996. A sympathetic biography of the great Ras Alula who participated in the Battle of Adowa.

Henze, Paul B. *Layers of Time: A History of Ethiopia.* New York: Palgrave Macmillan, 2004. A good general history that includes an introduction to the battle.

Holmes, George, ed. *The Oxford Illustrated History of Italy.* New York: Oxford University Press, 2001. Includes data on Italian imperialism in East Africa.

Jones, A. H. M., and Elizabeth Monroe. *The History of Ethiopia.* Oxford: Clarendon Press, 1955. A dated but still useful and accessible general history that includes information on the battle.

Marcus, Harold G. *A History of Ethiopia.* Updated ed. Berkeley: University of California Press, 2002. A very good history of the country with an excellent account of the Italian-Ethiopian crisis of the 1890s.

———. *The Life and Times of Menelik II: Ethiopia, 1844–1913.* Lawrenceville, NJ: Red Sea Press, 1995. An excellent biography of the great leader with extensive information on the battle.

Oliver, Roland. *Africa Since 1800.* 4th ed. Cambridge, U.K.: Cambridge University Press, 1994. Oliver's work is still worth reading and includes much relevant material that students will want to see.

Palumbo, Patrizia. *A Place in the Sun: Africa in Italian Colonial Culture from Post-Unification to the Present.* Berkeley: University of California Press, 2003. A scholarly study focused in Italian colonial ambitions in Africa.

Pankhurst. Richard. *The Ethiopians: A History.* Oxford: Wiley-Blackwell, 2001.

———. *Economic History of Ethiopia, 1800–1935.* Addis Ababa: Haile Sellassie I University Press, 1968. Provides valuable insights into the Italian interest in Ethiopia.

Pakenham, Thomas. *The Scramble for Africa: White Man's Conquest of the Dark Continent from 1876 to 1912.* New York: Avon Books, 1992. A standard work on European expansion in Africa that includes data on Italian colonialism.

Rosenfeld, C. P. *Empress Taytu and Menelik II: Ethiopia 1883–1910.* London: Ravens, 1986. An important dual biography of two leaders whose significant relationship had an impact on the people of Ethiopia.

World Wide Web

"Battle of Adowa." http://www.encyclopedia.com/doc/1O48-AdowaBattleof .html. A brief outline of the important facts concerning the battle.

"Battle of Adowa, 1896." http://www.militaryphotos.net/forums/show thread.php?t=103026. A useful summary of the battle with one photograph.

"Battle of Adowa, 1896." http://www.answers.com/topic/battle-of-adowa-1. A good fact-filled introduction to the battle.

"Battle of Adowa Timeline." http://africanhistory.about.com/library/timelines/ bl-Timeline-BattleOfAdowa.htm. An excellent timeline of the battle that covers it by the hour.

"Battle of Adwa." http://www.rastaites.com/Ethiopia/adowa.html. A good introduction to the background and causes for the conflict, which is critical of the Italians.

"Battle of Adwa (Adowa), 1896." http://www.blackpast.org/?q=perspectives/ battle-adwa-adowa-1896. A very good summary of the battle that includes an African drawing of the battle.

"Emperor Menelik II (1889–1913)." http://www.ethiopiantreasures.toucan surf.com/pages/menelik.htm. A very good biography of Menelik II with extensive information on the Battle of Adowa.

"First Italo-Abyssinian War: Battle of Adowa." http://www.historynet.com/first -italo-abyssinian-war-battle-of-adowa.htm. A very good introduction to the battle and to Italian imperial ambitions in East Africa.

"Menelik II." http://www.douglasyaney.com/mc895-bio.htm. A biographical statement on Menelik II with a photograph of the African leader.

"Ras Alula Abba Nega: An Ethiopian and African Hero." http://www.african idea.org/ras_alula.html. A fascinating account of the life of Ras Alula by Ghelawdewos Araia that includes detailed information on his role in the Battle of Adowa.

Multimedia Source

Adwa, An African Victory. Mypheduh Films, 1999; available through Sankofa. VHS. Directed and produced by Haile Germina. A critically acclaimed documentary, this is an excellent film that students working on this topic should view.

97. Fashoda Crisis (1898)

During the 1890s the longtime imperial rivals Great Britain and France were moving toward a colonial crisis in East Africa. Great Britain aspired to realize the dream of a Capetown-to-Cairo railroad through East Africa. At the same time, France wanted to expand its dominance in West Africa across the continent to the Sudan and to establish a presence on the headwaters of the Nile. In part, this goal was designed to block Britain's ambitions for the railroad. In 1896 French Foreign Minister Gabriel Hanotaux directed that a French expeditionary force of about 150 men under Commandant Jean-Baptiste Marchand should march across Central Africa from Gabon and establish a French presence on the headwaters of the Nile in the Sudan. Marchand succeeded in this secret assignment when he arrived on July 10, 1898, at the small outpost of Fashoda (now Kodok), which was upriver—south—of Khartoum. During the same period the British found themselves once again confronted by an Arab Islamic rebellion in the Anglo-Egyptian Sudan, an area that had been pacified by military action in 1885. The British-Egyptian army under General Sir Herbert Kitchener moved south from Cairo in the summer of 1898 and suppressed the rebellion at the Battle of Omdurman, which was followed by the seizure of Khartoum. Kitchener learned of the French force at Fashoda and moved farther south. The British force arrived at Fashoda on September 18, 1898, and the crisis broke. For several weeks the gravity of the diplomatic crisis threatened to drive the two powers into a war. However, new French Foreign Minister Théophile Delcassé directed Marchand to withdraw from Fashoda on November 4, 1898. British Prime Minister and Foreign Secretary Lord Salisbury and Colonial Secretary Joseph Chamberlain were satisfied, and the crisis abated. Through subsequent diplomatic efforts, the British and French governments brought an end to the crisis on March 21, 1899, when the British dominated East Africa and France had West Africa as a sphere of influence. This colonial crisis and its resolution resulted in a reorientation of Britain's strategy in foreign affairs. In 1904 the two nations entered into a colonial agreement (the Anglo-French Entente) that expanded into a relationship through which the former rivals were allies in the First World War.

TERM PAPER SUGGESTIONS

1. Compare and contrast the French and British policies that resulted in the Fashoda Crisis.

2. Write a paper describing Marchand's march across Africa.

3. Discuss and assess Kitchener's march from Omdurman to Khartoum to Fashoda.

4. Develop a paper on the diplomatic crisis between France and Great Britain that emerged from the Fashoda Crisis. Were the powers willing to go to war over this crisis or were they involved in diplomatic posturing to placate their publics?

ALTERNATIVE TERM PAPER SUGGESTIONS

1. Winston Churchill, serving as a war correspondent, accompanied the British army into the Sudan and was involved in a cavalry charge at the Battle of Omdurman. Imagine that you are Churchill and that you are with the British when they arrived at Fashoda. Develop a podcast of news reports on the immediate incident and the months ahead in which the two forces confronted each other.

2. As the new French Foreign Secretary Delcassé, you find yourself coming into office confronted with the crisis with Britain over Fashoda. Create a blog telling why and how you developed a policy of withdrawing from the crisis.

3. Develop an online map of East Africa in which you note the convergence of forces at Fashoda and provide an accompanying detailed narrative.

SUGGESTED SOURCES

Primary Sources

Boyd, C. W., ed. *Mr. Chamberlain's Speeches*. 2 vols. Boston: Houghton Mifflin, 1914. Provides primary materials by British Colonial Secretary Joseph Chamberlain on the crisis.

Churchill, Winston S. *The River War, An Account of the Reconquest of the Sudan*. 3rd ed. London: Eyre and Spottiswoode, 1951; originally published in 1899. Churchill served as a journalist with the British army in this war and participated in a major cavalry charge in the battle of Omdurman. While he was an eyewitness to much that occurred, he relied on others for much of the information on Fashoda.

Temperley, Harold, and Lillian Penson, eds. *A Century of Diplomatic Blue Books, 1814–1916*. New York: Barnes and Noble, 1966. An outstanding collection of primary materials—many of which address aspects of imperialism, including Fashoda.

Secondary Sources

Akol, Lam. *Southern Sudan: Colonialism, Resistance, and Autonomy.* Trenton, NJ: Red Sea Press, 2007. A revisionist account of the impact of European imperial actions and conflict in the Sudan. It is a readable and important recent study that relies on a balanced use of source materials.

Andrew, Christopher M. *Théophile Delcassé and the Making of the Entente Cordiale, A Reappraisal of French Foreign Policy, 1898–1905.* London: Macmillan, 1968. Andrew argues that Delcassé's withdrawal from Fashoda paid major dividends for the French in reorienting French and British foreign policies.

Bates, Darrell. *The Fashoda Incident of 1898: Encounter on the Nile.* Oxford; Oxford University Press, 1984. A reliable and detailed account of the Fashoda crisis with a good bibliography.

Chassaigne, Philippe, and Michael Dockrill, eds. *Anglo-French Relations 1898–1998: From Fashoda to Jospin.* New York: Palgrave, 2002. A collection of essays on the evolution of the Anglo-French relationship from the war-like atmosphere of the crisis to the diplomatic and economic partnership that had developed during the century after Fashoda.

Kubiecek, Robert V. *The Administration of Imperialism: Joseph Chamberlain at the Colonial Office.* Durham, NC: Duke University Press, 1969. An important study on Chamberlain's leadership and management style that provides insights on Fashoda.

Lewis, David L. *The Race to Fashoda: European Colonialism and African Resistance in the Scramble for Africa.* New York: Weidenfeld and Nicolson, 1987. An important and marvelous study by a trusted historian who considers the interests of the native population in the history of imperialism of the 1890s.

Marsh, Peter J. *Joseph Chamberlain, Entrepreneur in Politics.* New Haven, CT: Yale University Press, 1994. The best biography on Chamberlain. It is useful on his role in the Fashoda crisis.

Neiberg, Michael S. *Warfare and Society in Europe: 1898 to the Present.* New York: Routledge, 2004. The initial chapter of this important book is relevant on Fashoda and the war that almost broke out between France and Great Britain over it.

Neillands, Robin. *The Dervish Wars: Gordon and Kitchener in the Sudan, 1880–1898.* London: John Murray, 1996. The second half of this book provides an excellent account of British policies and actions through the Fashoda Crisis of 1898.

Porter, A. N. *The Origins of the South African War: Joseph Chamberlain and the Diplomacy of Imperialism, 1895–1899.* New York: Palgrave Macmillan, 1980. While focused on the origins of the Boer War, this book provides a broad perspective of British policies in Africa including Fashoda.

Smiyj, Hillas. *The Unknown Frenchman: The Story of Marchand and Fashoda.* Brighton, Essex: Book Guild, 2001. A well-written and reliable account of Marchand's march across Africa and his stand against Kitchener at Fashoda.

Wright, Patricia. *Conflict on the Nile: The Fashoda Incident of 1898.* London: Heinemann, 1972. Still a reliable and important study based on primary as well as secondary sources.

World Wide Web

"Fashoda Incident." http://www.en.encyclopedia.livepress.com/index.php/Fashoda_incident. A reliable, brief account of the incident.

Jones, Jim. "African History Timeline: The Fashoda Crisis." 1998. http://courses.wcupa.edu/jones/his311/timeline/t-fashod.htm. Very useful resource for gaining an understanding of the chronology of the crisis.

"The Open Door Web Site: The Fashoda Crisis (1898)." http://www.saburchill.com/history/chapters/empires/0055.html. Provides a brief account of the Fashoda Crisis (1898). Material by Shirley Burchill, Nigel Hughes, Richard Gale, Peter Price, and Keith Woodall.

Map, "Imperialism in Africa, 1880–1914." http://www.historyteacher.net/GlobalStudies/Readings/AfricaMap-Imperialism.htm. This can be used as a test map.

Multimedia Source

Empires: Queen Victoria's Empire. PBS Video, 2001. DVD. Narrated by actor Donald Sutherland, this documentary examines the evolution of the British Empire during Queen Victoria's reign (1837–1902). British political rivalries as well as the impact on the native populations are considered.

98. Hundred Days of 1898

The Hundred Days of 1898 in China was an attempt to reform Chinese political, economic, and social systems and move them in the direction of Japan, which had westernized its society. While it was motivated by China's defeat by Japan in the Sino-Japanese War in 1895, it originated in the earlier thoughts and writings of K'ang Yu-wei (1858–1927). During the 1880s K'ang produced *Grand Unity* and *Confucius as a Reformer* that won critical acclaim and placed him in the front ranks of the growing reform group. In response to the dismal state of Chinese affairs, the young Emperor Guangxu (1871–1908) met with K'ang and launched a comprehensive reform movement on June 11, 1898. It was designed to westernize

China through the establishment of a public school system, democratic elections at the local level, a plan for a national parliament, inclusion of Western ideas in all schools, reform of the Chinese bureaucracy and military, and tighter governmental regulation of the economy. Those opposed to these reforms rallied around the Empress Dowager Cixi (1835–1908) who supported their efforts. These opponents succeeded in overthrowing the Emperor on September 21, 1898, and placed him under house arrest until his death in 1908. Cixi assumed the position of regent. She acted immediately to end the reforms, and many of its principal supporters were executed. K'ang fled the country. The movement's failure further weakened China and its reputation among the great powers.

TERM PAPER SUGGESTIONS

1. Write a paper on the impact that K'ang Yu-wei had on the origins of the reform movement.

2. Develop a paper on the Hundred Days of 1898. What was planned and achieved? Had the reforms been implemented would they have made a difference in the history of China?

3. Why did the Empress Dowager Cixi and the conservatives oppose the reform movement?

ALTERNATIVE TERM PAPER SUGGESTIONS

1. Develop a podcast in which K'ang Yu-wei meets with Emperor Guangxu and discusses the condition of China and its need for reforms.

2. During the summer of 1898 you are excited about the reforms that are being discussed. You believe that they will restore China to a position that would command respect from all. Write a blog explaining why you support the reforms and describe your reaction to the conservative *coup d'etat* that occurred in September.

3. Develop an iMovie in which the Empress Dowager Cixi and conservative leaders meet to plot the overthrow of the reform movement.

SUGGESTED SOURCES

Primary Sources

De Bary, William Theodore, Irene Bloom, Wing-tsit Chan, Richard John Lufrano, and Joseph Adler. *Sources of Chinese Tradition: From 1600 Through the Twentieth Century.* 2nd ed. 2 vols. New York: Columbia

University Press, 2001. Includes relevant primary materials on the Hundred Days.

Correspondence Respecting the Insurrectionary Movement in China, Presented to Both Houses of Parliament, July 1900. San Francisco: Chinese Materials Center, 1979; originally published in 1900. British official documents that connect the reform movement of 1898 with the Boxer Rebellion of 1899–1901.

Ma, Jianzhong. *Strengthen the Country and Enrich the People: The Reform Writings of Ma Jianzhong (1845–1900).* Trans. Paul J. Bailey. Richmond, U.K.: Curzon, 1998. A useful contemporary memoir of an intellectual who was active during the 1898 reform movement.

Richard, Timothy. *Forty-five Years in China: Reminiscences.* New York: Frederick Stokes, 1916. Also available as an e-book at http://www.archive.org/details/fourtyfiveyears00richuoft. The recollections of a missionary who lived in China during the reform movement of 1898.

Secondary Sources

Cameron, Meribeth Elliott. *The Reform Movement in China, 1898–1912.* New York: AMS Press, 1974; originally published in 1928. Still an excellent resource for gaining an understanding of the reformers and their aspirations.

Chien-Nung, Li, and J. Ingalls. *Political History of China, 1840–1928.* Trans. Ssu-Yu-Teng and J. Ingalls. Stanford, CA: Stanford University Press, 1956. Provides a solid introduction to the movement with the context of Chinese political thinking and the mounting fear of foreign culture.

Cohen, Paul A. *Between Tradition and Modernity: Wang T'ao and Reform in Late Ch'ing China.* Harvard East Asian Monographs, no. 133. Cambridge, MA: Harvard University Press, 1987. A meaningful scholarly study that includes extensive information on the reform movement.

Compilation Group for the "History of Modern China" series. *The Reform Movement of 1898.* Beijing: Foreign Languages Press, 1976. A Communist interpretation of the reform effort in 1898.

Elman, Benjamin A., and Alexander Woodside, eds. *Education and Society in Late Imperial China, 1600–1900.* Studies on China No. 19. Berkeley: University of California Press, 1994. Integrates the development of education in China with the political and economic history of the nation.

Fairbank, John King. *The Great Chinese Revolution 1800–1985.* New York: Harper, 1987. The classic history by the preeminent twentieth-century American historian of China that includes information on the movement.

Karl, Rebecca E., and Peter Zarrow, eds. *Rethinking the 1898 Reform Period: Political and Cultural Change in Late Qing China.* Cambridge, MA:

Harvard University Press, 2002. Collection of essays on the reform movement and its impact on China.

Kwong, Luke S. K. *A Mosaic of the Hundred Days: Personalities, Politics, and Ideas of 1898*. Cambridge, MA: Harvard University Press, 1984. A valuable and useful study of the people who supported and opposed the reform movement.

Morton, W. Scott, and Charlton M. Lewis. *China: Its History and Culture.* 4th ed. New York: McGraw-Hill, 2004. Provides a good introduction to the Hundred Days' Movement.

Wang, Ke-wen. *Modern China: An Encyclopedia of History, Culture, and Nationalism.* Bristol, PA: Taylor & Francis, 1998. An excellent resource on all aspects of Chinese history.

Weston, Timothy B. *The Power of Position: Beijing University, Intellectuals, and Chinese Political Culture, 1898–1929.* Berkeley Series in Interdisciplinary Studies of China, no. 3. Berkeley: University of California Press, 2004. Beijing University developed as a major force in Chinese life during the 1920s and was involved in the Hundred Days' Reform.

Xiao, Gongquan. *A Modern China and a New World: K'ang Yu-wei, Reformer and Utopian, 1858–1927.* Seattle: University of Washington Press, 1975. A scholarly biography of the movement's leader.

World Wide Web

"Hundred Days of Reform." http://www.britannica.com/EBchecked/topic/276504/Hundred-Days-of-Reform. Provides a good introduction to the Hundred Days and its agenda.

"Hundred Days' Reform." http://encyclopedia.thefreedictionary.com/Hundred%20Days'%20Reform. Introduces the movement and includes some additional source information.

"Hundred Days' Reform." http://www.economicexpert.com/a/Hundred:Days:Reform.html. Provides accurate and extensive information on the movement and its consequences.

"Hundred Days' Reform." http://www.experiencefestival.com/hundred_days_reform/articleindex. Provides a list of articles and Web links on this topic.

"Hundred Days' Reform." http://www.bambooweb.com/articles/h/u/Hundred_Days_Reform.html. A very good and readable introduction to the movement that should be useful to most students.

"Hundred Days' Reform." http://www.knowledgerush.com/kr/encyclopedia/Hundred_Days'_Reform/. A useful statement that provides reliable data and some additional links.

"Hundred Days' Reform and Aftermath." http://www.workmall.com/wfb2001/
china/china_history_the_hundred_days_reform_and_the_aftermath
.html. Provides an extended statement on the movement and its impact
on China.

"Late Qing China: Reform and Rebellion (1898–1900)." http://www.thecorner
.org/hist/china/hdreform.htm. Emphasis is on the movement's place
during the collapse of Qing China.

"The Hundred Days' Reform and the Aftermath." http://countrystudies.us/
china/18.htm. Accurate description of the movement with additional
sources provided.

"The One Hundred Days of Reform." http://www.wsu.edu:8080/~dee/
CHING/HUNDRED.HTM. A succinct, precise statement on the contents of the reform movement.

Multimedia Sources

"China: Reform and Upheavel." http://encarta.msn.com/encyclopedia
_761573093/cixi.html. Provides more than a hundred images on China,
including maps that relate to this topic.

"Cixi." http://encarta.msn.com/encyclopedia_761573093/cixi.html. Provides a
portrait of the Empress Dowager who ended the Hundred Days' of
Reform.

99. Boxer Rebellion (1899–1900)

During the late nineteenth century, Europeans and Americans developed
an interest in exploiting the Chinese markets for finished goods and as a
resource for raw materials. This economic initiative was accompanied
by increased activities by Christian missionaries, both Catholic and Prot-
estant. During the 1880s and 1890s Chinese resistance to this exploitation emerged in a variety of ways. Some enjoyed the support of the
government while others did not. In the late 1890s xenophobia in China
was manifested through the Hundred Days of 1898 during which a wide
range of reforms were launched, Christian missionaries and merchants
were attacked, and societies such as the Society of Righteous and Harmo-
nious Fists, the Boxers, emerged in northern China. The Boxers feared
the impact of the Christian missionaries on Chinese culture, tradition,
and values. In the sway of martial arts, the Boxers believed that through
personal denial of comforts, rigorous physical training, and a regimen of

prayer, they would be capable of superhuman achievements. In 1899 Boxers began attacking Catholic missionaries and their followers, and during the summer the Boxers began actions against the foreigners in Beijing (Peking). The Empress Dowager Cixi (1835–1908) was persuaded by the reactionaries in her court to declare war on all of the foreigners on November 2, 1899. Chinese Imperial forces joined the Boxers and laid siege to the legation compound where the foreign embassies were located. For 55 days, the more than 2,000 Europeans and some loyal Chinese held back the Boxers and the Chinese army. An eight-nation relief force (Great Britain, Russia, Japan, France, United States, Germany, Italy, and Austria-Hungary) broke the siege and continued military actions against the Chinese until September 7, 1901, when the "Boxer Protocol" ended the Rebellion. China was humiliated by the multi-nation victory and the harsh peace that was imposed.

TERM PAPER SUGGESTIONS

1. Write a paper on the development of anti-Western sentiment in China during the 1890s.
2. Develop a paper on the emergence of the Boxer movement in northern China.
3. Write a paper on the siege of the European legations during 1899–1900.
4. Why did the Boxer Rebellion fail?
5. Write a paper on the "Boxer Protocol" of 1901 and its impact on Chinese history.

ALTERNATIVE TERM PAPER SUGGESTIONS

1. Develop an iMovie on the role that the Empress Dowager played in the Boxer Rebellion.
2. As a Catholic missionary who survived the Boxer Rebellion, create a blog based on the Boxer actions outside of Beijing (Peking).
3. Develop a podcast in which the European and American leaders are interviewed about their intervention in China. Was it more than a rescue mission?

SUGGESTED SOURCES

Primary Sources

Great Britain. *Correspondence Respecting the Insurrectionary Movement in China, Presented to Both Houses of Parliament, July 1900.* San Francisco: Chinese

Materials Center, 1979; originally published in 1900. Official British documents on the Boxer Rebellion and its suppression by the international force.

MacDonald, Claude Maxwell. *The Siege of the Peking Embassy, 1900: Sir Claude MacDonald's Report on the Boxer Rebellion.* London: HM Stationery Office, 2000; originally published in 1901. A valuable personal account of the siege and its lifting by a participant.

Price, Eva J. *China Journal, 1889–1900: An American Missionary Family during the Boxer Rebellion: With Letters and Diaries of Eva Jane Price and Her Family.* Introduction and annotations by Robert H. Felsing. New York: Scribner, 1989. Includes extensive information on the rise of Chinese xenophobia and the outbreak of the Boxer Rebellion.

Rockhill, William W. *Affairs in China: Report of William W. Rockhill, Late Commissioner to China, with Accompanying Documents.* San Francisco: Chinese Materials Center, 1975; reprint of 1941 edition. Important resource by the ranking American diplomat involved with the Rebellion.

Sharf, Frederic A., and Peter Harrington, eds. *China, 1900: The Eyewitnesses Speak: The Experiences of Westerners in China during the Boxer Rebellion, as Described by Participants in Letters, Diaries, and Photographs.* London: Greenhill, 2000. A valuable collection of materials from the recollections of many of those involved in the Boxer Rebellion.

Documents of the Boxer Rebellion (China Relief Expedition), 1900–1901. http://www.history.navy.mil/docs/boxer/index.html. Extensive documents from the archives of the United States Navy on the lifting of the siege at Peking.

Secondary Sources

Bickers, Robert, and R. G. Tiedemann, eds. *The Boxers, China, and the World.* Lanham, MD: Rowman and Littlefield, 2007. Includes ten useful scholarly essays on aspects of the Boxer Rebellion.

Bodin, Lynn E., and Christopher Warner. *The Boxer Rebellion.* Oxford: Osprey, 1979. A slender but useful study that focuses on the military aspects of the Rebellion.

Brandt, Nat. *Massacre in Shansi.* Syracuse, NY: Syracuse University Press, 1994. A well-written study of the isolation and fate of missionaries and their families in Shansi during the Rebellion.

Clements, Paul H. *The Boxer Rebellion: A Political and Diplomatic Review.* New York: Columbia University Press, 1915. Also available as an e-book at http://books.google.com/books?hl=en&id=dWZCAAAAIAAJ&dq=Boxer+Rebellion&printsec=frontcover&source=web&ots=9St06A23r1&sig=NBFlAM8qbSOs1b1mBqamMXKcaKU&sa=X&oi=book_result

&resnum=6&ct=result#PPP1,M1. An old classic but still useful. Clements had access to many primary materials and developed a scholarly synthesis of the Boxer Rebellion and its impact on Western policy in China.

Duiker, William J. *Cultures in Collision: The Boxer Rebellion.* San Rafael, CA: Presidio Press, 1978. Focus is on the cultural conflict between the West and the East—very good insights into the Western origins of the Rebellion.

Elliott, Jane E. *Some Did It for Civilisation, Some Did It for Country: A Revised View of the Boxer War.* Hong Kong: Chinese University Press, 2002. A relatively new study in which a revisionist interpretation is attempted with some success.

Fleming, Peter. *The Siege at Peking.* London: Rupert Hart-Davis, 1959. This well-written study includes 22 plates that should be of interest and value to students working on this topic.

Gray, Jack. *Rebellions and Revolutions: China from the 1800s to 2000.* 2nd ed. New York: Oxford University Press, 2003. A worthwhile study of the forces of change in China—both internal and external—during the nineteenth and twentieth centuries.

Harrington, Peter. *Peking 1900: The Boxer Rebellion.* Oxford: Osprey, 2001. Students working on the military aspects of the Rebellion should refer to this excellent work.

Martin, Christopher. *The Boxer Rebellion.* London: Abelard-Schuman, 1968. Includes useful photographs and maps on the Rebellion.

Nichols, Bob. *Bluejackets and Boxers: Australia's Naval Expedition to the Boxer Uprising.* London: Allen and Unwin, 1986. Provides an alternative (Australian) perspective on the international relief expedition.

O'Connor, Richard. *The Boxer Rebellion.* London: Hale, 1974. A dated standard on the topic that may be very useful and available to students working on this topic.

Preston, Diana. *The Boxer Rebellion: The Dramatic Story of China's War on Foreigners that Shook the World in the Summer of 1900.* New York: Berkley Books, 2001. An excellent resource for all working on this topic that is well-written and accurate.

Purcell, Victor. *The Boxer Uprising, A Background Study.* Cambridge, U.K.: Cambridge University Press, 1963. Scholarly study on the origins of the Rebellion. This volume provides insights and information not found in most other books.

Schoppa, R. Keith. *The Columbia Guide to Modern Chinese History.* New York: Columbia University Press, 2000. An indispensable resource for studying any topic in modern Chinese history.

Xiang, Lanxin. *The Origins of the Boxer War: A Multinational Study.* London: Routledge/Curzon, 2003. A recent and worthwhile volume that focuses on the international origins of the Rebellion.

World Wide Web

"1900—Boxer Rebellion." http://history1900s.about.com/od/1900s/qt/boxer.htm. A site developed by Jennifer Rosenberg that includes important links to other Web sites on the Rebellion.
"Boxer Rebellion." http://www.answers.com/topic/boxer-rebellion. Includes several useful descriptions of the Rebellion.
"Boxer Uprising/Movement (1900)." http://www.thecorner.org/hist/china/boxer.htm. A lengthy description and analysis of the Rebellion that may provide alternative interpretations on some aspects of the Rebellion.
"The Boxer Rebellion." http://www.smplanet.com/imperialism/fists.html. Good introduction with photographs.
"The Boxer Rebellion." http://www.wsu.edu:8001/~dee/CHING/BOXER.HTM. Useful introduction, fact-filled.

Multimedia Sources

55 Days in Peking. Atlantic Video, 1963. DVD. Directed by Nicholas Ray. A dramatic account of the siege of the foreign legations. Also see http://www.youtube.com/watch?v=t_rQTmcLxiU&feature=related for the opening scenes from the movie.
Cameron, Nigel. *The Face of China as Seen by Photographers and Travelers, 1860–1912.* Millerton, NY: Aperture, 1978. Provides valuable photographs on the Chinese reform effort and the Boxer Rebellion.
Ricalton, James. *James Ricalton's Photographs of China during the Boxer Rebellion: His Illustrated Catalogue of 1900.* Ed. Christopher J. Lucas. Lewiston, NY: Edwin Mellen, 1900.

100. Boer War (1899–1902)

Unlike the revolt in the Transvaal in 1880–1881, the Boer War of 1899–1902 was a major conflict that reflected the continuing animosity between the Boers (in the Orange Free State and the Transvaal) and the British in South Africa. The war started when negotiations between the British and the Boers over "rights" and access to gold deposits collapsed. In the early fall of 1899, British Colonial Secretary Joseph Chamberlain sent an ultimatum demanding "equal rights" for British citizens living in the Transvaal. The Boers countered with their own ultimatum demanding the withdrawal of British troops from the border areas. War followed and lasted through 1902. There is no doubt that both sides were extremely interested in the gold that could be extracted and sold. The Boers fought brilliantly throughout the war. Their knowledge of the terrain and their abilities as effective cavalry resulted in many victories over the British. The Boers laid siege to several British positions, and, for several months, enjoyed some success with these tactics. However, British numbers, firepower, and supplies prevailed and the sieges were lifted. Britain committed many tens of thousands of troops—including Canadian, Australian, and New Zealand units—to this very costly enterprise, which concluded with an agreement in 1902 that established the Union of South Africa. It was amended in 1907 when the Boers were given a level of autonomy that they desired. During the World Wars, the South Africans fought throughout the world in defense of British interests.

TERM PAPER SUGGESTIONS

1. Write a term paper on the background and causes of the Boer War of 1899–1902.
2. Develop a paper on the military aspects of the Boer War. Why were the Boers so successful in some operations against the British? Why did the war last so long?
3. Write a paper on the use of concentration camps during the war and the treatment of the prisoners.
4. Develop a paper on the consequences of the war. Did the British achieve their strategic objectives in South Africa?
5. Write a paper on the impact of the Boer War on the native population.

ALTERNATIVE TERM PAPER SUGGESTIONS

1. Develop an iMovie on Winston Churchill's capture and escape from the Boers. How did Churchill manipulate this event?
2. As a correspondent for the *New York Times*, you have been charged to embed yourself with British troops and to send a series of dispatches on the war and the common soldier. Develop these dispatches and provide commentary on

the living conditions that the soldiers experienced and their views on their own military leaders.

3. Develop a blog in which both British and Boer enlisted soldiers communicate their views on the war and its progress.

4. Develop a podcast on the negotiations that concluded the war. Be sure to include pre-negotiation conversations in which each side prepared for the deliberations.

SUGGESTED SOURCES

Primary Sources

Churchill, Winston. *My Early Life.* New York: Scribner, 1996; originally published in 1930. This book provides Churchill's personal narrative of his experiences during the war as a journalist, as a prisoner of war, and as a wanted escaped prisoner.

———. *Ian Hamilton's March.* Cedar City, UT: Classic Books, 2000; originally published in 1900. Churchill's dramatic but reliable account of the British operation that ended a Boer siege in Natal.

———. *London to Ladysmith via Pretoria.* Durban, South Africa: T. W. Griggs, 1982; originally published in 1900. Churchill's narrative of his experiences as a journalist during the Boer War.

———. *The Boer War.* New York: W. W. Norton, 1990. Includes Churchill's *London to Ladysmith via Pretoria* and *Ian Hamilton's March.*

Hancock, W. K., and J. van der Poel, eds. *Selections from the Smuts Papers, 1886–1950.* 7 vols. Cambridge, U.K.: Cambridge University Press, 1966–1973. An outstanding collection from the Boer leader who later became a defender of the British Empire.

Hobhouse, Emily. *Emily Hobhouse: Boer War Letters.* 2nd ed. Ed. Rykie van Reenen. Cape Town: Human and Rousseau, 1999. These letters by a prominent social worker during the Boer War provide critical insights on the concentration camps.

Plaatje, Solomon T. *The Boer War Diary of Sol T. Plaatje, An African at Mafeking.* Ed. John L. Comaroff. Johannesburg: Macmillan, 1973. A valuable personal narrative of an eyewitness at a major conflict during the war.

Reitz, Deneys. *Commando: A Boer Journal of the Boer War.* London: Folio Society, 1982. An absorbing and credible account of Reitz's experiences during the Boer War.

———. *Adrift on the Open Veld: The Anglo-Boer War and Its Aftermath.* Ed. T. S. Emslie. Cape Town: Stormberg, 1999. Another of the Reitz's personal narratives on the Boer War.

Riall, Nicholas. *Boer War: The Letters, Diaries and Photographs of Malcolm Riall from the War in South Africa, 1899–1902.* London: Brassey's, 2000. The personal reflection of Riall, an officer of the West Yorkshire regiment who used his inexpensive Kodak camera effectively.

Schoeman, Karel, ed. *Witnesses to War: Personal Documents of the Anglo-Boer War from the Collections of the South African Library.* Cape Town: Human and Rousseau, 1998. A valuable collection of documents by participants in the war.

Smuts, Jan Christian. *Memoirs of the Boer War.* Ed. Gail Nattrass and S. B. Spies. Johannesburg: J. Ball, 1994. An extremely important personal account by one of the most significant personalities in South African history.

Sternberg, Adalbert W. *My Experiences of the Boer War.* Trans. G. F. R. Henderson. London: Longmans, Green, 1901. A personal narrative by a participant who witnessed much of the war.

Throup, David, ed. *British Documents on Foreign Affairs: Reports and Papers from the Foreign Office Confidential Print. Part 1: From the Mid-Nineteenth Century to the First World War. Series G, Africa, 1848–1914.* 25 vols. Bethesda, MD: University Publications of America, 1995. Excellent resource of primary documents; volumes 8 and 9 are on the Boer War of 1899–1902.

Secondary Sources

Barker, Brian. *A Concise Dictionary of the Boer War.* Cape Town: Francolin, 1999. Excellent resource for anyone working on the Boer War.

Barthorp, Michael. *The Anglo-Boer Wars: The British and the Afrikaners 1815–1902.* Dorset, U.K.: Blanford Press, 1987. A very good history of the long-range hostility between the British and the Boers.

Bennett, William. *Absent Minded Beggars: Volunteers in the Boer War.* London: Leo Cooper, 1999. A worthwhile study of the British volunteer recruits who served in the Boer War.

Bourquin, S. B., and Gilbert Tortage. *The Battle of Colenso, 15 December 1899.* Randburg: Ravan Press, 1999. A reliable and readable account of the great Boer victory.

Caldwell, Theodore C., ed. *The Anglo-Boer War: Why Was It Fought? Who Was Responsible?* Boston: D. C. Heath, 1965. A very good and provocative volume that includes excerpts from sources that differ in their interpretation of the war and its aftermath.

Cammack, Diana Rose. *The Rand at War, 1899–1902: The Witwatersrand and the Anglo-Boer War.* Berkeley: University of California Press, 1990. An excellent scholarly account of the impact of the war on the Boers.

Carver, Michael. *The National Army Museum Book of the Boer War.* London: Sidgwick and Jackson in association with the National War Museum, 1999. Field Marshall Carver's excellent reference book on the Boer War, which includes illustrations and maps.

Coetzer, Owen. *The Anglo-Boer War: The Road to Infamy, 1899–1900.* London: Arms and Armour, 1996. A well-written and critical history of the war.

Evans, Martin. *The Boer War: South Africa 1899–1902.* Oxford: Osprey Publishing, 1999. A comprehensive scholarly account of the political and military aspects of the war.

———. *Encyclopedia of the Boer War, 1899–1902.* Santa Barbara, CA: ABC-CLIO, 2000. A marvelous and exhaustive reference work on all issues related to the Boer War.

Davidson, A. B. *The Russians and the Anglo-Boer War, 1899–1902.* Cape Town: Human and Rousseau, 1998. A seminal study of Russian interest in the Boer War and British geopolitical ambitions in South Africa and South Asia.

Farewell, Byron. *The Great Anglo-Boer War.* New York: W. W. Norton, 1990. A worthwhile and readable introduction to the Boer War and its impact on Britain.

Fremont-Barnes, Gregory. *The Boer War, 1899–1902.* Oxford: Osprey Publishing, 2003. A very good study of the advantages and disadvantages that the opponents had to confront and overcome.

Gillings, Ken. *The Battle of the Thukela Heights: 12–28 February 1900.* Randburg: Ravan Press, 1999. The best written history of the battle in Natal.

Gooch, John, ed. *The Boer War: Direction, Experience, and Image.* London: Frank Cass, 2000. A valuable and very useful scholarly account that includes several important essays.

Hall, Darrell. *The Hall Handbook of the Anglo-Boer War 1899–1902.* Pietermaritzburg: University of Natal Press, 1999. Another valuable reference work on the Boer War.

Hancock, W. K. *Smuts.* 2 vols. Cambridge, U.K.: Cambridge University Press, 1968. The best biography of Smuts by the foremost historian of the period and the conflict.

Holt, Edgar. *The Boer War.* London: Putnam, 1958. Still a good introduction to the political and military aspects of the war.

Jackson, Tabitha. *The Boer War.* London: Channel 4 Books, 1999. This work accompanied the BBC television series on the Boer War, and includes photographs, maps, and excerpts from primary sources.

Judd, Denis. *The Boer War.* New York: Palgrave Macmillan, 2003. A very reliable and well-written history of the war by a noted historian.

Knight, Ian. *Boer Commando 1876–1902.* Oxford: Osprey Publishing, 2004. A useful illustrated study of Boer life and the readiness for combat against the British.

———. *The Boer Wars, 1836–1902.* 2 vols. Oxford: Osprey Publishing, 1996. An excellent history of the war by a reliable military historian.

———. *Colenso 1899: The Boer War in Natal.* Westport, CT: Praeger, 2005. An excellent study of the Boer victory over the British—emphasis is on the military aspects of the struggle.

Krebs, Paula M. *Gender, Race, and the Writing of Empire: Public Discourse and the Boer War.* New York: Cambridge University Press, 1999. A seminal study of how the war had impact and was reflected in literature, by sex, by race, and on foreign relations.

Laband, John, ed. *Daily Lives of Civilians in Wartime Africa: From Slavery Days to Rwandan Genocide.* Westport, CT: Greenwood Press, 2007. Includes a very good chapter by Laband on the impact of war on civilians during the Boer War.

McCracken, Donal P. *MacBride's Brigade: Irish Commandos in the Anglo-Boer War.* Dublin: Four Courts Press, 1999. A very good account of the Irish brigade in the war by a military historian.

McFadden, Pam. *The Battle of Talana: 20 October 1899.* Randburg: Raven Press, 1999. An excellent examination of all aspects of the British victory over the Boers in Natal.

———. *The Battle of Elandslaagle: 21 October 1899.* Randburg: Raven Press, 1999. Very good history of the British victory with maps and illustrations.

Meredith, Martin. *Diamonds, Gold, and War: The British, the Boers, and the Making of South Africa.* New York: Public Affairs, 2008. A very readable, yet scholarly, study of the personalities and forces that led to the Boer War.

Pakenham, Thomas. *The Boer War.* Rev. ed. London: Folio Society, 1999; originally published in 1979. To many, Pakenham's history is still the standard on the Boer war. It is well researched and written.

Pemberton, William Baring. *Battles of the Boer War.* Philadelphia: Dufour Editions, 1964. An old but still useful military history of the war.

Sandys, Celia. *Churchill: Wanted Dead or Alive.* New York: Carroll & Graf, 2000. A very well-written and researched history of Churchill's capture by the Boers and escape, by his granddaughter.

Sibbald, Raymond. *The Boer War.* Dover, NH: Alan Sutton, 1993. Very good with an emphasis on the role and impact of war correspondents.

Smurthwaite, David. *The Boer War, 1899–1902.* London: Hamlyn, 1999. Includes personal narratives, information on social aspects, and pictorial works related to the war.

Torlage, Gilbert. *The Battle of Sploenkop, 23-24 January 1900.* Randburg: Ravan Press, 1999. A solid history of the Boer victory and its meaning in the war in 1900.

Trew, Peter. *The Boer War Generals.* Stroud, U.K.: Sutton, 1999. A critical account of British and Boer leadership during the struggle.

Van Hartesveldt, Fred R. *The Boer War: Historiography and Annotated Bibliography.* Westport, CT: Greenwood Press, 2000. A very valuable scholarly work on the historical literature on the war.

Watt, Steve. *The Siege of Ladysmith, 2 November 1899–28 February 1900.* Randburg: Ravan Press, 1999. An excellent study of the Boer siege of Ladysmith.

———. *The Battle of Vaalkrans: 5–7 February 1900.* Randburg: Ravan Press, 1999. A very good military history with maps and illustrations.

Wilson, Craig. *Australia's Boer War: The War in South Africa, 1899–1902.* Oxford: Oxford University Press, 2002. A valuable study on the role of Australian units in the war.

Wilson, Keith, ed. *The International Impact of the Boer War.* New York: Palgrave/Macmillan, 2001. A series of essays that consider the international ramifications of the war, which are quite interesting and may provide term paper topics.

World Wide Web

"Africa: Imperialism and Colonialism." http://www.emints.org/ethemes/resources/S00001799.shtml. Provides extensive list of links to Web sites on all aspects of European imperialism in Africa.

"Anglo-Boer War Museum." http://www.anglo-boer.co.za. An excellent site that provides a chronology, information on the principal personalities, the concentration camps, the fate of prisoners of war, and other data on the war. Multiple photographs and illustrations are also included.

"Concentration Camps." http://h-net.msu.edu/cgi-bin/logbrowse.pl?trx=lx&sort=3&list=h-africa&month=9803&week=&user=&pw=. A worthwhile H-Net Africa discussion on the concentration camps during the Boer War by Harold Marcus and Werner Hillebrecht.

"Concentration Camps during the South African/Boer War." http://library.stanford.edu/depts/ssrg/africa/boers.html. Compiled by John Rawlings, this site provides samples of the primary sources available in the Stanford University libraries on this topic.

"The Anglo-Boer War, 1899–1902." http://www.au.af.mil/au/aul/bibs/boer/boerwr.htm. A very good bibliography with Web sites on the war compiled by Janet L. Seymour of the Air University Library, Maxwell Air Force Base, Alabama. Numerous scholarly articles are included.

"The Battle of Belmont and Graspan." http://www.britishbattles.com/great-boer-war/belmont-graspan.htm. A description of the British victory

over the Boers on November 23 and 25, 1899, which includes a battlefield map and one photograph.

"The Battle of Colenso." http://www.britishbattles.com/great-boer-war/
colenso.htm. A good description of the Boer victory and British inept-
ness at Colenso on December 15, 1899, that includes a battlefield
map, three photographs, and two illustrations.

"The Battle of Elandslaagte." http://www.britishbattles.com/great-boer-war/
elandslaagte.htm. An account of the British victory on October 21,
1899, that includes a battlefield map, one photograph, and three
illustrations.

"The Battle of Ladysmith." http://www.britishbattles.com/great-boer-war/
ladysmith.htm. An excellent description of the Boer victory in northern
Natal on October 29, 1899, that includes a battlefield map and one
photograph.

"The Battle of Magersfontein." http://www.britishbattles.com/great-boer-war/
magersfontein.htm. A description of the Boer victory of December 11,
1899, in the northwest of the Cape Colony. Included are a battlefield
map and three photographs.

"The Battle of Modder River." http://www.britishbattles.com/great-boer-war/
modder-river.htm. A good account of the Modder River battle of
November 28, 1899, in which the British suffered heavy casualties but
forced the Boers to withdraw. Included is a battlefield map.

"The Battle of Paardenburg." http://www.britishbattles.com/great-boer-war/
paardenburg.htm. A solid account of the British victory on February
27, 1900, in which they suffered the highest single-day casualties
(1,270) of the Boer War, that includes a battlefield map, one photograph, and two illustrations.

"The Battle of Spion Kop." http://www.britishbattles.com/great-boer-war/spion
-kop.htm. A detailed description of the Boer victory on January 24,
1900, in northern Natal, which includes a battlefield map and six
photographs.

"The Battle of Stormberg." http://www.britishbattles.com/great-boer-war/
stormberg.htm. A very good description of the Boer victory of December
9, 1899, that includes a battlefield map and two photographs.

"The Battle of Talana Hill." http://www.britishbattles.com/great-boer-war/
talana-hill.htm. A very good description of the British victory over the
Boers on October 20, 1899, that includes a battlefield map.

"The Battle of Val Krantz and Pieters." http://britishbattles.com/great-boer-war/
val-krantz.htm. A description of the prolonged (February 5–28, 1900)
battle, which resulted in the end of the Boer invasion of Natal. Included
are a battlefield map and five photographs.

"The Boer War, South Africa, 1899–1902." http://www.geocities.com/Athens/ Acropolis/8141/boerwar.html?20086. A comprehensive introduction to the origins, development, and consequences of the Boer War, which includes maps, three illustrations, and numerous poems.

"The Siege of Kimberley." http://www.britishbattles.com/great-boer-war/ kimberley.htm. A description of the unsuccessful Boer siege at Kimberley (October 14, 1899–February 15, 1900) on the border of the Orange Free State and the Cape Colony, which includes a siege map and three illustrations.

"The Siege of Ladysmith." http://www.britishbattles.com/great-boer-war/siege -ladysmith.htm. A reliable and detailed account of the Boer siege of the British at Ladysmith (November 2, 1899–February 27, 1900), which includes a siege map and five photographs.

"The Siege of Mafeking." http://www.britishbattles.com/great-boer-war/ mafeking.htm. A description of the unsuccessful Boer siege at Mafeking (October 14, 1899–May 16, 1900) in the northern Cape Colony, which includes a siege map and one photograph.

Multimedia Sources

Barnes, John. *Filming the Boer War.* London: Bishopgate, 1992. A fascinating volume on the use of motion pictures in the Boer War. It includes a section on "British films of 1899" with a bibliography.

Breaker Morant. Image Entertainment, 2008 (original film, 1980). DVD. Directed by Bruce Beresford. Outstanding dramatic film focused on the court martial of three Australian soldiers in the Boer War for murder.

Churchill, Winston. *My Early Life.* Blackstone Audiobook, 2002. Narrated by Frederick Davidson. A quality reading of Churchill's 1930 autobiography of his early years.

The Boer War. Pegasus Entertainment, 2002. DVD. An excellent documentary on the outbreak, prosecution, and consequences of the Boer War.

The Boer War—A Bitter and Bloody Clash of Arms. Everlong, 2003. VHS. Directed by George Melford. A worthwhile film that provides insights on the level of violence during the Boer War.

The History of Warfare: The Boer War and Other Colonial Adventures. Cromwell Productions, 2007. DVD. A very good documentary.

Young Winston. Columbia Tristar, 1972. DVD. Directed by Richard Attenborough. An outstanding dramatic film on Churchill's early years, including his capture and escape during the Boer War.

Index

Adowa, Battle of, 370–371
Afghan Wars: First Afghan War, 137;
    Second Afghan War, 285–286
Algeria, revolt against France, 109–110
Ali, Mohammad: establishment of modern
    Egypt, 22–23; massacre of the Mamluks,
    30; Treaty of Unkiar-Skelessi,
    117–118
Anglo-Zulu War, 290
Argentinean War of Independence, 91–92
Armenian Massacres, 360–361
Arya Samaj Movement, 278
Ashanti Wars: First Ashanti War, 76;
    Second Ashanti War, 269
Australia: exploration, 7–8; Eureka
    Stockade, 192–193

Babism, 143–144
Barings Crisis, 347–348
Berlin Conference, 313–314
Bismarck, Otto von: Berlin Conference,
    313–314; Congress of Berlin, 281–282;
    Three Emperors' League and Alliance,
    273–274; Unification of Germany,
    263–264
Boer Wars: Boer War (1899–1902), 385–
    386; First Boer War, 305–306; and the
    Jameson Raid, 365–366
Bolivar, Simon: Bolivian independence,
    87–88; Colombian independence, 105;
    Ecuador independence, 101; Peruvian

independence, 64; Venezuelan
    independence, 27
Bolivia: Independence, 87–88; War of the
    Pacific, 298–299
Boxer Rebellion, 381–382;and the
    Hundred Days, 381–382; and White
    Lotus Rebellion, 5
Brazilian independence, 61
British North America Act (Constitution
    Act), 234
Burmese Wars: First Burmese War, 79–80;
    Second Burmese War, 179–180; Third
    Burmese War, 323–324

Canada: British North America Act
    (Constitution Act), 234; North-West
    Rebellion, 326–327; Rebellions in
    Upper and Lower Canada, 128; Red
    River Rebellion, 237–238; Ultramonta-
    nism in Quebec, 246
Cape-Xhosa Wars (Cape Frontier Wars or
    Kaffir Wars), 33–34
Carlist Wars, 121
Chile: War of Independence, 48–49; War
    of the Pacific, 298–299
Colombia: independence, 105
Congress of Berlin, 281–282; and the
    Straits Question, 44–45
Congress of Vienna, 40
Crimean War, 183; and the Straits
    Question, 44–45

Darwin, Charles, 213
Decembrist Revolt (Russia), 83–84
Discovery of Gold (South Africa), 341
Disraeli, Benjamin: and the Congress of Berlin, 281–282; and the Eastern Question, 12; and the First Boer War, 305–306; and the Suez Canal, 242–243

Eastern Question, 12; and the Straits Question, 44–45
Ecuador: establishment of, 101
Egypt: establishment of modern, 22–23
Eight Trigrams Rebellion, 37
Eureka Stockade, 192–193

Fashoda Crisis, 374
Ferdinand VII, 56–57; Carlist wars, 121; independence of Bolivia, 87–88; independence of Ecuador, 101

Gaelic Revival (Ireland), 320
Great Trek, 124
Greece: war of independence, 71–72

Haitian Revolt, 1
Herzl, Theodor, 367
Hundred Days (China), 377–378; and the Boxer Rebellion, 381–382

Indian National Congress, 333–334
Industrial Revolution, 16
Irish Home Rule, 337
Irish Republican Brotherhood, 205–206

Jameson Raid, 364–365
Japan: industrial revolution, 16; Meiji Restoration, 253; Sino-Japanese War, 357–358
Jewish State (Theodor Herzl), 367–368
July Revolution (France), 97

Leo XIII, Pope, 351
Liberia, establishment of, 150–151

Mamluks, 30
Maori Revolts, New Zealand, 140–141

Marxism, 157
Meiji Restoration, 253
Mexico: independence, 67–68; Liberal Revolt, 94; War of the Castes, 153–154
Mohammad, Sayyid Ali, 143–144

Nien Rebellion, 189
Nile River, 209
North-West Rebellion (Canada), 326–327

Opium Wars: First Opium War, 132; Second Opium War, 196
Origin of Species, 213

Panama Canal and the French, 294–295
Pandjeh Incident, 317
Paraguayan War (War of the Triple Alliance), 229–230
Pedro, Dom (Brazil), 61
Peru: independence, 63; War of the Pacific, 298–299
Pius IX, Pope, 225–226; Unification of Italy, 257–258

Raffles, Thomas Stamford, 53
Rebellions: Boxer Rebellion, 381–382; Eight Trigrams Rebellion, 37; Nien Rebellion, 189; Red River Rebellion, 237–238; T'ai Ping Rebellion, 175–176; White Lotus Rebellion, 5
Red River Rebellion (Canada), 237–238
Rerum Novarum, 351
Revolutions: Liberal Revolts of 1820, 56–57; of 1848, 163

San Martin, José de: and Chilean war of independence, 49; Ecuador independence, 101; Peruvian independence, 64
Schleswig-Holstein Question, 171–172
Scramble for Africa, 301
Self-Strengthening Movement, 217–218
Sepoy Mutiny, 199–200
Siamese Crisis, 354
Sikh Wars: First Sikh War, 146–147; Second Sikh War, 168

Singapore, 52–53
Sino-French War, 310
Sino-Japanese War, 357–358
Slavery: British abolish, 112–113
Social Democratic Party (Germany), 221–222
Straits Question, 44–45
Suez Canal, 242–243
Syllabus of Errors, 225–226

T'ai Ping Rebellion, 175–176
Ten Years' War (Cuba), 249
Three Emperors' League and Alliance, 273–274

Tientsin Massacre, 260–261

Uccialli, Treaty of, 344
Ultramontanism in Quebec, 246
Unification of Germany, 263–264
Unification of Italy, 257–258
Unkiar-Skelessi, Treaty, 117–118

Venezuela: independence, 27

War of the Castes (Mexico), 153–154
War of the Pacific, 298–299
White Lotus Rebellion, 4–5; and Eight Trigrams Rebellion, 37

About the Author

WILLIAM T. WALKER is Professor of History and former Senior Vice President for the College, Vice President for Academic Affairs, and Dean of the Faculty at Chestnut Hill College, Philadelphia. He is the author and editor of European History works for the Research and Education Association and a frequent writer on European History themes.